CHASING CHI

FBI Caveat

In accordance with my obligations as a former FBI employee pursuant to my FBI employment agreement, this book has undergone a prepublication review for the purpose of identifying prohibited disclosures, but it has not been reviewed for editorial content or accuracy. Because the FBI does not endorse or validate any information that I have described in this book, the opinions expressed within it are mine and not those of the FBI or any other government agency.

Some individual names in this book have been shortened, changed, or omitted to protect their privacy.

CHASING CHI

*The FBI's Groundbreaking Pursuit
of China's Most Prolific Spy Family*

JAMES E. GAYLORD

Prometheus Books

Essex, Connecticut

To contact the author or learn more about the story,
please go to ChasingChiBook.com.

PB Prometheus Books

An imprint of The Globe Pequot Publishing Group, Inc.
64 South Main Street
Essex, CT 06426
www.GlobePequot.com

British Library Cataloguing in Publication Information available

Library of Congress Cataloging-in-Publication Data available

ISBN 978-1-4930-9196-6 (cloth)
ISBN 978-1-4930-9197-3 (electronic)

*This book is dedicated to my beautiful and wise wife Melody,
my wonderful and intelligent daughters Kristen and Lauren,
their mature and responsible husbands James and Daniel,
and my gorgeous and clever grandchildren, all of whom make life a joy.*

CONTENTS

Preface: Why This Book? ix
Introduction: Red Storm Rising xi

PART I: Probe
CHAPTER 1: China Spy? 2
CHAPTER 2: Setting the Stage 7
CHAPTER 3: A Dark Cloud 15
CHAPTER 4: How Firm a Foundation 18
CHAPTER 5: Strange Subjects, Stranger Trash 21
CHAPTER 6: Promises Made to Be Broken 30
CHAPTER 7: Finding Friends in All the Right Places 33
CHAPTER 8: "Best Ever" 37
CHAPTER 9: SARA-4 Linguists Rock 42
CHAPTER 10: Enter the Dragon 46
CHAPTER 11: Enter the Dragon, Part II 58
CHAPTER 12: My "Go-To" Guys 63
CHAPTER 13: The Art of War 66
CHAPTER 14: Diamonds in the Rough 69
CHAPTER 15: Enter the Dragon, Part III 75

PART II: Pursue
CHAPTER 16: The Die Is Cast 82
CHAPTER 17: D-Day! .97
CHAPTER 18: Two Snakes Caged, One Loosed 103
CHAPTER 19: Denyin' Spyin' 110
CHAPTER 20: Big Needles in a Huge Haystack 125
CHAPTER 21: Bail or No Bail: Is That Really the Question? 135

CHAPTER 22: Witnesses and "Victims" 140

CHAPTER 23: Dazed and Confused: US Attorney's Office
at Work 147

CHAPTER 24: Cakes Need Frosting 160

CHAPTER 25: The Creaking Wheels of Justice 170

CHAPTER 26: It's a Bird. It's a Plane. It's a Subject
Matter Expert! 179

CHAPTER 27: Setting Up the Chessboard 185

PART III: **Prosecute**

CHAPTER 28: Traitor or "Victim"? 192

CHAPTER 29: "MIT Has No Keg Parties?" 207

CHAPTER 30: Closing Bang, Opening Whimper 224

CHAPTER 31: "Lies, Lies, Lies, Yea-ah" 250

CHAPTER 32: "Our Pal, Mr. Honesty" 281

CHAPTER 33: Et tu, Brute? 298

CHAPTER 34: Closing the Mak Door 313

PART IV: **After Mak**

CHAPTER 35: China Spy II? 334

CHAPTER 36: China Spy II! 357

Epilogue: China Spies! 383

Acknowledgments 391

List of Acronyms 393

Index 395

Preface: Why This Book?

In 1985, my FBI Academy criminal law instructor confessed to our class, "I love working bank robberies, but their importance pales in comparison to one successful espionage investigation, which can save thousands of US troops, or prevent or even win a war."

In 2004, I initiated the Chi Mak espionage investigation. Early on, my FBI Headquarters (FBIHQ) China Desk supervisor, Charles H. "Sandy" Kable IV, predicted a book was in my future. I had no time or energy to entertain that thought at the time. Yet with each new bizarre development, a colleague would declare, "You can't make this stuff up! Jim, you've *got* to write a book when this is over."

With the case's conclusion, I had the time, energy, and records to do just that. My Assistant US Attorney (AUSA) allowed me to save all the evidence, exhibits, correspondence, motions, transcripts, and other court documents he had slated for destruction, which I knew held great historic significance. I added "archivist" to my "case agent" title and set about documenting this case and its innumerable twists, turns, obstacles, outrages, betrayals, and victories.

In the end, I *had* to author this book, having run the investigation from start to finish, attending every meeting, reviewing every scrap of paper, and making every decision. It's a story that *had* to be told, for history and the legion of dedicated FBI counterintelligence (CI) agents who seek neither praise nor recognition, but deserve both. This book is for them, because they make all the difference.

Introduction: Red Storm Rising

*By Charles H. "Sandy" Kable IV, FBI Assistant Director (retired),
National Security Branch, and Director, Terrorist Screening Center*

CLARION CALLS BLARED FROM THE EAST COAST TO THE PACIFIC FLEET.
Mak family spy ring arrests were days away! The intelligence sources
responsible had done their jobs in spectacular fashion, intercepting
and reporting this deadly threat to the US Navy, its systems, and, most
importantly, its sailors. Warships and warrior engineers were quickly dispatched, skimming atop and beneath ocean waves to prevent the Communist Chinese Navy from capitalizing on these invaluable resources.
Who would get there first? Could they be secured in time?

Chasing Chi is powerfully accurate and anecdotally precise. I should
know. I lived it, having the great fortune to know and work alongside
a team of exceptional investigators, supervisors, intelligence analysts,
surveillance specialists, linguists, and attorneys, from a plethora of agencies, bureaus, centers, departments, offices, and services, all chasing Chi
Mak. My friend, retired FBI Special Agent Jim Gaylord, was a superb
investigator and mentor to his SARA-4 team, the counterintelligence
squad within the Los Angeles Field Office's Santa Ana Resident Agency.
Without Jim's tenacity, advocacy, and sheer willpower, Chi Mak and his
family would have escaped justice. But the Maks didn't, because SARA-4
personnel conducted the seminal Chinese espionage investigation in US
history, holding the entire clan, their associates, and the People's Republic
of China (PRC) government accountable for their treachery. *Chasing Chi*
is an extraordinary account of the men and women who actually did the
hard work. The members of SARA-4, and those who aided them, should

be extremely proud of their accomplishments, and all will enjoy reading about their heroic actions.

The threat of espionage has existed since this country's founding and continues today, as confirmed by the hundreds of active PRC investigations alone, with other treachery yet to be detected. Therefore, it is essential the FBI make this ever-present threat a primary concern. Why do nations spy? Clearly they want an advantage, economically, politically, technically, and militarily. But what motivates an individual to commit espionage? For hundreds of years, money, ideology, coercion, and ego have generally been the prime movers for betrayal. In the last decade, I would add activists to this list, the most prolific of whom was Edward Snowden.

In this case, though, Chi Mak spied for his native China because of his ideology; Chi believed "good ideas need to be shared." But to share, he first had to belong. Chi Mak had to have access to specific people and plans in order to transfer America's secrets for the advantage of the Chinese Navy. So, he immigrated to the United States, took an oath to be a good American citizen, foreswearing all other allegiances, and joined a team developing new systems and technologies to preserve his adopted nation as the premier fighting force upon the seas.

By the time an espionage investigation is opened, and long before its investigative crescendo, the country has already lost policies, plans, technologies, and other capabilities to a hostile foreign power. The primary reason there aren't more arrests and trials of traitors is because Assistant US Attorneys must first ask permission of, and coordinate every detail with, the Department of Justice's Counterintelligence and Export Control Section (DOJ/CES), which claims executive leadership over all prosecutions of espionage-related cases.

As you will read here, DOJ/CES and US Attorneys' Offices are rife with risk aversion and cowardice. Of the dozens of cases I personally advocated for prosecution with the chief of DOJ/CES, 98 percent were declined, usually bowing to political pressures and other influences rather than doing the right thing. They are the primary impediments to holding espionage suspects accountable.

Nonetheless, readers need to know that patriot sentinels remain on watch in the streets, in the air and oceans, and within cyberspace, tracking treasonous activity. To the spy and thief concealing their activities to sell out this country, your day is coming. Through your mistakes or our intelligence collection efforts, you will be discovered. It will be advantage FBI, but you won't know that until you hear the unforgettable metallic click of handcuffs tightening around your wrists.

Justice will be served.

Part I
Probe

CHAPTER 1

China Spy?

I DON'T WANT TO DO THIS! MY THOUGHTS SCREAMED.

My supervisor, Sal Valdez, had just told me I was the case agent on a new, high-profile, and sensitive espionage case involving the People's Republic of China (PRC). That was all he knew, along with orders to tell no one, and to fly to Washington, DC, the next day for polygraphs and a briefing by persons unknown. Neither of us had been polygraphed before, and as experienced counterintelligence (CI) agents, we found this level of secrecy extreme.

I diplomatically explained, "Sal, Joe is working China matters. He should have first crack. And Polly has more seniority." My philanthropy hid selfish motives, while my gut warned me this mysterious saga would become an albatross, entailing constant FBI Headquarters (FBIHQ) oversight and pressure. I had some great cases of my own in my field of expertise, countering the Socialist Republic of Vietnam (SRV).

Sal quickly countered, "Joe's too busy working undercover matters, North Korean cases, and has ticked off too many people on the squad. They won't work with him. Besides, he's transferring before year end. Polly's got seniority, but she's retiring this year. This looks to be big, and long-term. It needs someone who will stick around and can handle it. You're it."

Big and long-term—just what I was thinking.

"You've worked China stuff before," Sal added. "You're the most senior agent left, and the only one I can give this to and know it will be done right. You write well, do excellent paper, and know how things work." Sal was good at assigning an unpleasant task and making it sound complimentary.

All my life I'd wanted to contribute to a just society and protect this greatest of all countries. I joined the FBI in 1985 to thwart criminals and stop the spread of the most evil and powerful threat the world has ever seen—communism. Once I'd gotten a taste of this work, I was hooked. This was cemented when I became a member of Santa Ana Resident Agency squad 4 (SARA-4). SARA was the largest of the FBI's Los Angeles Field Office (FBILA) satellite facilities and covered all concerns within Orange County, California. SARA-4 handled all CI and counter-terrorism (CT) matters.

I had studied Vietnamese at the US Army's Defense Language Institute in Monterey, California, to work with Orange County's extensive "Little Saigon" community against the SRV, in addition to other CI matters—China, Russia, North Korea, Iran, etc. My partner was Special Agent Colleen McKay, who mentored me for years. I loved our work on behalf of Vietnamese Americans, and for over two decades we'd made an outstanding team. I didn't want to give it up for this new case.

But Sal had made his decision, and the die was cast, so I decided then and there that if I was going to work this major case, and endure the executive scrutiny it would entail, I would *not* be dictated to by others, something I'd seen destroy other FBI PRC espionage investigations. I would sink or swim doing it my way. I'd seen ignorant executives "manage" investigations into the ground countless times before. And when disaster arrived, they always blamed the case agent, since FBI executives always ran from their own bad decisions.

Their interference was also capricious. In 1999, during the Millennium threats, and after 9/11, cases I worked arbitrarily and rapidly heated up and cooled down, per the latest flavor or eccentric interest of my FBIHQ managers. Red-hot emergency orders mutated into cold disinterest a day or even an hour later, depending upon the motivations of the "blue flamers"—management sociopaths concerned only with their own career advancement, not the good of the country or family.[1] These

---

1. An academy instructor once told our class that you could identify these individuals by the "blue flame" shooting out of their backsides.

climbers, although lousy investigators, proved skillful manipulators of the system and thieves of others' credit. They have caused the FBI severe damage for decades. Not this time!

Sal and I flew to DC wondering what was about to be dropped on us. We checked into a Courtyard Marriott just north of FBIHQ and across from the old International Spy Museum location.[2] We discussed our pending polygraphs over dinner. I was looking forward to mine. Having worked with polygraphers before to test my assets—informants—I knew the tricks and routines well, including the "control" questions, and wondered what my "control lie" would be. The examiner needed to maneuver the test subject into an inconsequential lie to use as a standard point of comparison by asking questions like "Have you ever lied to a loved one?" This test proves stressful for honest people who qualify their answers to ensure absolute accuracy.[3]

The next morning, Sal and I were polygraphed. I figured out my control lie question: "Have you ever discussed classified information over an open line?" All agents have at one time or another, usually by talking around the subject matter or using an informal code. I answered, "No" to keep the process moving. That was it! The other questions regarded foreign contacts and aiding foreign governments. The worst part? They ran the session three times. Each time, with my arm elevated, cuffed for blood pressure, and instructions not to move a muscle, meant my arm literally turned purple and limp. The findings? "No Deception Indicated." Sal's findings were "Inconclusive," requiring a retest the next day, which bothered Sal.[4]

Next came our FBIHQ meeting with our incoming FBILA Acting Assistant Special Agent in Charge (A/ASAC), Mike, who was coming to LA from the Washington Field Office (WFO). My first impression

---

2. It would become our home away from home for years.
3. My wife Melody suffered this when she applied for a translator position, and barely forgave me! Her control lie questions included "Have you ever stolen something?" (Answer, "No, except for taking some of my daughter's Halloween candy") and "Have you ever lied to a loved one?" (Answer, "Only to spare their feelings"). Because the examiner kept pressuring her to stop qualifying answers and agree to the control lies, she exited the examination room in tears and focused wet, pitiful, accusatory eyes on me. She passed the polygraph.
4. I teased him later that night, asking what he had "withheld" during the test.

was not good, given his "mile-wide, inch-deep" blue-flamer bravado and dismissive lecture regarding WFO's "superior" anti-SRV work, in contrast to SARA-4's. I didn't appreciate his ignorance or belittling remarks.

We sat around a large conference-room table with a whole crew of people we didn't know. One engaging man, China Desk supervisor Randy Coleman, led the proceedings. He had a rare, upbeat, even-keel, and enthusiastic attitude for an FBIHQ manager. Introductions around the table gave us a sense of just how serious this case was. Various US intelligence agency representatives were there, as well as our FBIHQ Unit Chief, Section Chief, and CI Assistant Director representative. Randy told everyone we had passed our polygraphs, never mentioning Sal's "Inconclusive" result.[5]

Randy reported that an unidentified source had indicated someone within Power Paragon Inc., a company located in Anaheim, California, SARA-4's territory, was providing sensitive, proprietary, and US military data to the PRC. It was a power generation and distribution systems subsidiary of defense contractor L-3 Communications, where two hundred employees worked on US Navy (USN) contracts, installing their products on surface warships and submarines.

Since the US Navy was a victim, we agreed that the Naval Criminal Investigative Service (NCIS) would be brought into the investigation. This case presented an opportunity to catch a PRC spy red-handed, and therefore was Top Secret and strictly "need to know," assigned the code name "Glazed Stone," and would *not* be uploaded onto the FBI's standard Automated Case Support system.[6] Everyone working it must first pass a CI polygraph and be placed on a "bigot list" documenting everyone who had knowledge of the case. I would report results to Randy, who immediately proposed streamlined, time-saving measures and guaranteed us new standalone computers for our case and future visits to SARA-4 to gauge our needs. At last, I had an FBIHQ manager who believed in enthusiastically supporting field agents.

---

5. Randy decided the meeting would proceed with Sal reexamined later, demonstrating he was a pragmatist who cared more about the mission than the formalities—substance over form.
6. We discovered later during the case that the Automated Case Support system was riddled with security issues.

Sal and I discussed plans over dinner. Despite Randy's help, this case could become a nightmare of unfair management expectations and pressure. We still wanted out but saw no clear exit strategy. The next morning, Sal easily passed his polygraph retest before we flew back to SARA-4 to deliver the news that would forever change the squad's history and reputation, and the FBI's PRC counterintelligence program.

CHAPTER 2

Setting the Stage

ON THE FLIGHT HOME I KEPT THINKING *YOU'VE REALLY STEPPED IN IT now!* I'd handled smaller cases on my own. Larger ones required squad help. This one would be a Cecil B. DeMille production. I opened my code name investigation on February 28, 2004, and began writing lists of tasks to complete. First, we needed to corroborate the original sensitive source reporting, before committing extensive resources. Sal and I discussed case needs and assigned two agents to help, Sheldon Fung and Kevin Moberly.

Although relatively new to the Bureau, Sheldon had already run a big investigation, the Ford Weapons of Mass Destruction case, in partnership with the Irvine Police Department. Before the Bureau, he was a Sacramento police officer. Sheldon was young, energetic, enthusiastic, and flush with ideas. Given his family name, some might assume we chose him for his ethnic background, language ability, or cultural knowledge. We didn't. Sheldon spoke little Chinese and was 100 percent American-grown. He constantly poked fun at his own background, and that of others, and made me laugh, often because of his intentionally outrageous pronouncements.

Kevin was even younger and newer. He had arrived only months earlier, having served in the US Air Force as an intelligence officer. He had an intense manner and ability to focus on issues and see them through. He and Sheldon had similar interests and developed a natural affinity for each other. They also counterbalanced my more reserved, resolved, and single-minded personality and goals. We complemented each other beautifully.

Our early efforts confirmed the amazing accuracy of the initial source information, increasing our confidence that we were on the trail of an active, and unaware, spy. We took steps to protect this advantage. Too many investigators waste it, becoming prematurely aggressive to meet executive demands. In high-profile investigations, executives typically push for constant input and progress to justify resources and impress each other. We would be patient, not risking our advantage for an "Attaboy" or other short-term gain. It's a tough but essential balancing act.

In an espionage case, investigators must first decide whether to go public or remain covert. If public, you may remove access by getting the spy fired and/or making an immediate arrest, thereby preventing further damage. But you won't learn the full extent of the damage done, or likely obtain enough evidence to convict, thereby inviting public derision and future lawsuits. In addition, the spy might return to their activities later, with you thoroughly discredited. While remaining covert gives you time to build a solid case, develop the deeper story, identify associates and co-conspirators, assess the damage, and set the time and place of search and arrest, it also risks the spy stealing and delivering more US secrets, and if they detect your investigation, escaping and leaving you red-faced and empty-handed.

Catching and convicting a PRC spy was my goal. But I always had to weigh my options: the likelihood doing X could reveal our investigation, versus the potential gain of doing it. If the likelihood of discovery seemed anything other than very low, it was a no-go.

First, we did a deep dive into Power Paragon, documenting the company and personnel histories and its US Navy products. Directly recruiting an employee for help would be risky. The person could be the spy, or would likely know them, maybe as a friend. We needed to better our odds of success before doing that. We surveilled Power Paragon to understand its work shifts, routines, and daily rhythms. Many employees arrived in the early morning and left early in the afternoon. Some worked on Saturdays. Some ate in the cafeteria and some smoked outside in groups. We videotaped two-hundred-plus license plates in the parking lot, ran each for owner name and photograph, and then checked criminal records.[1] Assuming the spy was likely an engineer with access, we sifted our data accordingly, narrowing our suspect list.

I'll always remember the day I first heard the name "Chi Mak." A very excited and overly confident Sheldon walked up and announced, "I've got our guy!" You would understand my skepticism if you knew Sheldon. He had at times an irritating habit of making final, all-encompassing, definitive statements about things he couldn't possibly know for certain. I humored him as he showed me a picture of Chi Mak. "Look at the way he's dressed. I know engineers, and this guy is one," Sheldon said.[2]

I was doubtful—not that Chi Mak could be the man, but that Sheldon had enough facts to *know* he was. Being an engineer wasn't our only qualifier. Power Paragon was full of them! We had more digging to do. "We'll see," I said.

"*You'll* see," promised Sheldon.

Chi Mak was one of many engineers, and one of a handful of Asian American ones at Power Paragon, albeit the only ethnic Chinese one. We were looking at *all* engineers with access, regardless of race or ethnicity. Cries of "Profiling! Racism! Bigotry! Discrimination!" are as predictable as they are misplaced. The nation that actually profiles and discriminates based upon these factors is China, which specifically targets overseas Chinese to cash in on commonalities of race, ethnicity, heritage, and the ability to blackmail family members. China has declared that the world's ethnic Chinese belong to them, nationality and citizenship be damned. *That* is racial profiling!

We confirmed Chi Mak was an electrical engineer, what he did, and the technologies he had access to.[3] He fit the bill nicely. I checked our database for references to Chi Mak—what I learned was the Cantonese

---

1. Ironically, none of this included the spy because he was not at work then.
2. Chi's appearance? Glasses, goofy grin, wearing a plaid shirt with polka-dot tie!
3. His recent papers and presentations included "Circuit Design Optimization for High Power Density Electronic Assembly" at the 2004 Electric Machine Technology Symposium in Philadelphia, and a 2004 Applied Power Electronics Conference presentation session regarding "Soft-Switching and High-Density DC-DC Converters" at the local Disneyland Hotel. Tough stuff for a political science major like me to understand!

version of his name. Zilch. I then ran the Mandarin version and its Standard Telegraphic Code (STC) numbers.[4] Bingo! One hit, but it was a doozy: A 1994 FBI San Francisco teletype to Los Angeles identified Chi and his wife "Rebecca" Laiwah Chiu by their Mandarin names and STC numbers.[5] This teletype cryptically reported information indicating that Mai Dazhi (Chi) and Zhao Lihua (Rebecca) were married, living in Southern California, and had high-level, sensitive connections with PRC officials which that government wished to keep hidden. This lead went unpursued in 1994; if it had been, Chi and Rebecca would have been detected a decade earlier! We would correct this egregious error.

I've seen lackadaisical agent and supervisor work before, so I could imagine how it might have happened. But there was another possibility. This San Francisco lead came during a time a compromised agent supervisor, J. J. Smith, and his PRC-run asset, Katrina Leung, dominated FBILA's CI China squad. Might that have played a role? We'll likely never know. At least we could now confirm the Maks' long-term betrayal and our initial source's accuracy.

As we dug deeper, Chi Mak became the only possible suspect. His body of work included all the Power Paragon technologies leaked to China. He was Power Paragon's senior engineer and in 2004 led the US Navy's national working group to develop the Quiet Electric Drive (QED) propulsion system, a groundbreaking quieting system that reduced the acoustic signatures of our newest Virginia-class submarines and surface warships. Power Paragon was working with the Navy's Office of Naval Research (ONR), Naval Reactors (NR), and others to develop QED. FBIHQ informed us that our source reporting now confirmed our suspicions: Chi Mak was our spy.[6]

Incredibly, we also learned that much more had been known from the beginning but withheld from us by a certain US intelligence community

---

4. STC is the universal system that assigns unique numbers to each Chinese name, thereby avoiding confusion surrounding identification and name pronunciation. For example, STC allows you to determine whether "Chao" and "Chou" are the same name and person. Chi Mak's STC is 7796/2535.
5. Back then the Bureau communicated through three formats: the teletype—the most urgent communication with the highest-priority reporting—the airtel, and the memorandum. The latter two traveled via US mail.
6. Sheldon never let me forget it!

member, making us waste time while reinventing the wheel. Turns out, Chi Mak and the names of his accomplices, wife Rebecca and brother Tai Wang Mak, had been known from the outset. We now had three subjects. Peeved, we resolved to travel back east to demand a review of *all* the source reporting. Receiving it in dribs and drabs was unacceptable.

Now we were covering two residences: Chi and Rebecca's home at 8261 Blandwood Drive, Downey, and Tai's house at 1629 South Fremont Avenue, Alhambra. Tai's address was more entertaining and easier to watch. Fremont is a large, very busy street. Blandwood, a quiet, cramped, blue-collar neighborhood, proved more difficult and had no activity in the beginning. We didn't see Chi Mak, Rebecca, car movements, or evidence of any residents.

After days of this I called Chi's work number one Sunday, hoping for voicemail.[7] I was rewarded with the news I sought: "This is Chi Mak. I am on vacation from March first to the sixteenth. Please leave a message and I will call when I get back." Chi and Rebecca had been gone since our investigation began! But where, and why?

The next day we filed paperwork requesting FBILA Technical Agent support coverages under the National Foreign Intelligence Program and Foreign Intelligence Surveillance Act (FISA), including "Land Line, Cellular, Trap and Trace, Intercepts of Modems, E-mails, Facsimiles, Internet usage, Pagers, Interior and Exterior Closed-Circuit Television, Cellular and Vehicle Tracking, Microphones, Lock work, and Surreptitious Entry and Searches." This case was going to be done right.

I sent my first weekly case update to superiors on March 12 regarding Chi, Rebecca, and Tai. Surveillance, trash, and mail covers were scheduled, but we kept losing surveillance teams to counterterrorism (CT) case demands. CI and CT investigations share the Special Surveillance Group (SSG), the best surveillance specialists in the FBI. So, I requested permanent assignment of SSG teams to our cases, and we set up at LAX International Airport to cover Chi and Rebecca's return. I didn't place them on a Watch List to avoid the chance a sloppy customs agent might reveal our interest in them. Secrecy and security always came first. We

---

7. Working weekends would soon become my rule, rather than an exception.

Chi Mak, Tai Mak, and Rebecca Chiu in China, June 4, 1961 AUTHOR'S COLLECTION

obtained their immigration files and issued National Security Letters for their telephone, toll, and financial records. I also requested more agents to complement SARA-4's current six, along with dedicated linguists. And I began writing a FISA court application for more coverages. Since the initial source reporting was highly classified, I also requested that a Sensitive Compartmented Information Facility (SCIF) be constructed for document storage.

Meanwhile, NCIS Special Agent Gunnar Newquist was scheduled to join us by March 15. I was not enthusiastic. Experience had taught me that working jointly with another agency always slowed things to a crawl, inviting extra politics and drama, and that teaching someone our paperwork proved more trouble than they were worth. This partnership was unwelcome, but obligatory, given the US Navy was the victim.

I couldn't have been more wrong. Gunnar was just what we needed. He was intelligent, skilled, funny, friendly, enthusiastic, supportive, and a natural optimist. Even in the worst of times he'd exclaim "It's all good."

I would reproach him with, "No, Gunnar, it's not!" and we would both laugh and figure out our next move.

The day he arrived, I gained an essential partner and friend. We both were experienced investigators with complementary skills, and we easily bounced ideas off each other. When the work pace allowed, we relaxed by discussing our families and common interests, such as coaching our kids' soccer teams. Gunnar also respected and knew Bureau ways. His father had been an FBI Special Agent, and Gunnar worked extensively with FBI agents in San Diego, maintaining a desk, computer, and presence in their space. He knew our culture and paperwork, so there was no learning curve.

By mid-March we had a clearer picture. The Treasury Enforcement Communication System (TECS) reported Chi and Rebecca had traveled from LAX to Taipei, Taiwan, on China Airlines. The record stopped there, so we assumed they had continued into China. TECS also indicated past international travel to Hong Kong, Taiwan, South Korea, and Japan, as well as trips to Europe, South America, Australia, and Russia, but never Mainland China. Immigration and Customs Enforcement

Chi and Rebecca in China, March 12, 2004 FBI RELEASED

(ICE) identified the Maks' second-leg return flight but didn't tell us its arrival time until *after* it had landed at LAX, making us scramble for our first sighting of the Maks, upon their return to their Downey residence that night.

Our SSG surveillance teams began documenting Chi and Rebecca's contacts and routines while we studied Chi within his work environment. We met with representatives of the Defense Security Service (DSS), which oversees security for cleared defense contractors (companies that perform classified work). After much delay, DSS confirmed that Chi Mak carried a security clearance, and that Power Paragon's parent company, L-3 Communications, owned subsidiaries in Europe, Australia, New Zealand, and Japan, but not China.

Case manpower requirements soon increased exponentially, sucking in our whole squad. Data requiring analysis and action poured in. I was working twelve- to fourteen-hour days, six to seven days a week, and I needed to delegate, quickly. Sheldon became my co-case agent, taking over all technical coverage issues. Kevin became our surveillance coordinator, removing a huge burden from my shoulders and writing the template for all expanding, future coverages. Critically, once assigned tasks, Sheldon, Kevin, and Gunnar ran with them. No follow-up was necessary—truly an underrated, undervalued skill. Our investigative talent pool may have been small, but it was incredibly deep.

CHAPTER 3

A Dark Cloud

AT THE START OF OUR INVESTIGATION, THE FBI's SUCCESS RATE IN Chinese espionage prosecutions was bleak. In 1985, the FBI recorded one major success in the prosecution of Chinese espionage, in the form of defendant "Larry" Wu-Tai Chin. He had been recruited by Communist China near the end of World War II to spy against the United States. For forty years, while employed by the US Army and Central Intelligence Agency (CIA), Chin passed classified secrets to Mao's China. His subsequent arrest and confession led to his guilty plea for espionage and tax evasion. On the day of his 1986 sentencing, Chin was found dead in his cell, having asphyxiated himself with a plastic bag. Since then, the FBI's record of prosecuting China's spies had been abysmal.

The early 1980s had already witnessed two failed major prosecutions. The first investigation was in San Francisco, code name "Tiger Trap," targeting Chinese American scientist Gwo Bao Min, an employee of Lawrence Livermore Laboratories who was stopped at the airport on his way to China, carrying answers to technical questions his PRC handlers had posed regarding nuclear devices.[1] The FBI urged Gwo's prosecution, but prosecutors declined, claiming insufficient evidence.

The second case concerned Taiwanese-born nuclear physicist Peter Lee, who worked for TRW, Lawrence Livermore, and Los Alamos National Laboratories. He provided classified technical data to the PRC,

---

1. The FBI Special Agent who questioned him, Bill Cleveland, was later identified as having a sexual relationship with the subject of another Chinese espionage investigation, PRC spy Katrina Leung.

including advanced radar to track nuclear missile submarines, during numerous China trips. The evidence in this FBILA investigation, code name "Royal Tourist," was strong, but again its prosecution was weak. Its Assistant US Attorneys (AUSAs) complained that Department of Justice (DOJ) superiors blocked them from filing more serious charges. Lee pled guilty to one charge of espionage, making a false statement, and tax evasion, later receiving only a *one-year* sentence at a halfway house, three years' probation, 3,000 hours of community service, and a $20,000 fine.[2] Attorney General Janet Reno and her DOJ were heavily criticized for this weak result during US Senate hearings. Many FBILA CI agents began to say, "Why bother?"

The 1990s proved an impossible decade to prosecute PRC spies. When President Clinton put White House access up for auction, PRC representatives jumped in with both feet. By decade's end, Wen Ho Lee's investigation in Albuquerque, New Mexico, code name "Kindred Spirit," had ended disastrously due to mismanagement by the US Department of Energy and the FBI's Albuquerque Field Office, and the dawn of the loathsome "racism!" defense by Chinese American defendants.

This defense was extended into the new millennium by attorneys for PRC double agent Katrina Leung, code name "Parlor Maid," and her lover, FBILA Supervisory Special Agent (SSA) J. J. Smith. A special squad, National Security Division 9 (NSD-9), was created to investigate this case, but its prosecution ended badly due to weak prosecutors, some detestable FBI SSAs, and a left-wing judge. The finale flopped onto SARA-4's doorstep in 2004, permeating everything like a stinking fish just as our case began.

These Bureau failures became an ever-present cloud hanging over our investigation and were a primary reason FBIHQ assigned the Chi Mak case to SARA-4. Yet FBILA "experts" from the Leung/Smith case kept telling us what to do.[3] We still didn't want this investigation. The burden would be huge, and we were short of resources and lacked FBILA backing. But reading the tea leaves, Sal began closing or transferring all other SARA-4 case work to FBILA and adjacent Resident Agencies. We were

2. Future espionage defendant FBILA Special Agent J. J. Smith played a major role in this case.
3. If we had listened to these FBILA "experts," our case would have crashed and burned.

now only working this one case but had one more chance to avoid our fate. Chi Mak worked in Orange County, but he, Rebecca, and Tai lived in Los Angeles County, FBILA's jurisdiction. When Randy arrived from FBIHQ to visit, we would push for this case's transfer to other squads, maybe even to FBILA's "experts."

Randy arrived in April 2004, and we briefed him on all we knew. In little over a month, we had conducted a thorough investigation. Sal's leadership had allowed us to do our job, while he jumped in to obtain the support, personnel, and resources we needed, always ready and willing to battle on our behalf. Sheldon's contacts and energy gave us a head start, and the squad's full and unwavering support kept us ahead. Randy was astounded by our progress and the volume of amassed knowledge regarding our subjects. In a short time, we were up and running on multiple surveillances, trash covers, and "polecams" (closed-circuit cameras in public areas). Now we were collecting data on the subjects' associates.

We concluded our briefing with a pitch to transfer these cases to squads covering the Maks' residences. Randy's response was swift and emphatic: "No! This stays in Santa Ana. You guys have done a great job. You're on the right track, know where you are going, and have an excellent team. I have every confidence in you. Besides, Los Angeles management and their China squads are dysfunctional. Headquarters has no confidence in their ability to handle this. They are demoralized and disorganized." We countered, but it was no bueno. We were stuck.

We understood Randy's position, and our own. This investigation was now ours to run, for good or ill, and if anything went wrong, it would fall hardest on Sal and me, no matter the cause. Then and there, I decided I would yield my decision-making to no one, no matter their rank. My name and reputation would be attached to something of public, national import. If it failed, it would not be for lack of effort on my part. I would fight to the end.

I had no idea then just how important my determination would prove, or how much my resolve would be tested. In fact, it was a blessing that I didn't know what was to come.

CHAPTER 4

How Firm a Foundation

As the Glazed Stone investigation expanded, I wrote a strategy manual for my investigators. Any uncleared, mistaken case-related reporting could bring disaster to any prosecution. Our investigative goals included: 1) identifying all spy ring members; 2) developing assets within Power Paragon; 3) cataloging all sensitive data Chi Mak had access to; 4) obtaining FISA coverages on Chi, Rebecca, and Tai; and 5) utilizing every non-alerting coverage possible. I established new procedures based upon the new "paperless" filing system the FBI was initiating called "Virtual Case File" (VCF), proving I was no prophet. Within months, VCF crashed and burned, and was discarded, costing the FBI $70 million. We were stuck with this VCF-based system and had to make it work. Fact-checking each document before final submission and approval by me, Sheldon, Sal, and squad secretary Tanya prior to filing and uploading was paramount. Too many espionage prosecutions are sunk by sloppy paperwork.[1]

Confirming their team spirit and work ethic, our static surveillance personnel—"Lookouts"—volunteered to help Tanya with all the filing. It was outside the narrow duties their supervisor Tina kept trying to enforce, but their help proved essential. Tina earned my contempt for her ignorant, bureaucratic prohibitions while her Lookouts gained my admiration for ignoring her. They were a godsend, as their teamwork, selflessness, and flexibility kept our heads above water. Our paperwork

---

1. This required level of control and secrecy elicited derision from the criminal squads.

headaches were increased by FBIHQ experts' erratic, changing system requirements and prohibitions. For each system problem SARA-4 agents discovered, FBIHQ experts offered "solutions" that just created more work for us.

We eventually pulled the plug to build our own standalone system, with Randy obtaining new computers, monitors, printers, and scanners by hook or by crook. In the end, our system proved the most secure and user-friendly. Gunnar and his NCIS colleague "Rocky" helped set up this solution for us. Later, Sheldon, Kevin, and Doug took over administration of this system, which increased in size and complexity along with the investigation.

To increase efficiency and productivity, I needed accountability. Primary and secondary duties were assigned to all personnel to ensure consistent coverage. I was case agent for the overall Glazed Stone investigation, and Chi and Rebecca's cases. Sheldon handled Tai Mak, his wife Fuk, and their kids, and was overall FBI co-case agent. Gunnar was the NCIS case agent and took responsibility for review of US Navy technical data and personnel and asset (informant) development. Kevin managed our growing surveillance efforts—i.e., SSG teams, Lookouts, 24/7 polecams, and GPS vehicle tracking and communications—while other squad agents conducted background investigations of subject associates and weekly trash covers at four locations.

Sal used his advanced administrative and political skills to trade for additional invaluable additions like agents Jessie and Tom. Jessie was our invaluable surveillance, trash cover, trial evidence, and discovery coordinator. Whatever the job, she got it done.[2] Tom's exceptional organizational skills made him my invaluable partner in tracking, organizing, and retrieving the thousands of FISA technical intercepts and translations we accumulated, which would prove key to our prosecution. Tom kept it all straight.

While we had gotten the case off the ground, our estimated long-term needs included a separate SCIF off-site location, fifteen Special

---

2. She was also SARA-4's social activities manager and master baker, dubbed "Julie," as in the cruise director from *The Love Boat*.

Agents, one Squad Secretary, one Investigative Analyst, one CIA analyst, seven SSG teams, three Lookouts, and two full-time linguists.

Randy agreed, claiming our case was the "number-one PRC priority at FBIHQ." A/ASAC Mike fought our requests, repeatedly declaring the whole thing would blow over in ninety days.

Our estimated needs proved prescient. Mike did not.

CHAPTER 5

Strange Subjects, Stranger Trash

MOST INVESTIGATIONS BUILD GRADUALLY, BEGINNING WITH AN ALLE-gation, suspicious contact, or other unusual event. Inquiries are made, and if a threat is indicated, we go to the next level. The greater the threat, the more invasive the techniques, supported by the highest levels of substantiation. The highest authorizations came from the FBI director, attorney general, and the court which administers the Foreign Intelligence Surveillance Act (FISA). Since we had now confirmed that Chi Mak threatened our war-fighting capabilities with our greatest enemy, the PRC, we shot to FISA coverages practically overnight. But this meant FBI management wanted tangible results yesterday. We needed to quickly gain their confidence and buy some breathing room.

I requested polecam installations by FBILA's Technical Squad for the two Mak residences.[1] Although this was the highest-priority military-secrets espionage case, the response was crickets. Tony, our SARA-4 Tech Squad representative, claimed they were "too busy" with criminal cases. I knew Tony's reputation for lethargy. His superiors were no help, so we began our campaign of relentless arm-twisting and public shaming. Tony conceded with an angry telephone call, declaring he could only do the site survey at one a.m.

I was incensed with this brinkmanship. Getting caught near Chi's home would set off the whole neighborhood. Yet Sal agreed, beginning

---

1. Polecams are commonly used in drug cases to watch foot traffic at dealers' residences and places of business.

our first argument. I said this risked our biggest advantage—secrecy. Sal countered that Tony was bluffing, and we had to call it. Kevin got the unenviable job of meeting Tony, who never showed, giving Sal the ammo he needed. Tony's Tech Squad supervisor forced him to install the polecams, after two months of hemming and hawing. Unsurprisingly, he did a bad job, installing the Downey camera where its view of the front door was blocked most of the year by leaves on a neighbor's tree. Yet Tony and his Tech Squad refused to fix this poor work. I considered solving our frustrating visibility problem by driving a copper nail into that tree. In the end, we made do, but Tony's behavior initiated a maddening pattern of Tech Squad indifference to the mission.

We piped polecam closed-circuit television (CCTV) coverage back to the SARA conference room we had transformed into our command center. After more struggles with Lookout supervisor Tina, we obtained Lookout staffing 24/7 to watch the Maks' activities. This protected our covert investigation by enabling our SSG teams—"Gs" for short—to set up at convenient locations outside the neighborhood.

Hollywood has it all wrong. People can't sit in cars in neighborhoods for long periods of time without drawing suspicion and police inquiries. No one wants strangers loitering near their home. This positioning relieved the Gs from the nonstop eyeballing of targets' homes, assigning Lookouts the task of calling out surveillance instructions via radio or cellphone. This system worked flawlessly, drastically reducing our risk.

The Lookouts were worth every fight we had with Tina to get and keep them. They and the Gs proved to be our essential partners. These were elite surveillance personnel—experts. They are not Special Agents and look nothing like law enforcement. If or when you meet them on the street, you'll never guess they are FBI, and that's the point. Unfortunately our demand outstripped FBILA's supply, since other CI and CT cases also used them, so Randy at FBIHQ performed some horse-trading, acquiring teams from Field Offices in San Francisco, San Diego, Houston, Honolulu, New York, and Washington, DC, to name a few.

While they all proved excellent, I always believed FBILA had the best Gs, in part because they had the best supervisor, John, a man I greatly respected. The mission came first for him. He was forever cheerful, positive, and prepared to bend over backward to get us what we needed. My Vietnamese investigations had always been a low Bureau priority, so John often couldn't fully meet my case needs, but he *never* rejected my requests, always giving me something, even if it was just one body for half a shift. John didn't say no, even if it would have made his life easier. Instead, he said, "I'll see what I can do," did his best, and got back to me quickly. John and his teams always gave us their very best efforts.

Surveillance soon reported rigid and strange patterns of behavior by Chi and Rebecca, causing us considerable worry. We knew they were accomplished spies, having escaped detection for decades; thus, we readily assumed strange behaviors indicated intelligence activity. For instance, every weekday morning Chi strolled the neighborhood while Rebecca remained at home. When he returned, she went for a stroll. When she returned, he left for work, and she remained in their seven-hundred-square-foot home all day. Were they doing neighborhood countersurveillance while guarding something in the home? They never had any visitors. Chi's route to/from work never changed. Rebecca often checked their Plymouth Voyager minivan parked at the curb in front of their home, closely examining its tires, as if to look for signs of tampering or movement. And she constantly peeked out the house windows, calling Chi at work to report the "Mexican kid" from the neighborhood hanging around outside.

I always worried over our investigation being detected, so we ran very loose surveillance. Long-term surveillance must always consider: "What's worse—being identified, or losing the subject?" since the time always arrives when the risk grows into one or the other.

My answer? "*Never* get made!" This meant holding back and sometimes losing them during strange behaviors and movements. Our tracking devices would tell us their general location. Line-of-sight surveillance is eventually spotted, blowing up a covert investigation. One way to detect compromise is identification of surveillance detection routes (SDRs), target behaviors which may indicate conscious attempts to detect or lose surveillance, such as sudden changes in speed, direction, or route, excessive stops and turns, running lights, driving on the shoulder, looking around, etc. In this regard, Chi and Rebecca put us through the

Chi and Rebecca under surveillance FBI RELEASED

wringer, not intentionally or through clever tradecraft, but thanks to their strange personalities, which produced apparent SDRs, making us wonder whether Chi and Rebecca were on to us. My younger, more excitable co-case agent, Sheldon Fung, was usually the first to express these concerns, proclaiming, "They're going operational!" I laughed it off, but often pondered the same as a question.

Eventually we learned the truth: Rebecca was naturally paranoid and antisocial. She didn't like anyone, stranger, friend, or relative, suspecting them all. What she did inside of her house all day, every day, remained a mystery until later.[2] And we learned to attribute Chi's strange driving habits to his poor sense of direction. If he hadn't drawn a map beforehand, he became lost easily, meaning frequent U-turns. Other SDR-like behaviors originated from the Maks' fanatical thriftiness. We followed them endlessly around stores, only for them to buy nothing, although Rebecca did shoplift batteries on occasion. Once, after an hour of shopping, they tried to purchase a single box of Top Ramen but left without it. Why? Their coupon had expired. How much does *one* box of Top Ramen cost?

---

2. We did rule out one thing upon first entry into the home: It certainly wasn't housekeeping!

They saved the soda cans they received during airline flights. Their house trash lacked bottles or cans, consisting only of fruit peelings wrapped in Chinese-language newspapers. They didn't want to wash dishes, which costs time and money for soap and water, so they ate their fruit, wrapped its remains, and threw it out! Simple.[3]

Once, during a two-night work visit to Las Vegas, they moved to another hotel for the second night. Since Power Paragon paid Chi a per diem, he could pocket the $2 difference between hotels. And although they visited Europe, they never bought souvenirs or ate in restaurants, only at sidewalk vendors. When they toured Hawaii's Big Island, using earned flyer miles, each night they stayed in a sketchier, cheaper, more decrepit hotel than the last. During business trips, Chi wore the clothes on his back and carried one change of underwear in his briefcase, washing and drying the worn pair every night. The Maks bought all their clothes at Goodwill and never upgraded or renovated their home. All of these behaviors saved them some bucks, to the tune of nearly $1 million in the bank, but at what personal cost? The greatest irony: Most of those hard-earned savings were later lost to US government seizures and large defense attorney bills. The axiom "You can't take it with you" was never truer!

Their weekend behaviors were even more bizarre. Chi and Rebecca rose early every Saturday to drive to a local park and briefly play a bad game of tennis, then post a letter at the same mailbox.[4] We never saw indications they were marking the mailboxes.[5] The Maks then drove to the same gas station to refuel, using the station's squeegees and paper towels to wash their *entire* car at the same time. This seemed a great countersurveillance technique, allowing them a casual 360-degree view of their surroundings. Turns out this was just another way to save time and money—no need to pay for water, soap, hoses, sponges, towels, or squeegees. After that, they entered the one big front door of the "All American Store," a large hardware business, immediately walking to the lumber section, where they remained until finally exiting the store and driving home, never purchasing anything.

---

3. You've got to admit, there is a weird sort of efficiency to it.
4. The Gs thereafter "mailed" markers, allowing later retrieval of what were always bank payments.
5. Mailboxes with signals marked upon them, often with chalk, have a long history in Soviet Union spycraft.

We were confused. Was this countersurveillance, using the front-door funnel, as it were, to watch from the lumber section for a tail? Were they servicing a dead drop within the lumber, leaving/retrieving messages or other signals to handlers?[6] We requested an NCIS surveillance team to stake out the interior one Saturday before the Maks arrived. Their findings? Mak hyper-cheapness was once again to blame. Every Saturday morning this hardware store offered free coffee to its customers, so the Maks grabbed a cup, quickly drank it within the stacked lumber section, threw the cups away there, and left. No dead drops, no communications, no countersurveillance.

Covering Tai Mak and his family was more interesting. As head of Phoenix TV's audio department, Tai's schedule was unpredictable, often requiring odd hours to troubleshoot. Tai ran errands all over Los Angeles, and often ate breakfast or lunch with his son Yui or daughter Suet Li, known as Billy and Shirley, respectively. Some errands were for his wife, Fuk. Tai was a cautious, better driver, easier to follow. Occasionally, he hosted Phoenix and Asia TV representatives visiting from China, many of whom behaved like intelligence officers. Not surprising, since PRC officials ran both companies.

Fuk won the prize for most interesting to follow. She had no legal occupation and followed no schedule, operating at odd hours day and night, meeting people at various locations. She was emotional, erratic, and highly intelligent, with a self-destructive bent. Fuk certainly made it challenging. One day she left her house and walked around the block to the parallel street behind her home, jammed with parked cars from nearby apartments. By the time the Gs arrived, Fuk had vanished.

After this had happened several times, the Gs parked a car back there and waited. This time they saw her walk to a waiting car, which then drove her away. It was owned and driven by Mr. Zhang, who we nicknamed "ZZ," as in "ZZ Top." He took Fuk to apartment complexes, offices, restaurants, and malls to meet with others. In one restaurant, the Gs overheard them discussing a "marriage contract" and a $10,000 charge with a third party. At a different restaurant, we saw Fuk and Zhang sift-

---

6. A dead drop location is used to exchange information, items, or communications with confederates.

ing through driver's license photographs. Turned out they were partners in an illegal marriage fraud immigration business.

Zhang was a suspicious character in his own right. Years earlier he had visited the United States as a representative of a PRC government company. Shortly thereafter, he requested asylum, claiming to be a PRC-persecuted follower of the Falun Gong religious movement. Our government granted him asylum and he claimed residency in New Jersey, yet he obtained a California driver's license within days. It all stunk to high heaven, especially since Zhang had continuously lived in Southern California and remained on very good terms with PRC consulate officials. Another demonstration of our porous immigration system.

In addition to polecams and SSG surveillance, we instituted trash covers, a basic technique that is often overlooked by agents.[7] They involve the collection, sifting, documentation, and retention of relevant items from a subject's trash. Although not a glamorous duty, it often provides valuable evidence. I had enjoyed great results in previous cases, from incriminating love letters to external hard drives. Trash covers will also produce bank records, telephone numbers, phone messages, personal identification numbers, travel receipts, business transactions, plane tickets, and other activities. While the possibilities are limitless, the methods used are not, usually determined by circumstances. Most trash covers are short-term, one-man jobs—grab and dash—performed in the dark of night. I did these myself. The advantage was little to no foot or vehicle traffic to witness your actions. The disadvantage was the quiet. Any suspicious noise or activity witnessed was amplified by the night air and quiet street. If seen, you might compromise the investigation, and you could never return to that trash.

Less cautious agents had more harrowing experiences, including local police response or jumping hedges and injuring themselves while making their escape. How long one should tarry and what should be seized was another issue. The longer you linger and search, the greater the chance of discovery. If you take too much, the subject might notice the next morning, and in the darkness, it's hard to see what should be taken,

---

7. I also tried mail covers, which proved difficult and unproductive. We saw one cryptic Chinese New Year postcard from someone in Hong Kong. Colleen and I believed it was a PRCIS handler's message, but we could never prove it.

or left. You dare not use a flashlight. Trash also often contains noisy items like cans and bottles, with neighborhood dogs ready to bark. This method remains covert only if it's done a few times, *and* you're not caught. Daytime trash covers allow for quick selection and collection but are tough to pull off unwitnessed. I knew these methods wouldn't work for the Maks' trash, so I went with door number two. While much harder to detect, it involves more outside players.

We approached the trash collection company's route supervisor, who then introduced us to his drivers. We paid them directly to collect the trash for the Maks' block—without providing the Maks' name or address—and deliver it to a safe location where we could sift through it. This system worked exceptionally well for over a year at both Mak residences, without compromise. Paranoid Rebecca suspected nothing. The drivers delivered their smelly loads, dumping them onto a vacant parking lot where agents waited to jump in, culling through the haul efficiently with shovels, rakes, rubber gloves, booties, jumpsuits, plastic tarps, and face masks—the latter especially necessary in hot, rancid summer months.

Clear plastic garbage bags held our best finds. Any damp trash collected was separated and dried in the sun on the top floor of our SARA parking garage before filing, to prevent smell and rot. Because the Maks used unique, cheap trash bags of an unusual color and texture, agents soon could avoid culling a whole block's worth of trash, only needing to locate the Maks' bags. Those containing addressed bills, Rebecca's electrical engineering magazines, and junk mail confirmed the Maks' ownership. Agents found no cans, bottles, or discarded letters, but plenty of Chinese newspapers, travel brochures, fruit peelings, coffee grounds, empty Top Ramen containers, and juice boxes. While collection became monotonous, with diminishing returns, our people remained disciplined.[8] This was a repulsive, time-consuming duty, so we rotated the agents performing it. Jessie and Scott did more than their fair share of this, but everyone pitched in, except, ironically, me. Although I was the trash cover's main proponent and wanted to join them on occasion, for old times' sake, if nothing else, I never did. In three years, I just didn't have the time. I still regret not joining them.

---

8. Their conscientiousness later proved critical to our investigation.

Gunnar helped with this often, despite his initial doubts regarding its efficacy, because he was a team player. And being a natural storyteller, he often had the squad and me in stitches with his slightly exaggerated "Trash Tales." There was the time he was hit by palm nuts while sifting trash on the asphalt. He looked around, saw Sheldon, and told him to knock it off. Sheldon denied it, saying Gunnar was hallucinating. Gunnar went back to work and was hit again, and again. Finally, he realized parrots flying overhead were dropping them on the pavement (and sometimes on Gunnar's hard head) to break them open.

Another time Gunnar and other "gringo" agents were questioned by neighborhood kids as to why they were going through trash in an abandoned parking lot. Had they lost something valuable, and could the kids help? On more than one occasion, Gunnar expertly mimicked his gag reflex after moving some trash, thereby releasing an army of cockroaches and maggots wiggling over his gloves and shoes. The intimate details of his nausea whenever he entered the back of the garbage truck to shovel out its contents made you feel as if you were there. Others had similar experiences, of course, but Gunnar made it come alive for the listener.

Jessie, who worked more of these trash runs than anyone, personally "thanked" me for her experiences on challenging trash days, i.e., hot or rainy days. Her valuable lesson? "When you go in the back of a garbage truck filled with plastics, coffee grounds, rice, toiletries, and other filth, if the rice moves, *it's not rice!*"

The trash cover of Tai's home initially proved even more fruitful. We recovered completed marriage fraud contracts identifying Fuk's clients and associates, as well as Tai's business cards for an import/export company, Mak Professional Stereo Engineering Company, Ltd.[9] We also collected business cards for a Hong Kong auto lighting business Billy ran with his rich girlfriend. And we learned of daughter Shirley's abysmal high school and community college grades.

Significantly, and ironically, our first trash recovery was a fax invoice sheet, which became the most important piece of evidence collected from Tai's trash, although its true importance would only emerge years later.

---

9. Tai's attorney would try to use it as an alibi two years later.

CHAPTER 6

Promises Made to Be Broken

IT WAS SOON APPARENT TO ALL BUT A/ASAC MIKE THAT THIS CASE was growing and would be long-term. SARA-4 needed to at least double its seven-agent contingent and add analysts, Lookouts, SSG teams, and linguists. We submitted our estimate of everything needed, knowing we would be lucky to get half. Getting and keeping resources became a never-ending battle with management. I documented every need, sending my Weekly Investigative Update to FBILA and FBIHQ. We submitted our requests to FBILA Assistant Director in Charge (ADIC) Richard Garcia, and he invited us to brief him at the next FBILA Special Agent in Charge (SAC) conference. Mike tried to muzzle us, saying we would embarrass ourselves. My response? "I don't care." With my name attached to this case, it was going to be done right. I would not be nickeled and dimed into failure. Mike had been downplaying our case; clearly, he didn't want to look foolish.

As we entered the ADIC meeting, a frustrated Mike made one last appeal: "Let's keep this in house. I'll make sure you're taken care of." We didn't believe him. Surprisingly, ADIC Garcia opened with a declaration that SARA-4 had a huge case, and Los Angeles would meet all its needs. Apparently, FBIHQ Assistant Director (AD) Dave Szady had notified Garcia of his intense interest.[1] I'm sure Randy at FBIHQ also had something to do with it.

---

1. When I first briefed him about this family of spies, Szady exclaimed, "This is another 'Walker' case!" John Walker, a US Navy communications officer, recruited others, including his brother and son, to spy with him for the Soviet Union between 1967 and 1985, helping it decipher over one million US Navy–encrypted messages. Many consider him the most damaging spy in history.

Garcia asked for SARA-4's request and I presented it. Before I could finish, Garcia interrupted, saying "Okay. Here's what we need to do," laying out a plan that promised us more than we had requested. Surprised, I naively thought, "With this kind of support, success is guaranteed!" The cooperation Garcia promised was staggering, rivaling that given the J. J. Smith/Katrina Leung case. In shock, Sal and I said, "Thank you, sir!" and we were all dismissed. A morose Mike told us, "Well, he's on board. You got what you wanted. I don't know why. Don't screw up!"

The next day felt like Christmas! ADIC Garcia sent an email to us and FBILA and FBIHQ bigwigs documenting the copious resources SARA-4 would receive: a secure off-site location to be staffed with two SSAs; twenty Special Agents; six SSG teams; six FBI, CIA, and military analysts; one squad secretary; and six Language Specialists (linguists). The off-site location would include rooms for monitoring surveillance coverages, storing evidence, processing mail, and maintaining equipment, breakrooms, and restrooms.

Sal forwarded this email to Sheldon and me with instructions: "Let's identify a building before they find one for us!" If only Bureau upper management was always so decisive; too many good CI cases die due to shortsighted, backbiting Bureau and DOJ politics. Sadly, my admiration for Garcia proved short-lived. Almost immediately he began backpedaling on his promises. It was the usual theater to look decisive and responsive to FBIHQ with no intention of following through. Garcia actually failed to provide this support, and later attacked us for documenting his broken promises.

ADIC Garcia's directives pretending to support a SCIF for SARA-4 made us waste months pursuing it. The project was led by Dennis, a former SARA-4 squad mate turned SSA who had his own experiences with twisted, immoral Bureau politics.[2] He secured a wonderful off-site location in Cerritos, under budget, but it all eventually fell through when Garcia wouldn't overrule a low-level DC bureaucrat's escalating mandates. The final requirement that killed the deal? The private landlord of this large, commercial, multi-tenant property had to guarantee an

---

2. Dennis was the consummate agent, professional in every respect, the sort of manager who made effective decisions. But he was only one man in a sea of sociopathic sycophants.

appropriately "diverse" landscaping and maintenance crew. DC telling LA how to be diverse? What a joke![3] Garcia refused to lift a finger.

That was that. A year's worth of work up in smoke. A low-level FBIHQ clerk was allowed to kill an off-site location and SCIF that the ADIC had claimed "essential" to our high-priority PRC espionage case. We were ordered to do what they had said shouldn't be done—expand our current SARA space, without real support from FBILA. This simply made us enemies to all the SARA criminal squads we now had to fight for space. Sal and I became SARA's favorite villains.

Criminal agents have always held CI agents in disdain. The problem comes down to a lack of publicity: Whereas criminal agent work is public and rewarded accordingly, CI work is secret. There are no newspaper articles, televised news programs, prosecuting attorneys, public announcements, or other community recognition. The few national CI awards don't provide case details because they're classified. Criminal agents aren't cleared to know our cases or even enter our SCIFs.[4] So, they make the lazy assumption, "No publicity means no work done." Most CI classified investigations never generate criminal cases, which means no public acclaim or reward. Those that do receive recognition are rarer than four-leaf clovers.

Through sheer determination (my specialty) and brinkmanship (Sal's forte), we gained the bare minimum of resources to continue, at great cost in time and energy. A temporary partition wall giving us more space was derisively called "The Great Wall of Sal" by criminal agents. It was poorly constructed, and beneath CI or safety regulations, but otherwise served its purpose, keeping criminal agents out, and our information in. Our "essential" SCIF never happened. FBIHQ and FBILA refused to certify one small file room we had that was already SCIF-compliant, meaning we would waste hundreds of man-hours over the years, making the two-hour drive each way in horrible traffic, to use the SCIF at FBILA headquarters.

---

3. Apparently, not enough Swedes and Armenians would be mowing the lawn.
4. Even our own families can't know the details about our work.

CHAPTER 7

Finding Friends in All the Right Places

SUCCESSFUL INVESTIGATIONS OFTEN REQUIRE HELP FROM AN "INSIDER" who can provide essential information and access. We needed this to learn about Power Paragon and its employees, so Gunnar and I worked to recruit one. Asking the wrong person about Chi could end our investigation before it even began. We needed to know where his workspace was, who his friends were, what technologies he had access to, and so forth.

Gunnar, Sheldon, and I drew up a short list of search parameters and potential candidates and asked our agents and analysts to build profiles for each one. They produced one excellent candidate I will call "Pat." Pat was a calm, levelheaded, patriotic person with great company contacts; someone who could be trusted to choose America over China *and* employer. Too many these days won't.

Now came the question: How to approach Pat? We ruled out at home; we didn't want to look like we were trying to intimidate them. Approaching during the morning commute wouldn't allow us enough time for the pitch, leaving an undecided Pat to possibly let this slip to coworkers. Contact at work was an obvious no-go. If done by phone, Pat might disbelieve us and mention it to a coworker. The safest approach, with the greatest chance of success, was right after work. If Pat didn't bite, this approach from "NCIS agents" wouldn't scream "espionage investigation" like an FBI inquiry would.[1]

---

1. If rejected, our interest would more likely be interpreted as representing a general government fraud investigation.

So, we set off on our first recruitment pitch. I drove with Gunnar as passenger and parked near Pat's vehicle. We were dressed business casual to avoid the "G-man" look. Right on time, Pat exited Power Paragon and walked toward their car.

Gunnar got out and met Pat there, discreetly displaying his NCIS credentials at his hip to avoid a scene. "Good afternoon. My name is Gunnar Newquist," he said. "I'm a Special Agent with the NCIS. You are not in any sort of trouble, but I have a very serious and sensitive matter to discuss with you, in which you could be of great help. Do you have time to talk to me now?" With the answer "Yes," Gunnar directed Pat to meet us at Mimi's Restaurant nearby, which contained few customers at the time. Gunnar reentered my car and we followed Pat's vehicle to the restaurant, where we met inside.

The first meeting was guarded. I identified myself as Gunnar's colleague, letting Pat assume I was also NCIS, in case this contact went poorly. We were assessing character, gauging whether Pat was trustworthy and had the access to people and information we needed. Pat was trying to figure out if we were genuine, what we wanted, and if we could be trusted. The meeting went smoothly and professionally, and by its end we told Pat there was an issue at Power Paragon concerning proprietary and sensitive US Navy information being lost, explaining the company was not under any suspicion, and that we had contacted Pat due to their personal reputation for honesty and patriotism. We emphasized that no one else could know of our interest, or the fact we'd made contact. Pat agreed to help, and to meet us again the next day. Pat appeared to like us both and appreciate our low-key approach and easy manner (Gunnar and I made a very effective team).

We had a good feeling about Pat, and the next day told them about the compromised technologies and asked who the "leaker" might be. Pat knew everyone, including Chi, but named no suspects. At our third meeting, we indicated that our evidence pointed to Chi. Pat was surprised, finding it hard to believe, but did confirm Chi had access to the relevant material. Pat reported that Chi was well-liked and known for his cheerful, can-do attitude, and agreed to help us, believing cooperation and our investigation would clear Chi's name.[2]

Pat's recruitment was an essential first step and provided intelligence that guided our investigation and got us into the facility for covert technical surveys. Pat also identified another trustworthy Power Paragon employee who could get us continuous covert access to the facility: Fred Witham, director of security. Fred's background was impeccable. We would talk to him next.

Although Fred wouldn't be a formal asset, we stuck with the same winning formula. He parked in back of the facility and farther away, so the risk of other Power Paragon employees seeing us was even less of a concern. When Fred exited right on schedule, Gunnar walked up to him near his truck. In my driver's seat, with parked vehicles between us, I could only see the tops of their heads.

Within seconds, Gunnar returned.

A new record! I thought.

Gunnar flung the door open, angrily sat down, and shouted, "Go!"

As I backed up, I asked, "What happened?"

"Just go!" Gunnar barked.

We left, but told our SSG team to continue covering Fred.

I drove back to our office as Gunnar muttered exclamations of anger and frustration at himself and Fred. Gunnar told me that before he could finish his first sentence, Fred angrily declared his credentials were fake—he wasn't an NCIS agent—and demanded to know who he really was. When Gunnar reassured him that he was genuine, Fred pulled out his walkie-talkie, did an about-face, and quickly walked back toward the Power Paragon facility, shouting instructions to point outside CCTV cameras at Gunnar, who by now was beating his own quick retreat to my car.

Gunnar couldn't figure out what went wrong. Why had Fred reacted that way? What had Gunnar done? I assured him it wasn't his fault, assuming Fred was just having a very bad day.

---

2. Pat's belief in Chi's innocence remained until the prosecution phase. Once our evidence became public, Pat reluctantly came to the sad conclusion that Chi Mak had betrayed his coworkers, company, and country.

Our SSG team later reported that Fred once again exited the facility with others in tow, searching around his truck and the general vicinity where my car had been parked. Fred eventually headed home in his truck, but then abruptly turned off the freeway and drove back to Power Paragon. Turns out he had accomplished the rare feat of spotting our coverage. After returning to Power Paragon, he called the police. I told our SSG team to stand down, and we hoped the whole thing would quickly blow over. The next day, Pat and other sources indicated Fred was more nervous than usual but eventually calmed down.

Although somewhat concerned about Fred's behavior, we were grateful our initial approach didn't reveal our purpose, keeping our investigation secure. Pat told us Fred only told his superiors about the incident, and they didn't know what to make of it.

I notified my FBIHQ desk supervisor, Charles H. "Sandy" Kable IV, of this development. He was unfazed, and suggested we go over Fred's head to his boss to get the cooperation we needed. Sandy said Fred's boss "Scott" had an excellent reputation for integrity, so he scheduled a meeting with him "regarding a national security matter." Sandy flew west while I flew east, meeting in Salt Lake City. We explained our need to covertly investigate an unnamed Power Paragon employee for suspected espionage. Scott, a calm, composed man, assured us Fred would be a trustworthy partner, and that our bad first contact wasn't a problem. He promised that once Fred knew the details, he would be a great asset. Scott was an impressive man and strong patriot. It was refreshing.

And he was right about Fred. Once we explained our mission, Fred became a great ally. When we needed to electronically surveil Chi at work, he arranged covert cover and entry for our Tech Agents, who brought the wrong-colored coaxial cable to use. No worries! On his own initiative, Fred provided the same cables L-3 used so our cables would blend in. He also ran interference for us with questioning L-3 personnel, helped us identify employees for later interviews, forewarned and interceded for us regarding L-3's "damned attorneys" (Fred's words and my shared sentiments), and later warned us about defense and L-3 Washington Operations (WashOps) actions designed to sabotage our case. He proved a true friend to Gunnar and me, the case, and the country. It just goes to show, first impressions don't have to be lasting.

CHAPTER 8

"Best Ever"

THE MAK INVESTIGATION TOOK ME TO A WHOLE NEW LEVEL OF FISA coverages. In less than two years, and nine applications, we accumulated nearly forty interception techniques, including home and office telephone landlines, cellphones, microphones, CCTVs, emails and email traffic, internet and computer usage, vehicle microphones and trackers, and surreptitious home, office, hotel-room, and vehicle searches. I was submitting FISA reauthorization renewal requests to FBIHQ every sixty days to guarantee no drops in coverages.

Our first FISA coverages revealed Chi and Rebecca had no cellphones and used email and the internet sparingly, including America Online (AOL) dial-up! Being younger, larger, and more dynamic, Tai's family consumed the lion's share of our coverages, requiring considerable hours from linguists, surveillance specialists, and agents, the personnel tripod that supported our investigation. Each FISA renewal application justified more intrusive coverages.[1] We had to know for certain that no more sensitive data would flow to China. Obtaining that level of assurance would require use of the most intrusive techniques, including covert home entries.

---

1. The next time you hear claims that we're watching everything Americans do, know that it is said in ignorance. Our government lacks the time or resources to accomplish this. Covering the two Mak families we *knew* were spying required hundreds of investigators and millions of dollars. Add 350 million more people, and you'll understand it's an impossible charge that could handcuff our ability to counter actual bad foreign actors in our open and free society.

SSG teams had covered the Maks for months, documenting their every movement. Our three Lookouts—Nancy, Jack, and Jaime—used SSG reporting, and their own 24/7 CCTV observations, to build a database of the Maks' and their neighborhoods' natural rhythms. Using this 24/7 coverage, both teams worked to answer every relevant question: Who had dogs, especially "barkers"? When did they walk them, and where? What households had teenagers? Who were the neighborhood busybodies?, etc. We often joked that dogs and teenagers—two of our biggest variables—had much in common: both were noisy, oversexed, and unpredictable. We learned who the insomniacs were, who used bathrooms in the middle of the night with windows facing the Maks' homes, which neighbors smoked on their front porch at two a.m.[2] We also learned who had criminal records and what their work schedules were.[3] We had to thoroughly understand this neighborhood.

Sal suggested we meet with Downey's chief of police to request his assistance. After I briefed him generally on the timetable, rough location, and anticipated events, we learned he was a graduate of the FBI National Academy.[4] He proved extremely helpful, even offering the idea of posting a squad car nearby manned by a Downey officer and an FBI Special Agent to handle any problems that might arise, such as a neighbor's "suspicious activity" call. The chief didn't ask what person or address we were targeting, only needing to know the neighborhood and selecting a handful of patrol officers and the desk officer to help us.[5] The chief also recommended the perfect local, fenced, and isolated Dennis the Menace Park to stage our entry operations. His cooperation was a welcome surprise, given the cold shoulder we'd received from Alhambra PD, a relationship of constant friction, forcing our SSG teams to play cat-and-mouse games every time a suspicious neighbor called in. Thankfully, over time that relationship improved.

---

2. We also were interested in who owned guns.
3. For instance, this was a blue-collar neighborhood with resident contractors coming and going at all hours.
4. A prestigious fifteen-week training program for superior law enforcement officers nominated by their departments.
5. Downey PD's help prevented possible case compromise during our later covert entries.

Downey residence, aerial view TRIAL EXHIBIT 127

The Lookouts kept documenting neighborhood movements while we requested help from covert "Flaps and Seals" experts in Quantico, part of a highly skilled and experienced covert entry group of former agents hired back as contractors due to their unique skills, experience, and training. These people participate in many covert entries, crisscrossing the country to meet the CI and terrorism operational needs of FBI Field Offices.

We weren't sure what to expect but prepared ourselves for every conceivable question. These specialists proved an interesting lot, disciplined in their methodology but creative in their approach, tailoring each entry plan to the unique demands of that environment. To the outside world they looked like regular guys, maybe even slobs, but definitely not FBI agents. I'll call our main guys Paul and Doug. Paul was the smoother, more diplomatic one. Dealing with him didn't require a thick skin or great patience. Doug, on the other hand, was crusty, sarcastic, and belittling, with the mouth of an old sailor—fun to listen to as long as you weren't the target of his ire. They made a good team and obviously enjoyed their work.

In our first meeting, we briefed them generally on the case and the environment. The three Lookouts briefed Paul and Doug on the neighborhood and its inhabitants. They concisely covered every relevant question. Encrypted radio communications in the area were unreliable, so Bureau-encrypted cellphones and FBI radio channels locally boosted and enhanced would be used, with code language when referring to people and locations, ensuring that identifying information would never be provided.

Since the beginning, the Lookouts and SSG teams had referred to the Mak families using names from TV sitcoms. Chi Mak was Homer (Simpson), while Rebecca was Marge.[6] Tai Mak's family was based on *Married with Children*. Tai was Al (Bundy), Fuk was Peggy, Billy was Bud, and Shirley was Kelly. And their dog "Dong-Dong" was Buck. Flirty Fuk and boy-crazy Shirley differed little from their TV counterparts![7]

I was very proud of my team. Each had worked hard at knowing their assignments and fulfilling their roles. Coincidentally, Paul and Doug, with big smiles, stated they were extremely impressed with what they labeled "the best covert entry site preparations ever!" This boosted our confidence greatly, since we felt like we were doing all of this by the seat of our pants. A target entry date and entry method were selected, and future tasks were identified. Paul and Doug completed their neighborhood survey, including methods to defeat the Maks' locks, and consulted with FBILA's Tech Agents for support before leaving. We began final preparations for entry to take place during an Alaska cruise Chi and Rebecca had been planning.

We began scheduling for the immense manpower and equipment required for the entry and reserved use of the park with Downey PD. It would be an ideal staging area and command center, surrounded by a fence and locking gates, with bathrooms (very useful in an all-night operation) and quick access to the freeway just southeast of the Maks' home.

Covering the Maks' Alaska trip also required special preparations. We needed agents to tail the Maks throughout their trip, to ensure we weren't surprised by an early return, and to watch for suspicious behav-

---

6. If Chi and Rebecca, who considered themselves PRC intelligentsia, had known this, they would have felt insulted, given the dimwitted nature of this bourgeois American TV cartoon couple.
7. Tai's family, having more contemporary interests and taste, might have even been flattered.

iors or meetings. The choices were obvious: Polly was our most seasoned agent, a Bureau expert in CI and terrorism, smart, personable, with loads of common sense.[8] The second agent, Jessie Murray, had recently joined CI and our squad to work this case and was running our surveillance and trash coverages. She had a great work ethic, and despite her husband's Irish-sounding surname, she had a youthful Asian appearance and spoke Mandarin fluently, a very useful skill.

The Maks' route to Vancouver, Canada, in order to board an American-flagged cruise ship to Alaska presented a complication. Randy at FBIHQ told me we had to bring the Canadians in on the planning. I resisted. Polly and Jessie could cover the Maks, and our original source reporting was too sensitive to risk. Worried over possible compromise, I pointed out that we could skip watching the Maks during their few hours on Canadian soil.

It didn't matter. Protocol required Canadian notification.

With grave concerns, I flew to Ottawa with Gunnar, Dennis, Sheldon, and Sal, where we met at the US embassy with Randy, our FBI legal attaché, and representatives from the Canadian Security Intelligence Service (CSIS). With a knot in my stomach the whole time, we briefed our northern neighbors, who enthusiastically volunteered to surveil the Maks in Vancouver. Despite my misgivings, it appears our secrets remained safe with the Canucks, who admirably and professionally supported our operation.[9]

With this final international piece in place, we were ready to take our next huge step in the Mak investigation.[10]

---

8. I was sorry we would soon lose her irreplaceable expertise due to her upcoming retirement.

9. I was fascinated to learn that the CSIS was a hybrid of our CIA and FBI, with severe restrictions upon its powers.

10. This trip's greatest drama still lay before me. While returning to our hotel, our group stopped at a convenience store. At the cash register, the Syrian immigrant owner and his young American wife learned we were from the United States and made jokes about our "violent" and "stupid" president, George W. Bush. Dennis and I pushed back, while Sal, Gunnar, and Sheldon watched in amusement. The business-minded shopkeeper quickly moderated his stance, but his wife proved intractable, shrilly shouting the most outrageous anti-American lies. Finally, her shopkeeper husband told her to shut up. I marveled at her ignorance and hoped she would move to Syria and learn just how fortunate she was to be an American and living in Canada. Her husband certainly knew his good fortune.

CHAPTER 9

SARA-4 Linguists Rock

BEFORE OUR FIRST COVERT ENTRY, WE NEEDED SOME TRANSLATION
work. After our FISA coverages began, we were drinking from a firehose
of spoken Chinese, yet our requests for full-time linguists repeatedly hit a
brick wall—until Sal and I began banging our heads against it. We would
do whatever was necessary to ensure this case succeeded.

Some resistance came due to the recently failed J. J. Smith/Katrina
Leung case, which had sucked up linguists for years but produced little
to show for it. Other ongoing CI and criminal cases required translation
work, meaning linguists with clearances to work CI cases, especially our
hypersensitive one, and they were rare and in high demand. I understood the challenges, but they didn't justify the FBILA language unit's
apathetic, disinterested response. They offered us intermittent services of
inferior translators, i.e., those who couldn't or wouldn't do the job, denied
China was a threat, or were outright sympathetic to it. We required the
very best from FBILA and FBIHQ, especially since many of the current
PRC cases soaking up linguists produced little of value.[1]

Our dogged pursuit of skilled Chinese linguists became critical
as Tai's family cellphones tripled our translation workload.[2] And the
complexity increased with the discovery we were dealing with *three*
dialects—Mandarin, Cantonese, and Shanghainese, which are as dif-

---

1. This principle also applied to the situation regarding the availability of Lookout personnel.
2. Especially Fuk's and the kids, the latter two mostly being irrelevant and therefore filtered out and
not translated.

ferent from one another as separate languages.[3] Chi and Rebecca spoke Shanghainese, Cantonese, and Mandarin, often changing mid-sentence, while Tai's family spoke Cantonese and Mandarin. As well-educated electrical engineers, Chi and Rebecca discussed topics at a high technical level, requiring linguists capable of translating the same in three dialects. Although initially a nightmare, this helped us separate the chaff (poor/ lazy linguists) from the wheat (great linguists). One awful linguist in particular was both lazy *and* a PRC sympathizer, claiming, "No Chinese would ever betray the United States," and therefore, the Maks were innocent victims of US government prejudice. And he kept intentionally mistranslating damning Mak statements as innocuous ones! After a huge fight, we kicked this linguist off our case. They assigned him non-CI cases. He should have been fired.

Another hurdle was the FBI's archaic practice of segregating the linguists from the agents, anathema to basic efficiency and effectiveness, by locating them at a secluded, covert off-site location. First, the site was difficult for agents to reach. Second, unhealthy, ingrown, ingrained "old world" subcultures were formed, whether Russian, Chinese, Korean, or Iranian, each a law unto itself and reinforcing harmful, counterproductive norms and practices.

For example, pressure within the Chinese linguist group dictated that an individual's work should not stand out, following the Asian saying, "The nail that sticks out gets hammered down." Older members were assigned the prominent cases likely to garner acknowledgment and awards. Meritocracy was *not* practiced. We ended up with an elderly linguist who literally could not hear what was being said in our intercepts! This subculture also dictated that younger linguists couldn't tell us anything that might cause an elder linguist to "lose face." Third, this physical and psychological distancing kept linguists disinterested when it came to case agent needs. We became disembodied voices on the telephone who held less sway than the elder linguist in the adjacent cubicle.

In addition, we were forced to farm out electronic intercepts—what we called "tech cuts"—around the country for translation. This meant no

---

3. With distinct pronunciations and divergent spellings.

matter how high our case priority was, it was always put at the bottom of another field office's work pile. Out of sight, out of mind. Local work always took priority.

The delays were intolerable; translations became outdated before we saw them. Even worse, we received useless product, with conversations between Chi, Rebecca, Tai, Fuk, and their kids labeled as "Asian Female 1," "Asian Male 1," "Asian Female 2," etc. The solution was simple: co-locate investigators and linguists. This caused the biggest fights and provided the greatest rewards. Once accomplished, the linguists became our allies and teammates and proved invaluable and essential to our success, the very definition of the overused word "synergy." Now we received cultural and linguistic context, along with informed translation. This benefit was undeniable. We, and they, got immediate feedback, so any misunderstandings were quickly rectified. We all loved this arrangement. Our embedded linguists became students of the Mak families and went with us on all later entries and search warrants. Not a second of their productive time was wasted. Our final linguistic team of four was absolutely all-star. They all later testified for us.

First was Len Pi, a former electrical engineer who spoke Chi and Rebecca's technical language in both Mandarin and Cantonese dialects. He was passionate about our investigation, never caring about the "old world" linguists' criticisms.[4] Len had been a linguist for the NSD-9 J. J. Smith/Katrina Leung case but never tried to tell me what to do. He always strove to contribute and was responsible for alerting me of that treasonous linguist's words and intentional mistranslations. Sadly, Len has since passed away, but I will be forever grateful for his support and unrelenting enthusiasm for the case and our nation.

Next came Henry Dean, a highly educated and cultured gentleman who knew Mandarin, Cantonese, *and* Shanghainese. He was our stabilizing force, circumspect and always careful not to overstate the issue. Henry personified the axiom, "Still waters run deep." Born in China, he held a master's in Chinese linguistics, taught Chinese grammar and translation, authored a guide on proper Chinese, and served as a master linguist for

---

4. The "old world" clique's official motto was "As an elder, take it easy. Do as little work as possible."

state and federal courts, law firms and private corporations, and several US intelligence agencies. Whatever Henry translated, it was 100 percent accurate. If Len Pi was the team's heart, Henry Dean was its head.

Then came "Rick" Zachary Yoo, on loan from the Chicago FBI Field Office.[5] A native Shanghainese speaker with a PRC linguistics degree, he was a conscientious whirlwind, pumping out extremely accurate Shanghainese translations of conversations that were difficult to even hear. We heard about Rick from other linguists and never regretted following their recommendation. He wiped out our backlog in no time and was a delight to work with. It was hard to get and keep him, but when you need the best to convict a spy, you don't give up.

Finally came humble "Harriet" Hao, my rock and sounding board.[6] She was helpful, cheerful, and popular for her people skills. One of the sweetest, smartest, and most conscientious people I know, she understood the PRC and communism like no one else. I'll always remember the day after the Beijing Olympics' opening ceremonies. Harriet approached me noting the mass display of robotic-like performers, bemoaned the Chinese people's submissiveness under the CCP (Chinese Communist Party), their willingness to follow its orders, and warned that China's sheer numbers, the CCP's all-consuming hunger for power, and its willingness to destroy any person or nation in its way, could one day flood the world like a red tsunami. Harriet demonstrated remarkable objectivity. No ethnic pride or racial loyalties for her! She loved America, what it stood for, and what it meant to her family.

---

5. Alias provided at "Rick's" request.
6. Again, alias provided at "Harriet's" request.

CHAPTER 10

Enter the Dragon

BEFORE OUR FIRST COVERT ENTRY, SPECIAL AGENT KEVIN MOBERLY, IN charge of communications, arrived at Dennis the Menace Park to set up our command post. The park was quiet, a striking contrast to the beehive it would become. Kevin staked out areas for personnel and equipment while Downey PD officers cleared the park of its remaining few occupants, mostly teenage couples making out.[1] Curious members of the public were told a law enforcement exercise was under way. The gates were locked, and the keys handed to Kevin.

Soon, personnel and equipment began arriving. The mobile command center (MCC) parked in the center, with antennas raised and signal strengths tested, to ensure uninterrupted communications between the MCC, SSGs, SARA-4 Lookouts, and entry agents. The Mak residences' polecam videos were now playing on MCC screens, as the stand-alone generator hummed in the background.

I had arrived very early in the morning at SARA-4 to finalize plans and calm management nerves, so I hoped for an afternoon nap at home before the big, all-night show, and urged my team to do the same. I managed to get a couple hours of sleep before arriving at the park around 7:30 p.m. On the drive there I wondered, *What have I forgotten?* I hadn't actually forgotten anything, but I did later discover a wardrobe issue which caused me grief. During all the planning, I had never asked our

---

1. Periodically, we would continue to unromantically shoo away young lovers who snuck into the park.

covert entry experts about proper attire. As case agent, I would be the only investigator participating in the first entry. My intuition, and some Hollywood brainwashing, told me the darker the clothing, the better. So, dark jeans, socks, and long-sleeved shirt—no problem. But what about shoes? I had no black tennis shoes, and the rest all sported reflective tape. I grabbed the next best thing: my Adidas soccer cleats from my soccer refereeing days. I put black electrical tape over the three stripes and left, leading to a very uncomfortable evening standing on asphalt and concrete. As it turned out, that wouldn't be the worst of it.

Thanks to Kevin, Sheldon, and others, everything was well in hand when I arrived. Our transport to and from the Mak residence that evening would be a beat-up blue 1998 Plymouth Voyager, which our LA Tech Agents had gone to great and admirable lengths to procure. Why? Because it was an exact match for the Maks' own 1998 Plymouth Voyager, which was currently in LAX's long-term parking lot, where they had left it.[2] Our agents had searched it and implanted tracking and microphone devices. Since the Maks' neighbors knew nothing of this trip, they would expect to see what they saw every evening: the Maks' Voyager parked on the curb in front of their home. Except now the neighbors would see *our* Voyager, serving as our transportation. To carry more, we removed its back seats.

Entry around midnight was possible, although it was likely to be closer to 2:00 a.m. First, we waited for darkness, then for our "witching hour." We were primed to strike, like a coiled snake. Thankfully, Sal kept A/ASAC Mike and other executives far away from those running the operation. I wanted to enter as soon as possible, but frustratingly, the east neighbor's teenagers had not returned home.[3] From early that morning, our surveillance teams had been watching Tai's family and other relatives and friends who might conceivably swing by to visit Chi and Rebecca, which seemed unlikely, since we'd never seen anyone visit them. Nevertheless, we wanted no surprises. All were safely down for the night.

---

2. The Maks also owned a rarely used brown 1988 Oldsmobile Cutlass, which was usually parked in their garage.
3. They were a concern with every covert entry we performed.

Downey residence at night TRIAL EXHIBIT 150

Tai in Alhambra was the closest. If he headed toward Downey that evening, we would have little notice. One pleasant discovery: The 24/7 din of nearby Interstate 5 traffic created a white noise that masked any sounds we might accidentally make in the house or neighborhood.

Paul and Doug, our Flaps and Seals guys, had us send someone to the Maks' front door days earlier to knock and unscrew the porch light, disconnecting it. That way, neighbors were acclimated to seeing no Mak porch light days before our entry, thus hiding our movements.[4]

At 1:00 a.m., we got the "All Clear" call from our Lookout and SSGs. The teenagers next door had come home, the neighbor across the street had finished his front-porch smoke, and the insomniac with the westward-facing bathroom next to the Maks' home had returned to bed. The neighborhood was quiet. Paul walked down the block and up to the Maks' door to gently knock and ring the doorbell. Receiving no reply, Paul unlocked the door using duplicate keys and then walked on down the street.

---

4. This demonstrates why everyone should leave a porch light on at night.

Thirty minutes later, Paul and Doug returned in the Voyager and parked on the front curb. Upon receiving the "All Clear," Doug and Paul exited the minivan, crossed the lawn, and walked up the steps and through the unlocked front door while I held my breath. Surveys indicated no Mak residence alarms, but we couldn't be sure until entry and search, which they now did.[5] They reported back, "House secure. Good to go!" and began preparing the home for the rest of us. It was now nearly 2:00 a.m. I worried we would have little time for searching, copying, and installations, given this neighborhood of early-rising blue-collar workers and contractors.

Finally, the time had come. The Tech Agents, their equipment, and I squeezed into the Voyager in a slow version of Tetris: grown men hugging their equipment, laying on their backs, stomachs, or sides in fetal positions, with Paul driving. The unloading and loading of men and materials in front of the Mak home would be the riskiest part—big, clumsy shadows tumbling out of a clown car. We had to keep such incidences to a minimum.

That was why the biggest problem sprung on me that night was so vexing. Doug and Paul had confirmed that the Maks' home contained multiple computers and laptops, which was great news. We had an approved computer forensic expert from Quantico there to copy all computers and digital media. But copying hard drives takes time. The problem? Doug and Paul only *at this moment* decided to bar this expert's participation, because he was *not* a Special Agent, and therefore unarmed. This "All covert entry personnel *must* carry firearms" requirement was new, and ridiculous. They said, "What if things go south, leading to a firefight?" As head of the overall entry operation, I insisted we proceed as planned. I would take responsibility.

But they claimed absolute authority over the entry and dug their heels in. No gun, no entry. Outrageous! They had helped develop this plan and selected our Quantico expert and said nothing about this. It was too late now to procure someone else. Their "requirement" might have been justified if the Maks were militant, violent criminals or terrorists,

---

5. Thankfully, Ring cameras didn't yet exist.

and this was their hideout. But this was the vacant home of an elderly couple suspected of stealing information, within a quiet suburban neighborhood. Lookouts, surveillance, and Downey PD had the neighborhood covered.

With nine armed agents, one unarmed employee made *no* difference. A "firefight." Really? Weigh the small chance of that against the real threat of compromising a sensitive espionage investigation if a neighbor happened to peek out a window to see men coming and going from the Mak house carrying computers—and even stranger, the men reappearing to return those computers.

But not to Doug and Paul, who kept repeating this "safety of the team" mantra. It made no sense, and sounded more like union rules protecting labor jobs. They proposed three options: 1) Suspend entry operations until a specially trained Special Agent Forensic Computer expert was found (completely unrealistic); 2) ferry the computers out to the computer expert to copy as he lay in the vehicle (crazy risky and completely impractical); or 3) carry the computers out to the vehicle, transport them to the command post for the expert's examination and copying, and then return it all to the Mak home (only slightly less risky or impractical).

Since Flaps and Seals had a stranglehold on entry decisions, I chose the best option, allowing us to proceed that evening: door number three. That night we ferried computers back and forth as I silently cursed them for this manipulation. Thankfully, these many extra trips were never detected, but if they *had* been, I would have never forgiven Doug and Paul for their petty, last-minute declaration.

Our Voyager took off for the Mak home carrying its cramped cargo. It was an eerie feeling, lying down on the stripped minivan bed, watching lights dance across its ceiling, and listening to radio traffic documenting our progress. Before I knew it, we were parked at the Mak home, waiting for the "Go" signal. Although a driver in a parked car at night might seem suspicious, more so is the sight of many men exiting a vehicle and carrying equipment into a house. We needed to *not* be seen. The Lookouts, Gs, and nearby Downey PD officer's squad car carrying Sheldon gave the

"All Clear."[6] Whenever neighborhood threats emerged, we waited them out while lying on the minivan floor, or drove away and circled around. Receiving this green light, we slowly slid the side door open, exited the Voyager one by one, and walked head down directly to and through the front door, which Paul was holding open from inside. The last man to exit quietly slid the door closed with a whispered *click*.

Stepping into the house for the first time was surreal. With all the house lights off, I crossed the threshold into pitch-blackness as the door closed behind me. It had been a hot summer day in Southern California, so the home's built-up heat was stifling. We couldn't use the air-conditioning. "Empty" houses don't use AC, and opening windows would allow noise to escape. This was a tiny, seven-hundred-square-foot house which had never been expanded, remodeled, insulated, or updated by its spartan owners. It was now a small "hot box," with our nine working bodies heating it up even more by the minute.

I dared not move initially for fear of bumping into the eight other men there or breaking some unseen lamp or decoration. Any damage risked later discovery by the Maks. I remained still until my eyes fully adjusted. I then used a small five-inch flashlight I had been given for this entry. Red film covered its lens. We were to *always* point it downward and away from windows to prevent visible light from alerting neighbors of activity within the home. This proved an effective, albeit slow, method to search the house covertly.

I carefully made my way over to Paul to seek his advice on next steps. I was there to direct and prioritize the search, handle any questions, evaluate the value of anything found, and weigh in on best places for listening device installation. I first addressed the digital media discovered. The home office contained five computers—two desktops and three laptops—and many discs. FBILA's Computer Analysis and Response Team (CART) disconnected, labeled, and sent each to the Quantico forensic expert back at the command post.

I reviewed the tall stacks of documents we found around the house while other searchers photographed them and searched other areas

---

6. Scott later took over the Downey PD ride-along role once Sheldon began making entries with me.

jammed with junk and old clothing. A covert search can *never* be as thorough as a criminal one, since it requires everything be left as originally found. Absolute stealth is paramount, leaving no sign we were ever there. This means some things can't be searched then, or sometimes ever, to protect our secret. That requires patience, discipline, and hard decisions.

It was strange creeping around an unfamiliar home in low light, while other spectral figures silently glided around you, performing their own ghostly tasks. Periodically, one of these phantoms would float up to ask a whispered question, then return to the ether. Great care was exercised throughout the house because *everything* was covered with a thick layer of dust. This appeared to be how the Maks lived and made our stealthy jobs that much harder. The entry experts were convinced that this dust was the Maks' countersurveillance technique, akin to placing a hair across a doorjamb. Anything moved on a dusty surface left a trail. Each item selected had to be examined without disturbing surface dust. The Maks even covered decorative knickknacks on the furniture with sandwich baggies, which in turn were covered with dust.[7]

In the backyard was a small shed, but we didn't search it, in order to avoid detection by neighbors. We knew Chi Mak mowed his lawn and stored yard tools there.[8] I visited the attached garage and confirmed it contained the Cutlass and typical garage items. The garage became the lowest priority, along with the old, little-used, and meagerly stocked kitchen.[9]

The small combination living and dining room, containing furnishings equally decrepit, was more of the same. The corner plastic lampshade was yellowed and brittle as old book paper, and stood next to a sunken, dirty, threadbare couch, which was fronted by a small coffee table also covered with a heavy layer of dust. The room was a high search priority, along with the master bedroom and home office, thanks to their tall stacks of sensitive technical papers by the doorways and on each table.

---

7. It later became clear that Rebecca was simply a very poor housekeeper. Exhibit number one: Their little-used vacuum cleaner stood in the hallway, covered by a plastic garbage bag, itself covered by a thick layer of dust.

8. Our criminal search there nearly a year and a half later found nothing other than yard tools.

9. The kitchen sink's old, brittle, rarely used plastic soap dispenser was cracked and leaking congealed soap like lava from a volcano. The dishes, utensils, and cookware were cheap, grimy, and chipped.

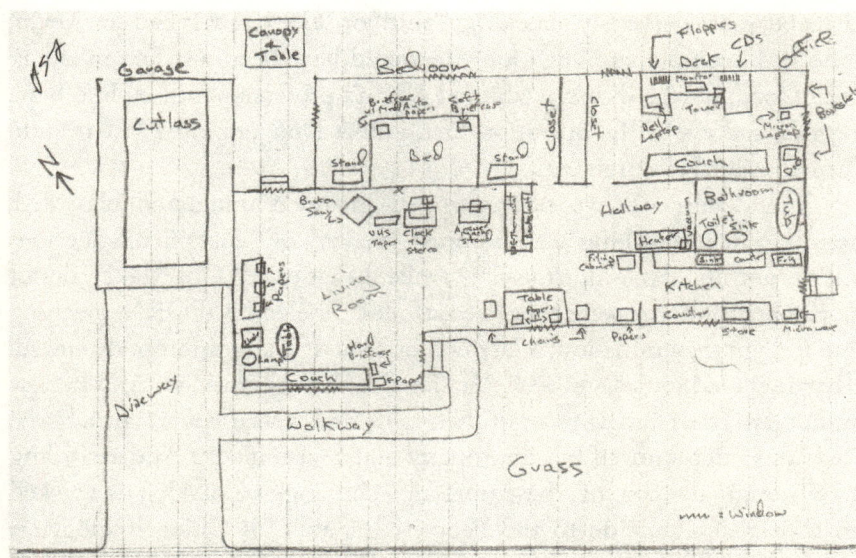

Downey residence diagram JAMES E. GAYLORD

Teams of two, a searcher and a photographer, tackled each stack, careful to remove, peruse, and photograph each document before replacing it in its original order. The top dust-covered paper was left separate and unmolested, to preserve its layer of dust. Although painstakingly slow, the method was as effective and efficient as circumstances allowed. By the end of our investigation, we had produced hundreds of document photographs which served as important proof of what *was* and *wasn't* there, and *when*. This photographic evidence convinced our superiors, and the FISA Court, that our continuing investigation had "just, probable cause."

We transported the digital evidence to and fro throughout the night. Constant, clear communication, which Kevin was charged with, was essential. He did it well, but it rubbed Doug the wrong way.[10] After a few instances of Doug and Kevin stepping on each other on the radio, i.e., inadvertent simultaneous broadcasts, Doug broadcast a barrage of curses and f-bombs at Kevin over the airwaves. We all knew Doug had a quick temper and sailor's vocabulary, but everyone cringed with this

---

10. *Many* things rubbed Doug the wrong way.

diatribe, most nervously chuckling "Shit!" or "Geez!" I felt bad for Kevin, who had been doing a great job. He would have been justified in laying into Doug, but he didn't. I admired Kevin's professional discipline here, putting success of the operation first, unlike Doug, or their last-minute "armed agent" requirements.

The documents we photographed included unmarked classified, sensitive data. Nothing was stamped "Secret" or "Classified," but that meant nothing. Spies don't usually make it that easy.[11] Chi Mak's piles of documents at home were export-controlled, labeled NOFORN, meaning "no foreign dissemination," classified or sensitive, and improperly stored. They included topics and technologies Chi did *not* work on. And he was prohibited from having most of them outside his secure work area. Some he had written himself but improperly under-classified.[12] And according to our original reporting, these were all technologies Chi Mak was tasked to collect and provide to the People's Republic of China intelligence services (PRCIS).

Our entry also meant installation of concealed microphones to pick up conversations. Tech Agents explained the options, pros and cons of potential locations, levels of concealability, collection ranges, maintenance needs, strength of signal, etc. Again, compromise was required, but the deciding factor was always which option held the least chance of detection. We also had to sacrifice some collection quality due to the decrepit nature of the Maks' home wiring, which they had never upgraded or repaired. It could barely handle a dial-up tone, let alone the 24/7 audio feeds we wished to install. So, at taxpayer expense, the Maks were treated to a free rewiring upgrade of their home in late June 2004.[13]

---

11. This is something I would expect to explain to laymen in court, but not so-called CI specialists. Yet this became a continuing source of irritation for Gunnar and me as we battled ignorant, impatient, agenda-driven individuals within our agencies and the DOJ. Petty rumors also circulated that we had no case because nothing found was *marked* classified. They were all flat-out wrong, but that was of little consolation or help at the time.

12. No doubt as part of his plans to transport them covertly to authorities in China.

13. Tai Mak's two hardline telephones and cellphone were also tapped, but his home was modernized, and therefore required no similar upgrades. Ironically, we never had the chance to enter or microphone Tai's home, as they never took vacation, and Tai, Fuk, and the kids were constantly coming and going between school, work, and play.

These people, cheap to a fault, were once again getting something for nothing, but this time it was to their detriment. The locations for listening devices and cameras were very important, not just to intercept, but to *not* intercept some things. Defense attorneys might later falsely charge the government with "outrageous conduct." In the Katrina Leung case, due to some rational, case-related reasons, a concealed CCTV was placed within a hotel bathroom, which later proved damaging to the prosecution because Leung had been filmed using the toilet. To avoid any hint of impropriety, I prohibited any device implantation within or near the bathroom or bedroom. Husbands and wives can have some telling, candid conversations there, which I was giving up any chance of intercepting.

I probably worried for nothing. Over our years of investigation, we never saw one instance of affection between Chi and Rebecca—no hand-holding, or a single kiss, peck, pat, or "I love you," in public or private. Anything intimate seemed inconceivable within this political, contractual marriage. Even so, the defense would still make outlandish claims, so I removed that possibility. This doesn't mean I would never bug a bedroom. I would if I knew relevant conversations took place there.

As we approached five a.m., our night's cover was ending. Contractors and workmen were beginning their early commutes, so we put everything back, as depicted by our pre-search photos. It took three vehicle runs to empty this small home. We congregated near the front door and Paul took the first group out. Doug began methodically checking the backrooms for any evidence of our presence, including inspecting the flooring for marks, shoeprints, or dropped items, like a movie character in a Western using a branch to sweep away his prints in the dirt.

As Paul was coordinating the second group for departure, my most embarrassing moment in this whole investigation occurred. Doug suddenly shouted, *What the hell? What dipshit did this?!* (I've left out his more colorful adjectives.) Doug continued cursing a blue streak—a little too loudly for a covert entry, I thought. Fortunately, traffic on good old Interstate 5 continued to mask the noise.

Doug had discovered—and was now painstakingly removing—thousands of pockmark indentations in the carpeting. "It looks like the damn house has smallpox!" he swore.

I immediately knew the source: *my soccer cleats!* They'd left round indentations all over the house. It would be hard to leave a more obvious sign that a stranger had been there. The guys appeared confused as to the cause. I wasn't, but didn't fess up, instead meekly stepping off the carpet. Doug kept cleaning up my mess on his knees, working his way to the front door, loudly grumbling the whole time. I made the "command decision" to leave with the second group, preventing Doug from seeing my cleats and really losing it. I saved myself an embarrassing and loud tongue-lashing, rationalizing that what we needed was a quiet and professional exit. My group's return to the command post was uneventful. Fortunately, Doug was able to brush away all the pockmarks I had left.

Later that evening I asked Paul what attire they wanted those making covert entries to wear. He said nothing bright, but also not all dark or black colors, because if something did go wrong and we were detected, we needed to appear normally dressed while talking and walking our way out of it. (So, sneakers were okay!) It's not like the movies, he explained. Ninjas don't talk their way out of discovery; they just kill all the witnesses, which is definitely not Bureau policy.

That first night wasn't enough to accomplish all our tasks. But Chi and Rebecca's Alaska cruise was a week long, over a thousand miles away, and under Jessie and Polly's watchful eyes. Therefore, we had several more nights for entries, with "Dipshit" Gaylord's cleats never making a return appearance. Sometimes Gunnar and Sheldon covertly entered as well. During the Voyager transports, Gunnar and I remained in a fetal position, right next to each other. (He later told others of our "special, intimate times." Don't believe him—no spooning or snuggling ever took place.)

The time, scope, and parameters of our covert searches were severely limited. One area we couldn't inspect was a two-drawer filing cabinet in the living room corner. Our imaginations ran wild speculating over the valuable evidence lurking inside, but there was a hitch: Spiderwebs stretched from the adjacent wall to the cabinet's handles. Pulling either drawer open would break the web. It wouldn't be an issue in a criminal search, but here the Maks might notice. Since we didn't have a spider on retainer to re-sling its handiwork, we left the apparently little-used filing cabinet undisturbed, hoping it didn't contain much evidence.[14] Rebecca's poor housekeeping: 1, FBI: 0.

By week's end we'd collected plenty of evidence to prove Chi Mak was a PRC agent, including classified, sensitive technologies Chi had stolen, per PRC taskings and frequent, concealed travel to China. We suspected much more evidence remained under the surface, much like an iceberg, which only a thorough criminal search would reveal.

Chi and Rebecca's return home proved uneventful. We watched and listened, half expecting our visit to be discovered. Had we tripped any covert traps they had set? Was something in the home left askew? Did they find one of my pockmarks? Did the house smell of sweaty men? Time provided the answer: No change. Our investigation was secure.

We also gained insights into Chi and Rebecca's strange world from Polly and Jessie. Rebecca had refused to socialize with any other plane or ship passengers, talking only to Chi in hushed whispers. She also mimicked his every move, walking two steps behind while displaying the "old world" meek, deferential Asian wife stereotype, despite being anything but.

What was consistently demonstrated was her extremely suspicious nature. On the plane, she was seen staring at and examining a can of Coke as if it was an IED. Chi, however, proved sociable, comfortable and engaged with his surroundings. Polly and Jessie saw no signs the Maks ever met or communicated with covert agents, or otherwise engaged in intelligence activities.

---

14. Over a year later, we eagerly searched that cabinet upon seeing the web was already broken. It contained no sensitive technical data, but it did hold valuable travel records refuting the Maks' later denials of travel to China.

CHAPTER 11

Enter the Dragon, Part II

THE TRICKIEST QUESTION OF AN ESPIONAGE INVESTIGATION IS WHEN TO end it. If you make an early arrest, you may halt the damage but lack enough evidence to convict. If you wait too long, the enemy may obtain devastating data.

Chi Mak with statue of Shanghai's first communist mayor, Chen Yi FBI RELEASED / AUTHOR'S COLLECTION

I knew Chi had already passed data to China. We couldn't allow that to continue. Preventing this required total surveillance coverage: comprehensive physical and electronic surveillance ensuring nothing went to China. I believed we had that, but paranoid doubts returned with every eccentric behavior Chi exhibited and each conference he attended. Chi had dramatically increased his conference attendance, thereby fanning our anxiety levels, because it meant increased contact with other engineers and possible foreign agents, which can be hard to spot at such crowded events.[1] Our informants reported nothing unusual during sponsored or spontaneous gatherings, sessions, meals, hotel room meetings, and other exchanges, but my nightmares persisted.

When Chi attended a sensitive naval conference, we sent Gunnar and surveillance teams to cover him. I submitted an emergency FISA request for a covert search of Chi's hotel room, luggage, and rental car, since Chi would be mixing with individuals working the very technologies China wanted. To accomplish these coverages—hotel and rental car searches—Gunnar had to reveal government interest in Chi Mak to select civilian managers, who had to sign non-disclosure agreements.

Gunnar's searches revealed that Chi was submitting papers to the conference.[2] We learned later that this was Chi's modus operandi, to submit sensitive, unmarked, and unauthorized classified technical papers to conferences for publication. Chi exploited most conferences' chink in the armor. They did not vet technical papers for clearance to be published before releasing them. In Chi's case, the work was classified, and meant to meet PRC requirements.[3]

We also discovered Chi was grooming a Chinese American materials engineer for recruitment, which began with a luncheon at an Applied Power Electronics Conference. Months later, Chi called this engineer and reintroduced himself, softening him up with talk of their shared memories of being born and raised as "Hong Kong Chinese," having

---

1. We later learned this increase was in response to taskings he had received from PRCIS handlers in 2004.

2. These were sensitive technology papers he was *not* authorized to publish.

3. We also saw how lightly Chi traveled. He typically carried one change of underwear and socks, one shirt and pair of pants, and a toothbrush, washing everything each night in the sink and hanging them out to dry.

never visited Mainland China. Chi's lies continued with a request that a "colleague" needed help with materials issues. He asked if his "coworker" could call the materials engineer in the future with questions. The engineer agreed. Chi had no such colleague, and in fact was laying groundwork for a PRCIS officer to make this pretext call. Chi's arrest aborted his plan.

We had a broad range of technologies to protect from Chi Mak: QED submarine propulsion technology; carrier Electromagnetic Aircraft Launch Systems (EMALS); electromagnetic guns; DD(x) destroyer specifications;[4] AEGIS SPY-1 radar power requirements; ship combat survivability studies; launched and space-based interceptors; torpedoes; and other sensitive, classified technologies.

Chi had proven an enthusiastic collector for his Chinese masters. To increase his efforts, Chi's conference attendance and paper submissions accelerated, including a QED white paper for the American Society of Naval Engineers (ASNE) Advanced Naval Propulsion Seminar and a Solid-State Switch paper to ASNE for its Reconfiguration & Survivability Symposium. He lied to L-3 each time, denying he was submitting papers. He also collected data from the Institute of Electrical and Electronics Engineers Electric Ship Technologies Seminar and a Future of Power Electronics Conference sponsored by the USN Office of Naval Research (ONR) and the Defense Advanced Research Projects Agency (DARPA).

The Mak "vacations," which proved strange, spartan affairs, always made us nervous. These fanatically frugal people splurged on nothing, scrimped and saved everything, yet traveled to Alaska, Europe, and Hawaii. We had to assume these trips held a more sinister, intelligence purpose. CI history is chock-full of spies using trips abroad to signal, meet, and pass information to intelligence contacts. The Mak's European trip especially worried us. If it had been to England, one of the "Five Eyes" allies, we would have requested their help.[5] But it wasn't, so we requested a special multi-intelligence agency surveillance team, codenamed "Wrangler's Roundup."

---

4. Later designated as Zumwalt-class; three such specialized destroyers were built.
5. Canada, Australia, New Zealand, and the United States are the other four.

A common theme from that team's surveillance emerged. The Maks were just as cheap on foreign soil as they were in America, staying in threadbare, run-down hotels and hostels and never entering restaurants, preferring to grab pretzels or fruit from street food carts. When they entered stores, they rarely purchased anything and often left through a back, obscure exit, as if already knowing the store's layout. These behaviors set off that team's warning bells, but we on SARA-4 were more skeptical of claims of intelligence behaviors. We knew how weird the Maks were.

But one behavior did catch our jaundiced eye: The Maks occasionally peeled off from their group tours to photograph the undersides of public park benches, bridges, and dark corners of railway stations. Tourists don't do that. Intelligence operatives do, to service dead drops or identify future ones. While this screamed intelligence activity, we never got answers to these puzzles, and likely never will. No meetings or exchanges were seen. In any case, that team returned convinced the Maks had engaged in intelligence activities in Europe.

While the Maks were in Europe, we executed a second wave of entries into the Mak residence to search and add/update technical coverages. I was excited to get CCTV and better microphones installed.[6] Our squad was a well-oiled machine, producing flawless entries. The problem? We were stuck with a dysfunctional Tech Squad under the mismanagement of Kenny, a supposedly legendary tech figure. Some individual Tech Agents were great, but Kenny was a bottleneck, not a facilitator. Orders and authorities weren't getting through to them. So, despite FISA Court authorities sent *months* in advance, and Tech assurances of preparedness, *no* preparations had been made to switch in better microphones or install covert CCTV devices. Rare opportunities were being squandered.

The Tech Squad did have its good moments, however, especially when Kenny was *not* involved. GPS was easily mounted onto Chi and Rebecca's two vehicles during Mak vacations. On the Voyager, it was done while the van sat in LAX's long-term parking lot.[7] GPS for the Maks' brown 1988 Oldsmobile Cutlass was done during covert entries into the home garage.

---

6. I got neither.
7. Lot managers never detected us.

GPS installations within Tai's black 2001 Audi A6, Fuk's blue 2004 Mercedes, and the kids' silver 2002 Toyota Celica were another matter altogether. Since their home never remained unoccupied for long, we couldn't do covert entries. Luckily, they had a helpful parking problem. With a small driveway and busy street that didn't allow parking, they had to park most of their vehicles on the parallel street behind their home, giving them no direct line of sight. Starting there, we executed riskier GPS installations after researching each car model and obtaining duplicate keys. We towed each car away in the middle of the night, on different occasions, to a nearby secure garage, where Tech Agents installed GPS and microphones. Then we towed the car back to its original spot. Due to the professionalism of the Lookouts, SSGs, and Tech Agents involved, Tai's family and neighbors were never the wiser.

Alhambra residence, aerial view FBI RELEASED

CHAPTER 12

My "Go-To" Guys

SUCCESSFUL ESPIONAGE INVESTIGATIONS REQUIRE THE HARD WORK AND talents of many agents and support personnel. And strong, supportive leadership is essential. While Sal provided that on a local level, FBILA's executive leadership was inconsistent, one minute supporting us, the next, hanging us out to dry in daily attacks, frontal or covert, from units in all directions—technical, language, static surveillance, facilities, personnel, computer services, etc. We always tried diplomacy first, but that rarely worked. Some challenges were sincere, but most were clearly in bad faith. We responded accordingly. Those in bad faith were met with force and power politics because that's all they understood. We fought ferociously, and when put under the gun, we proved formidable opponents indeed. We didn't want this, but ours was a righteous cause, so we did what was necessary to succeed.

It shouldn't have been this way, especially "friendly fire" from our own RA, Field Office, and United States Attorney's Office (USAO). Before Chi Mak, I'd fought many investigative battles. The norm is Field Office support against some numbskull at FBIHQ mucking everything up through laziness, incompetence, or both, because many FBIHQ managers are blue flamers with little investigational experience and fewer accomplishments, yet carrying huge egos.[1] What is good or bad for the nation is not part of their calculation. This is why FBIHQ has always

---

1. Blue flamers guidelines: Climb by playing it safe. Use the ideas of those better qualified. If they work, claim credit and advance. If they don't, blame others and advance. Hard decisions risk bad results, so don't make them, instead pushing them onto others. Repeat process.

poorly represented the FBI rank and file. Whenever the news reflects poorly on the FBI, it is invariably due to bad executive decisions and behavior. FBIHQ is usually the problem, not the solution.

Our Mak investigation proved the exception thanks to two extraordinary FBIHQ supervisors, Randy Coleman and Sandy Kable. Randy was on the Chinese CI desk, an enthusiastic, supportive, motivated, breath of fresh air. From the start he promised to be there for whatever we needed, and he was. Previous FBIHQ managers said similar things but always ran for the hills when it counted.[2] When Sal and I needed computers to build a standalone case network, Randy pledged to obtain them for us, "even if [he had] to steal them off of FBIHQ basement pallets." And he did—obtain them, not steal them. When we needed immediate linguistic, Lookout, and surveillance help, he got it. Whenever we met FBILA resistance, he pressured them on our behalf, and if his own rank wasn't sufficient, he had his superiors make the call. We didn't always win, but we rarely lost, and never completely, always gaining some concessions. Randy's reputation for success often defeated opposition before it could get started.

Unfortunately, the typical one-and-a-half-year term of FBIHQ desk managers meant Randy left halfway through our case.[3] He notified me of his departure, promising a great replacement. I was morose. Randy had been the rare exception. Surely, lightning wouldn't strike twice, meaning our case was in trouble. A typical FBIHQ manager replacement would kill it. Too many solid CI cases wither on the vine and die. Success requires dedication, energy, and enthusiasm. And the timing couldn't have been worse. I had a pending Emergency FISA needing signatures from his replacement, and soon, requiring a very fast learner. Fortunately, Sandy Kable was that guy. He got us our authority with hours to spare. Surprised, I called Sandy to introduce myself and thank him. Randy had fully briefed Sandy about our case, so he hit the ground running with

---

2. A great example was Vince Z., who fled every request I made of him concerning "Sam," a PRC spy. Thanks to Vince hiding from case needs on the golf course during work hours, Sam escaped prosecution and deportation, receiving a green card and permanent resident status instead.
3. He eventually became the FBI's executive assistant director, one of the few who actually *earned* that title.

skill, experience, and hard work. In fact, he was bouncing off the walls! His was a boundless enthusiasm, determined to attack the long-standing Chinese espionage problem.

Before reaching FBIHQ, Sandy had been a case agent on an active Chinese Counterintelligence Squad, specializing in counterespionage investigations. He knew firsthand the frustrations of case agents. Turns out Randy and Sandy were close friends, two peas in a pod. Prior to the Bureau, Sandy had been a US Navy surface warfare officer who specialized in shipboard propulsion, combat systems, and antisubmarine warfare—a perfect match for this case. His appointment was a godsend, and his personal mission was to see us succeed.

I invited Sandy to Orange County to see our operations and meet the squad. Like Randy, once Sandy arrived, every team member loved him for his enthusiasm, support, attitude, and appreciation for our efforts. He witnessed the obstacles we faced in FBILA, and they astounded him. Sandy became the other FBIHQ manager without whom our case would have failed. He would help see me through some of my darkest days. Eventually, Sandy also moved on and up in the Bureau, passing through FBILA later as a CI ASAC, eventually becoming the FBI's Assistant Director of its National Security Branch, and Director of the Terrorist Screening Center.[4]

---

4. When later assigned to FBILA, Sandy worked alongside Sal, also an ASAC by then. Ironically, Sal oversaw the linguist, technical, mobile, and static surveillance support programs and some of the supervisors who had been such thorns in our sides. Sandy and Sal also worked with another of my later supervisors, ASAC Chris Nicholas, who managed the CI China program. Sandy and Chris later had front-row seats to the outright lies and reprehensible conduct the local CIA supervisor and officers practiced against my squad to steal our top investigation and recruited asset.

CHAPTER 13

The Art of War

Battles with various FBIHQ and FBILA support units were literally a daily occurrence. We made it an art form. Each morning Sheldon, Gunnar, and I met Sal in his office to discuss current obstacles, strategize solutions, and develop tactics for attack. Could FBIHQ be used to pressure FBILA, or vice versa? Which one of us should apply the pressure, and how? Could NCIS or USN officials be used to shame the FBI into doing the right thing?

Sometimes it was the reverse. Encouraging one-upmanship and rivalries between agencies often got us needed resources. Sometimes, scheduling a meeting with an obstructing manager and inviting a supportive superior to attend did the job. Other times the visit of an FBI, NCIS, CIA, or US Navy "expert" from back east moved the ball. You name the political leverage game, we played it, thanks in large part to Sal, who was a political genius and superb arm-twister. Sal arranged the meetings and asked us to be 100 percent prepared with counterarguments. We always were, and he always supported us.

Sometimes Sal began a meeting by breaking a verbal two-by-four over an obstructionist's head. That also worked frequently. Other times he sat quietly while we agents presented our requirements and arguments, only for him to later pounce ferociously on our opponents. Sal's loyalty to his agents was a rare quality, difficult to find in most FBI managers. I cherished it, having seen too many supervisors cut and run, throwing their people under the bus to protect their own career. Sal was a counterintuitive, brilliant politician who got us results.

Early on, NSD-9 personnel repeatedly lobbied to take our case, whispering to FBILA executives that SARA-4 agents were inexperienced and unequal to the task. To them, we were rubes and hicks who should be seeking daily NSD-9 "expert" involvement and advice. "Experts in what?" I asked. "Everything CI" they answered, claiming we were doing everything wrong.

Getting nowhere, Sal announced a change in tactics at one particular weekly squad meeting. He was setting up a rotating daily schedule for each squad agent—except for me, Sheldon, and Gunnar, the case agents—to call NSD-9 squad members with stupid questions. The dumber, the better, and whatever the answer given, SARA-4 agents should pretend to be confused and pose equally stupid follow-up queries. I objected, afraid to confirm NSD-9's claims about us. But Sal insisted they would tire of our inane questions, beg for it to stop, and write us and our case off as hopeless.

It worked! Weeks later, NSD-9 wanted nothing more to do with our investigation. Besides Sal, much of the credit for success must go to Scott. He accepted this assignment with glee, making more calls than required. He would later regale us at weekly meetings with hilarious reenactments of his moronic questions and the irritated answers he received. I still laugh at the thought of this, Sal's insight and Scott's flawless execution. The lesson here? Regular head banging might have made our heads sore, but it built up calluses, nurtured creativity, overcame hurdles, dumped poor workers, and defeated opponents.

We had frequent battles to retain our linguists working alongside us. We were initially given many excuses why our proposal was "impossible." We overcame the FBILA language manager's objections, but then another storm kicked up back east from Ling-Ling, head of the FBIHQ Language Unit. She began dismantling our language team and farming out all our work. This proved disastrous, so Sheldon and I flew back to DC.

I'll never forget the day we met her in her office. Like in some bad movie, Ling-Ling was wearing a full-length, bright red, Mandarin-collar Chinese gown, decorated with dragons. It was her power dress, to make a statement, although not the one she likely intended. It matched her imperious attitude. From then on, I dubbed her "The Empress Dowager." Sheldon went with "Dragon Lady," because she reminded him of his loud, obnoxious aunt who habitually overdressed and wore too much makeup and perfume.

Ling-Ling listened to nothing we said. She was oblivious to the individual worth of each linguist and made it clear she considered them interchangeable cogs, one easily replaced by another. She insisted she knew "[her] people" better than we ever could. Once again, I saw smug pride and racism rear its ugly head. She was clearly a petty person who had risen to responsibilities and powers beyond her abilities.

We ended our frontal assault and regrouped, inviting her to come out west to see our operation and meet our people. She accepted and came two weeks later. Sheldon and I prayed she would maintain her appearance and persona, wanting the entire squad to observe this marvelous caricature. She did not disappoint. Ling-Ling met my team and made the same grandiose gestures and claims, astounding everyone. We then set her loose to visit with the linguists, having forewarned them that if they wanted the old ways to give way to the new, they had to speak up and stop this walking anachronism.

It worked, with Len leading the charge. The visit proved disastrous for the Empress. She maintained a brave face during departure, but the linguists had given her both barrels, insulted by the "interchangeable cog" linguist theory she promulgated. Len had directly dressed Ling-Ling down for her condescending attitude toward them. Our linguists also told her that we investigators respected and treated them as equals, and they loved the work. The Dragon Lady returned to Washington with her scaly tail between her legs, and we never experienced serious trouble from her again. Having lost her power over our case, she quietly slid into obscurity. We, however, were back on track, firing on all cylinders.

CHAPTER 14

Diamonds in the Rough

At the one-year mark of our investigation, we had a lot of smoke, a few embers, but no raging fire. We'd gained excellent intelligence and confirmed source reporting, but had nothing we could charge in open court. There was a suspicious invoice for $17,276.50 from Tai's trash, but we couldn't prove it was intelligence-related. The stacks of technical and unmarked classified documents throughout Chi's home matched sensitive reporting but could be explained away as a sloppy engineer's flotsam. There was a huge gap between what we knew, and what we could present in open court. A simple charge of illegal possession would be too easy to downplay or refute. We needed proof of collection done *for* the PRC.

We sought US Navy subject matter experts (SME) to sift through our collections to help us piece it all together. They would support our opposition to internal forces pressuring us to switch out our prosecution intentions in favor of pure intelligence collection. These forces wanted to take back our resources, so they urged us to "recruit" Chi, which was a ridiculous suggestion. Chi was a true believer. And what if recruitment failed? Chi was a US citizen, so deportation was off the table.[1] That path meant lower expectations and smoother sailing for the blue flamers, but if we didn't pursue espionage here, when would we? Some declared we would never be able to make such a case. These alternate paths led to injustice, surrender, and another Bureau defeat and PRC victory. They were anathema to me.

---

1. Deporting naturalized US citizens is a practical impossibility, although it shouldn't be.

Then, a routine trash cover of Chi's home on February 7, 2005, changed everything. Usually, little of use was found. This time, the little we found proved game-changing. Our incredibly professional, methodical, dogged, and conscientious agents found tiny bits of paper, many smaller than a dime, amongst the rotting garbage. Some bits contained Chinese characters, some handwritten, some machine-printed. *One* of these paper bits had "DD(x)" handwritten in English. Once notified of these finds, I directed that the bits be immediately reassembled and translated and the results forwarded to me.

On this rare occasion, our well-oiled machine sputtered and misfired for a moment, allowing this task to temporarily fall between the cracks. The next week, I realized I hadn't seen the results, and inquired. Jessie reported that no assembly or translation had occurred. I was frustrated—not with anyone in particular, as we all had a lot on our plates—but

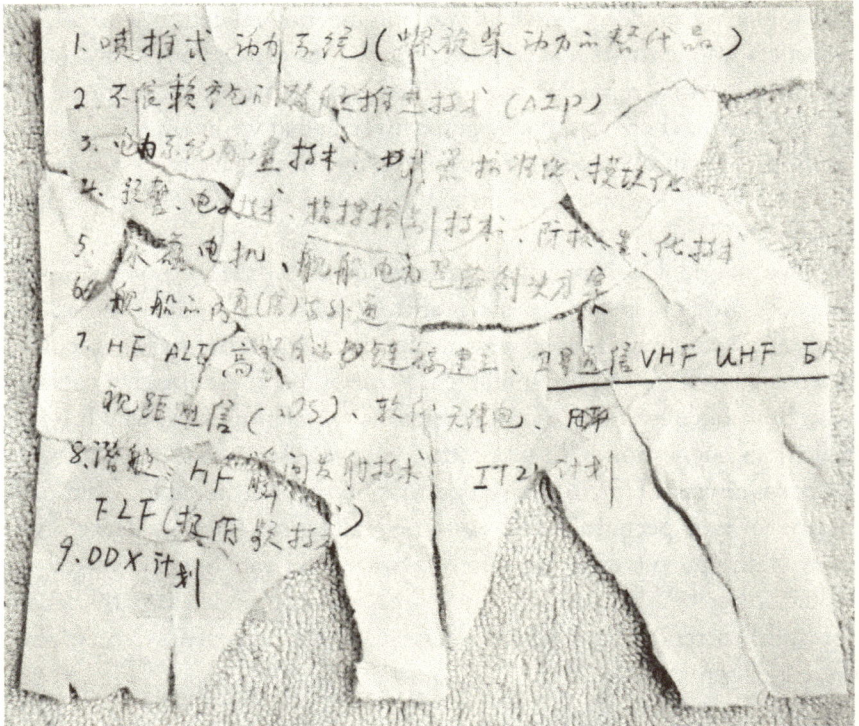

Handwritten tasking list found in trash TRIAL EXHIBIT 44

because this item sounded so promising and came from a technique that had produced so little to date.

I asked Jessie to locate the items and meet with me and a linguist to sort them out. Jessie dumped the pieces on the floor. They were stained but had been dried out, explaining the reason for the delay. The three of us crouched on the carpet, assembling what turned out to be two tiny puzzles, both missing some pieces. Thankfully, we recovered the vital fragments. Once reassembled, we taped them together, and that was how they remained—no fancy forensics lab work required.

Jessie and the linguist translated the documents for me. They were technology collection tasking lists from China! One was handwritten, the other machine-printed. This was unlike anything we'd found before. We could now publicly link what Chi had gathered, and had in his home, with what China was tasking him to collect.

Below are translations of each note: { } indicates translator explanations, // indicates broken sentences and words due to rips in the paper, and [ ] indicates insertion of implied meanings/terms:

{A.   Handwritten, numbered list in Chinese characters}

1. Jet propulsion power system (replacement for propeller power).

2. {Illegible} . . . ship [submarine] propulsion technology (AIP), non–air reliant . . . {illegible}.

3. Power system configuration technology, weapons standardization and modularization.

4. Early warning and electronic technologies; command and control [systems] technology; defense against nuclear attack technology; defense against chemical-biological attack technology.

5. Permanent magnetic motor, integrated solution for shipboard power [system].

6. Shipboard internal and external communications [systems].

7. HF, ALE, establishment of high frequency // self linking, satellite communications, VHF, UHF, EHF, Line-of-sight communications (?OS) [LOS], software, antenna package.

8. Submarine: HF transient launch technology // IT21 Plan, ELF (Extremely Low Frequency technology).

9. DDX Program

{B. Machine-printed instructions and list in Chinese characters}

[You] can learn more through joining more associations and participating in certain symposiums. [The information from] one symposium can [could] be compiled onto a disc, and later on it will [would] be very meaningful to do research on it.

Space-based electromagnetic intercept system, space-launched magnetic levitation platform, electromagnetic landing platform for carrier-based aircraft, electromagnetic // artillery system, submarine torpedoes, electromagnetic launch system.

Aircraft carrier electronic systems // Handbook of systems configuration and operating parameters, // types, models, and specifications for electronic systems, including electromagnetic shielding techniques for TR [transmit/receive] tube [or barrel], amplitude limiter, electromagnetic shield, etc.

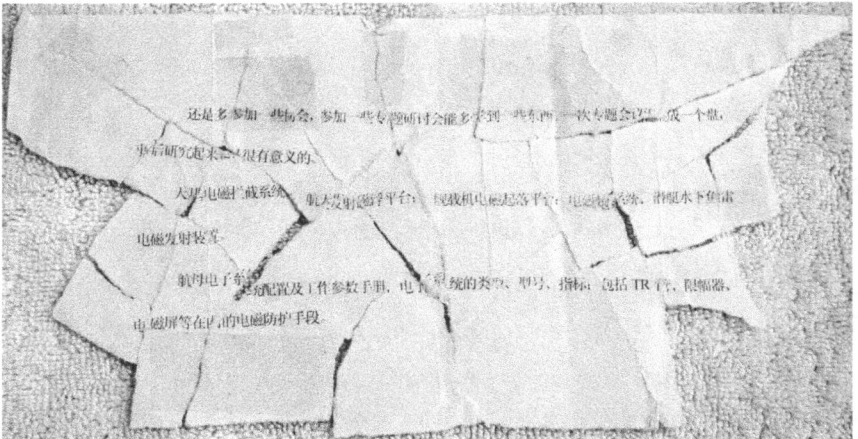

Machine-printed tasking list found in trash TRIAL EXHIBIT 45

Adding to our excitement, data matching taskings 1, 2, 3, 5, and 9 on handwritten List A were found within Chi's residence, and Chi had collected *all* of the technologies requested within the machine-printed list B and followed *all* of its instructions.

We could now prove Chi Mak was a willing, active spy for China! This strengthened every argument for a criminal prosecution and our resource requests, and temporarily silenced our many critics and armchair quarterbacks. Handwriting comparisons confirmed none of the Maks had written List A, a broad, general tasking for many technologies, some of which Chi Mak could *not* access. But Chi was an expert in electromagnetic submarine motors and their quieting technologies, such as QED, even serving as the US Navy's 2004 national QED chairman. This list appeared to be scrawled by someone who knew Chi Mak worked with the US Navy but was ignorant as to his exact access. Its final item listed our newest stealth destroyer, DD(x), which Chi had never worked on, yet he had somehow found a way to obtain its data and send it to the PRC in early 2004.[2]

The machine-printed list gave us even more. Since Chi's home and work computers and printers couldn't print Chinese characters, someone else had created and printed this list for him.[3] More importantly, it told Chi *what*, *where*, and *how* to collect data, and processing procedures thereafter, i.e., collect data at "certain symposiums," to be "compiled onto a disc," for them later to "do research on it." We had seen Chi follow this template, proving he was obeying China's taskings, and linking PRC orders to Chi's collection in his home. Chi's access to *all* the technologies in List B proved it was meant specifically for him. And the final "etc." meant Chi Mak should collect whatever else he could get his hands on, which he had!

With these finds we reevaluated our earlier recovery from Tai's trash of the fax invoice sheet. Tai's import/export business, Mak Professional Stereo Engineering Company, Ltd., appeared to be a front. Who was Mr. Lee Po Fat (aka, Pu Pei Liang), the man it was addressed to in

---

2. We were later able to prove Chi had taken DD(x) project data from his employer's shared drive.
3. Chi Mak later admitted he had no way to print out this list.

Hong Kong?[4] And what about the Po Fat Electronic Trading Company, Ltd. (aka, Pu's Good Fortune Electronic Trading Company)?[5] Tai and Pu each listed phony businesses as their front companies. This invoice requesting payment of $17,276.50 for installation of audio equipment was dated just days before Chi and Rebecca traveled to China and when our investigation began. We would later learn that Chi had carried the DD(x) information himself during their 2004 trip; Pu was the Maks' PRC intelligence handler; and the payment requested was Tai's bill for having encrypted Chi's stolen DD(x) data onto a disc for Chi and Rebecca to carry to China.[6]

The pieces were falling into place.

---

4. Chinese name spelling and pronunciation differ by dialect. "Pu" is the Mandarin form, while "Po" is Cantonese.
5. Pu's cellphone number later proved a critical link at trial between the Maks and PRCIS officers.
6. Tai wanted Chi to bring back Pu's payment, but Pu never paid up.

CHAPTER 15

Enter the Dragon, Part III

IN THE SUMMER OF 2005, OUR INVESTIGATION WAS BALANCING MANY spinning plates. While our navy experts cataloged the technologies Chi was collecting for the PRC per its trashed tasking lists, our linguists were falling behind due to the thousands of poor-quality microphone intercepts of the Maks, forcing time-consuming, painstaking replays to ensure comprehension. We'd also lost Gunnar to the NCIS San Diego office, which reclaimed him. His replacement, NCIS Special Agent Omar Lopez, had to make his own nightmarish daily commute from Point Mugu, north of Los Angeles, but was providing us invaluable help, given his background as a military lawyer. Omar was also a quick learner whose high energy and sharp mind proved essential as we worked to frame charges against Chi. The NCIS remained our essential partner. Still, Gunnar, a beloved team member, was a tough loss.

Another blow came when Sal went on medical leave for an ankle injury, just before our coverages indicated Chi and Rebecca were planning a weeklong trip to Hawaii's Big Island in late September 2005. Jessie coordinated SSG coverage of the Maks with FBIHQ and the Honolulu Field Office, to be supplemented with our own Gs, who knew the Maks best. She was the natural choice to lead this surveillance, although it brought some good-natured ribbing, having also had the cushy assignment of tailing the Maks during their 2004 Alaska cruise.[1] Jessie and Sheldon coordinated surveillance plans, while I concentrated

---

1. She had not watched them on their European vacation, however.

upon a third covert entry opportunity, likely our last chance to install home CCTV and better microphones.

Jessie and our FBILA SSGs arrived in Hawaii days early to coordinate and prepare with Honolulu's Gs. By the time the Maks arrived, the team constituted one well-oiled, ready-to-roll machine. This was good, because the Maks' movements, while entertaining, didn't make it easy. Their usual ultra-cheap, eccentric methods of sightseeing would have alarmed the uninitiated, but that's where the FBILA team's experience shone.

After landing, the Maks stopped for a few groceries and then headed to the worst dive of a hotel you can imagine, filled with all manner of prostitutes, drug dealers, and other shady customers. This dangerous environment made it difficult to blend in and maintain personal safety, posing a unique challenge for our unarmed Gs.[2] Staying at the Maks' hotel proved too dangerous. The normally gung-ho Gs agreed, so they stayed in safer hotels nearby, requiring two car rolling surveillances to watch the Maks—and each other's backs. I've conducted surveillances in dangerous neighborhoods. It's hard to blend in, and you spend as much time with your head on a swivel, checking to ensure you aren't jumped by neighborhood thugs, as you do surveilling the target.

By now we were well versed in the Maks' cheap ways. These Maoists were the tightest wads one could ever meet. Their hotels only needed to meet one criterion: Be Hawaii's cheapest hotel.[3] The Maks stayed in a different hotel every night, making their way around the island, each hotel cheaper and sketchier than the last. One aspect of it became easier. We knew that once the Maks were tucked in for the night, they wouldn't leave until morning. They were too cheap to eat out, and even they weren't crazy enough to go out after dark. Among all the drug dealer and prostitute activity, we saw that the Maks met with no one.

---

2. FBI criminal squads use surveillance teams composed of armed Special Agents. SSG teams are made up of non-agents because CI work isn't usually exposed to criminal elements or life-and-death scenarios. This is a huge plus for us. Surveillance units using Special Agents, no matter how good, tend to have a sameness of appearance, personality, and behavior, due to the Special Agent vetting process. For example, I think I'm excellent at conducting a surveillance, but I also know I have that generic look of a "government man."

3. Is there a travelogue market for cheap Maoists? Frugal Marxists of the world unite!

Each morning brought an interesting ritual witnessed by SSGs: Rebecca and Chi Mak walking out onto their balconies, leaning over the railing, and vigorously scratching their heads, their version of a shampoo and rinse. Some SSGs swore they saw particulates cascading from the Maks' heads during their vigorous scratching sessions. Their pattern of driving around Hawaii in an extended circle, staying in a different bad hotel each night, and eating groceries for every meal continued.

Meanwhile, on the mainland, we watched nearby relatives and friends as we began our third series of covert entries.[4] My primary goal this time out was ensuring the installation of interior CCTV cameras and improved microphones, with no more Tech Squad excuses. This Hawaii trip had been an answer to prayer, giving us one last chance to force these installations. Sandy, Sheldon, and I had brought maximum pressure to bear, no longer relying on Kenny to do his job. Instead, we engaged in constant, unremitting telephone calls, emails, court orders, and meetings with Technical Unit managers, exploiting FBIHQ advocacy and pressure, bordering on harassment, to achieve this. *We* obtained the proper equipment for the Tech Agents, and handed them authorizing orders, in triplicate. No more wiggle room. Heather, SARA's Tech Agent representative, and the rest of the Tech Squad had their written orders.

Our requests were not greedy or excessive: I requested one CCTV pinhole camera covering the Maks' home office's desktop and one camera covering their small dining room table, the two locations most likely to support paper- and computer work. And the audio collected from the new upgraded microphones were to synchronize with the new CCTV for integrated transmission directly to our SARA-4 command center, creating a seamless product. I was happy the installations would finally be accomplished.

This being my last covert entry, I took time to ponder how this whole thing had started, what we had accomplished, and what remained to be done. Maybe too much time! As I stood between the couch and coffee table in that cramped living room, surrounded by eight other guys, waiting my turn to walk out to our getaway Voyager parked outside, I turned

---

4. Again, the Maks told no one of their trips, and no one ever visited their home while they were away.

around to get more comfortable. With that turn the hard rubber antenna on my walkie-talkie, clipped to my hip, punched a hole in the yellowed, stained, brittle lampshade next to the couch.

No one else in the darkened room noticed, but I was horrified. On my first entry it had been my cleats, which I had long since banished. Since then, I had been careful to leave no trace of my visits, even ensuring spiderwebs remained unbroken. Now, on my *last* visit, I had punched a hole in a lampshade that I had no time to fix or replace. I did the only thing I could. Like an embarrassed guest, I quietly, sheepishly, turned the lampshade around so the hole faced the wall, and said a silent prayer that Rebecca wouldn't notice it, or assume Chi, or age, were the cause. Whenever this happened to TV's Control Agent 86, Maxwell Smart of *Get Smart* fame, he would look around, lick his fingers, and "repair" the broken item with his spit. It never worked. Now I was Max, meekly turning the lampshade and hoping Chaos agents wouldn't notice.

The next day, our Flaps and Seals guy Paul had to reenter the Mak home because a Tech Agent couldn't locate a tool and feared it had been left in the Maks' home. We didn't like going back in during the day, just hours before their return, but we had to be sure. With heavy SSG and Lookout support, Paul covertly reentered their home, swept it, and found no missing item. My relief was measured but not total. I still imagined the Maks later finding that tool between the couch cushions, alerting them enough to also discover their torn lampshade. Only time would tell.

With our work completed, we waited with bated breath for the Maks' return and anticipated our long-sought opportunity to observe them within their home. We had finally forced the installation of CCTV coverage within two rooms of the Mak residence, the computer and dining rooms, and allegedly, better home and vehicle microphones. From experience I doubted the microphone clarity would improve, and it didn't.

Then there were the CCTV pinhole camera installations. As requested, one camera was recording over the dining room table, with the other over the computer room desk. Installation had gone relatively smoothly over a few days. I was assured that everything tested well, according to plan. Then they dropped the hammer, *after* the installations and entries were done. Heather informed me the CCTV camera feeds would *not* be synchronized with the audio *or* be directly fed to our SARA-4 command post. Instead, they would be transmitted from the Maks' attic via microwave, requiring SSG teams in their cars to record the transmitted signals using handheld mobile receivers.

I was flabbergasted. This was *not* what I had requested, or been promised. When I asked why, she explained the Maks' home wiring was too old, unable to support the load necessary to hard-wire out the video or audio feed. We had known this since 2004, and I believed we'd already addressed it when Tech Agents upgraded the Maks' home's electrical and cable systems. Yet now they were saying they couldn't—or wouldn't—support the CCTV! They'd literally had *years* to plan for this well-documented request yet had done nothing to address it. Moreover, this microwave transmitter signal was very weak, at best transmitting under a hundred yards. Our Gs were given big, clumsy, obsolete Rube Goldberg contraptions to operate within Chi Mak's neighborhood, an area we had avoided for years to ensure the security of our long-term investigation. This negligent installation also meant the audio and video recordings would not be synchronized, and that both recordings would be received erratically, forcing upon us immense manpower requirements and confusion now and in the future. I was fit to be tied!

Heather defended the work as the best that could be hoped for, but you could see she knew it was a lie. To be fair, she wasn't the installer, and was subordinate to Kenny, her supervisor, but I didn't care anymore. I'd had it with this lazy incompetence and sloppy mediocrity, and told her so. I threw up my hands and walked away, sick of the endless battles to force others to do their jobs competently.

It ended up being even worse than Heather had described. The signal was so weak that SSG teams had to get as close as fifty feet from Chi's home before capturing the signal, which kept blinking in and out, depending on the day, weather, antenna angle, neighborhood activities, and alignment of the planets! The Gs had to literally drive around the Maks' home, waving their arms while holding antennas out their windows, in hopes of catching the elusive signals. It was a bad dream and another *Get Smart* moment, which would have been comical if not so outrageous. This sloppy negligence threatened the success of our investigation.

The Maks returned home and entered their residence. We received choppy, intermittent, streaked, and grainy black-and-white footage of their movements whenever they were near the dining room table or home office desk. It was underwhelming, to say the least. We requested better focusing, boosted signal strength, and more robust receivers, but were told we were lucky to have this. Knowing whom we were dealing with, I believed it. So, we worked with what we had, knowing it should have been much better. The good news? The Maks never mentioned the damaged lampshade, or discovering a strange "tool."

Within days of installation, the CCTV camera in the computer room went dark, with no explanation. These daily events seemed more like satire than reality, more Laurel and Hardy or Keystone Kops than Federal Bureau of Investigation. I said this and much more to Heather. She didn't care; she'd fought this case from the beginning because of the resources it consumed. Fortunately, due to the strong dedication and skill of our team, and the grace of God, we were able to cull enough evidence from this seriously flawed product to later make our court case, without alerting the Mak neighborhood to our presence. Once again, it came down to the extraordinary efforts of our own agents, linguists, SSGs, and Lookouts.

In the weeks following the Maks' return, we saw little relevant activity, so I worried that the computer room's failed CCTV was missing all-important computer activity. At least the Maks' time in Hawaii had helped our linguists catch up somewhat. We were only a couple of weeks behind at this point. Meanwhile, our SSGs did their best to collect signals from the surviving dining room CCTV, which I prayed would continue functioning.

On Sunday, October 23, 2005, we caught a *huge* break that I attribute to God's direct intervention. Given the computer room camera failure, poor audio and video feeds, and lag in translations, it is the best explanation for our sudden and dramatic change in fortune.

Part II
Pursue

CHAPTER 16

The Die Is Cast

AT 8:50 A.M., SUNDAY, OCTOBER 23, 2005, WHILE SITTING IN THEIR cars, the Gs watched Rebecca stand over Chi's shoulder at their dining room table as he copied compact discs (CDs).[1] Rebecca constantly critiqued Chi's efforts as she handed him additional discs. Credit for this discovery goes to the Gs, who worked diligently with inferior equipment and circumstances to capture this monumental event. By 10:27 a.m., the Maks finished copying data and packaged three discs for transport. Shortly thereafter, they headed north on I-5, arriving at Tai Mak's Alhambra home and carrying the CDs inside, thus marking the first and only passage of data we witnessed between the families. Since we knew Tai was Chi's courier, this was a huge event.

Thirty minutes later, both families drove to Homestyle Restaurant in Monterey Park for lunch. Chi and Rebecca left Tai's home without the package. Lookout Jaime called me at home that same day with the news. My hairs stood on end—We had passage! I called an all-hands meeting for early Monday morning and arrived even earlier for what promised to be a momentous, exhausting day. First, I called Sandy with the news and my plans. He suggested a teleconference Tuesday morning with FBI and NCIS superiors to discuss what we knew and next steps.

Monday morning, the Gs reported their observations and showed their footage. We peppered them with questions because the video

---

1. Had the Maks logically used the computer room with its malfunctioning hidden CCTV, our case conclusion may have been disappointingly different. It is a what-if scenario I do not enjoy pondering.

TC +09:22:31:14

RC: Little Bu/Pu's carefulness is useless. He/she does not understand. He/she does not understand. This is not his/her field. He/she does not read it. He/she does not read it. People before him/her read it. But people before him/her did not read it, either.

FBI video cut: "Pu is useless. He won't understand." TRIAL EXHIBITS 192 AND 212

remained grainy, repeatedly dropped out, and had no accompanying audio. But the activities were clear enough. Chi methodically copied three CDs onto his laptop, then made three more copies, labeled each, and wrapped them in a bag which they delivered to Tai's home. Lookouts, SSGs, and linguists knew of nothing explaining this activity other than the obvious. Since the linguists were still two weeks behind in their translations, I ordered them to make Mak translations their *only* job and priority, and immediately tell me of any pushback so I could report it to FBIHQ, NCIS, and US Navy brass.[2] I required additional information before my scheduled Tuesday-morning meeting with Washington executives, who expected answers. Summaries of Chi and Rebecca's Sunday discussions had to be on my desk long before then.

---

2. "Ordered" is too strong a word. Our linguists were all over this case, working it 24/7 if left on their own. Their FBILA and FBIHQ language managers were the problem, still assigning them other casework as well. I said that would stop *now*, phrasing it as an FBIHQ order to protect the linguists from their management.

Then I outlined next steps for the linguists *after* completing Sunday's summaries. I needed rough summaries for all Mak intercepts, including emails, going backwards and forward from Sunday. They were to be sent immediately to myself, Omar, Sheldon, and Acting Squad Supervisor Randy.[3] We *had* to get a handle on the background for Sunday's events, and quickly. A deadly serious, excited mood descended on us all, realizing where this was heading. Omar, horrified to learn how difficult it was for the Gs to collect good CCTV signals, drove north to join them and look for a better way.

That afternoon I visited Assistant US Attorney (AUSA) Deirdre Eliot at the Santa Ana branch of the Los Angeles US Attorney's Office (USAO).[4] She'd been assigned our case over a year earlier, being the only Santa Ana AUSA handling national security cases there, meaning mainly terrorism matters. Initially, I had visited her office, introduced myself, and lightly briefed her of the threat, since most of our reporting was too sensitive to discuss, unsuitable for open court, and therefore worthless for prosecution. Deirdre was courteous and interested, but way too busy with terrorism cases to invest more time. She said I was to continue my investigation, following standard CI methods and reporting procedures.

A year later, I updated her on the trashed tasking lists we recovered and our FISA coverages. She noted our progress, requested I keep her informed, and said to continue documenting our investigation as an intelligence case, not a criminal one. This meant we continued reporting all progress via Electronic Communications (ECs) and Memoranda rather than FD-302s.[5] This later horrified "experts" on NSD-9, and elsewhere, but not Sandy or other FBIHQ management. Our CI methods of documentation aided our overall success, creating a clean, definitive CI record until the point it became a criminal matter. Upon my third visit, I alerted Deirdre that the case had clearly crossed over to criminal, since we expected a Mak family member to soon travel to China to transport Chi's data to the PRCIS.

---

3. Supervisory Special Agent (SSA) Sal Valdez was on medical leave during this time.
4. This ten-minute drive, as opposed to the hour and a half it took on a "good" day to reach the main downtown Los Angeles USAO, proved a huge advantage as the case progressed.
5. The FBI form for recording all evidentiary matters.

Deirdre understood, and since she was swamped with terrorism cases, promised to seek help from another Santa Ana AUSA she knew who had recently gained clearance to handle classified cases. By day's end the linguists had briefed me on their translations covering Sunday, and the days before and after. Their news gave me an adrenaline rush and near heart attack.

Our string of events began the prior Tuesday, October 18, when Fuk called Tai to report she had booked their travel to China for Friday, October 28, 2005, returning November 9.

The next day, October 19, Tai called intelligence handler Pu Pei Liang's cellphone, 13922702332.[6] During this brief, stilted exchange, Tai used coded phrases, opening with "Chief Pu. This is Mr. Mak, Red Flower of North America," then asking, "Have you been busy with the trade fair lately?" Pu answered, "Yes. We're getting more clients." Tai replied, "Actually, I'll be coming over to attend the trade fair too." Tai provided Pu his flight information, adding, "I'll be with my assistant." Pu promised to pick Tai up at the airport and told him to contact Pu upon arrival by using his magnetic calling card. Tai agreed, and Pu responded "Good-bye, Chief Mak" before hanging up.

To this day, we don't know what or who initiated this China trip, but it spawned a flurry of related conversations.

The next afternoon, Thursday, October 20, Fuk and Tai had a lengthy, revealing conversation about this trip. Tai mentioned he had been unable to reach "Elder brother (Chi)" before they discussed both Chi and Rebecca.

Tai: Let the couple get nervous about it next week. Or whatever it is, it doesn't matter. I know they are definitely nervous about it.

Fuk: It is better not to carry than carrying them. Carrying that stuff is kind of heavy.

Tai: I know. Now it's only a disc.

---

6. Soon thereafter, we began referring to Pu's continuously resurfacing cellphone number by its last four numbers—2332.

Fuk: Doesn't he know how to do it—disc?

Tai: He has to give it to us to do it—on my computer, on my notebook. . . . He definitely has to give that to me; he cannot do it.

Fuk: (confused) Uh! After he has to give us . . . his papers first and then—

Tai: (interrupting) No, no. He had to give me a disc, but I still have to take his disc and then have it encrypted at my place, then it is okay. . . . They don't have it over there. It can only be done on my IBM—I mean the one in the second floor, the notebook we brought over. . . . But he must give me the disc. The couple is really nervous about it. They'll come to your house and watch you how to do it. . . . I mean a series of activities will bother you for five or six days for sure. That's how they are.

Fuk: (chuckling) It is better to know it later than to know it sooner.

Tai: So next week they'll bug you for five or six days for sure. They're really nervous about this kind of stuff. . . . Like last time he was given the disc, watching him how to do it.[7] This, this, that. He wanted to know how you do it. Anyway, very nosy, and very nervous. . . . I'm not going to bother with it. Today is Thursday and tomorrow is Friday. I'll give him another phone call and it is done. I'll call him again next Monday. I'll be leaving next Friday. Whether he is going to have it ready or not, I don't care. . . . They will definitely do it. They tear off page by page from the whole book—they tear off a couple of pages at a time, I know their stuff. I know them. . . . Last time, Choi mentioned that if the stuff is not important, don't bring it over.[8] They mentioned that they know that it's a book.

Fuk: Also, [the pages] are non-consecutive, giving half and not giving the other half.

---

7. This describes the 2004 encryption of the DD(x) data disc by Billy, with Chi watching over his shoulder.

8. "Choi" is the Cantonese version; "Cai" is the Mandarin. Choi/Cai is another PRC intelligence officer.

Tai: (agreeing) Every time—next time, a couple of pages are torn out; next time, a couple of pages are torn out. Wow! I said, if you are afraid, don't do something like this [unintelligible].

Fuk: Don't bother with him. He's just carrying out his duty.

Tai: [finishing this topic] I don't have anything to report. I don't need to report it if I don't have anything. For that many years, I am still the same, right? I feel free and easy. I am not going to bother with it. I'll get in touch with him again next week. . . . Nothing special then.

They finished this call with a discussion of Fuk's criminal marriage fraud business.

The next day, Friday, October 21, Tai called Chi. After initial discussions about their elder sister Shouling Barnes's travels in China, Tai changed the subject.

Tai: I'll be going back to Hong Kong next week.

Chi: Oh really? Going next week? What day?

Tai: Next Friday.

Chi: We might as well meet, or what?

Tai: It's the 28th.

Chi: We might as well get together, okay? . . . You, you're only going to Hong Kong?

Tai: I'll also go to China. . . . But it'll be short. Mainly in Hong Kong.

Chi: Good. So, it'll be beneficial to meet.

Tai: I'll probably be back in about ten days.

Chi: For this trip, is the company asking you to go or—?

Tai: [interrupts] It's both. That is, everybody has made a request.

Chi: What's the reason for asking you to go back?

Tai: Not much. It's just that we haven't seen each other for a long time.

Chi: It's probably like a work report.

Tai: Yes, yes.

They discussed the need for occasional contact with organization leaders and Tai's Asia TV employer.[9] Chi learned Fuk would be going, but not the kids. The conversation continued:

Chi: Leaving on Friday. . . . I think, I mean it's better that we meet before you leave.

Tai: Sure, sure.

Chi: How about let's meet this Sunday?

Tai: [agrees that Chi will come to Tai's home beforehand] Good. So, there's enough time and no problem.

Chi: [again verifies departure date, length of stay, hotel, and other travel details] Would this be considered a business trip? I mean, do they pay you?

Tai: They'll pay for it.

Chi: The weather should be okay, I think. There's no typhoon or whatever, right?

Tai: Yes.

Chi: Actually, when you go there, besides meeting with them—when you're in Hong Kong, besides meeting with them, there isn't much to do. [Chi suggests that Tai visit the mainland]

This was excellent, exciting news—Chi would meet and give Tai something to carry to China; but what?

The Sunday CD copying conversations indicated technical data gathered in "2004" and "2005," and copied onto discs, one titled "Reconfiguration," another "Propulsion," and a third unnamed CD containing "US Naval Academy" presentations. Chi and Rebecca had discussed the merits of the data they were copying: "Power Simulation . . . Carrier Program . . . Advanced Motor . . . Automatic Control . . . Power Conversion . . . 5 Megawatt QED," etc., discussing each topic's "usefulness" and mentioning their copies were for a collector in China called "Little Pu/Gu."

---

9. We didn't intercept a request for Tai to travel to Hong Kong, and his boss later testified Asia TV didn't request Tai's travel.

They also reminisced about their last trip to China, and the royal treatment they received in Guangzhou and Shanghai—chauffeur, luxury car, and hotel. Then Rebecca interrupted Chi—a common occurrence—to criticize his slow method of copying CDs. Once copies were completed, she told Chi to label each disc. The two of them then mentioned "these three original packaged pieces [were] okay to go to their home," and briefly discussed getting the data past US authorities: "Customs people . . . These kinds of people, even if they do the inspection, they will not be able to find it." Why? Because the discs' data will be "encrypted."

Chi and Rebecca then wrapped the three CDs in a plastic bag as they watched the movie *Enough* on TV. Its plot confused Rebecca. Chi's explanation proved amusingly Maoist.[10]

Soon thereafter, they drove to Tai's home and delivered the CDs before having lunch with Tai's family at a nearby restaurant. During the drive home to Downey, our implanted vehicle microphone recorded portions of an interesting conversation.

Chi: It is good that I made three CDs this morning for him to take to Little Gu/Pu.

Rebecca: He said that he still needs to work on them further.

Chi: Yes. He has to encrypt them.

Then on Monday, October 24, Tai called his son Billy at the University of California at Los Angeles (UCLA), telling him, "When you come back, no matter where you go, go to buy several CDs—the recordable CDs. . . . Buy three or four. . . . So, buy them. I have something to do with them." Chi later called to pester Tai as to whether "[E]verything [was] ready?"

Before our own critical meeting the following Tuesday morning with FBIHQ, NCIS, and US Navy brass, I had some big decisions to make. But the Maks' vaguely worded intercept conversations didn't specifically describe *what* was on those CDs Chi and Rebecca had created.

---

10. "A female was oppressed by a male. After having been oppressed, the wife escaped. Later, she wanted to avenge herself. She said she [unintelligible] abused [by the] husband."

We couldn't risk them going to China, but what if we stopped them and found only unrestricted or undecipherable data? Our case would be blown. We needed to decrypt the CDs' data, but what if we or Tai's laptop couldn't decrypt it? We'd have a theory, but no criminal charges. Chi would be disrupted, but not permanently stopped, and an investment of a year and a half and millions of dollars would just end up as another failed FBI Chinese espionage investigation. I also feared Murphy's Law if we rushed a massive takedown operation in *four* days, involving simultaneous arrests, searches at multiple locations, and interviews of non-English-speaking persons, all while using many extra FBI and NCIS personnel with no CI experience or familiarity with our specific case.

Fortunately, I received a good piece of news: Gunnar was returning to rejoin us! As Gunnar, Sheldon, and Omar all shared my misgivings about rushing this case, we developed an alternate plan: We'd use Fuk's marriage fraud immigration business to our advantage.

We knew that Fuk already feared she was a target of law enforcement, since many of her competitors had been recently arrested. Therefore, we would arrest Tai and Fuk at the airport and charge them with immigration fraud, while simultaneously having US Customs seize all belongings as evidence. That way, we could intercept the CDs, take a crack at breaking the encryption, and then destroy the digital data in a manner providing plausible deniability. The discs' data would never reach China, with the reason appearing to be Fuk Li's criminal activity. This would put them in the PRCIS doghouse, Chi would appear to remain untouched by it all, and we could take the time to build a bigger case, maybe even arresting him months later when he retired and moved back to China, transporting his *entire* collection of technologies. This would guarantee many more serious charges.

It was a good plan that met everyone's concerns. After a long day of planning, we went home satisfied and ready for the next morning's big meeting.[11] Because each lived two hours away, Gunnar and Omar stayed in a local hotel that night, and many nights, weeks, and months

---

11. East Coast management being three hours ahead meant *very* early morning meetings for us West Coasters.

thereafter. I went home thinking about the next day's decisions, and that a conclusion was finally in sight.

The Tuesday morning video teleconference included a large cast of players. Gunnar, Omar, Sheldon, and I represented SARA-4. FBILA CI SAC Pete Brust also sat in, a good guy and exception to our string of bad FBILA executive managers. I had briefed him the previous evening, and he supported our plan. Sandy at FBIHQ was on the line, along with his unit chief, Tony, and an unidentified CIA representative. Finally, from the Navy Shipyard in DC, we were joined by Gunnar's NCIS boss, Barry Marushi, sitting with some high-ranking USN officers representing stakeholder groups Naval Reactors (NR) and the Office of Naval Research (ONR).

Sheldon and I gave everyone the background and what we currently knew. Omar and Gunnar outlined the technologies Chi had access to and what was in his home. The USN officers drilled down on Chi and Rebecca's references to "Carriers" and "QED," wanting to know what was on the discs. We couldn't say for sure, and that bothered them. When asked for our next steps, we laid out our immigration and marriage plan regarding Tai and Fuk. We also explained the dangers of rushing these arrests and search warrants.

The CIA official and Pete Brust expressed enthusiasm for this option, while Sandy, Tony, and Barry remained noncommittal. But the navy officers adamantly opposed it, saying it risked QED data getting to China. I repeatedly pointed out there was *no* chance of that happening, since we would seize the CDs no matter what. Either they weren't listening, or they didn't comprehend. They insisted they were comfortable with only one option: immediate arrest, search, and seizure based upon QED-related charges.

Wasting my breath, I pointed out that their option added nothing while threatening the whole prosecution. Sandy, Tony, and Barry at NCIS sided with the navy, while SAC Brust and the CIA rep were with us. An actual vote was taken, but since my team didn't get a vote—more executive snobbery!—we lost. We were ordered to proceed with the navy's plan, as if they were the authorities on the US legal system.

I hung up with palpable anger. Sheldon felt the same. We were sick and tired of doing all the work and then being ordered what to do by ignorant higher-ups. Omar and Gunnar took it in stride, with Omar's first words being, "Okay, the first thing we need to do is . . . ." I appreciated his professionalism but stopped him, unwilling to throw in the towel yet. Eighteen months of successfully pushing back against similar executive foolishness had conditioned me to think I could still win this fight. They needed *me* to successfully prosecute Chi Mak, and I still had some cards to play.

First, I called the CIA official to thank him for his support—a first and last in my career—and requested he ask his superiors to contact their FBI counterparts and express a preference for our proposal. I then called Sandy and said, "What the heck? How could you let those navy officers, knowing little about the case, and unconcerned about a successful prosecution, dictate what *we* are going to do? It may be their technology, but it's *our* case. And either way, we guarantee keeping their secrets out of China!"

Sandy explained, "Those guys represent Naval Reactors, [an] East Coast government behemoth with its hands in nearly every navy program. If we get on their bad side, they can shut down our prosecution through lack of cooperation, so that no matter how good our result, NR would falsely claim we ignored its wishes and put QED at risk."

No NR cooperation meant no technology experts, no QED background information, and no successful path to Chi's prosecution. This was hard to swallow. Sandy was skilled at compromising for the greater good, and I understood his reasons but didn't accept them as valid. "Politics" was interfering with justice.[12] My team and I had earned the right to make this call. I also called SAC Brust. Although he was sympathetic, he didn't believe the course could be altered.

Undeterred, I continued my lobbying efforts while simultaneously undertaking my marching orders. I visited AUSA Deirdre Eliot and filled her in. There was much to do. She opened a prosecution file and

---

12. This "political" path leads to abuse, as I learned years later when my SAC Jim Struyk rewarded outrageous CIA behavior by stripping my squad and case agent of a fantastic asset my agent had skillfully developed, giving it to a rapacious, incompetent, deceitful CIA officer and her chief of station. Sandy and my ASAC Chris Nicholas went along with the whole thing for similar "political" reasons.

stored it in their poor excuse for an SCIF, a stifling, cramped, windowless former broom closet. She agreed that rushing to write the paperwork needed for multiple espionage arrests and searches in under four days was foolish. We visited with her manager, Tom O'Brien, a former fighter pilot who marketed himself as a fearless man of action. Deirdre hoped O'Brien would slow all this down. Agitated that the navy was dictating our actions, he pledged to stop this runaway train. My lobbying efforts were working!

O'Brien also told us to begin writing an affidavit supporting arrest and search warrants, just in case. Given her overwhelming terrorism workload, Deirdre requested the help of fellow AUSA and friend Greg Staples. O'Brien assigned Greg to my case full-time.[13] I met Greg, and we all began writing the affidavit. Jessie shipped all my Mak files to the AUSA offices to support the drafting process. I remained optimistic O'Brien would halt this nightmare and cooler heads would prevail.

My delusion of success was shattered by a pre–six a.m. telephone call Wednesday morning. Given the early hour, I assumed it was Sandy back east. But it was SAC Brust in Los Angeles, who sounded beaten down. Counterintelligence Division Deputy Assistant Director Timothy Bereznay, livid, had called about my lobbying efforts with CIA and DOJ officials, demanding I stop immediately or be removed from the case. Brust bravely supported me, but Bereznay cut him off. I would either get with his program or he would send an espionage team from the Washington Field Office (WFO) to handle the case. This was a ridiculous threat, but one that blue flamer Bereznay might just be stupid and arrogant enough to carry out, given the East Coast superiority complex I had witnessed throughout my entire career.

Pete was in a tough spot. We both knew how it would all unfold if I continued to resist:

1. They would order me to carry on until their "experts" arrived;

2. Once there, these experts would criticize every decision made and proclaim us unprofessional and/or incompetent;

---

13. At the time, I didn't realize how monumentally important Greg Staples's assignment to this case would be.

3. Their ignorant decisions would then sink our case; and

4. They would blame us for their failure.

I'd seen it before. This would be Wen Ho Lee 2.0, with NSD-9 crowing, "I told you so!" from the sidelines. I wouldn't let that happen, so I made the only decision I could, telling Brust to tell Bereznay I didn't appreciate his foolish threats, but nevertheless would manage a Friday-night arrest. However, I expected FBIHQ to provide *whatever* immediate assistance we required, *whenever* we required it. My answer relieved Pete, and he promised me anything I needed from FBILA. I responded, "A lot of manpower for Friday," and said we would follow up with a list of other needs soon.

That morning, I informed my team of this final forced decision. Sheldon would organize our aid requests to Brust, SARA-4, and the adjacent RAs of Long Beach, West Covina, and Riverside. I delivered the news to Deirdre and headed to her office.

Ironically, that same Tuesday afternoon, October 25, Billy called Tai. The translation I received Wednesday morning confirmed the wisdom of our now-overruled plan to create corrupted, unreadable discs.

Billy: I was making that disc for you, but . . . I need the small diskette in order to do it. Where did you put the small diskette?

Tai: It is in my drawer. I mean, in an envelope in the drawer of the night stand close to my bed. The first drawer. Go and look for it now.

Billy: Which drawer?

Tai: The one on the side where I sleep. Open the drawer. There is a white envelope, right?

Billy: A white envelope?

Tai: Isn't there a floppy—a diskette inside a box?

Billy: I don't see the envelope, but I see the diskette.

Tai: That's it.

This call demonstrated that Billy had previously encrypted Tai's data.

Then, later that afternoon, Tai called Billy from home and discussed Billy's computer writing error.

Tai: I saw that your computer up there is just running.

Billy: Oh, yes. That's because I am burning that disc for you.

Tai: You have to click "OK" or something like that. It is making that *quack quack* sound continuously.

Billy: It doesn't matter. I am coming back to do it.

Tai: I clicked "OK" to stop it, but it's still spinning and making that *quack quack* sound.[14]

The next three days were spent writing the supporting affidavit, with Greg doing the typing. It was a compelling tapestry of Chi's treachery. Greg and Deirdre provided the legal framework for all the facts I supplied. I wasn't the Bureau's smartest or most experienced CI Special Agent, but when it came to this PRC espionage case, I was all in. For years, I was unrelenting, ignoring all those encouraging me to ease up. Stubbornness is my superpower. I'd memorized every fact and now regurgitated every tidbit of incriminating evidence, something no one else on earth could have done, especially the "experts" from NSD-9, WFO, or FBIHQ. I knew every report, interview, intercept, and scrap of evidence. No one knew that case like me.[15] I stitched together every incriminating thread to form a damning picture, with Colleen, Jessie, Scott, Sheldon, Tom, Omar, and Gunnar helping to locate each supporting piece cited.

Deirdre and Greg made wonderful teammates. She was a conservative, a rarity within DOJ, and enthusiastic, while Greg was a lefty, not unusual, but with a sense of humor, which was. And Greg loved catching those he called "cheaters." The USAO viewed Greg as a bit of a maverick, since he didn't care about promotion or managing others, happy with

---

14. Forensic experts later determined that a writing error had occurred, requiring Billy to redo his encryption that evening.

15. One of the factors that killed the Wen Ho Lee case had been the revolving door of over nine different case agents. So much knowledge is lost with every case agent change. I had been the *only* Mak case agent, beginning to end—another thing blue flamers don't understand.

just prosecuting criminals. His office wasn't dominated by legal degrees, plaques, and awards but by posters of the Sex Pistols and Jimmy Hendrix. And he and Deirdre respected FBI agents, treating us as peers, not subordinates. Most AUSAs disdain our work, intelligence, and judgment. If their case goes wrong, we are their favorite default fall guys, despite the fact we produce the cases and do the majority of the work.

While we three drafted, others performed their own miracles. Sandy told me of extraordinary measures being taken to protect our original reporting source from compromise once public arrests were made. Sheldon and the team were recruiting and coordinating manpower for our huge, rushed Friday-night operation, being forced by circumstances to use many personnel with little or no CI experience. It would include surreptitious and simultaneous removal of all our electronic devices. The SARA-4 team performed magnificently under great pressure, for which I am eternally grateful.[16]

---

16. At the risk of leaving someone out, I feel compelled to identify the following individuals for their noteworthy participation in this takedown: 1) FBI: SAC Pete Brust, ASAC Jim Struyk, Sandy Kable, Sheldon Fung, Kevin Moberly, Jessie Murray, Colleen McKay, Len Pi, Henry Dean, Harriet Hao, Tom, Scott, Jaime, Lisa, Dennis, Doug, Than, Tanya, Mike M., Mike G., Randy, Joe J., Joshua, Will, Sylvia, Dan Bolick, Sharon K., Peter, Mike K., Rodney, Rita, Kevin S., John P., Steve L., Joe A., Thom, Gerald, John A., Mederick, Dave, Todd, Steve I., Kevin A., Mark L., Thomas, Sandra, Tommy, Teresa, Sharon L., Duncan, Do, Young, Kenny, David, Troy, Steve K., Tarik, Catherine, Marvis, Angela, and Michael, our invaluable Gs of whom there are too many to name, Kenny, Chad, Heather, Warren, Craig, Rob, Mark O., Cathy, and Marc; and 2) NCIS: ASAC Barry Marushi, Gunnar Newquist, Omar Lopez, Tim, Scott W., John P., Mark P., Leanne, Pete, Tracy, Andrew, Jennifer, Gary and Rocky. They all played a personal role in this takedown, which went off without a major hitch.

CHAPTER 17

D-Day!

FRIDAY, OCTOBER 28, 2005, CAME QUICKLY.

I arrived very early, anticipating many decisions that day, but hoping to squeeze in an afternoon nap since I'd be pulling an all-nighter. I had all day to swear to the completed affidavit and warrants to gain the magistrate's signature. Gunnar and I also needed to prep for Chi Mak's interview, which we would conduct at FBILA headquarters after his late-night arrest. I told Sandy we were on schedule, then met my team to review preparations and new developments. Everything was well in hand.

I drove to the AUSAs' offices to learn when I would see the magistrate. We agents had long advocated the simple, easily proven initial charges of "Acting as an Agent of a Foreign Government" (18 USC. § 951) against Chi, Rebecca, Tai, Fuk, and Billy, "Use of Property to Aid a Foreign Power" (18 USC. § 957) against Tai and Billy, "International Traffic in Arms Regulations" (ITAR—22 USC. § 2278(b)(2)) for Chi, "Conspiracy" (22 CFR 127.1) against all five of them, and Marriage Fraud (18 USC. § 1325 (c)) for Fuk.[1] Criminal searches and interviews would produce evidence for more charges, including espionage, later. Every affidavit detail had been double-checked—every address, name, serial number, date, factual claim, etc.—leaving no exposure to legal challenges.[2]

---

1. Espionage charges were called for, but DOJ and the USAO had repeatedly scuttled that possibility.
2. Our legal system has mutated over the years to allow even the most trivial of errors to bring about a case dismissal.

Yet I found Deirdre and Greg on edge when I arrived. The problem? Competing armchair attorneys at the Los Angeles USAO and in the DOJ Counterintelligence and Export Control Section (DOJ/CES) in DC were arguing over the proper charges, leaving Deirdre, Greg, and my squad caught in the middle, powerless. Two teams of attorneys equally ignorant of our case were deciding everything.

One team was led by Acting US Attorney George Cardona, someone Greg expressed respect for, something I never understood. He was a mealymouthed hand-wringer, a Doubting Thomas who only said what couldn't or shouldn't be done, never offering a better alternative. His ideas always involved scaling back, downplaying, retreat, or outright surrender.

The other side was commanded by the cautious, cranky King of Unkept Promises, John Dion of the DOJ/CES, who always sought the minimum charge. The irony was that these two similarly wavering, warring sides despised each other. Dion and his attorneys were snobs who had tried few if any cases personally. Yet they looked down on USAO attorneys as ignorant rubes who didn't know the law. Cardona and his USAO lackeys saw DOJ/CES lawyers as naive, unprincipled academics who didn't know the real world and made promises they wouldn't keep. The scary thing was, each side was right! And each was willing to betray everyone else to save their own skins if things went south. They were two sides of the same miserable coin. In bad times, agents always got it in the neck from both. History was about to repeat itself.

These two sides fought all day, treating this like a law school exercise. While my team did the heavy lifting, these idiots couldn't get their act together or their egos under control, thus jeopardizing the entire operation. If the warrants weren't authorized in time, the Maks would go to China with US Navy secrets. I'd never conceived of such a possibility!

The scheduled time for me to swear to the affidavit and warrants before the judge that morning came and went. Greg and Deirdre kept rewriting the paperwork each time the latest dictate came down, while nervously assuring me I could swear before the after-hours duty judge *in downtown Los Angeles*. I was steaming! This eleventh-hour pissing contest was inexcusable and unconscionable. While each team of lawyers jockeyed for dominance, my after-hours duty judge had retired to his northern San Fernando Valley home. Getting his signature now meant a trip of more than two hours![3]

It wasn't until 3:30 p.m. that both sides signed off on common charges. Now I had to wait for Greg and Deirdre to alter the affidavit and warrants accordingly once again, and make multiple copies of each, based upon charges we had *never* contemplated.

These charges proved "The words of committees do harm merely by existing."[4] The two Mak couples—Billy had been dropped as a defendant completely—were charged with "Theft of Government Property" (18 USC. § 641) and "Conspiracy" (18 USC. § 371). These violations were completely inadequate and legally flawed, but we had no time to argue. Our window for arrest was closing fast. We would be lucky to get everything done before Tai and Fuk flew off to China.

Greg, Deirdre, and their staff quickly made the drastic changes required, performing admirably given the many critical details and limited time involved. The reckless USAO and DOJ/CES morons had endangered our whole prosecution. The slightest mistake now risked utter failure.

Around 6:00 p.m., I was given banker boxes filled with the new documents (I had long since missed the 4:00 p.m. SARA-4 "all-hands" pre-takedown meeting, as well as the chance to grab a power nap or prep for Chi's interview with Gunnar). These battling buffoons had put us in a horrible position. Without my fantastic team it would have been a complete disaster, yet if anything had gone sideways, they still would have blamed us, claiming "poor execution."

I jumped in my Bureau car and launched like a rocket, careening through downtown Santa Ana streets to reach the traffic-choked I-5 north and head toward Duty Judge Jeffrey Johnson's home in the San Fernando Valley hills. Greg and Deirdre had alerted him of my anticipated arrival. I was in the middle of Friday evening's rush hour, meaning a two- to three-hour drive. I was literally shouting curses at Cardona, Dion, and their groveling minions as I weaved through traffic. If they had

---

3. About as far from Orange County as Los Angeles County gets.
4. Freeman Dyson quote.

been there with me, violence likely would have ensued over their petty, egotistical, moronic interference.

As I alternately careened and crawled through the I-5 traffic, my team leaders kept calling to give, and get, updates. They were keeping everything together but couldn't act until all the paperwork was signed. I continued bobbing and weaving north, using the HOV lane when it wasn't clogged, and even the freeway's shoulders, inviting angry honks. I prayed the California Highway Patrol would notice, stop me, and then escort me. But they didn't. There's never a cop around when you need one!

Meanwhile, our whole operation had kicked into gear. As 9:00 p.m. approached, SSG teams reported Billy was driving his parents to LAX for their flight.[5] Meanwhile, Chi and Rebecca had settled down at home for the evening. I was finally pulling up to Judge Johnson's home, my radio crackling with anxious people asking if the documents were signed yet. Judge Johnson's wife answered their door. I must have looked a sweaty and stressed-out mess, but she showed no surprise, offering me a drink and a seat in their living room as she got her husband.

Judge Johnson entered and jokingly commiserated with me about the drive I'd just endured. I apologized for the late hour and mentioned our time constraints as he sat down to read my affidavit and warrants. He asked clarifying questions as he went, like how I knew my factual statements were true, the importance of the data Tai and Fuk were carrying, etc. He concluded by stating he found the documents sufficient and asked me to raise my right hand and swear to their truth. By now I was receiving near-panicked calls from agents in the field asking about the warrants. Tai, Fuk, and Billy had turned off I-405 at Century Boulevard and would soon arrive at LAX. Fortunately, they parked in the Terminal 5 garage and walked. If Billy had simply dropped them off, we would have had real trouble. Still, they were minutes away from the planned arrest—*after* they passed through airport security—yet not a single document had been signed.

Judge Johnson began signing just as the Maks approached the Delta Airlines counter.

---

5. During this LAX trip, our vehicle microphones recorded Tai discussing the CD they were carrying for Chi, how Billy had encrypted it, and how nervous this whole thing made Chi.

I kept excusing myself to go to another room to field these increasingly intense calls. Hearing their distress, Judge Johnson asked about the situation. After my explanation, he replied, "Tell them that for their purposes the affidavit, arrest, and search warrants have all been signed as of now, and that they are cleared to proceed."

It was 9:15 p.m.

I thanked him for his consideration and forwarded the good news, triggering a collective sigh of relief across the airwaves. We were a go!

At 9:42 p.m., Tai and Fuk checked their one small bag. Billy said good-bye at 10:01 p.m. and left his parents to walk to the security line. At 10:13 p.m., Tai and Fuk exited security and were immediately and professionally arrested without incident by FBI and Customs agents. Few bystanders even noticed.[6]

Meanwhile, in Alhambra, Shirley Mak had left home to party with friends. The arrest of Chi and Rebecca, and searches of the Mak homes in Alhambra and Downey, began minutes later. I listened to these events unfold over the radio while I sat watching the judge sign each copy. Finally, I took my leave, banker boxes in tow, thanking Judge Johnson and his lovely wife for their hospitality and understanding. He wished us good luck.

It was a long drive from north San Fernando Valley to FBILA, but at least some pressure had been lifted. All arrests had gone smoothly, with subjects in custody and searches begun. I still needed to get to FBILA quickly, to deliver the signed documents, and more importantly, to interview Chi Mak.

Tai and Fuk's interviews began at LAX at 10:31 p.m. Chi and Rebecca were arrested minutes later and transported to FBILA. They now awaited interviews in separate rooms. And Billy had returned home to find FBI and NCIS agents searching it. By 11:30 p.m., Rebecca's and Chi's interviews had begun. Gunnar handled preliminaries with Chi as he waited for my arrival, because we worried that the longer Chi sat alone, the angrier he might become, and the likelier to invoke his Fifth Amendment rights against self-incrimination. Knowing Gunnar to be

---

6. *One* did: Chinese national Luo Zhi Xiong. SSG had been watching him tail Tai and Fuk.

an excellent, likable interviewer, I told him to start without me, knowing he would make a good impression on Chi and keep him engaged and wanting to talk. Once more I cursed the attorneys whose destructive interference had messed with the most important interview of this case, and my career.

Upon arrival at FBILA, I maneuvered my rickety dolly of document boxes to its front door and knocked on the glass until a guard answered. I waited while he confirmed I was allowed entry, then took the cargo elevator to the seventeenth floor and walked into the command center, once more a hot, sweaty, frustrated mess.

Colleen updated me on our status: All defendants had waived their Miranda rights and denied wrongdoing. At LAX, Fuk was testing her feminine wiles on Omar, cooing over how handsome he was. Billy had disappeared upon seeing his home was being searched, while sister Shirley partied the night away at a nearby club. When approached for an interview, she swore at agents and threatened to shoot them.[7]

And Rebecca? She proved a formidable opponent, aggressively arguing every point, no matter how ridiculous or obvious. I glanced at the monitors and saw Sharon, a Special Agent fluent in Mandarin, along with our linguist Henry, interviewing a stoic and argumentative Rebecca.

I then sat down to watch Gunnar's friendly, rapport-building conversation with Chi. Gunnar hadn't yet pressed him about the evening's events, instead complimenting Chi's engineering background and his "work for this country." I tried to time my entry to begin this most tricky part, interviewing and confronting the Mak family patriarch and head spy.

---

7. Upon hearing this, AUSA Greg Staples facetiously declared he was in love; Shirley was his kind of girl! She was fortunate she wasn't arrested then and there. I wish she had been.

CHAPTER 18

Two Snakes Caged, One Loosed

THE LINCHPIN TO THE OPERATION WAS TAI AND FUK'S ARREST *AFTER* clearing LAX security. If we had arrested them before that point, they could have claimed no intention to transport the prohibited materials to China. After passing security, that claim disappeared. Our Gs volunteered to work double shifts—they wanted to see this case to the end.[1] Sheldon and Dennis assigned them a secondary outer perimeter, an investment which produced great returns. As Tai and Fuk checked their bag, those Gs reported a suspicious Asian male covertly watching and filming the Maks through the terminal window. He was surveilling them! Who was this guy? Dennis told these perimeter Gs to stay on him and report back once we'd arrested the Maks.

When Tai and Fuk stepped into the security line, this same man stepped in right behind them. While in line, Fuk and the man made eye contact but showed no signs of recognition. This guy followed them right out of security, towing his carry-on bag. SSG teams then covertly filmed the Maks walking into the waiting arms of law enforcement. It was a low-key, quick, professional arrest by FBI Special Agents Jessie Murray, Sheldon Fung, and Doug, accompanied by some Border Patrol officers.

It was so quick and quiet that no one else noticed this event, *except* one guy, a Mr. Luo Zhi Xiong, who slowly walked by, absorbing the whole

---

1. Like the linguists and Lookouts, I believe how we treated the SSGs made a huge difference. They weren't interchangeable cogs. Each was a valued and unique team member. I'm convinced that's why they each gave us so much bang for our buck. They were motivated and invested to go the extra mile.

unfolding scene. After going a few feet more, he stopped and watched Tai and Fuk being led off. He then sat down and began fidgeting and looking around nervously, while placing calls and sending texts on his various cellphones. Eventually he moved to a different terminal from his scheduled flight, the same flight for which Tai and Fuk were ticketed. SSG teams informed Dennis, who came by once Tai and Fuk's interviews had begun.[2]

Given his good looks and easy manner, we had Omar interview Fuk, the incorrigible flirt. Tai, the PRCIS's official courier, was also a very important interview, so we had Dan Bolick, an experienced, Mandarin-fluent CI agent, handle him, since Tai's English was practically nonexistent. We hoped this would streamline things, but it did put Dan at a disadvantage, since he was unfamiliar with our case. Tai waived his rights and Dan began the interview around 10:30 p.m. by gathering background information.[3]

Tai immediately began lying, claiming:

1. He had no older brother in the United States;

2. He was taking his first trip back to China;

3. He never lived in Mainland China;

4. He was his family's only source of income;[4]

5. He'd created the CD we recovered to listen to music during the trip;[5]

6. He'd told Fuk nothing about the CD;

7. He had no laptop computers at home;

---

2. While audio for both interviews would be recorded, no video-recording capabilities were available.
3. Tai led off by declaring that he had never completed junior high.
4. Fuk earned up to $30,000 a month with her criminal marriage fraud immigration business. Billy also worked.
5. Tai's answer never wavered, even after he was reminded that he carried no means to play that music.

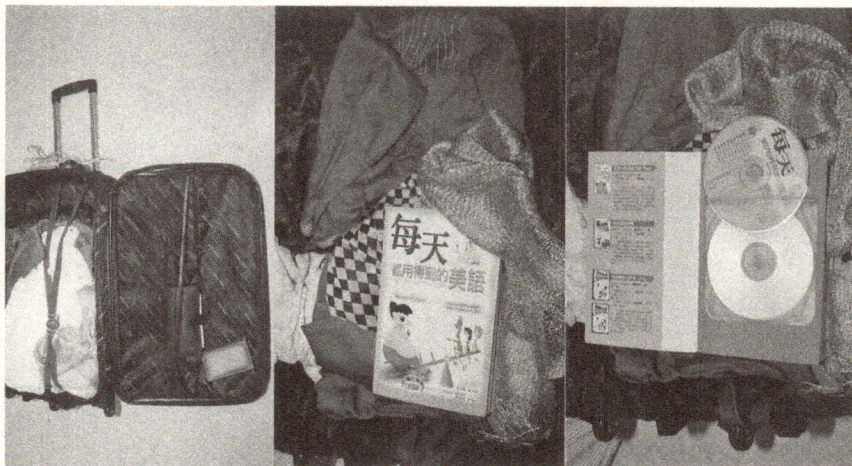

Concealed encrypted disc seized at LAX TRIAL EXHIBITS 13, 15, 21, 22, 25, 172

8. He had no connection to PRC intelligence organizations or individuals; and

9. He'd never carried anything for Chi Mak.

Tai's first lie of having no older brother in the United States bogged down the interview early on, something our linguists later claimed was Tai's intention. Tai later admitted to having a laptop at home, but claimed he'd purchased it for Billy, another lie. At one point, he requested an attorney, but almost immediately thereafter revoked his request. But when Dan asked about the Asian male at LAX, showing Tai a picture, he denied knowing him and again invoked his right to an attorney. Tai was transported to FBILA for processing before delivery to the Santa Ana Jail around 4:00 a.m.

Fuk was a wholly different kind of animal. Along with linguist Len and Thuan, the immigration fraud case agent, Omar was taken on a verbal roller coaster of ridiculous emotions, conflicting lies, and surprising truths, all embellished by Fuk's histrionics. Claiming to be "just a housewife," she intentionally confused the proceedings as much as possible. Despite Fuk's efforts, Omar documented some useful, obvious lies:

1. Fuk and Tai were never given CDs, knew nothing about encrypting or transporting them to China, and never "carried heavy things" there for Chi;

2. Fuk never broke the law—there was no marriage fraud business;

3. Son Billy didn't understand English;[6]

4. Billy only loaded the LAX CD with traveling music for Tai;[7]

5. The FBI was framing Fuk;

6. Tai didn't know about Fuk's marriage fraud business, which was run by a woman named "Carol"; and

7. The Asian man at LAX had no link to Fuk.

Wading through Fuk's verbal swamp, Omar managed to pull to the surface a surprising number of admissions:

1. Fuk and Tai *had* traveled to China previously, contradicting Tai;

2. They told Chi about this China trip, met him for Sunday lunch, and had dreaded his subsequent "nagging";

3. The laptop in Billy's room was a "gift" from a "Hong Kong friend," which Billy used to encrypt data onto a CD per Tai's request;

4. Fuk handled "marriage introductions" for money, which Tai knew about and helped with;

5. Her business partner was Mr. Zhang, someone of whom Billy disapproved;[8]

6. Tai and Fuk despised Chi and Rebecca;

7. Chi would soon retire;

---

6. That would be news to Billy's UCLA professors!
7. Yet the CD was in the checked luggage.
8. Did Billy suspect "monkey business" came along with the illegal business?

8. An "audio friend" was picking Tai and Fuk up at the Hong Kong airport; and finally

9. The Asian male filming Fuk and Tai at LAX was Mr. Luo, a past marriage business client.

Throughout the interview, Fuk was masterfully obtuse and unconcerned with whether her lies made sense, lurching between dispassionate discussions and crying jags.[9] But she never admitted working for Communist China. The agents ended the interview and delivered Fuk to the Santa Ana jail, after FBILA processing.

Other players we interviewed that evening included Billy Mak, who initially left our Alhambra home search but later returned to watch. Billy acknowledged being a senior Molecular Cell and Developmental Biology student at UCLA, as well as a part-time "broadcast control room technician" at Phoenix Satellite Television for his dad. He confirmed summer 2004 travel to China to visit friends and his grandmother in Guangzhou, and possessing a laptop which Tai used with Billy's help. He denied encrypting discs for Tai, only admitting to creating music CDs for Tai to listen to. Soon after, Billy shut down, repeatedly acting confused and answering, "I don't know." When his interview ended, Billy was released.[10]

Sister Shirley Mak proved the hardest with whom to hold a civilized conversation. She broke all the stereotypes, earning Fs at community college, partying every night, and swearing like a sailor, proving this apple didn't fall far from the Fuk tree! At 2:00 a.m. in the parking lot of one of many nightclubs she visited that evening, agents approached a combative and agitated Shirley. She refused to be interviewed. Jessie Murray requested consent to search her parents' 2004 Mercedes that Shirley was driving.[11] She gave it, but reneged when asked to sign the form.[12] When Jessie told her the search would happen anyway under judicial warrant, Shirley screamed demands to talk to her parents and brother Billy; to

---

9. From her poor ninety-three-year-old mother to her "no-good brother" in China.
10. The warring USAO/DOJ attorneys had dropped all of our planned charges against him.
11. Asking for consent often calms people and encourages cooperation. Not in this instance!
12. FD-26 Consent to Search.

call the police; to take pictures of the agents' "licenses";[13] and to call her "car attorney" (whatever that is!). When Jessie gave her an FBI business card, Shirley threw it on the ground. When the car search began, Shirley shouted "I will shoot you!" Once informed that threatening a federal officer was a federal crime, she provided the valet ticket and car keys, which agents used to search the vehicle.[14]

"Mr. Luo," aka Luo Zhi Xiong, who surveilled and filmed Tai and Fuk, was the evening's bonus. It seemed he had been issued orders to surveil Tai and Fuk and report.[15] Dennis arrived and spoke with the SSG team. They believed Luo, currently in the bathroom, was a PRCIS surveillance specialist. Dennis and a Border Patrol agent walked in to detain and question Mr. Luo, and seize his possessions: four cellphones, a personal digital assistant (PDA), a digital camera, a digital camcorder, and various documents, including "employment" papers identifying him as a PRC biomedical firm "marketing consultant." He also possessed a signed contract with Fuk to marry an American woman.[16] Yet Luo claimed he didn't know the Maks and couldn't explain his signed marriage contract with Fuk. Then he admitted knowing Fuk, barely, before denying filming her.[17] Mr. Luo admitted to being a PRC citizen, native of Guangzhou, and a graduate of Zhongshan University.[18]

Luo's video of Fuk and Tai contained additional footage of Zhongshan University delegations visiting Harvard, MIT, and the University of Minnesota. His PDA proved a gold mine, listing hundreds of PRC and US contacts, which we would pass on to the CIA, NSA, and other members of the US intelligence community.[19] We had enough to arrest and charge Mr. Luo with conspiracy, but USAO executives predictably

---

13. We never allow our credentials to be photographed, to prevent counterfeiting attempts, among other things.
14. Shirley was fortunate that night. If I had been there, she would have spent the weekend in jail.
15. When reviewed, his cellphones revealed text messages asking for status and why he had stopped texting.
16. We had recovered a copy of this same agreement from Tai and Fuk's trash on July 8, 2004.
17. Review of his film proved otherwise.
18. Tai and Fuk were from Guangzhou, and Zhongshan University contained the Center for Asian Pacific Studies (CAPS), where PRC intelligence officer Pu Pei Liang covertly operated as a "Research Fellow."
19. None of them ever sent us a "thank-you." Par for the course.

Luo Zhi Xiong at LAX AUTHOR'S COLLECTION

intervened with their same old timid playbook. We were forced to cut Luo loose, so he jumped on the next China-bound flight. But we kept his stuff, analyzing the crap out of it.[20] If Luo ever returns, he might face arrest on foreign agent and co-conspirator charges—that is, *if* USAO and DOJ executives ever grow a backbone. No matter. Luo's name is on the Prohibited Traveler Watchlist, blocking his return to America.

Our goal had been to get honest answers, and we got some. But even documented lies helped us, demonstrating rehearsal and organization. *Every* defendant claimed Tai took the LAX CD to listen to its "music," the very definition of coordinated co-conspirator answers. Their biggest miscalculation? Tai carried nothing on which to play this music.

---

20. Eighteen months later, during Chi Mak's trial, AUSA Greg Staples whispered to me that he had been contacted by an American attorney retained by Mr. Luo, who was safely in Guangzhou. Mr. Luo wanted his items returned. Greg asked for my answer. I said Mr. Luo could have all his stuff back (we had copied and analyzed it all by then), but only if he returned to the United States to sign for it. We still have his stuff.

CHAPTER 19

Denyin' Spyin'

ONCE TAI AND FUK'S LAX ARREST OCCURRED, WE EXECUTED "KNOCK and announce" arrests and searches at Chi and Rebecca's home, using two uniformed Downey Police officers to avoid confusion, resistance, or delay. The Maks, who were preparing for bed, were arrested on federal charges and their house was searched. Once delivered to FBILA, each was processed, visited the bathroom, and received water before placement in interview rooms. Chi requested and received hot tea.

Both rooms were videotaped by order of SAC Brust, overruling my objections.[1] I had never conducted a videotaped interview, so I thought it unwise to begin with arguably the most important interview of my career.[2] Because I had been placed chronically behind schedule, Gunnar waited on me by plying Chi with tea and introducing himself as a reasonable professional just doing his job. Finally, able to wait no longer, Gunnar obtained Chi's signed Miranda rights waiver. Chi thought he could talk his way out of this, as we'd expected. Gunnar began with softballs, verifying Chi's background, birth, education, training, employments, etc., demonstrating to Chi that we'd done our homework. He also established some common ground between these two "navy guys," with Gunnar identifying Chi as the engineer who'd "done a lot of good work for the navy over the years."

---

1. This was not standard procedure at the time. Bureau policy has since reversed, requiring subject interview recordings, unless otherwise authorized.
2. I was never so happy to be wrong! These recordings later proved a gold mine for the prosecution. I only wish we had videotaped Chi's third interview as well.

When I arrived, carrying Chi's third cup of tea, they were discussing Chi's work, including the national QED project he'd headed. Gunnar introduced me and summarized their discussions about Chi's favorite subject, electrical engineering. He was obviously very proud of his work. We encouraged him to educate us laymen, to be our instructor. Gunnar had established rapport, so I stayed in the background, just asking the occasional clarifying question. Chi boasted he'd taught at UCLA, Cal State University Long Beach, and in Hong Kong, and confirmed he'd never worked on DD(x)—an important point.

Chi Mak had a unique way of answering questions. If he liked the question, his English-language answer was complete, detailed, and grammatically correct. Those he didn't like were answered with cryptic, ambiguous, partial responses trailing off into unresponsive answers. In fact, they were gibberish, allowing him to later deny saying anything substantive, or that he'd been misunderstood. While he did acknowledge that his work for Power Paragon and the US Navy was "proprietary" and would threaten our sailors if provided to foreign adversaries, any admission was accompanied by caveats and exceptions. And once he realized how damaging some of his initial admissions were, he backtracked to fantastic lies. For instance, saying that he'd given Tai the data discs to guide Tai's purchase of QED books in Hong Kong bookstores. This, of course, was ridiculous. QED was an experimental US Navy technology, and Tai hadn't even finished junior high. Here is a sample of Chi's practiced answers of incoherent gibberish:

Gunnar: Did you give your brother some information about the QED?

Chi: QED is still, long time ago, let me see, not long time, he let me, try to think, a meeting or whatever things I think I talk with him before.

Chi later let slip that Tai had traveled to Hong Kong once before, confirming Fuk's answer and disputing Tai's.[3] He acknowledged understanding export-control laws and knowing "NOFORN" data could

---

3. We later confirmed this covert trip took place in December 2001.

not be exported, but he declared none was in his home.[4] Chi proudly declared he had easily passed his recent L-3 Ethics test (he meant to say his Export Compliance Quiz).[5] While admitting prior China travel,

---

Export Compliance Quiz

Thursday, March 3, 2005

Name: _CHI MAK_   Associate #: _2823_ Department #: _2755_

Match the words at the bottom to their correct definition.

1) _Foreign Person_ An individual who is neither a U.S. Citizen nor a permanent resident alien.

2) _Defense article_ Any item or related technical data which is specifically designed, developed, configured, adapted, or modified for a military application and does not have predominant civil applications and does not have performance equivalent to those of an article or service used for civil applications.

3) _Export_ When a commodity or technical data are shipped to a foreign country, or the transfer of technical data to a foreign person, in any manner, whether in the U.S. or abroad.

4) _Export License_ One type of approval from the Department of State giving permission to discuss or ship a commodity listed on the application.

5) _export Compliance Coordinator_ The title of the Point of Contact at PSG that will assist in export issues.

6) _Red Flag Indicator_ A checklist for exporters indicating suspicious transactions

7) _Unclassified Foreign Visitor Request_ A form completed by a PSG employee prior to the arrival of a foreign visitor.

8) _Technical data_ Information other than software, which is required for the design, development, production, manufacture, assembly, operation, repair, testing, maintenance or modification of defense articles.

9) _sanctioned countries_ Cuba, Iran, Iraq, Libya and North Korea

10) _Unclassified Foreign Visitor Request_ Required for foreign visitors prior to gaining access into L-3/Power Paragon.

11) _Defense Service_ The furnishing of assistance (including training) or technical data to foreign persons, whether in the U.S. or abroad

Foreign Person	*Defense Article*	*Defense Services*	*Export*	*Approval*

Export Compliance Coordinator (ECC)	*Export License*	*Sanctioned Countries*

Unclassified Foreign Visitor Request	*Red Flag Indicators*	*Technical Data*

Chi Mak Export Compliance Quiz, March 3, 2005 TRIAL EXHIBIT 83

---

4. Our previous surreptitious entries and searches proved otherwise.
5. Ironically, after retiring from the FBI twelve years later, I became L-3's Director of Global Investigations—Corporate Ethics.

Chi Mak in FBI interview room, October 29, 2005 TRIAL EXHIBIT 189

Chi vastly understated its frequency and totally denied his 2004 trip and retirement plans.

At 1:00 a.m., Saturday, October 29, Gunnar and I took a break to coordinate and get updates before exploring Chi's relationships with his wife and brother. We got nowhere. He was unconcerned for either's welfare. Information and lies continued coming in dribs and drabs: Chi had worked the EMALS program;[6] his PRC travel would be recorded in his US passport;[7] Chi had *no* contacts in China; and *did* provide Tai access to DD(x) data prior to Chi's 2004 trip to China. Every admission came with a caveat you could drive a truck through.

> Gaylord: [Tai] was given access to DD(x), correct?
>
> Chi: Uh, correct, and not completely correct. Because DD(x) I can find in published paper, even in newspaper.

---

6. Electromagnetic Aircraft Launch System (EMALS), for use on future US Navy aircraft carriers.
7. Chi knew no PRC trips were recorded, since none of the Maks' flights had been nonstop to or from China.

113

At 3:00 a.m., we took another break to consult with colleagues. FBILA's general counsel said we had to wrap it up, believing Chi's age, the length of the interview, and the lateness of the hour, would support any later "under duress" challenges by a defense attorney. Bogus advice! If anyone was exhausted, it was Gunnar and me. The videotape clearly demonstrated Chi was alert and energized, given plenty of tea and bathroom breaks, and eager to convince us of his innocence. But once again, foolish "experts" held sway. The interview had to end.

We had listened patiently, documenting Chi's responses while gently probing answers that didn't match known facts, to stay on his good side. Now we switched tracks to ramp up the pressure. Given that most of our proof was still classified, we were hamstrung concerning the information we could use to challenge him, and we didn't know yet what evidence had been recovered from the searches.

Gunnar began by reminding Chi that he had provided sensitive US Navy information to Tai on the three CDs before his travel, claiming Tai had told us all about it. Chi didn't bite, but the tension built. We mocked Chi's story of a poorly educated, English-illiterate Tai buying QED books in Hong Kong. Chi's responses were increasingly incoherent, useful only for later impeachment. We had *one* LAX disc—not the three we'd seen created—and couldn't yet prove what it contained. We weighed all this against one other huge consideration: Chi had not yet requested legal representation.

We decided our final push would walk him through the tasking lists recovered from his trash. If that produced no substantive admissions, *we* would call it a night, expressing disappointment with Chi's deceptions, while maintaining our ability to question him later. If we pushed too hard, he might invoke his rights and end our access, something we didn't want.

I played our last card—his trashed tasking lists—ratcheting up the tension. After dramatically informing him I had personally collected and reassembled the trash lists, giving me some credibility, I directed Chi to read the printed trash list out loud. Knowing this was his biggest test, Chi stalled for time, sipping his tea and holding the cup in front of his face for long periods. He also pretended to have trouble translating his own list. Chi's lies became contradictory: He had created the lists but had no such data; and he had *not* written the list, while also admitting his computers, printers, and software couldn't print Chinese characters. Chi kept changing claims from "we" did this to "I" did this, realizing "we" indicated a conspiracy.[8] He refused to explain the lists' origins, simply denying they came from the PRCIS. Then he changed his story, nonsensically claiming he never threw these lists, which he made for himself, in his trash. This demonstrated how blatant and shameless a liar Chi could be, which later proved invaluable.

Gunnar then hit Chi with a flurry of accusations, demanding the truth. When Chi refused to give a straight answer about the lists, we told Chi we were done (knowing that allowing Chi to continue would have undermined our credibility with him). Gunnar began putting away his "files" with flair as Chi, obviously disappointed, appealed for us to continue. I asked him a final question:

Gaylord: What was the purpose of these [trash] lists?
Chi: So we can learn something, or something like this, that's all.

Again, the royal, plural, conspiratorial "we." Chi claimed the handwritten trashed tasking list reflected magazine articles.

We stood up to leave, saying he had squandered his chance to be honest with us.

Chi looked hurt and confused. He didn't want the interview to end, and that was good; it meant we'd preserved our ability to make a run at him later that weekend. With Miranda rights still waived, the door remained open.

Rebecca's interview proved very different from what we'd been told to expect. Our vaunted Behavioral Science Unit (BSU) at Quantico had labeled her a fearful, cowed, subservient woman who would collapse and tell all under a professional female's questioning. Sharon, a seasoned Chinese American CI Special Agent and fluent Mandarin speaker,

---

8. This was *not* a simple mistake. Chi's conversational English never mixed up genders, singulars, or plurals.

got Rebecca to waive Miranda, then followed BSU's instructions. As it turned out, their assessment couldn't have been more wrong. I wasn't surprised, having never seen a good BSU product when immigrants from very foreign cultures were involved.

Rebecca proved an impossible nut to crack, then and in later years. Unlike Chi, she presented no pretense of courtesy. She was hostile, dismissive, sarcastic, and condescending, from beginning to end. Thus, I tip my hat to Sharon for the admissions and lies she *did* pry out of Rebecca. The truth is best, but blatant lies are also useful, undercutting their later credibility and demonstrating malicious intent. Rebecca provided us with both fiction and truth.

Fiction:

- She knew nothing about Chi creating, copying, or giving CDs to Tai.
- She didn't know what Chi's employment was.
- Tai carried CDs with him to listen to music.
- Chi and Rebecca only traveled to Hong Kong, never Mainland China.
- She, Chi, and Tai were never in the People's Liberation Army (PLA).
- The Cultural Revolution was not a difficult time for people in China.

Truth (often clashing with earlier lies):

- She *did* know what Chi did for work, and some of it was classified.
- She understood what QED was.
- Chi brought work home and copied it onto CDs.
- Chi had technical discussions with her about his work.
- Chi was retiring soon.
- Accurate information about her formative years in China.

Chi Mak at the Great Wall of China, July 19, 1994 AUTHOR'S COLLECTION

Rebecca Chiu at the Great Wall of China, May 1996 AUTHOR'S COLLECTION

While Chi and Rebecca were being delivered to the Santa Ana City Jail nearing 6:00 a.m., just two hundred feet from our own SARA offices, Gunnar and I were briefing management, receiving reports on the night's events, and racing to the Maks' Downey residence to join the search before it concluded, only to arrive minutes before it ended. The Alhambra search had already finished. Sheldon, Omar, Gunnar, and I agreed to rest and regroup later that day at SARA-4 for another run at Chi.

I had one more stop to make, Power Paragon, where our search warrant for Chi's cubicle would soon begin. I wanted to ensure a smooth start, so I met our team at the facility's doors, briefed them, and emphasized that Power Paragon was a cooperating party. I introduced them to Fred Witham and ensured he received a copy of the warrant. I then went home to grab a short nap and shower. Our collected evidence would be stored to await analysis. Most agents took the rest of the weekend off. I greeted my wife Melody and daughters Lauren and Kristen, summarized the results, ate a quick breakfast, and flopped into bed.

At noon, my team caught each other up and kicked around our options. Gunnar and I would visit Chi in jail but would listen to no more lies. We doubted Chi would come clean, but we had to try. We didn't seek to record him for a few reasons: Policy prohibited recording interviews without authorization; we were exhausted; and we fully expected Chi to continue lying.

To ensure that Chi had plenty of sleep, we waited until nearly 8:00 p.m. before visiting him. We again had him sign our Waiver of Rights form (FD-395), just to be safe. Chi was happy to see us, but complained he had received no pillow, blanket, or toothbrush because someone had put him on suicide watch.[9] He also worried about missing work the following week, and how to contact a contractor scheduled to fix his roof leak on Monday.[10] We pledged to address the bogus suicide watch, told him Power Paragon already knew of his predicament, and said he could reschedule his contractor with a call from jail.

---

9. Not us! Chi would never commit suicide. To this day, I don't know who requested this. Suicide wasn't a concern we harbored regarding any of the Mak suspects.
10. We had just dodged a bullet, as a roofer would likely have discovered our attic-mounted cameras.

We then said it was time to tell us the truth. No more lies.[11] Chi insisted he had been completely truthful, and then began lying again. We cut him off and exited his cell, leaving a distressed Chi wanting more, and again leaving on good terms and with Chi's Miranda waiver intact. We canceled Chi's suicide watch and obtained promises his amenities would be restored.

After returning to SARA-4, we realized we were too exhausted to think straight, so agreed to rest and return at noon on Sunday to discuss our remaining options before Monday morning's initial court appearances.

I arrived Sunday to find Gunnar and Omar already in enthusiastic discussion. I was still exhausted. Although hopeful about the case, I was less so about our chances of getting Chi to be honest. I refused to sit through any more of his insulting lies. Gunnar and Omar were more optimistic, each advocating a third shot at Chi. Monday morning, that option would vanish.

I knew Gunnar had a better rapport with Chi. It wasn't personal: Gunnar was the fellow navy guy who wanted to "understand" Chi and "appreciated" his contributions to the US Navy. After my horde of FBI agents in raid jackets descended to arrest and jail Chi and search his home, we decided they would assign me the role of bad guy. Since Gunnar was willing, and Omar was absolutely enthusiastic over a third try, I agreed, despite being skeptical. What did we have to lose? Gunnar would play the older, senior (or senile!) agent who needed things explained to him. Omar would be the younger, hipper, smarter agent who understood Chi's viewpoint. Omar and Chi would together "explain" things to Gunnar to convince him of Chi's claims. We drafted our plan over lunch.

As 2:30 p.m. approached, Gunnar and Omar walked to the jail. Again, recording wasn't considered an option. As they began this third quest, I reviewed the weekend's events and wrote my now-overdue weekly activity report for FBI management.

As it neared 7:00 p.m., I called it a night, surprised I'd heard nothing yet from my NCIS colleagues. I assumed Chi was talking, and still lying, forcing them to work hard for every tidbit of truth. I had just left the

---

11. We had already counted the twenty-nine different lies he'd told the previous night.

office when Gunnar called. I couldn't understand him at first. He and Omar were laughing, talking, and yelling over each other as they drove to a nearby In-N-Out Burger for dinner. Chi was eating his jailhouse meal in his cell.[12]

The interview was going great, with Chi admitting to almost everything! He'd only denied sending "classified" data to China, logically explaining, "Because then you would have to charge me with espionage." Gunnar and Omar had played their roles perfectly, appealing to Chi's ego-centered need to be the smartest guy in the room. Their depictions of the FBI as the bad cop "with its own agenda," Gunnar as the "old, *slow* cop," and Omar as the "young, *smart* cop" got Chi to open up. Whenever Gunnar was "confused" about a Chi Mak claim, Omar would supportively explain Chi's reasoning, which Gunnar then came to "understand." This tactic took time but slowly convinced Chi they were on his side. He came to trust them, as opposed to the FBI, which they portrayed as only looking to mount a Chinese scalp on its wall.[13] This trust allowed them to revisit Chi's big lies, trading their support for Chi's other claims for more reasonable answers from him regarding the CDs he gave Tai, the trashed tasking lists, and other topics. They explained that they couldn't credibly lobby the FBI on his behalf if he stuck to incredible lies.

By dinnertime, they had documented major corrections and admissions. By taking a dinner break, they ensured Chi's continuing goodwill and cooperation. He didn't want to miss his beloved jailhouse meal. I was ecstatic, telling them they'd each earned Double-Double hamburgers, with cheese, fries, and a shake, on me.

Monday morning, they wrote their FD-302 interview report and filled me in on the exciting details. Chi had thoroughly discussed the importance of the US Navy's sensitive and classified QED program, especially regarding its newest Virginia-class submarine, and acknowledged that release of QED data would damage US national security, enabling enemies to track our submarines. He named two engineering

---

12. One might assume Gunnar and Omar enjoyed their meal more, but we later learned that Chi *loved* jail food, especially the fried chicken which he said came in tastier and larger portions than anything he'd received at home.
13. I loved that we could turn this scurrilous charge to our own benefit!

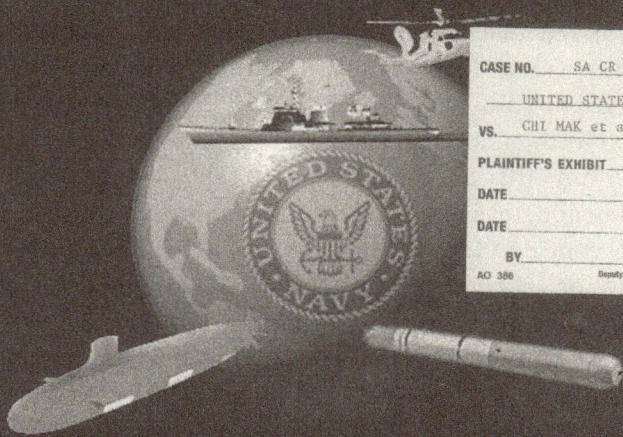

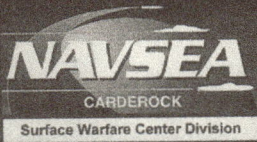
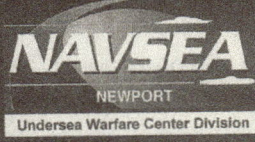
Chi Mak copy of classified symposium articles TRIAL EXHIBIT 186

friends who understood its technology and believed as he did that good ideas must be shared, whether or not the data was restricted.[14]

Chi admitted to sharing restricted data and hand-carrying it to Tai in China, with Rebecca's help, since 1983. It included USN data regarding installation of Electromagnetic Aircraft Launch Systems (EMALS) on future aircraft carriers. The couple also provided the PRC information on other projects, including QED; a 5,000-amp hybrid breaker; DC/DC converters for submarines; autobus transfer systems; the MARF (USN reactor prototype) Program; advanced power systems for battleships; the AEGIS SPY-1 radar power distribution system; and battleship survivability studies.

Chi agreed that he provided this publicly unavailable data to the PRC's "Science and Technology community" to help China. He normally gave the data to Tai, who gave it to "Mr. Pu," a "representative" of that same S&T community. He knew Pu as a non-relative who looked after Fuk's infirm mother in Guangzhou. Chi explained the stages of his passage: 1) emailing or hand-carrying a thumb drive or disc to Chi's home laptop; 2) copying the prohibited data onto CDs for transport to China; and 3) Chi or Tai hand-delivering the CDs and other materials to PRC officials in China.

Chi also admitted repeatedly lying to us Friday night. He now confessed that on Sunday, October 23, he gave Tai three CDs containing USN data for passage to Pu Pei Liang. Chi didn't know whether Pu was with the PLA or another PRC intelligence agency, but he did know the CDs contained export-controlled QED program data protected by International Traffic in Arms Regulations (ITAR) law, which prohibits passage to foreign governments or individuals.

Chi's confession exactly matched the data we later found on the decrypted LAX CD, proving the accuracy of their FD-302 report. This third Chi interview also confirmed Chi's trashed tasking lists came from Pu, who used Billy as a courier. The lists were hidden within a "small orangish-yellow colored Chinese health book" Chi received at a family dinner after Billy's return from China in 2004. Our SSG surveillance logs

---

14. Each man held alarming, naive, China-friendly views and would later figure prominently in Chi Mak's defense.

confirmed Billy's passage of materials to Chi back then. Chi knew the lists represented Pu's instructions on what to collect, making Chi angry. He declared that he didn't take orders from Pu! So, Chi admitted tearing them up and throwing them away. Two weeks later, we intercepted Chi's telephone call to Tai dismissing the health book contents received from Billy, perfectly explaining Chi's actions of trashing Pu's lists, and how he originally received them.

Chi also explained that once Tai moved to Los Angeles, Tai was supposed to carry Chi's data to China. Rebecca was fully informed of this

PLA propaganda officer Tai Mak in Hunan, China, October 18, 1970 FBI RELEASED

plan, and helped Chi copy the latest data offerings. She knew what they were doing was illegal.

Chi claimed he was never compensated by China for his services.[15] His covert China travel was aided by use of their Hong Kong residency cards, which meant they could avoid getting a PRC stamp in their US passports. Finally, Chi admitted he and Rebecca were PLA members, recruited while engineering students in China, and that Tai had served as a PLA propaganda officer. Photographs and documents recovered from our searches later confirmed the truth of Chi's confession to Gunnar and Omar.

With all major topics covered, and Gunnar and Omar still on Chi's good side, they ended the interview approaching 10:00 p.m. on Sunday, and returned to their hotel rooms to crash. Now our efforts would turn toward prosecution and conviction of Chi and his family of spies.

---

15. We knew this claim was a lie, but it was one of little consequence given the bigger picture.

CHAPTER 20

Big Needles in a Huge Haystack

THE MAGNITUDE OF OUR SEARCH WARRANT HAUL DIDN'T BECOME CLEAR until months later. With it, through painstaking research and analysis, Colleen, Omar, and others created a magnificent mosaic of the Mak family's guilt.

First came our seizures at LAX. Tai and Fuk's checked bag carried the encrypted-data disc, hand-labeled "10/25/05," hidden within a commercial Chinese-language DVD set entitled *How to Easily Learn American English*, wrapped in Fuk's clothing.[1] That date was the day we heard Billy encrypting Chi's three discs for Tai. Only two files were viewable on this disc—one with New Age music, the other with Billy's UCLA school papers. The remaining files were gibberish, appearing to be internal program files, like one labeled "DLL," apparently a drivers file.

Using what we found at the Alhambra house, that being Billy's laptop from Pu Pei Liang and diskette encryption keys, we decrypted this "DLL" file, demonstrating it was actually a compressed and encrypted version of all three CDs Chi had given Tai that previous Sunday. Billy mislabeled the file "DLL" to hide it. Once decrypted, we saw all the classified QED, export-controlled, ITAR-protected, and proprietary trade-secret data from three US conferences: 2004 ASNE Advanced Naval Propulsion; 2005 Reconfiguration and Survivability; and 2005 ONR-DARPA Future of Power Electronics.

---

1. Linguist Len Pi later proved this set was likely purchased at a local Chinese bookstore.

The unmarked classified information resided within articles Chi had written and submitted. Why, if this data was unrestricted, as Chi claimed, did Billy take steps to conceal and encrypt it? And they used "Exclusive-OR" or "XOR" encryption, which was "almost unbreakable through brute force methods," according to software engineer Alex Allain. "It is susceptible to patterns, but this weakness can be avoided through first compressing the file to remove patterns. [This is exactly what Billy did.] This encryption requires both encryptor and decryptor have access to the encryption key, but the encryption algorithm, while extremely simple, is nearly unbreakable."[2] The LAX search also uncovered multiple references to PRCIS handler Pu Pei Liang and his 2332 phone number, handwritten on Tai's business card, and inside Fuk's calendar book.

No one was home when we began searching Tai's home at 1629 South Fremont Avenue, Alhambra. Besides the encrypting laptop and encrypting diskettes, we recovered Chi's original three discs, thereby proving the chain of events. The IBM laptop was upstairs in Billy's bedroom.[3] Our forensic examination documented each step Billy took to encrypt all of Chi's data onto the one DVD-R disc. The encryption program's author, "Dr. Cheng Qiming," built it to mimic an actual commercial encryption program named "DTI." We could now prove Billy had seen every US Navy article as he encrypted each within the "DTI" file he later renamed "DLL."

Billy knew what he was encrypting and hiding for his parents and Uncle Chi to take to China. We found the two 113-bit encryption "diskette" keys—one green, one pink—in Tai's bedside table drawer, just as he'd told Billy. The green one was deceptively hand-labeled "Old friends' phone #s" in Chinese. It contained no such thing. Along with these diskettes we found more treasures in the white envelope near it. First were pictures of Tai in a PLA uniform showing propaganda films, just as Chi had told Gunnar and Omar. On the back of each was written, "Tai Wang, 1970.10.18, Hunan."

2. Alex Allain, "XOR Encryption in C++," Cprogramming, accessed November 25, 2024, https://www.cprogramming.com/tutorial/xor.html.
3. Fuk and Tai's telephone calls identified the laptop as a "gift" from Pu to use for encrypting Chi's data.

Second, it contained a code word sheet handwritten by Chi on a realtor's notepad page distributed by Downey realtor Ken Gonzales of Century 21.[4] The email address "JACKIEWDF@YAHOO.COM.HK" was written at the top. Although it ended with an "HK" extension, this address was actually created in Guangzhou in March 2004, where Pu and other officers were based while Chi and Rebecca were there visiting. Its registered owner resided in Beijing. Underneath this email address was the number "1" with Chinese characters written next to it, saying "US to China." Below this were four phrases in English, followed by an equal (=) sign and Chinese translation: "HOSPITAL = Something wrong"; "HAVE DINNER WITH FREIND [sic] ON XX DATE = Coming to Guangzhou on XX date"; "CINEMA = Retirement"; and "SEND A CARD = Check on Tai's mother-in-law."[5] These were phrases to be used when communicating with handlers in China. Below these four phrases were two more code translations: "WE = Tai" and "I = Chi."

Underneath them, the code word sheet's second half began with "FAX: 020-87319358." Like the email, this was an accommodation address, a place handlers could be contacted. We later verified the fax was a special covert line used to communicate with the PRCIS home office. Under the fax number was a "2," next to a Chinese character meaning, "China to US." PRCIS handlers used the phrases that followed to communicate with US-based agents. Further down were three phrases in English, followed by an equal sign and equivalent Chinese character: "WEATHER FINE = Everything is good"; "WEATHER UNCOM-FORTABLE = Come back to Guangzhou for work";[6] and "I HAVE TO PAY VISIT TO AN OLD FREIND [sic] FROM ABROAD = Mother-in-law emergency. Come back soon." This code word sheet was frosting on our cake!

Forensic examination of the Pu IBM laptop revealed Billy had also copied and encrypted DD(x) information just before Chi and

---

4. The rest of the Ken Gonzales notepad was found within Chi and Rebecca's Downey home.
5. Handler Pu was assigned this last primary care task, and it was one he didn't want.
6. This explained Chi's telephonic question to Tai regarding whether there were any typhoons in China. He wanted to know if sending data would be safe. If Tai had confirmed a typhoon (danger), Chi would *not* have given Tai anything to carry there.

Rebecca's 2004 departure for China, just before our investigation began.[7] Intercepts of Tai and Fuk conversations indicated Chi had nervously watched Billy encrypt the data on that previous occasion. Now we knew what and when: On February 11, 2004, DD(x) data was copied and encrypted onto a disc, two weeks before Chi and Rebecca traveled to China. We could now forensically document each stage:

1. Chi copied DD(x) data onto a CD from Power Paragon's share drive;

2. Billy copied the CD's data onto Pu's laptop;

3. Billy encrypted the data and placed it onto a new CD; and

4. He gave the new CD to Chi to carry to China.[8]

We also recovered the three CDs Chi created and delivered to Tai at the Alhambra home, and they were a perfect forensic match for the LAX

Code word sheet in Chi Mak's handwriting found at Alhambra TRIAL EXHIBIT 10

---

7. Remember, "DD(x) Program" was number nine on Pu's handwritten trashed tasking list to Chi via Billy.

8. Billy also returned Chi's original DD(x) CD to him, which we found within Chi's home.

disc. Within other Tai family computers, we found addresses for PRCIS intelligence officers Pu Pei Liang and Chen Rong Dong, along with Guangzhou numbers for their "company": 8767 1016 8777 7757, pager 86-20-8737-5888/5313, fax 87671017, and the 2332 cellphone number. Mak links with PRCIS intelligence just kept piling up!

The Alhambra residence further produced evidence of Tai and Fuk's covert, illegal travel to Guangzhou, China, via Vancouver, Canada, in November 2001, while awaiting their US green cards. Their Hong Kong residency cards made this possible.[9] This trip caused Fuk to complain about carrying heavy papers for Chi, and PRCIS handlers' criticism of Chi for providing only portions of a "book." We also found confirmation of Billy's 2004 travel to Guangzhou and later identified intercepts verifying Billy had met there with "Uncle Pu" several times.[10] These included a failed visit to the US Consulate in Guangzhou with Pu to try to obtain a US visa for his grandmother. Billy then returned to the United States and delivered Pu's tasking lists to Chi.

The search of Chi's house at 8261 Blandwood Road, Downey, began around 11:00 p.m., utilizing over a dozen FBI and NCIS personnel.[11] I was excited to see what we would recover from a criminal-style search there. No more covert sneaks and peeks or having to carefully cover our tracks. I directed seizure of any scrap of paper that "could" be linked to espionage activity, foreign contact, or foreign travel, in essence, tasking agents to be human vacuum cleaners.

Overall, we seized:

1. The three conference CDs Chi and Rebecca used to create the three CD-Rs for Tai;[12]

2. Thousands of technical documents Chi had illegally stored—classified, NOFORN, Department of Defense sensitive, restricted, export-controlled, and proprietary trade secrets;

---

9. During interviews, Tai denied this trip, but Fuk and Chi acknowledged it.
10. During his 2004 China trip, Billy's parents told him via telephone, "Uncle Pu will provide anything you need."
11. A CNN reporter described the Blandwood home as "drab."
12. These CDs were exact forensic matches with the data copied onto Chi's laptop, the three CDs Chi created, the data on Pu's laptop, and on the one DVD-R LAX disc Billy encrypted and produced for Tai and Fuk to carry to China.

3. PRCIS tradecraft, including the tracking of US Navy warship movements during wartime;

4. Evidence of frequent covert travel to China; and

5. Dozens of references to various PRCIS handlers.

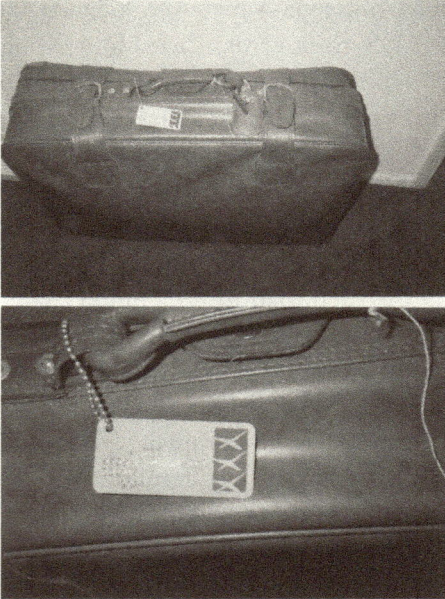

"Go bag" at Downey residence TRIAL EXHIBIT 18

Within a small suitcase in their bedroom, we found a cache of information about Chi Mak's time in Hong Kong, six brand-new $100 bills, and denominations of various other countries, along with British passports, citizenship papers, Hong Kong residency cards, and other travel documents. It was a "go bag" to use for a quick escape.[13]

We also found Chi's past employment documents from Hong Kong, as an electrical engineering professor at Hong Kong Technical University, and a "tailor" representing US Navy Purchasing, a job sister Shouling got him through her husband's tailor business. Chi wasn't just an ordinary tailor; he serviced US Navy personnel exclusively, using the pseudonym of "Johnson" to sell suits and uniform repairs. The photograph we found of a smiling "Mr. Johnson" in company uniform was classic.

In reality, this was more than a job; it was an intelligence assignment, proven by the ledger we recovered. From 1968 to 1973, Chi meticulously tracked any movements of the 295 active-duty US Navy

---

13. I always figured any Mak emergency escape plan would be a quick drive to the Mexican border, followed by a Mexico City flight to Manila, Taipei, Tokyo, Seoul, or Singapore, then a connecting flight to Hong Kong.

warships passing through Hong Kong harbor back then. While the United States was fighting North Vietnam, China's ally, Chi was reporting our ships' movements to our enemies by ship name, class, hull number, and visitation dates, along with photos of any ship personnel he encountered. Examples of such reporting included "USS *Lyman Swenson*, DD [destroyer] 729, 7/8/70"; "USS *Ranger*, CVA [carrier] 61, 2/2/73"; and "USS *Hawkbill*, SSN [submarine] 666, 8/26/72." This was Chi's first intelligence assignment outside China. When provided to North Vietnam's military, this intelligence could translate to American servicemen lives lost.

Chi Mak as Hong Kong tailor "Johnson," June 1971 TRIAL EXHIBIT 220

Many documents linked the Maks to PRC government officials and intelligence, whom they visited every few years via unrecorded travel, thanks to their untraceable Hong Kong residency cards. Recovered address books, business cards, hotel bills, photographs, notes, letters, and bus, train, movie, and laundry tickets filled the gaps and contradicted their blank US passports and travel denials. A PRC hotel receipt billed the Maks for calling Pu's 2332 number minutes after arrival. Documents in two dozen locations, including an old Fuji cassette tape cover, listed PRCIS handler Pu Pei Liang's 2332 cellphone number, which Pu predecessors "Cai Hu" and "Engineer Yan Feng" also shared.

Intercepted discussions between Shouling and Chi regarding covert China entry and exit routes that would produce no PRC stamps on travel papers now made perfect sense and explained references to past Mak "deliveries" to, and meetings with, handlers Cai, Yan, and Pu. Chi and

Rebecca also gave technical briefings to PRC academics and manufacturers, carried "instruction papers" (code word sheets and tasking lists), and means of contact (PRCIS accommodation addresses), while enjoying luxury hotel rooms, cars, and chauffeurs.

Chi also kept business cards of high-level PRC officials, such as:

1. Zhao An Tai, senior engineer and professor, Shanghai Mechanical and Electrical Industries;

2. Han Xiang Song, deputy director and senior engineer, Department of Facilities and Financial Support, State Science & Technology Commission, Beijing;

3. Ma Fu Bang, China National Nuclear Corporation (founder of China's nuclear navy) and member, Chinese Academy of Engineering, Beijing (Ma's personal email address was written on the back; we also recovered photographs of Chi and Rebecca with Mr. Ma and his wife at their Beijing home); and

4. Several business cards for Gu Wei Hao, senior engineer at the Ministry of Aviation, Beijing (handwritten on this card was Gu's personal email address). Gu represented aerospace, *not* the PRC navy, so why contact Chi? And why had Chi and Gu met at Griffith Observatory, per a dated photograph of them we recovered? Chi associate "Greg" Dongfan Chung would later provide the answer.

Judging from all the boxes of materials seized, it appeared the search had been exhaustive (we discovered later it wasn't). Property receipts for items seized were left, along with a search warrant copy, on the kitchen counter. We locked the doors and left.

Our final search location was Chi Mak's cubicle at Power Paragon, 901 Ball Road in Anaheim.[14] We found good evidence—some expected, some not. We confirmed Chi's work computer had downloaded the com-

---

14. I had asked the search team to disrupt the workplace as little as possible, as Fred Witham and Power Paragon had been very cooperative, and this would be the first time Chi's coworkers learned of his treachery. Quite a shock.

pany's DD(x) share drive data and contained files on *every* technology Pu had requested. We were pleasantly surprised to discover dozens of PRC officials' business cards within Chi's desk, with Gu Wei Hao once more making an appearance. Yet Chi had told coworkers he was a Hong Konger who had never visited Mainland China.

Our biggest surprise was discovering stamped classified documents stored within Chi's file drawers, including illegally copied and stored classified articles regarding submarine propulsion "quieting" technologies. Chi kept illegal copies he'd made of two classified articles within his assigned booklet from the Secret/NOFORN December 2000 session of the Third Naval Symposium of Electric Machines in Philadelphia. Each booklet had spiral plastic binding, *no* punched holes, and articles printed on both sides of the page. Attendees were prohibited from removing these booklets from their meeting room. When the symposium concluded, the booklets were sent to each attendee's employer's security unit and locked away.

Chi's booklet went to Power Paragon security manager Bob Miller in April 2001, where he documented its receipt and storage within Power Paragon's safe. Months later, Miller contacted Chi, asking if he wished to review the booklet. Chi did briefly, on September 17, 2001, under Miller's watchful eye. It was then returned to the safe, without any copies being made. Chi never accessed it again.

So why did Chi have copies of the first and third classified articles from his booklet? These one-sided copies were clearly made not from the original conference booklet, but from previous copies which had been three-hole-punched for a binder. So, where were the first three-hole-punched copies? Chi was known for collecting technical papers at work in three-hole binders, but none contained these two classified papers. It seemed obvious Chi had illegally copied, transported, stored, and delivered them both to China through Tai and Fuk's trip there in 2001. That was the "book" with "missing pages"—the second classified article—Fuk and PRCIS handlers had criticized.

Although pleased with our haul, after speaking with the searchers, I suspected that we had missed a large volume of evidence. Colleen and the linguists reported that our analyst Mike had searched Chi and Rebecca's bedroom dresser, finished quickly, and seized very little from it, leaving photographs, undeveloped rolls of film, and untranslated Chinese writing. Mike confirmed this, explaining that since he couldn't identify the other people or foreign locations pictured, he hadn't seized them. He'd also passed over Chinese letters without seeking translations, directly contradicting my broad search parameters: Seize *anything* which *might* be evidence of foreign travel, meetings, and contacts. Mike had followed his own interpretation: Seize something only if you *knew* it was evidence of espionage.

In Mike's defense, he was not an agent and had little search experience, yet he had ended up assigned to a small but critical area. On the other hand, he had been our case analyst for over a year, and I expected more. I did appreciate his honesty, which allowed me to pivot. Uncertainty over items missed both agitated and motivated me, and now I knew where to look.

Judges don't normally give you a "second bite at the apple," which seems both foolish and unfair. Defendants and their attorneys are constantly given second chances, including whole retrials, even when they are based upon their own mistakes. Why shouldn't we search again? It's an unnecessary, arbitrary restriction that only serves injustice, and protects the guilty, not the innocent.

I had to try for a second search.

CHAPTER 21

Bail or No Bail:
Is That Really the Question?

MONDAY MORNING, OCTOBER 31, 2005, WAS GOING TO BE A GLORIOUS day. Four Maks had spent the weekend in jail, I'd finally caught up on my sleep; and Chi had admitted to the majority of his crimes. Gunnar, Omar, Sheldon, and I visited our AUSAs early to update them and discuss the defendants' initial appearance. They were happy to hear of Chi's confession and surprised to learn that Gunnar and Omar were still on good terms with him.

At the appearance, our squad sat on the stage left side, behind the AUSAs and me, to demonstrate support.[1] The right side was for the defense. There was one exception that day: Gunnar and Omar sat in the back row of the defense side and didn't interact with our team. They wanted to continue their charade for Chi that the "US Navy" was at odds with the FBI. This fiction had long passed its expiration date, since Chi's attorney would prohibit him from talking, but they wanted to prove their claims to us.

When Chi entered the room, he scowled at me and my squad but lit up when he saw Gunnar and Omar. He gave them a big smile and a wave with his handcuffed hands. They returned his gestures. It was all we Bureau folks could do not to laugh. Point, NCIS!

---

1. We maintained this practice throughout every court appearance and trial day.

The appearance before Magistrate Marc L. Goldman was brief, as he tentatively agreed to detain each defendant. Each defendant claimed indigency, requesting government-paid counsel, and that they didn't understand English, even Chi. He'd worked decades next to English-speaking coworkers, authored papers, and given English presentations at conferences. We challenged Rebecca and Chi's claims of indigency, reporting they had over $1 million in savings. Better to force the Maks to spend their ill-gotten gains on attorney fees than ask the taxpayer to do it. We succeeded. Chi and Rebecca had to hire their own lawyers. Fuk and Tai got counsel at government expense.

The attorneys were little better than legal circus clowns. Chi hired the firm of Kaye, McLane & Bednarski LLP. They proved incompetent, verbose, and insulting, more interested in furthering their progressive agenda than their client's interests, and hoping to use Chi's defense to expand their practice to national security cases.[2] Rebecca's, Tai's, and Fuk's lawyers proved little better.

Due to the USAO's faulty initial charges, the subsequent appropriate ones appeared less severe, causing Magistrate Goldman to reverse his initial detainment decision.[3] He tentatively granted Chi Mak bail and called for a second hearing to finalize it. Fortunately, this second hearing was before Cormac Carney, the assigned trial judge. What a difference! Greg superbly summarized our overwhelming evidence against Chi, presenting simplified arguments to protect our classified sources. Then he presented me for cross-examination by defense attorneys. His advice had been simple: "Be yourself. Answer directly. Don't get into a fight with them. You'll be fine. You're smarter than any of them."

I was grateful for the trust he displayed in me. I testified that the Maks had high-level PRC connections and relatives, Guangzhou family property, and faced serious charges, sentences, and evidence, making them extreme flight risks. Defense counsel countered with "model citi-

---

2. After our case, they continued taking anti–US government cases, including Abu Ghraib prison claims.
3. These changed charges, and false claims from USAO spokesman Thom Mrozek, stoked defense declarations that we had overstated the case. Feckless USAO/DOJ executive indecision and cowardice was already undermining us.

zen" claims supported by "upstanding citizens" and quotes from Katrina Leung and Wen Ho Lee case judges, as if the facts and rulings must be identical because those defendants were also Chinese Americans. Talk about racial profiling! Judge Carney overruled Goldman, citing "substantial evidence" that Chi had engaged "in espionage for over twenty years" and the "many factors that indicate Mr. Mak is likely to flee." Chi was remanded for trial.

Tai's second detention hearing with Magistrate Goldman began one hour after Chi's hearing before Judge Carney concluded, and went much the same way, with similar testimony from me, while Tai's attorney, John Early, tried to argue factual differences without a distinction. After I finished, Magistrate Goldman began pronouncing a long, illogical decision to grant Tai bail, but suddenly reversed himself upon learning Judge Carney had minutes earlier overruled Goldman's bail decision for Chi. Declaring he couldn't free a non-citizen when a US citizen was held for the same crimes, Goldman remanded Tai until trial. Timing is everything!

A final detention hearing was scheduled in early 2006 so that I could be cross-examined about my declaration. It became a mini trial. First, Chi's retired power electronics engineering friend Bob Lee downplayed the importance of QED technology. Lee clearly valued his friendship over his duty to testify truthfully. Next, Chi's sister Shouling testified he was no spy—the pot testifying the kettle wasn't black. Then, Kaye claimed Chi's confession was fake, and that Rebecca was released on "downgraded" charges, citing USAO spokesman Thom Mrozek's shameful "explanation" blaming the FBI.[4] I'd expected defense mischaracterizations, exaggerations, and lies, but not USAO and DOJ blockheads supplying their ammo!

Kaye also called two Chi coworkers as character witnesses, before challenging our translation of *two* words among the millions we'd processed. *Again* he quoted Wen Ho Lee's Judge Parker. Different time, accused, case, charges, and facts, but same dead "racism!" horse.

---

4. Both female defendants were also extreme flight risks, yet USAO executives refused to support their detention because they were women. Sexism personified!

Our primary prosecutor Greg, and reluctant second-chair AUSA Craig Missakian, countered well, with expert declarations and questions that buried defense arguments. I testified at great length, including under cross-examination from Kaye's female co-counsel, Marilyn Bednarski. She attempted to rattle me with aggressive questioning. Little did they know I had fifty years of experience sparring with my older sister Susan, a Stanford-trained attorney. Bednarski reminded me of her, so I welcomed and enjoyed the experience, and my advantage. She attacked on all fronts, but lost each time. She never had a chance.

Greg's redirect questioning was superb, giving me succinct, simple, effective questions to answer, sinking each defense point. He conducted a legal clinic that day for hapless defense attorneys, and in a third of the time they had taken.[5] We slammed the door with testimony from Office of Naval Research (ONR) engineering program manager Steve Schreppler and Naval Nuclear Propulsion Program/Naval Reactors (NR) engineer Ed Chabay. The Mak crimes "contribute[d] to the vulnerability of Virginia Class submarines." It was here the phrase "kill chain" surfaced, terminology the defense counsel loathed for its accuracy and gravitas.[6] After Fred Witham's description of company employee security and training, Chi's videotaped interview by Gunnar and me was shown, demonstrating his easy, shameless proclivity to lie. After admitting he'd given defense attorneys great leeway, Carney ruled "No bail."

Winning this detention mini trial was huge, especially since we continued finding more damning evidence. My initial answers of "We don't know that" or "We have no evidence of that," soon became "We now know that for a fact because . . . !" Judge Carney's resulting written decision declared:

> *[There is] no condition or combination of conditions that [would] reasonably assure the appearance of Mr. [Chi] Mak as required. The Government has presented substantial evidence that Mr. Mak is an agent for the People's Republic of China and that there are several compelling reasons to suspect that he would flee the United States if he*

---

5. This one-to-three ratio for *every* defense or prosecution witness would hold throughout the trial.
6. "Kill chain" refers to the chain of events leading to the destruction of a US submarine.

were released on bail. The Government has presented substantial evidence that Mr. Mak has been engaging in espionage for over twenty years. . . . The Government also has presented substantial evidence that Mr. Mak passed the sensitive naval technology to the PRC in a very covert and suspicious manner. [After listing every piece of evidence we presented as convincing, his footnote added.] The Court is obviously making its findings for the purposes of detention only and is expressing no opinion of Mr. Mak's guilt or innocence with respect to the charge returned in the indictment.

This judge *got* it!

CHAPTER 22

Witnesses and "Victims"

GIVEN THE ARRESTS, WE COULD NOW INVESTIGATE AND INTERVIEW openly. I was eager to contact witnesses and erase the knee-jerk complaints by ignorant talking heads and "community activists" that we were squelching academic freedom and scapegoating Chinese Americans. On local TV, one Chi Mak neighbor lied that she "knew the Maks very well," and that we were "railroading" a loyal immigrant American because he was Chinese. But then Maryanne Deem was the outlier. Although she lived across the street from the Maks for twenty years, we never saw her exchange a word with them. And Deem had an ax to grind. Her brother was R. W. Miller, the first FBI Special Agent ever tried and convicted for espionage. His incompetence as a Special Agent was legendary before he was seduced by a female Soviet spy. When Miller's good Mormon wife discovered this, she threw him out. Thereafter, he lived for a while with his sister Deem, meaning that Miller, a Soviet spy, had lived directly across the street from Chi Mak, a PRC spy. What are the odds?

To prevent any other surprising claims, I drew up a list of witnesses to interview, and agents to conduct them. Successful interviews require skill and preparation, questions with purpose and proper framing. And follow-up questions are essential. If an initial answer misleads, follow up with a clarifying question. For example: Chi's engineer friend may admit to taking NOFORN materials home. Left there, the defense would say, "See? Everyone does it!" The follow-up questions should ask, "What did your training say about this? Can you identify other engineers who took work home? Did you keep it at home for months/years, or only overnight? Was it done to meet a pressing deadline? Did you tell anybody what you were doing? Why not? Would you ever want the PRC to have this technology or data? Why not?"

Now you have context. Unless the interviewee is completely oblivious to employment requirements (also helpful for us), their answers to these follow-ups will limit or reverse the damage. Context is everything. We needed to lock in testimony to counter the defense's twisted, fact-free questions designed to pervert the truth. An agent with excellent interviewing skills is invaluable! They get you so much more than one with a "check the boxes and get this over with" approach. Our Chi Mak witnesses generally fit into one of five categories: neighbors, friends/relatives, fellow engineers, work associates, and "other."

The other Mak neighbors' responses were predictable: "Don't know them . . . Where do they live? . . . I've never spoken with them . . . What do they look like? . . . I don't know *who* lives there . . . They [the Maks] don't interact with neighbors . . . They keep to themselves." None had ever visited the Maks or their home or invited the Maks over, including Deem, who didn't even know if the Maks had children.

Friends and relatives provided tidbits. Relatives called Chi "Jack" or "Uncle Jack," and confirmed his planned March 2006 retirement in China. Chi's sister, Shouling Barnes, played games with us, canceling a scheduled interview *after* Colleen and I drove over two hours to her Lancaster home, using her son Andy and his wife Christine to deliver us her message at the doorstep.[1] After I refused to leave until I'd served her a subpoena for handwriting samples, Shouling came out to accept it. We parted, exchanging disdainful looks. During her later provision of handwriting exemplars in Santa Ana, she provided false information on the form and claimed eyesight problems, after first undergoing acupuncture treatments on her writing hand to compromise her sample's integrity.[2] She was a perfect representative of the Mak family, fitting right in with

---

1. I'd telephoned to make the appointment, which she only agreed to *after* I informed her she would otherwise be interviewed under subpoena in Santa Ana.
2. Her embarrassed son corrected some of her false written answers, including how many brothers she had.

Rebecca, Fuk, and Shirley. The Mak men were liars. The Mak women were ornery liars.

Interviews of Chi's fellow engineers supported evidence of Chi's technical knowledge, access, training, interactions, origins, and travel. Many liked Chi and were shocked by his arrest, disbelieving he was a PRC spy. They confirmed NOFORN materials could never be taken home; that all published work had to be pre-cleared by the company; and that Chi claimed to be a Hong Konger who had never visited the Mainland. Many worried about the damage Chi had done as a spy, having access to "pretty key technology."

Defense subject matter expert (SME) witness Bob Lee proved a combative interview for NCIS agents. "Hogwash" was his normal response. His arguments proved emotional, not logical. The two had worked together for over twenty-five years, yet Lee's ignorance of security requirements was staggering. He concluded his interview by declaring Wen Ho Lee was innocent and FBI agents lie to frame people.

One interview burned into my memory is that of engineer Liemeng and his wife Alice, which Gunnar and I conducted at a Marie Callender's restaurant. Alice immediately declared we were targeting her husband because he was Chinese.[3] Nonsense! Liemeng was in Chi's address book. Alice slammed a recorder on the table, announcing she was taping our interview. I told her Liemeng was free not to talk to us and she would *not* be recording us. Liemeng smiled, shrugged an apology to us, and told Alice to put it away. He said he respected Chi as an engineer and considered him a friend for over twenty-five years, yet he knew little about his personal life, and proved uncooperative, claiming ignorance of nearly everything about him. He believed the propaganda that America is a racist country and picks on Chinese Americans and other "people of color."

This matched a disturbing pattern. Some Chinese Americans displayed loyalties based upon ethnicity and race, siding with the PRC, not America. The irony was that most of them had taken extraordinary steps to escape PRC authorities for the good life in the United States, yet their identity as "Chinese," not "Americans," led them to aid our totalitarian

---

3. Apparently, she hadn't looked around; our restaurant was filled with Chinese Americans we would *not* be interviewing.

enemy. Nonetheless, they didn't want to live there, preferring America's freedoms. Slavery for fellow Chinese, freedom for themselves. How twisted is that? I often heard the statements, "Chinese would never do that!" and "We don't discuss that. It makes 'our people' look bad." Newsflash: Ethnic Chinese are just as capable of evil as anyone else.

We interviewed "Greg" Dongfan Chung of 7412 East Grovewood Lane, Orange, California, and his wife Ling Jia, both of whom reeked of this insidious brand of racism. We'd seen them socialize with Chi and Rebecca. On April 24, 2006, Special Agents Jessie and Scott interviewed them. Chung was a structural engineer for Boeing, Ling Jia a painter and community college professor, and they had raised two sons. The Chungs said they met "exchange scholar Mr. Gu" in 1985 at Qing Hua University during a China trip, and first met the Maks in 1992 when they picked Gu up from the Mak residence. The Maks and Chungs thereafter became friends, staying in contact every few months. Yet they claimed Greg and Chi *never* discussed engineering topics, their employers, or trips to China. The Chungs confirmed some China trips and interactions with university groups, and claimed Greg had reported China travel to Boeing and was never approached by PRC officials. We knew the Chungs were lying, so we kept them on our radar.

Work associates provided interesting, useful, and objective information. We figured out how Chi got his hands on the copied classified documents we found in his work desk: by sneaking the Philadelphia conference's classified booklet out of the meeting room during a break to copy it on machines near the bathroom. Doing this covertly, and probably feeling rushed, he neglected to copy the middle article. In response to later criticism from handler Cai that his reporting was incomplete, missing the middle article on pages 6–12, Chi later sought a copy from its author, Robert Ashton, professor of electrical and computer engineering and power electronics and systems at the Naval Postgraduate School in Monterey, California. Professor Ashton denied Chi's request.

Having known Chi Mak from ten years of government project work together, Chi's request struck Ashton as strange. First, the document contained classified algorithms for submarine propellers—not pertinent to Chi's unclassified project work. Second, Ashton and Chi had never discussed classified data. Third, no one had ever asked Ashton for a classified document before. He told Chi that was not how things were done. He must go through official channels to obtain it. Chi dropped his request and asked that the matter be forgotten. Ashton now was worried that if Chi gave China access to any of the classified QED algorithms, it would help the PRC acoustically track USN ships and submarines. Chi and his lawyers were never able to concoct an explanation for this contact.[4]

Power Paragon's export control officers never authorized Chi Mak to present data or white papers at conferences and proved his training prohibited it.[5] In fact, Chi had actively lied to company officials to cover his activities. Others worried over Chi's vast knowledge of US Navy systems, and the harm he could do to its navy. Without notes, Chi could teach an advanced course on the electrical system of the world's most advanced warship, our Arleigh Burke–class destroyer. Chi's access was broad and deep.

Some ONR QED program managers held alarming positions. One PRC apologist I'll call "Terry" aimed to keep as much QED research publicly available as possible, despite admitting QED was export-controlled, on the US Munitions List (USML), and that its compromise would damage US National Security. "Lynn," another program manager, alarmingly predicted Chi's compromises would cause "a great deal of damage to US national security because it would be far more difficult for USN submarines to operate without being detected." He said Chi's access also threatened other USN platforms, programs, and personnel.

Our interview of Richard, Power Paragon's technical writer, proved illuminating. Chi Mak had used him to transfer data onto CDs, allowing Chi to bypass Power Paragon's five-megabyte email restriction. Chi explained that he wanted "to give it to people," or that "I have to give these to somebody."[6] Chi attended more conferences than anyone else,

---

4. If Chi only needed the data, it sat feet away in Power Paragon's safe. He needed the whole article to give to Cai in China.
5. Valerie Hampton later made a heroic appearance when she, in the face of unethical and illegal pressure from L-3 corporate compliance superiors, wrote a detailed email explaining why they were wrong. Chi's white papers violated company regulations and US federal law.
6. Finally, Chi told the truth, albeit obliquely.

and always brought home conference CDs with export-restricted data, and then asking that it be converted to PDF files.[7]

Meanwhile, Tai Mak's work associates claimed little knowledge about him. Younger workers called him "Old Mai," and confirmed Tai claimed to be "Hong Kong Chinese." He was quiet, good to work for, but didn't socialize. One subordinate, "Owen," once saw Chi and Rebecca visit Tai's workplace, and was familiar with Billy, Shirley, Fuk, and Mr. Zhang, the latter being Owen's landlord. He reported that Billy returned from a Hong Kong trip once with a laptop for a coworker. Tai's supervisor and coworkers confirmed he never took a work-related trip to Hong Kong or China, and most were shocked by his arrest, saying he wasn't a "young, smart, handsome, stylish, sexy" man, and therefore "didn't fit [the] James Bond model." Tai's boss was Wu Xiaoyong, president of Phoenix International, who I believed to be a PRC intelligence officer like his boss, Liu Chang Le, Phoenix founder and majority stockholder. Wu claimed Tai came highly recommended by a Mr. Feng, Tai's supervisor and mentor in Hong Kong (we knew the Maks reported to Chinese intelligence officer Yan Feng), and had visited Phoenix many times.

Other interviews included Fuk's marriage fraud participants. One American participant, "Dirk," came from a life of crime, drug addictions, and vagrancy. Through Fuk's arrangements, Dirk married PRC citizen and stranger Xaioyan in a simple ceremony. They spoke no common language, yet posed for "marriage" pictures together. He received $3,000, after which he and his "bride" went their separate ways.

Months later, they met to prep for their immigration interview, practicing answers to anticipated questions like "What side of the bed do you sleep on? What kind of soap does your spouse use? What is your spouse's favorite TV show?" They passed the actual interview easily. Dirk and Xaioyan then took more pictures in a nearby park, and he received another $3,000 installment. Dirk's problem? The marriage was supposed to be annulled, at which time he would receive his last $3,000 payment. Even though this never happened, Dirk now wished to marry a local

---

7. I understand Richard later resigned in guilt over the help he innocently provided—another Chi Mak casualty.

woman "for real," but couldn't locate Fuk or his Chinese "spouse," so he offered to help us in a "sting" operation. Ain't love grand?

Then came our most innocent witness, Ken Gonzales, of realtor notepad fame. He brought an attorney but quickly relaxed once told the interview's topic, confirming he'd only distributed notepads in Downey (Chi's city), never Alhambra (Tai's). This demonstrated that the code word sheet at Tai's home had come from the notepad in Chi's house.

Gonzales rued the unfairness of life: He'd stopped being a Century 21 Realtor in 2001, yet he'd spent money to hire an attorney for a ten-minute FBI interview in 2006. All of this because cheap Chi Mak had used Gonzales's old advertisement for spy stuff! We sympathized.

CHAPTER 23

Dazed and Confused:
US Attorney's Office at Work

THE SEARCH WARRANTS JUDGE JEFFREY JOHNSON SIGNED ON OCTOBER 28, 2005, sought every conceivable form of evidence, down to the smallest piece of paper, thumb drive, or sim card, and were supported by my twenty-seven-page affidavit.[1] The following ridiculous charges, however, were forced on us by foolish DOJ and USAO "experts."

1. 18 USC. § 641: "Whoever embezzles, steals, purloins, or knowingly converts to his use or the use of another, or without authority, sells, conveys or disposes of any records, voucher, money, or thing of value of the United States or of any department or agency thereof, or any property made or being made under contract for the United States or any department or agency thereof";

2. 18 USC. § 2: "Whoever aids, abets, counsel, and induces the commission of an offense is punishable as a principal";

3. 18 USC. § 371, "Criminal penalties for those who conspire to commit an offense against the United States"; and

---

1. I had tried to include Tai's and Billy's workspaces at Phoenix International but lost that argument with the USAO.

4. 18 USC. § 2314: "Whoever transports, transmits, or transfers in interstate or foreign commerce any goods, wares, merchandise, securities or money, of the value of $5,000 or more, knowing the same to have been stolen, converted or taken by fraud."

You don't need a law school degree, which I have, to know these did *not* apply to intellectual property!

Once USAO managers realized they'd badly screwed these charges up, they dropped them. Needing *something* to charge, I went to Los Angeles for my first grand jury appearance on November 15, 2005, to support an 18 USC. § 951, "Acting as an Agent of a Foreign Government" charge.[2] Greg and Deirdre warned me to arrive early, since grand jury members didn't like to be kept waiting. I did, and as we discussed my upcoming testimony and request that Billy be made a defendant, we were interrupted by Chief Assistant US Attorney George Cardona's summons of Greg and Deirdre.[3]

They returned much later, fifteen minutes into our scheduled grand jury appointment! Greg was somber and Deirdre angry, denouncing USAO interference. Cardona wanted all charges against the wives dropped, claiming it was "mean-spirited" to hold wives "hostage as leverage" against their husbands. "We are charging and holding them because *they* committed knowledgeable and culpable crimes," I argued. "Why treat women differently?"[4] Deirdre and Greg relented regarding Fuk, but held firm on Rebecca. Cardona told them they would be sorry.[5]

I was angry. Cardona's bizarre logic meant that indicting son Billy was out of the question. His hand-wringing left me poorly prepared to testify before the grand jury regarding Chi, Rebecca, and Tai—a grand jury he had ticked off by making us twenty minutes late. Thanks, George!

Despite this, my testimony went well. When jurors asked questions, the AUSAs asked me for clarification. One exasperated juror asked, "If

---

2. This was the charge we investigators had *always* advocated for. Grand jury sessions in Orange County and Los Angeles alternated weeks. LA was the first appearance possible.

3. As second in command to USA Debra Yang, Cardona was to prove my greatest hurdle within the USAO.

4. Where are the true feminists when you need them?

5. The only regrettable thing was that the AUSAs followed any of Cardona's timid, irrational instructions.

Billy was involved in the copying and encryption of the restricted materials, why hasn't he been arrested yet? And why hasn't Fuk been charged?" *Why indeed?* I thought. The AUSA's question to me was designed to temporarily mollify the jurors with a response that the investigation was "ongoing [blah, blah, blah] and that other future charges might be brought." This practiced deception made me uncomfortable. Two minutes after we left the grand jury room, they returned a "True Bill," authorizing all of our new indictments. This slam dunk confirmed we agents knew the "man on the street" jurors better than the DOJ, USAO, or AUSAs. Agents had requested "Foreign Agent" charges all along. They were accurate, easily proven, and screamed *Spy!* and later played an outsized role during trial. All of my grand jury appearances became cakewalks.

I paused to consider past experiences with DOJ and the USAO when seeking charges against intelligence agents of the Socialist Republic of Vietnam (SRV). Colleen and I spent most of our careers protecting Vietnamese Americans from SRV oppression and blackmail. We built many such cases against SRV agents in America, but we were always rebuffed. AUSAs dismissively claimed, "It's just a bullshit charge, a placeholder. No one uses that as a main charge." Colleen had the perfect candidate and evidence for that charge. Mr. Bien was a well-known snake who wielded the SRV's power and influence to cow and terrorize Vietnamese American communities, particularly Orange County's. Thanks to the USAO, he never faced justice on earth.

We initially got the same reaction pushing these charges for Chi, but now we had more experience, people, determination, and firepower. Since Chi Mak's trial, the "Foreign Agent" charge has become fashionable because we proved it could be successful.[6] The law didn't change, just AUSA perceptions of success, trends, and comfort levels. The same applied for the charge of "Economic Espionage." It didn't see trial for its first ten years of existence, but once we forced the issue in a later case, and won a conviction, suddenly it was charged across the country! Most prosecutors are cowards, more worried about their record and reputation than justice. Greg Staples proved an invaluable exception. Meanwhile,

---

6. It seems DOJ and USAO charges are based more upon trends and fads than facts.

Bien and other communist henchmen terrorized Vietnamese American immigrants because most AUSAs fear looking bad.

To hide their initial Mak charging screwup, the USAO did what it does best—go to Plan B: Blame the agents! When their spokesman Thom Mrozek announced the new charges, the press noted the new penalties were less severe.[7] Mrozek responded that FBI agents had "misled [them]. . . . Prosecutors decided not to press the initial charges against the defendants because the information about submarine technology wasn't classified. It's sensitive but not classified. Some of the stuff they had talked about is openly at conferences." He told damaging lies to cover USAO mistakes! The press, led by the *Los Angeles Times*, enthusiastically reported these four Mrozek lies:

1. Our prosecutors made no such decision;

2. The switch was made because 18 USC. § 641—Theft of Government Property—was the wrong charge;

3. Those charges had *not* required that Chi's documents be of a classified nature; and

4. We *did* intercept "Confidential" and "Secret" classified data on its way to China.

I demanded an apology and retraction from Mrozek's office but never received one, just mealymouthed excuses and advice to not take it personally.

And it got worse. When I complained to FBIHQ and DOJ, the USAO reflex was to lie some more, telling FBI management that our squad was endangering the overall prosecution and demanding we work 24/7 through the end of the year to "catch up." That meant no Thanksgiving break and restricted Christmas leave. It was outrageous, and FBI management knew better. My squad had done *everything* in its power

---

7. 18 USC. § 951 threatened a maximum sentence of five years, while the 18 USC. § 641 maximum was ten.

to support the case.[8] But our upper management canceled all leave to smooth things over. My fellow agents, who had performed admirably and diligently, had to cancel travel plans and eat penalty fees. The USAO had proved not only cowardly, deceitful, and treacherous, but petty and vindictive as well.

A meeting was scheduled for 8:30 a.m., December 7, 2005, at the USAO to plan a way forward. Sheldon and I had prepared binders supporting more criminal charges against Chi, Rebecca, Tai, Fuk, *and* Billy.[9] Attendees included USAO Criminal Division Chief Tom O'Brien, Sal Valdez, FBIHQ's Sandy Kable, NCIS San Diego and Office of Special Projects management, and DOJ/CES Attorney Simpkins, representing John Dion.

The day began on the wrong foot. Sheldon and I got stuck in horrendous morning traffic between Orange County and downtown Los Angeles, arriving twenty minutes late to a room filled with pissed-off executives unaccustomed to waiting for underlings central to the meeting. Normally, I would have been horrified, but not this time. My built-up anger from being screwed over so many times by these stuffed shirts burst forth, and soon Sheldon and I were multiplying and reflecting their anger right back at them. In hindsight, it worked out great. When USAO and DOJ/CES executives threw attitude our way, Sheldon and I were ready and loaded for bear, lighting into them for their slanders against our team, canceling our leave, mischarging errors, and Mrozek's lies. Taken aback, they attempted no defense or apology. They just sat there dumbfounded as Sheldon and I berated them.

I denounced their ever-shifting espionage finish line—each time we crossed it, they moved it! We'd proved Chi had sent classified data to China. *Now* they required it to be *stamped* classified. Chi was many things, but "fool" was not one of them. He had removed and omitted classified labels before shipping it to China. We could still prove it was

---

8. Years later, when the trial concluded, Greg, Deirdre, and others thanked us, saying they had never seen such stellar and comprehensive support for a case from agents.

9. 18 USC. § 957—Possession of Property in Aid of a Foreign Government (Chi, Rebecca, Tai, Fuk, and Billy), 18 USC. § 1001—False Official Statements (Same), 18 USC. § 951—Agent of a Foreign Government (Same), 18 USC. § 1030—Fraud Using a Computer (Chi, Tai, Billy), 22 USC. § 2778—ITAR (Chi), as well as Economic Espionage (Chi).

classified; they were just cowards hiding behind this new standard which, if followed, would prevent all but idiots from being charged with espionage. Sheldon tore them a new one with facts and well-placed expletives, which was his forte.[10] These "one-two" angry case agent punches put these attorneys on their heels. They didn't dare say anything, embarrassed by this public parade of their incompetence in front of FBILA and FBIHQ managers who were clearly enjoying the show.

After a long, awkward silence, Simpkins backpedaled, claiming they *would* sign off on espionage under the "Mosaic" theory.[11] He explained we could combine all the sensitive national security information together, like a completed puzzle, to demonstrate that the larger, stronger, aggregate whole was classified. DOJ/CES would welcome it and approve espionage charges. Naively, we took him at his word, leaving the meeting satisfied. We had vented in defense of our team, publicized USAO and DOJ/CES incompetence and deceit for all to see, *and* received assurances of future espionage charges. Months later, we would learn the actual worth of a DOJ/CES promise.

What followed were multiple superseding indictments, adding and removing charges at the whim of USAO executives. Meanwhile, we organized expert review of materials seized and classification assessments to create Simpkins's "Mosaic" espionage charge. We also inaugurated our "Kill Chain Working Group" of USN engineers, led by Steve Schreppler. Despite our well-documented charging books supporting a variety of violations, the USAO refused to consider many of them. They wouldn't charge Chi's sister Shouling and fought indicting Billy, Fuk, and even Rebecca, rejecting our displayed mountain of supporting evidence. I strove to make it as difficult as possible for USAO executives to decline charges. They also had a practice of combining multiple charges into a single charge that struck me as ludicrous—an absolute invitation for disaster.[12]

---

10. I've always been grateful for Sheldon's full-throated support at that moment. We made a great team.

11. Also known as "Classification by Compilation."

12. It caused the later loss of our most consequential DD(x) charge, which multiple charges would have prevented.

In April, we met at NCIS headquarters in DC to hear the Kill Chain Working Group's "Mosaic" espionage charge findings presentation for John Dion. Simpkins was *not* there. Before this trip, USAO executives had warned us, "Don't believe what CES tells you. They will screw you every time." Naturally, I was skeptical of anything they said, but their warning turned out to be prophetic.

I was proud of the engineers' excellent presentation. They'd invested much time and hard work, following Simpkins's guidelines to the letter, and proving the case for an espionage charge. But upon their conclusion, a habitually sourpuss Dion leaned over to Greg and snapped, "I want to see you in my office this afternoon!" He stood and stormed out, without a word of thanks to these brilliant engineers. King Dion's demeanor deeply embarrassed me. We thanked the engineers for their hard work and promised to get back to them. Greg looked concerned. Craig was absolutely terror-stricken. He wanted *no* part of this meeting (no doubt to protect his career aspirations), but I wanted in, and to his credit, Greg agreed. Greg treated me as an equal partner, not a peon, as Craig and most USAO/DOJ attorneys did.[13] That's all any agent can ask.

That afternoon, we met with Dion. Maybe because I didn't realize how important and legendary a DC figure Dion was, or maybe because I was fed up with being jerked around by DOJ attorneys, I arrived agitated, ready for a fight. No sooner did we sit down than Dion began lecturing Greg, demanding an explanation for proposing an espionage charge based upon the "Mosaic" theory. Dion was livid, declaring he would *never* use that theory because it would collapse in court and destroy espionage case law.

Greg took it calmly, without objection or excuses. Notably and honorably, he did not blame agents or engineers. I was thankful Craig wasn't there to do that, but I couldn't take it anymore. I interrupted, saying I realized DOJ didn't care what I thought, but it was Dion's man, Simpkins, who'd told us to pursue the "Mosaic" model! I declared that I was sick of being manipulated by USAO and DOJ lies, and I cited all the times this

---

13. To them we were just lesser cogs, there to demonstrate their brilliance. When they succeeded, it was due solely to their outstanding talents and efforts. When they failed, they claimed agent failures and stupidity as the cause.

had happened. I then mentioned the *stamped* classified documents found in Chi's work desk drawer which he'd illegally copied, transported, and stored. I angrily asked, "Why aren't those getting addressed?"

That got Dion's attention, and his disposition noticeably changed. He was clearly taken aback. I imagine few people, especially of my station, ever spoke to him that way. But I was right, knew it, and was mad as hell. In a polite voice I'd never heard him use, Dion asked me questions about that classified evidence. While quietly confirming "Mosaic" charges were out, he promised he *would* support espionage charges for illegal duplication, transportation, and storage of the two classified Philadelphia symposium documents, using 18 USC. § 793, "Gathering, transmitting or losing defense information." But he concluded with a warning: "You've got a wacky USA office out there." That was it. No apology for his rude behavior or Simpkins's misdirection.

Nonetheless, Greg and I returned to our hotel that afternoon walking on air. Greg practically skipped! He was off the hook with the big guy, who had also given us the go-ahead for an espionage charge. Finding ourselves between a rock—USAO—and a hard place—DOJ/CES—we had not only survived, but prospered! Later betrayals might come from both sides, but the future looked bright.

Upon our return to California, Greg added 18 USC. § 793 against Chi to his Prosecutive Memorandum (PM) and submitted it for review to USA Debra Yang.[14] Greg asked me to review it for accuracy first, a practice the USAO foolishly prohibits. I gave him my input and corrections, including that the PM was still deficient, since it didn't include charges for Fuk. After expressing skepticism over the new espionage charge, the USAO signed off on it upon learning John Dion approved. Weeks later, at the eleventh hour, George Cardona again announced his cowardice, calling Dion to say they would approve the espionage charge, *as long as* they were free to pull it later. Dion responded absolutely not. Unless the USAO was 100 percent behind the charge, it should *not* be brought. They each had now found a way to excuse the other's inaction! When I challenged

---

14. Dion had explained 18 USC. § 793(b), "Gathering Defense Information" was an easy espionage charge to prove given Chi's theft, copying, storage, and attempted transmission.

them, each side claimed the other had blinked.[15] Each side had warned me about the duplicity of the other, and *both* had been right.[16]

And yet, we kept discovering classified data Chi had embedded within the discs headed to China.[17] I met with USA Debra Yang after her return from a trip to China to urge espionage and Economic Espionage (EE) charges. "Untested" EE—her words—was a hard "no," and espionage would only be possible *if* a defendant turned state's evidence against a fellow family member. She knew that was a nonstarter, and when I confronted her with that, her real reasons surfaced: "Political considerations."[18] Yang abruptly ended our meeting and walked out.

Criminal Section Chief Tom O'Brien then walked up and whispered, "We understand your frustrations, Jim, but we gotta protect Deb." Finally, the truth. Yang was afraid of the Chinese American "community activists" and their claims that Chinese people were being "unfairly targeted" for prosecution.[19] What can be done in the face of such corrupt, idiotic, racist reasoning? Once again, Debra Yang had proven herself to be an empty suit.

That same day I met with incoming ADIC Stephen Tidwell, who was one of the rare good ones. He was a no-nonsense former marine officer who understood our case, backed his people, and agreed to speak to USA Yang about espionage charges over the phone. Because USAs hold FBI executives in almost as much contempt as they do street agents, he was handed off to Criminal Section Chief O'Brien. It ended in a shouting match, with Tidwell pronouncing O'Brien a "pussy!" and slamming the receiver down.[20] Not diplomatic, but true. I admired Tidwell for his passion and loyalty.

---

15. Thanks to Yang's, Cardona's, and Dion's cowardice, the charge was never brought, although I continued to lobby fiercely for it up until the very last minute.

16. Greg submitted another Prosecutive Memorandum in October 2006, attempting again to add the 18 USC. § 793(b), "Gathering Defense Information" espionage charge, but it died on the vine.

17. The NCIS worked tirelessly to collect all the previously distributed conference discs containing Chi's white papers with embedded and unmarked classified data.

18. USAO and DOJ "political considerations," not justice, always determined what charges were brought in this case.

19. Our poor excuse for a US Attorney had caved to this silly, baseless, tired canard.

20. O'Brien marketed himself as a former, fearless fighter pilot. The emphasis should have been on "former," because when it came to hard decisions, he was a coward and apologist.

As trial approached, Billy remained uncharged; he would soon graduate from UCLA and return to Hong Kong for his automobile lighting import/export business, where we couldn't touch him. I pressed Greg for charges. He responded, despite USAO resistance. My haranguing also produced charges for Fuk, including for marriage fraud and aiding and abetting.[21] We were finally charging both Fuk *and* Billy. The grand juries kept requesting espionage charges and we kept falsely promising them. Again, this subterfuge bothered me. Then came the grand jury "True Bill" finally indicting all five defendants for 18 USC. § 951, "Acting as an Agent of a Foreign Government" and ITAR charges, long delayed by US Department of State (DOS) dithering.[22] We arrested Fuk and Billy that same day.

Billy's arrest should have been easy, since we knew his college schedule. But he was going to UCLA, a public institution hostile to law enforcement. Although arresting Billy on campus was safer, FBILA worried about faculty and student sensitivities, so they made us arrest him at his girlfriend's home. We arrested Fuk at home. Thankfully, Judge Arthur Nakazato agreed with my declaration seeking Billy's detention as a flight risk. We were batting a thousand on requested detentions.[23] Unfortunately, the USAO still refused to seek Fuk's detention, following its foolish, and false, "wife as leverage" denunciations.

Our last chance for an espionage charge arrived in July 2006. Brave emails by SAC Brust and ADIC Tidwell regarding DOJ/USAO intransigence produced a visit from Acting CI Assistant Director Tim Bereznay, who promised to "hear [agents] out."[24] His legendary predecessor was CI Assistant Director Dave Szady, who had been a big supporter of our investigation. We strategized visit plans at our all-hands

---

21. 8 USC. § 1325(c), "Marriage Fraud Regarding Immigration," and 18 USC. § 2, "Aiding and Abetting."

22. Previous to this, my Weekly Investigative Updates to FBI managers had reported "US State Department behavior borders on obstruction."

23. This detention time provided some justice, given the anemic plea deals the USAO would later dishonestly force upon us.

24. Brust and Tidwell both made excellent, passionate arguments for espionage charges. Tidwell threatened to go to the deputy director, and Brust said USA Yang's comparison of the Chi Mak case to past failed Chinese espionage cases was "comparing rotten apples to fresh oranges." The bravery and loyalty of these two men was refreshing.

team meeting, hoping to convince Bereznay to push espionage charges during his scheduled conference later that day with USA Yang.[25] Sal said only team leaders should speak, in order to keep Bereznay focused on the goal. No questions! Sal turned to Scott, slowly repeating this instruction. Everyone chuckled, because Scott always asked questions, some relevant, some not. Sal worried that a silly, off-topic question could derail our careful choreography. Scott responded with "But what if—" a couple of times, which Sal kept cutting off, making us laugh harder each time. Scott finally got the message: *No* questions.

We picked up Bereznay, who was already in a foul mood, and we had no clue why.[26] We followed our plan flawlessly, leading up to our thirty-minute pitch. Bereznay's sour expression remained unchanged. At the conclusion, I asked for his thoughts, and I'll never forget his answer. It *wasn't* "Lots of good work here, but . . ." or "This is good stuff, but . . . ," or a hundred other similar phrases. His words were angry: "This is the weakest espionage case I have ever seen!"

I was shocked, but I shouldn't have been. Bereznay was showing his true blue flamer colors—ego, ignorance, and disdain for agents. As the collective air left the room, we did what we could to salvage the situation, asking for his specific criticisms or advice. Predictably, he had none, simply parroting John Dion's distrust of the Los Angeles USAO's ability to prosecute espionage charges. Bereznay had already decided long before *not* to support espionage, no matter the evidence presented. Unfortunately, someone at FBIHQ had told Bereznay that EE was the charge to push with USA Yang.

Curtly dismissing our inquiries, he angrily asked if we had any *other* questions. All eyes drifted toward Scott. His struggle to resist temptation was visible and palpable. Like us, he couldn't understand Bereznay's attitude. Just as Bereznay closed out his disingenuous question with an "All right, then," Scott blurted out a "But what about" question. You could see our collective eye rolls and smirks, and Sal's eyes burning holes through

---

25. After all, both DOJ/CES and the USAO had authorized an espionage charge before Cardona's knees had gone weak.

26. I often wondered if it was because he was a chain smoker. Fanatical California is very hard upon such people.

Scott. I was amused. What harm could Scott do now, given Bereznay's predetermined stance? And we needed this moment of comic relief. I still laugh thinking about it. Bereznay brusquely brushed Scott off. He was a rude, dismissive, arrogant man, and I wanted nothing more to do with him. Unfortunately, a squad lunch was already scheduled.

Sal drove Bereznay to the nearby El Torito Restaurant while the rest of the team carpooled. Finding Bereznay's demeanor and reaction unbelievable, during the drive we schemed further runs at him over lunch. Upon arrival, I grabbed the seat on Bereznay's right. Sal sat on his left, and others perched directly across from him. During a lull, I leaned over and quietly implored a scowling Bereznay to push espionage charges with USA Yang, warning him that she would react viscerally to any proposal to charge EE, which she claimed was seriously flawed.[27] Bereznay grunted, glared at me, and turned back to his food. My teammates fared no better. After lunch, Bereznay met with Yang (I was glad to be rid of this disagreeable character). As predicted, Yang rejected Bereznay's EE pitch with the same words I'd heard. The battle of empty suits had ended: politics—1, evidence—0.[28]

The NCIS executive assistant director tried to intervene for us with DOJ and the USAO regarding espionage charges, with similar results. We became so frustrated with the USAO that we discussed with Dion the option of separating out an espionage charge and having a DOJ attorney come out west to manage it. We preferred Greg Staples, but the USAO was impossible. This made waves, and a worried Greg approached me privately to warn that such a move would weaken our overall efforts. I understood his concerns, and had no confidence in DOJ attorneys, but was frustrated with USAO cowardice, politics, and stupidity. In the end, we ruled this option out. The deciding factor was my loyalty to Greg, the only attorney—other than Deirdre—I trusted. He had earned it.

By October 25, 2006, we'd won most of our charging arguments, and my Orange County grand jury appearances added charges of "Conspiracy

---

27. I smelled Chief AUSA George Cardona's tainted legal opinion here. Yang had always been a sock puppet for other USAO actors.
28. Suffering no consequences for incompetence, Debra Yang moved on to a lucrative position at a private firm.

to Export Defense Articles" against all five defendants, three counts of "Attempted Unlawful Export of Defense Articles" (ITAR) against Chi Mak, "Possession of Property in Aid of a Foreign Government" against Tai concerning the encryption laptop, and "False Statements" against all five.[29]

29. For the "False Official Statements" (18 USC. § 1001) charges, we had many whoppers to choose from for each defendant. Greg directed me to pick only the strongest lie for each defendant to avoid multiple charges. I wanted multiple charges but reluctantly followed instructions.

CHAPTER 24

Cakes Need Frosting

SEVEN MONTHS AFTER THE FIRST ARRESTS, I WAS WORKING ON second-look search warrants, especially for Chi. I believed too much had been missed. But we needed fresh probable cause to accomplish this. Chi's tale to Gunnar and Omar of Billy's "orangish-yellow health book" from Pu fit the bill. Evidence review allowed us to verify its passage to Chi, as well as PRCIS officer "Uncle Pu's" close relationship with the Maks.[1] I requested a second search to find the Pu "health book" Billy gave to Chi, and to search other books that could contain similar lists. We hadn't known of this practice *prior* to our previous search and Chi's admission, and finding it would again defeat defense claims that Gunnar and Omar had made up Chi's admissions. We had already verified that many details he had confessed were accurate, proving Chi and the defense attorney claims since were full of crap.

Mid-2006, I sought a second search of both Mak homes, simultaneous with Billy's and Fuk's arrests. Along with the "health book," I wanted the receipt for Billy's purchase of CD-Rs for use in copying and encrypting Chi's disc data, along with anything verifying Billy and Shirley's 2004 China travel and Tai's claimed side audio/video business. While I built this justification, NSD-9 "experts" and some FBI and NCIS executives urged me not to waste time and resources, believing too much time had passed. Surely, Rebecca and Fuk had destroyed any remaining incrimi-

---

1. In an intercepted telephone call, Fuk told the kids that Pu's favors were compensation for Tai's work for Pu, who held a "special" position.

nating evidence.[2] We needed to focus on the evidence we had, and not take our eye off the ball. Nonsense. For well over a year, I *never* took my eye off the ball.

I believed the Maks assumed the worst was over, and, having seen the condition of their homes, was convinced they themselves didn't know where everything incriminating was.[3] These searches were smaller and more tightly focused, utilizing only our best, most knowledgeable searchers. On June 7, 2006, we did another "knock and announce." Rebecca was inside, along with Chi's older sister Shouling and her latest husband (#4), Phillip Paul. The couple left, while Rebecca remained and called her attorney, using our agent's cellphone. I assigned Colleen the sole task of searching Chi and Rebecca's bedroom dresser. Eureka! Her intense review produced amazing results, unearthing a whole new vein from a gold mine others believed was tapped out. Some drawers were jammed with envelopes and photographs. It took Colleen hours as she methodically pulled these absolute gems from the dross.

Her first find was the original scrap of paper Chi copied to create the "Ken Gonzales" code word sheet in Tai's bedside table drawer. Chi's original differed slightly from the copy he'd made. First, it was written almost entirely in English, unlike Chi's half-and-half English/Chinese version for Tai. Second, it was in someone else's handwriting, and on the front and back of "Hualida Biotech" stationery. Third, some additional code phrases had been crossed out and therefore omitted from Tai's copy. The two redacted phrases, for use by US-based spies communicating with Chinese authorities, were "supermarket = good material" (did Chi find this useless or insulting, since he provided China only good material?) and "car can't work and have to take the taxi = emergent [*sic*]" (was this deemed redundant since the "weather uncomfortable" phrase already addressed exigent circumstances?).

Colleen's second valuable discovery was a postmarked envelope addressed to Chi from sister Shouling which contained an aviation tasking list handwritten on two sheets of yellow-lined legal pad paper. Most

---

2. They hadn't, and don't call me Shirley! But seriously, Rebecca and Fuk were only at home because both had been released on bail per sexist USAO decisions, and over my very strenuous objections.
3. This also later turned out to be true for Greg and Ling Jia Chung.

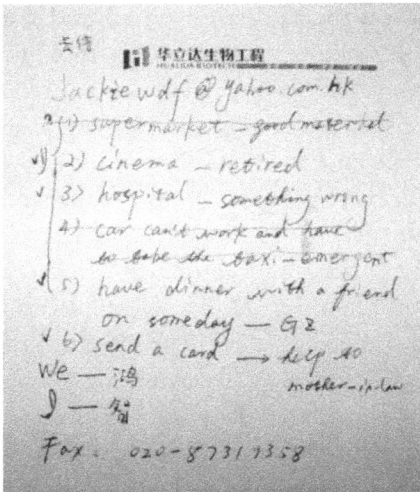

Front of original code word sheet found at Downey residence TRIAL EXHIBIT 61

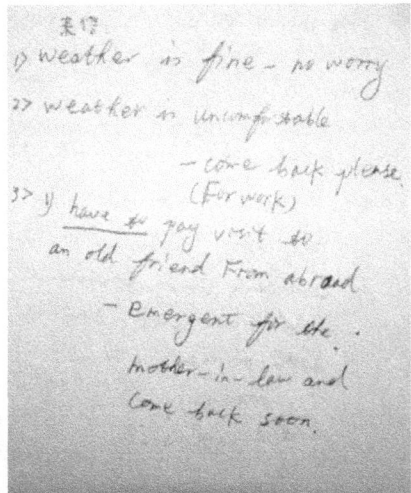

Back of original code word sheet found at Downey residence TRIAL EXHIBIT 61

of the list was in Chinese. We translated the taskings: "Urgent need: War Plane Process Manufacturing Specifications . . . Other fighter-jets, Strikers, Navy jets . . . Complete sets are best. Partials are needed as well . . . Any fighter-jet aero-electronic solution software mainstream technology . . . Chemical cutting processes." Specific technologies of interest included McDonnell Douglas's F-15, F-16, and F-18; Grumman Aircraft's F-14; "Fire control"; "Navigation"; and "Black 25 Aircraft." It also requested modeling software for "Structural Analysis," "Finite Element Modeling," "NASTRAN," "Robotics," and other Boeing, McDonnell Douglas, and General Dynamics technologies. Here was evidence sister Shouling was also collecting technology for the PRC, raising more questions: How deeply involved was Shouling, and for how long? Why send an aviation tasking list to Chi Mak, a naval expert? To find answers, we dug deeply into Shouling's background.

Born in Beijing on February 10, 1929, eleven years Chi's senior, Shouling Mak married Kingman Ma, owner of the Sea Sea Tailor shop that had employed Chi. In 1965, Shouling and Kingman traveled to Northern California to seek business opportunities with partner William Barnes, an American they'd befriended in Hong Kong. When Kingman returned to Hong Kong, Shouling remained and had an affair with Barnes. Despite Kingman's filed affidavit detailing Shouling's fraud, she successfully fought off US deportation efforts, secured a green card, and divorced Kingman, marrying Barnes four days later in Reno, Nevada. She obtained her US citizenship in 1972, and the two settled in Lancaster, California, working at Barnes Aviation, a flight school founded by William's mother "Pancho" Barnes, located adjacent to Edwards Air Force Base.[4]

Years later, William Barnes died when his P-51 mysteriously crashed in the desert. Shouling took over the business and grew her contacts with families and officers stationed at Edwards, becoming a regular on the base. She also maintained an aviation business in China, owning several planes and regularly meeting PRC officials there. Shouling became the very definition of an embedded PRCIS agent, collecting US aviation data per PRC taskings. Now we knew why Shouling received aviation tasking lists from China. But why forward them to naval expert Chi?

Colleen's third discovery answered this question. Shouling wanted Chi Mak to relay her PRCIS aviation tasking list to his friend, aerospace expert and Boeing structural engineer "Greg" Dongfan Chung. Buried within Chi Mak's dresser, Colleen found copies of candid, uncoded correspondence between PRC aviation official Gu Wei Hao and Greg and Ling Jia Chung, carried by Chi. It identified Chi as Gu's trusted courier and agent. Below is a verbatim translation of one such letter:

Mr. & Mrs. Chung,
How are you?

I hope you've received the letter that I sent to you in April. Since I haven't received your letters for a long time, I'm thinking of you.

I went to the US for official business this year, but I didn't have a chance to meet and have a detailed discussion with you. It's deeply

---

4. A PBS documentary describes the life of Shouling's mother-in-law, "Pancho" Barnes, a famous female aviator, contemporary of Amelia Earhart, and friend to Chuck Yeager and other test pilots and US astronauts. At that time, Pancho ran The Happy Bottom Riding Club on Edwards AFB. The documentary's finale mentions William Barnes, and identifies his wife, Shouling, as Pancho's daughter-in-law, and displays a photograph of them together. I wonder what patriot Pancho would say now about her son's choice in wives.

regretful. But I do have some important things to discuss with you personally.

I am very excited to learn that my relative, Mr. Chi Mak, is in Los Angeles. (Mr. Mak studied electrical engineering. He is a Chinese American, same as you, working in the US. He has opportunities to come back often. He is a good person, loyal, dependable, and totally trustworthy.) I have specially asked him to come visit you (using my handwritten letter and a signed business card as identifiers) and bring you a small present to show my and old Chen's appreciation. Please accept it. Since Mr. Mak has not been in the US for long and is unfamiliar with the environment, please take good care of him.

At present, China is in the process of discussing and approving the trunk line airplanes (150-seaters) and planning and arranging the space shuttle issues. I hope these products will be flying sky high soon.

There are some difficult technical issues that need your assistance. I hope to have a chance to consult with you in person. I was wondering if it is possible for you to help collect some information on airplane design for the trunk line and the development of the space shuttle. In the past, I have asked you to collect some quality control information at your convenience. This will greatly help to enhance our product warranty and quality.

For all the expenses that you [plural] have incurred on collecting or purchasing information, I will find a way to pay you cash in person, and you will be allowed to carry it outside the country.

If it is going through me, I can guarantee you that I can do this. It was through Managers Yang and Chen in the past, but they probably couldn't do this! I still press them on this from time to time.

I very much hope you can allocate some time this year to come to Guangzhou. This way it would save some time and expenses. When the time comes, I will try my best to arrange for a few colleagues to go down south to Guangzhou with me to discuss with you in a small setting, which is very safe.

Moreover, I plan to arrange for Mrs. Chung to meet with her counterparts at the Guangzhou Fine Arts Center or Guangzhou Academy of Fine Arts to discuss fine arts. We'll be responsible for all the expenses of your international travel and stay in Guangzhou. You can discuss the time and route of your trip to China with Mr. Mak in person. I'd be greatly delighted if you will come to my house for a visit in Beijing.

You may use "traveling to Hong Kong" or "visiting relatives in China" as reasons for traveling abroad, or we can ask the "Guangzhou Fine Arts Center" or the "Guangzhou Academy of Fine Arts" to extend an invitation to Mrs. Chung and have you, in the name of accompanying your wife, travel abroad together with her. To sum up, if you have any suggestions or if you have anything that I can help you with here, you can have Mr. Mak convey it to me. Normally, if you have any information, you can also pass it on to me through Mr. Mak. This channel is much safer than others.

It is Your Honor and China's fortune that you are able to realize your wish of dedicating yourselves to the service of your country.

I can't say enough with these few words.

Wish your family well!

Gu Wei Hao

May 2, 1987

Before these letters, we only knew Greg Chung as a Chi Mak engineering associate, having once observed the Chungs and Maks together at a restaurant. Chung was a Space Shuttle structural engineer for Boeing, while Ling Jia taught art at Saddleback Community College. The Chungs, older than the Maks, came from a higher social class and Nationalist background. Both spouses' families fled to Taiwan when the communists won China's civil war and obtained undergraduate degrees there before moving to the United States, gaining citizenship the same year as Shouling. Chung went on to earn a US graduate degree in engineering and could answer many of the requests on Shouling's list, having worked on F-15s, F-16s, structural analysis, NASTRAN and other finite element modeling programs, and chemical cutting processes. Most importantly, since 1973 he had been an expert on the US Space Shuttle program.

The unfiltered discussions in these letters between PRCIS handler and agents clarified many things:

1. Greg and Ling Jia were both PRC agents;

2. The correspondence was mutual;

3. Gu visited them in the United States on PRCIS business and introduced them to the Maks;

4. Chi traveled to China regularly as a "loyal, dependable, and trustworthy" courier carrying sensitive, illegal materials for his handlers;

5. Chung and Chi worked together to help China with "difficult technical issues";

6. Chung repeatedly fulfilled Gu's taskings;

7. China reimbursed the Chungs for expenses;

8. Chung sent information to at least three different handlers in China;[5]

9. "Safe" PRCIS debriefings of Chung were performed in secure Guangzhou locations;

10. Pretext invitations, cover stories, and backstopping involving Ling Jia were used to cover the Chungs' intelligence travel to China;

11. Travel was coordinated with Chi and included visits to Gu's Beijing home;

12. Chung communicated with Gu through Chi; and

13. The Chungs saw their primary duty and loyalty as service to the PRC, despite being naturalized US citizens for over sixteen years.

My obvious conclusion? The Chungs merited their own PRC espionage investigation.

Human vacuum cleaner Colleen had also sucked up every scrap of evidence covering China travel and contacts. Two other letters from Gu, addressed to Chi, discussed the Chungs. Also recovered were photographs of the Maks with Gu in the United States, eating out with the

---

5. Competition between handlers for agent services is a well-known PRCIS practice.

Chi Mak in China, May Day, 1971
AUTHOR'S COLLECTION

Chi and Rebecca in China AUTHOR'S
COLLECTION

Chungs, with family members and government officials in China, with PRC nuclear official Ma Fu Bang and his wife in their Beijing home, etc. There was even a younger "beefcake" shot of Chi Mak back in China. Many photographs were dated, with the names of those pictured written on the back.

Colleen also recovered a handwritten copy of the Mak family tree, helping us to identify relatives in China, their PRC government connections, and who was *not* a relative, like Gu Wei Hao, Ma Fu Bang, and officer Cai Hu.[6] Colleen also discovered a Mak family deed to property in Guangzhou. By the time of trial, she had two banker boxes of travel evidence, what I called "Colleen's Web," supporting a timeline of covert Mak travel from which they could never extricate themselves.

---

6. The defense later erroneously claimed otherwise for each.

Chi and Gu at Griffith Observatory FBI RELEASED / AUTHOR'S COLLECTION

Rebecca and Gu at Newport Beach's Wedge TRIAL EXHIBIT 62

The second Alhambra residential search didn't produce Downey's volume. After all, Colleen couldn't be everywhere. But it still proved valuable. Along with accomplishing Fuk's second arrest, we seized Shirley's diary, which contained illuminating references to the many and varied services "Uncle Pu" provided the family, and why.

The moral of this second search story? Don't be lazy. Always be methodical and thorough on your first search, and if you miss something, search again!

CHAPTER 25

The Creaking Wheels of Justice

WE WERE NOW A FINELY TUNED MACHINE WITH MANY FUNCTIONS. To meet discovery requirements, we sent a huge number of microphone, email, video, internet, and telephone intercept summaries to Sandy at FBIHQ requesting declassification for court use. That made them nervous, but not us. We knew the only thing classified had been our interest in Chi Mak and the original sources. The former was now public, and the latter never would be. The intercepts themselves contained nothing remotely sensitive. Our navy experts were examining all technical materials seized, and Power Paragon personnel were consulted regarding valuation, regulation, and sensitivity of the materials Chi had stolen.

We scanned all our evidence, the first massive batch requiring six full-time workers from FBIHQ to spend two weeks processing over 120,000 documents.[1] A second search at Power Paragon was executed of storage containers we discovered Chi had used, producing twenty-six more boxes of evidence. More scanning ensued. We released hundreds of intercepts to defense attorneys, and whatever transcript summaries we had for them.[2] Digital copies of all evidence were provided to each defense team.

---

1. Everything has a cost. Three scan team members were injured in a "Bucar" (FBI-owned car) accident, which we had to investigate.
2. We never received a single intercept declassification request from the attorneys for Rebecca, Tai, Fuk, and Billy, demonstrating their lack of work ethic, client dedication, or intent to go to trial. Yet they still got paid!

The remaining months before trial were filled with hard work and defense attorney demands. Handwriting exemplars from Chi, Rebecca, Tai, Fuk, and Shouling were taken to compare with the tasking and code word sheets, with no real results due to tainted samples and poor lab work.[3]

The US State Department did us one timely favor, quickly certifying that none of the defendants were registered foreign agents. Unfortunately, the ITAR certifications proved ridiculously slow and unwieldy, mainly due to ICE incompetence, which also had sought to wrest the export-control ITAR charges from us entirely so they could claim some stats. We parried that ICE thrust. I should have listened to Gunnar and used NCIS to submit the ITAR determination request.[4] ICE had simply added itself, a confused chef, to the kitchen. The ICE and State Department process involved lengthy, duplicative review stages.[5] The wait was interminable and inexcusable. If defense counsel hadn't kept delaying the trial, we would have had no ITAR charges.

A few weeks before Chi's trial, we lost the third ITAR DD(x) charge because the submitting ICE agent had mislabeled the article he sent to the State Department, rendering the resulting certification letter useless. There was no time to resubmit it. Presto, the charge was lost. ICE had *one* job to do, and it failed! Also, the USAO's inane policy of charging only *one* ITAR article per disc, not each violating article, meant many more DD(x) charges were never brought, and therefore lost.[6] It was the only technology we could prove had actually reached the PRC.[7] Adding insult to injury, ICE insisted we let that same agent testify before the grand jury to help him gain "experience" and promotion potential! I was in no mood.

---

3. Chi, with his distinctive all-capitals printing style, was the obvious author of the "Ken Gonzales" code word sheet, yet no such finding was made.

4. For many reasons, I later greatly rued that decision, which cost us dearly.

5. Three reviews and three certifications for *each* document; only the final, third one of each was trial-worthy.

6. If all the ITAR articles on each disc were printed out and sent to China, each article would have been charged. Silly, right?

7. The 2004 trashed tasking list demonstrated how important DD(x) was to the PRC. Chi had *never* worked on it, yet he strove to obtain it, watched Billy's encryption of it, and carried it to China in 2004.

Getting creative, Frank, SARA's Forfeiture Unit specialist, filed an Application and Affidavit for Seizure Warrant for a portion of Chi and Rebecca's bank funds, under the legal theory that Chi defrauded his employer, Power Paragon, all those years by accepting a salary despite giving its technologies to China, a competitor, thereby reducing their value and efficacy. Frank seized $250,000 of Chi's funds before Judge Arthur Nakazato refused to sign off on any more such seizures. No matter. Defense attorneys would strip the rest.

Some clueless FBI managers began declaring, "You've made your arrests. The case is solved. Time to give back the resources." Nothing was further from the truth. We now needed *all* hands on deck. Evidence had to be located, collated, and organized, verbatim translations produced, witnesses interviewed, testimony and testifiers selected, and reliable, relatable expert witnesses located. We defeated NCIS efforts to take Gunnar and Omar and FBILA efforts to remove Lookout Jaime and our linguists.[8] Sal's and Sandy's lobbying, and our new and improved FBILA CI management, proved crucial. Linguists were now producing court-certified verbatim translations for every possible evidentiary intercept and document and summarizing the rest. Our Chicago Field Office again lent Shanghainese linguist extraordinaire Rick Yoo to us for an extended period so he could rip through our backlogged Shanghainese intercepts.[9] When the language units pulled all funding support for our linguists, we pivoted by paying for them through case funding.[10] They were worth every penny.

Greg Staples began working on plea deals and requested we create a presentation for Fuk's attorney, Tom McDonald, as a good faith "proffer."[11] McDonald proved a difficult, argumentative jerk, even when simply asked to listen. He said that our offer—guilty plea to Unregistered Agent and False Statement charges, with reduced sentence, in exchange for cooperation with the government—was "feasible." Yet he never dis-

---

8. Each of them possessed phenomenal institutional case knowledge essential for trial preparation.
9. He was the primary reason we produced fully certified verbatims for all Shanghainese trial intercepts.
10. Talk about sabotage!
11. Boy, did I *hate* that term and the deception it came to represent.

cussed it with Fuk before rejecting it *months* later. He lied to us, and it wouldn't be the last time!

Greg shrugged it off as normal defense attorney behavior. I soon tired of performing tasks for non-reciprocating defense counsel. I told Greg, "No more offers." We had the Maks dead to rights, and our evidence got stronger every day, especially with recent searches of the Chungs' home. And the lab, for once, had come back with something useful—Billy's fingerprints on the encrypted LAX disc.

The problem of intermittent, unsynchronized audio and video intercepts the Tech Squad had saddled us with proved almost intractable. The video and audio feeds had randomly blinked off and on due to weak signals. Every recording break returned synchronization to square one. Our Forensic Audio, Video, and Image Analysis Unit's (FAVIAU) one effort at synchronizing the October 23, 2005, recordings was amateurish. Greg told me if we didn't turn over a product to the defense soon, we wouldn't be able to use it at trial. So, I assigned this impossible task of putting Humpty Dumpty back together again to Scott and linguist Len Pi. They used a private lab back east, investing hundreds of hours, with their only markers being the sounds or sights of chairs sliding, objects dropped, footsteps, doorbells, etc. It took months of drudgery, and many false starts and failed versions. But they kept at it and got it done, days before Greg's deadline. It proved an airtight product the defense never challenged, for which Scott and Len deserved full credit.

Our Cryptologic and Electronics Analysis Unit (CEAU) at Quantico proved no better. Omar found whole folders of PRC contact names, numbers, and addresses within Mr. Luo's PDA from LAX that CEAU's examination had missed. That was the whole purpose of their examination and reason for existence. This, combined with FAVIAU's defective product, poor handwriting examinations, and the Behavioral Science Unit's botched interview advice for Rebecca soured me on the quality of Quantico "experts." I was done with them.

On the defense side, Chi's attorneys had done most of the work, while the other defense attorneys merely rode their coattails. But by the fall of 2006, Tai's attorney John Early contributed to their collective effort, moving to sever Chi from the other defendants, arguing that a joint trial brought "a serious risk of 'spillover' stemming from the antici-pated substantial evidence in the case relating to . . . defendant Chi Mak."

I understood. If I were Chi's co-conspirator, I wouldn't want to stand trial next to him either. Too much damned evidence! It's a good sign when defense counsel complains there's too much evidence against the ringleader for a follower to receive a fair trial. This became the only major motion we lost. The silver lining? Judge Carney's ruling indicated the evidence against Chi was overwhelming. Now there would be two trials, with Chi going first. Early did Chi's co-defendants a huge favor. If there had been just one trial, they all would have been convicted and given longer sentences.

Kaye's next move was a "Hail Mary" motion to "suppress evidence obtained and derived from [the] Foreign Intelligence Surveillance Act," claiming my FISA requests were full of lies. He called for suppression of all evidence as "fruit of the poisonous tree of the FISA surveillance," claiming the law itself was unconstitutional.[12] Kaye sought to read my FISA applications. He knew we would pull our case before letting that happen to protect our sources and methods. When other cases had been pulled for that reason, defense attorneys publicly and predictably lied, declaring the case was "weak" or "flawed."

To meet this threat head-on, I asked squad agent Tom, who tracked all things FISA-related, to write the sworn affidavit, classified "Secret," detailing our every step. He documented our extensive, progressive mini-mization efforts, meaning we didn't listen to irrelevant conversations. The more we learned, the more conversations we minimized. First came tele-marketing calls, then conversations between Tai's kids and their friends, and so on. For Chi Mak, this meant no monitoring of home microphones and video when only Rebecca was at home. I don't care two figs for the privacy of PRC spies, but I *did* want to safeguard our FISA against likely defense claims. Minimization risks missing some things, like "Uncle Pu's" calls, which first appeared to be innocent family discussions. Fortunately, FISA collection records everything. Once we knew what to look for,

---

12. Though boilerplate, these claims still irked me. I would *never* perjure myself in a FISA appli-cation. It would destroy my self-image, reputation, and career. Everything I swore to was airtight, documenting every detail, necessary correction, and "minimized" interception.

we went back and translated relevant unreviewed calls, gaining insights regarding discussions concerning intelligence officer Pu. This is how we also learned that Billy was telling friends he would soon move to Hong Kong.[13]

FBILA, FBIHQ, the Office of Intelligence and Policy Review, and DOJ's Counterintelligence and Export Control Section each filed oppositions to Kaye's FISA challenge, demonstrating how seriously they took it. Greg Staples's in camera, ex parte response classified "Secret" countered each Kaye FISA challenge and quoted my applications and Tom's affidavit to demonstrate their accuracy.

Eight FISA applications and renewal requests were delivered to Judge Carney by a special armed government courier who waited while Carney conducted his long in camera, ex parte review.[14] Once done, the courier returned to DC with the briefcase's contents handcuffed to his wrist. Carney rejected all defense motions:

The Court engaged in a thorough and exhaustive review of the FISA material and found none of the above factors [raised by the defense] present. Instead, the targets of the surveillance were clearly identified, the facts justifying surveillance were amply supported by the available materials and certified by responsible officials, and the information retained is well within the bounds set by the minimization procedures. Accordingly, disclosure is not necessary . . . there is substantial evidence to support the FISC [FISA Court] judge's conclusion that there was probable cause that Mr. Mak was an agent of a foreign power. . . . The Court found no material inconsistences or misstatements anywhere in the FISA applications, nor is there any evidence to suggest that the government omitted material information that would have altered the FISC judge's determinations. . . . The Court is satisfied that the government has exercised good faith in attempting to minimize the retention of non-public information obtained during surveillance of Mr. Mak. It has similarly been diligent in its efforts

---

13. This aided efforts to detain him until trial.
14. FISAs were renewed every ninety days over a nearly eighteen-month period.

to discern and separate information that is relevant to foreign intel-
ligence from information that is irrelevant.

This ruling was expected but still deeply appreciated, producing a large, collective sigh of relief. Another hurdle cleared, yet no chance to rest.

Defense attorneys immediately created a series of harassing, meritless motions, attempting to exhaust and overwhelm the prosecution. Once again, agent efforts proved key. We suggested, located, collected, organized, and presented the rebutting evidence our prosecutors then used to defeat every baseless defense argument, from "violated" Miranda rights to insufficient discovery.

The most annoying one was Stanley Greenberg's and John Early's claim that their clients' rights to "a fair and unbiased" trial were violated by anonymous "Senior Justice Department officials," quoted in reporter Bill Gertz's *Washington Times* article. They declared grand jury proceedings were intentionally leaked to taint our jury pool—hypocritical hogwash from defense attorneys who daily broadcast lies designed to do just that. Gertz's reporting was vague and contained within an obscure newspaper three thousand miles away. Judge Carney ruled against Greenberg, but I warned FBIHQ and DOJ to find the East Coast leakers, knowing Greenberg would pursue this like the Holy Grail because he had nothing else.[15] I proved prophetic. Greenberg's motion ended up outlasting the Mak prosecutions.

Our trial dates were now set—March 20, 2007, for Chi Mak, and May 15 for the rest. We saw a glimmer at the end of this tunnel, yet Kaye tried to snuff it out with new motions constituting legalized whining. One sought a videotaped deposition of a PRC official *in China* for testimony, knowing full well he could perjure himself with no consequences. Greg's counterarguments were sustained after the NCIS demonstrated the official in question regularly traveled to the United States, where per-

---

15. They took too long, fueling Greenberg and angering Carney. By the time FBIHQ CI Section Chief Clayt Lemme told me the investigation had begun, Judge Carney was demanding an immediate progress report.

jury laws applied. That was the last we heard of that. Just another cynical, dishonest defense ploy.[16]

Another Kaye motion whined that our forensic copies of Mak computers were "too hard" to review. He wanted "logical" format copies that were easier for his paralegal to read.[17] But such copies allow changes to be made to the original, a big evidentiary no-no. One time, our expert, Special Agent Chris Pluhar of the Computer Analysis and Response Team (CART), spent three hours helping Kaye's paralegal navigate the data. But nothing was ever good enough for Kaye. He complained again. So, I wrote a declaration educating him on why only forensic copies were used. If we *had* provided a logical copy, Kaye would miss evidence and then scream, "Brady violation!"[18] Bottom line, Kaye and the other lazy defense attorneys always tried to force us to do their discovery work. Judge Carney thankfully nixed this.

But defense attorneys never say die. Kaye wanted courthouse visitors' metal detectors relocated so Chi wouldn't look guilty (?!) and objected to our expert witnesses.

I had no idea the extent to which the government . . . intended that its experts would apply background information and directly conclude at trial that Mr. Mak is a spy for the PRC, or that multiple government experts would opine that the goal of the documents given to co-defendant Tai Mak was part of a "kill chain" to harm the security of the United States.

Really? He didn't realize our experts were going to add two plus two and say it equaled "spy"? He wanted to ban our experts, despite admitting, "Our office also retained experts to educate the jury about these issues." Carney rejected this as well.

---

16. "Truth" is not a defense value. Winning at all costs is, even if it aids a totalitarian communist PRC regime.
17. Kaye was too cheap and incompetent to hire a forensic examiner.
18. Criminal prosecutors must turn over all evidence to the defense. When we did, they *still* claimed "Brady" violations!

Kaye then moved to exclude our strongest evidence, claiming "unfair prejudice." While *all* of our evidence was prejudicial to Chi, he particularly didn't like our use of Chi's ledger of US Navy ship movements, Gu's letters, and, in his words, "prejudicial surplusage [like] kill chain." He sought to wordsmith the case to death, washing it of all negative connotations and prosecution testimony about PRCIS tradecraft, military and foreign policy goals, technology sensitivities, and classifications. He was trying to fix the fight before it began.

Even in the midst of jury selection, Kaye submitted a stack of motions over six inches high to exclude government evidence regarding the Gu letters, Mak cover stories and immigration patterns, and Chi's ship logs. Greg and Craig skillfully shot them all down as "prior statements or conduct by co-conspirators allowed by law."[19] In a losing defense motion that would nonetheless cause us trouble later, Kaye claimed the statutory, nonreviewable decision regarding whether "technical data [was] subject to export control" belonged to the jury, *not* the State Department. The USAO's warning—"Watch out for CES. They'll screw you every time!"—would again prove prophetic.

At least our pole cameras provided us some levity by contrasting Mak extremes: antisocial Rebecca barricaded within her home alone, while Fuk "entertained" gentleman callers round the clock and Shirley and her boyfriend partied all night, as Chi, Billy, and Tai languished in jail.

---

19. Reading my mind, they also noted for the court, "Relevant evidence is inherently prejudicial."

CHAPTER 26

It's a Bird. It's a Plane.
It's a Subject Matter Expert!

CRIMINAL CASES MAY REQUIRE A FEW SUBJECT MATTER EXPERTS (SME): a fingerprint examiner here, a DNA scientist there, maybe a blood splatter analyst for violent crimes. Our trial required thirteen, due to the complex, sensitive nature of the technologies Chi Mak stole, the history and methodology of the PRC's military and intelligence services, and the three Chinese dialects spoken. We needed engineers who thoroughly understood this maze of technologies—which was above the understanding of agents with college degrees—yet could explain it all in "layman's" terms. If we couldn't understand it, neither would the jury. I tried to get US Navy experts through FBIHQ. Crickets! So, Gunnar became our secret weapon. Using his navy contacts and personality, and after conducting interviews of all prospects for screening purposes, we found the perfect SME for each task.

Our first engineering SME was a godsend: Steve Schreppler, Office of Naval Research (ONR) Program Officer for Ship Signatures. He was alarmed by what Chi was collecting and shared our horror over the apathy many engineers and officials had displayed regarding the China threat. In fact, there was a "China lobby" within our government that preferred to look the other way rather than face the threat. But Steve could see the whole technology forest, not just one tree, and the threat to our national defense. He became our invaluable SME whisperer for spotting and recruiting others. And he himself matched the technologies found in

Chi's home to those on the trashed tasking lists and could easily discuss the nature and importance of each. Steve and Gunnar then teamed up to identify the best experts to help us.

They recruited Ed Chabay, a nuclear engineer at Naval Sea Systems Command (NAVSEA), Reactor I&C Division, also known as Naval Reactors (NR). A former naval officer and current manager of the Instrumentation and Control Division for the newest CVN-21 Gerald R. Ford–class aircraft carrier, he had over twenty years of experience in naval nuclear propulsion and ten years managing the Advanced Submarine Branch, including oversight of the Virginia-class submarine.[1]

Since both sides were required to disclose their experts, I appointed two of my agents and an analyst to assemble impeachment files for each defense expert, identified by collecting any and all publicly available background information on them, especially derogatory, for our AUSAs to use if the time came. This being a time-honored defense tactic, I thought we should do the same. We got some good stuff!

Opposing Steve and Ed were retired octogenarian Bob Lee and Professor Thomas Lipo. Lee would claim QED was in the public domain and reject its "NOFORN," "classified," and "sensitive" labels as nonsense. Professor Lipo, a commercial power expert from the University of Wisconsin, Madison, boasted a powerful résumé, and would challenge our assertions that Chi's QED data could help detect acoustic signatures. But both had derogatory personal and financial ties to Chi that we could now point out.

Our three main linguists would also testify, and they were the best of the best. Opposing our all-stars were two brothers, Eddie and Stephen Yip, who would prove no match in background, experience, methodology, or skill, on or off the witness stand.[2] They never produced a single translation, only attempting to unconvincingly challenge a couple of words here and there.

To tackle our forensic digital evidence—desktops, laptops, hard drives, thumb drives, CDs, and floppy disks—we needed two experts.

---

1. The development of the Virginia-class sub, "the first navy ship design post–cold war," took over fourteen years.
2. The other Mak defense attorneys never produced *any* opposition linguists.

Special Agent Chris Pluhar from the Computer Analysis and Recovery Team (CART) was the perfect fit, being one of the few members who remembered what the "A" in CART stood for. And he could explain it in layman's terms.

But we also needed an expert in encryption. Since all members of Quantico's Cryptologic and Electronics Analysis Unit (CEAU) quailed at the thought of testifying, Gunnar found us the ideal SME in NCIS Investigative Computer Specialist Nick Mikus, who showed us how the Maks' PRCIS encryption worked. Nick could also demonstrate how he retrieved the stolen data, while exhibiting this great vibe as a young, savvy, intelligent computer geek, garnering him instant respect and credibility. The opposing defense SME quickly bolted, probably because we had discovered he'd lied on his résumé about working with the FBI and had helped to defend Alejandro Avila, the infamous rapist murderer of young Samantha Runnion.[3] Avila was convicted, sentenced to death, and sent to San Quentin.[4]

Then we lined up some SMEs to which the defense had no counter. Bob Gerrity, division head of the China Naval Forces Division, Strategic Assessment and Warning Department, Office of Naval Intelligence, would testify about specific goals of the People's Liberation Army Navy (PLAN), its primary goal to retake Taiwan, and its secondary purpose of projecting naval power globally. The PLAN was building itself specifically to fight the US Navy in a war. That fact sank Chi's defense that helping China was not hurting the United States.

USN captain Kevin Eyer would discuss tactical warfare advantages provided by AEGIS-class ships' SPY-1 radar, characterized as a quantum leap paradigm shift in capabilities—advantages lost when China "obtained" these same capabilities decades ahead of schedule due to Chi's betrayals. Again, this meant future US lives lost.

---

3. Avila had been acquitted in 2001 of molesting two girls, who had testified against him. Law enforcement believed that that experience caused him to kill Samantha this time around, after molesting her, to prevent another witness from testifying against him.
4. California governor Gavin Newsom's immoral pledge to stop executions, plus the Left's stranglehold on the state, means that day sadly will never arrive.

Then came Rear Admiral William Hilarides, program executive acquisitions officer for our nuclear navy, who oversaw acquisition and life-cycle maintenance of submarines, weapons, countermeasures, sonar, combat control, and imaging systems.[5] He would explain the value of QED, AEGIS SPY-1 radar, and EMALS, all of which Chi compromised. His knowledge, high rank, and personality lent our claims real gravitas. And per ITAR charge requirements, our last technology SME, Mal Zerden from the State Department's Directorate of Defense Trade Controls, Bureau of Political-Military Affairs, would certify that these technologies were on the US Munitions List.

Our two PRCIS tradecraft SMEs were only identified just before trial, thanks to heavy-handed CIA interference.[6] FBIHQ could or would not produce such an expert, so we widened our search, interviewing dozens of candidates from government and private sectors. But every time we chose a candidate, the CIA stepped in, uninvited, and said no. When we refused their unwanted input, they blackmailed our candidate into withdrawing, threatening exposure of personal details and/or withdrawal of that person's government contracts. Utterly outrageous. The CIA's justification each time? "[The candidate] attended or taught at 'The Farm' [the CIA's training facility] or worked on a CIA project, and therefore knows too much to testify." Just plain stupid. This case was about Chi Mak's spying, *not* "The Farm"! Our SMEs would testify only about *our* evidence, not what they did for the CIA. The CIA was blackmailing US citizens! I ordered a total CIA blackout. We would no longer tell them *anything* about our case. As we continued our search, the Agency kept finding ways to interfere with our efforts. It became obvious we had a rat somewhere. Here's how we found out who it was.

One day we were interviewing Rear Admiral Eric McVadon, USN, retired. His distinguished service had included acting as defense naval attaché in Beijing from 1990 to 1992 and personal experience with the

---

5. Hilarides went on to become a vice admiral and the forty-third commander of NAVSEA, the largest of the USN's five system commands. He eventually retired from this position in 2016 after thirty-nine years of service in the US Navy.
6. From that moment on, I would experience nothing but CIA interference and deception for the rest of my career.

Center for Asian Pacific Studies (CAPS) in Guangzhou. He was superb. As we finished our interview, a female DOJ/CES attorney accompanying us began asking McVadon about his past work for, and relationships with, the CIA. To his credit, Craig pounced on the attorney like a cat, demanding an explanation. Craig aggressively pried out of her that she was doing the CIA's bidding, having received instructions to ask these questions. The DOJ/CES was the rat! We shouldn't have been surprised. Once again it was interfering, doing its best to "screw us."[7] After asking McVadon to leave the room, Craig tore this DOJ/CES attorney a new one at a volume all could hear. I did not pity her, believing she was receiving what she so richly deserved. I had never seen Craig so righteously angry and passionate. Despite all this, McVadon agreed to be our SME, stating he didn't care what the CIA thought. He was an impressive man, sticking with us despite immense pressure from the Agency.

The defense SME counterpunch to McVadon was University of Southern California (USC) history professor Dr. Stanley Rosen. His background reminded Colleen and me of the typical old Communist Party USA member: knee-jerk defense of all things PRC while downplaying its oppressive and murderous totalitarian regime. Rosen's previous testimonial appearances defended Communist China and those accused of conspiring with it, including Katrina Leung. Rosen's livelihood depended upon maintaining good relations with that regime. He would explain away even its most barbarous acts.

But our tradecraft SME shotgun had two barrels. We also recruited Rudy Guerin, retired FBI acting deputy assistant director of operations, Counterintelligence Division, after Rudy hit a grand slam during his interview. His deep CI background gave him insights into just about every piece of evidence, linking it all together into one integrated, reasonable narrative, just like I wanted. And he spoke not like an executive or egghead analyst, but as an agent, with self-assurance, confidence, and earthy common sense and humor, all of which go a long way with a jury. Greg and I loved him! Ironically, CIA interference had ended up giving us the two best possible tradecraft experts for our case.

---

7. In the words of the USAO.

Ron Kaye produced a *weak* tit for our tat, retaining their own retired Bureau executive, I. C. Smith, who was anything but a PRC expert. He had served as section chief of Analysis, Budget and Training at FBIHQ and as an SAC at the Little Rock Field Office. In his 2004 autobiography he wrote, "I am not an expert on China." Case closed! But what he lacked in experience he made up for in ego, hubris, and ignorance. In classic blue-flamer fashion, Smith worked as a Special Agent investigator for only eight or nine years, four of them on criminal matters, before moving up the management ladder. His book also declared, "In Chinese counter-intelligence, you aren't going to catch them red-handed." I couldn't wait for Greg to dissect this egotistical, self-important blowhard on the stand.

CHAPTER 27

Setting Up the Chessboard

ALTHOUGH A SEASONED COUNTERINTELLIGENCE AGENT, I WAS A NOV-
ice when it came to criminal matters. Fortunately I'd learned two basic
truths during my criminal work at my first office in Minneapolis:
AUSAs agree to ridiculous plea bargains over agent objections, *and* I
excelled at testimony.

As a new agent in Minneapolis, I testified in a defense hearing
seeking to exclude their client's confession to me. She was an attractive,
likable young woman who, as a bank teller, had embezzled a few thousand dollars. Her attorney aggressively grilled me to prove coercion. I
remained calm, ignoring his insults while dispassionately answering his
questions. The calmer I was, the more agitated he became. I enjoyed it!
The judge ruled her confession was informed and voluntary, and publicly
complimented me for my honesty and demeanor. The beaten defense
attorney accepted the AUSA plea bargain he'd previously rejected, sarcastically sniping I should be "very proud" for intimidating a young woman
into a felony confession, thereby "ruining her life." Earlier, I had told
the AUSA that the defendant was young, made a foolish mistake, and
demonstrated true regret, so had urged she be offered generous terms,
including no jail time. But defense attorneys don't care about that, or that
she'd committed a felony, or that we were helping her to make restitution
and move on with her life. He was angry that he lost. The next day, the
judge sent notes to the AUSA and my supervisor complimenting my
candor and professionalism, an event both men told me was a rarity.

After my transfer to SARA-4, I was re-called to testify in a marijuana farm case I'd conducted before reassigning it to a senior agent in Minneapolis. I had seen the defendant leaving the farm years earlier as we drove past each other on a small country road. She looked now as I remembered her back then, a strung-out drug addict, the only differences being her combed hair and nice clothes. On cross, the defense attorney showed me her driver's license back then—she looked *very* different—and asked, "How can you possibly sit there and say that you identified this defendant while passing her at a combined speed of 40 mph, using this photograph?" I replied, "That's not the photo I used." Defense counsel looked at the judge, who looked at the prosecution. The case agent and prosecutor shrugged and swore there was no other photograph, thereby hanging me out to dry. The defense attorney accused me of lying. I pushed back: There *was* another photograph!

The judge ended testimony that day so I could search the file for it. I went to the FBI office with the case agent, a lazy man who again declared no such picture existed.[1] I examined my old case file and quickly found a 1A envelope.[2] On it was written the defendant's name and "mug shot." Inside was the picture I remembered, a mug shot from her prostitution days depicting her *exactly* as she looked now. It was right where it should have been.

I couldn't *wait* for testimony the next day. The defense attorney's narrative was destroyed, and the senior agent and prosecutor had mud on their faces, having not produced it for the defense in discovery. They had to crop the picture for the jury to try and hide the defendant's prior conviction.[3] But mug shots are impossible to disguise. I happily sat on the stand, stoic on the outside but grinning on the inside, my credibility exonerated and elevated. The jury would see this photo and recall the defense's withering cross-examination and my calm certainty and tes-

---

1. My previous Minneapolis experiences demonstrated that *all* of the GS-13s (older agents) on its Organized Crime squad in the 1980s did only the required minimal work, i.e., low-hanging fruit only. This man had taken mine and given it his minimal efforts.
2. 1A subfiles are used for storage of miscellaneous items such as photographs, notes, and record check results.
3. Just more of our criminal system's nonsense, hiding inculpatory evidence in the name of "justice."

timony linking the defendant to the marijuana farm. Ultimately, they found her guilty.

I recalled all of this as the Chi Mak trial date approached. I was confident I could rely on my common sense and character judgments while sticking to my guns. I've always known what a defense attorney is after, and how to answer cleverly and honestly. A little advice for giving successful cross-examination testimony:

1. Agree with the defense attorney whenever helpful to build credibility with the jury for the times you *politely* correct their misstatements or provide answers the defense attorney doesn't like;

2. The jury will believe you on the big stuff if you volunteer little things to defense counsel "for clarity"; and

3. Always appear—and actually be—truthful, calm, confident, and relaxed.

To prepare for the fast-approaching trial, I had to complete our "Government's Exhibit List," which I'd been building from the beginning. For some reason, Craig wanted it arranged in a strange way. Having little trial experience, I deferred to his judgment. Big mistake! His "system" used no recognizable organizing principle, scattering crucial evidence willy-nilly throughout the nearly 250 exhibits, thereafter making it difficult to find anything easily. Craig also announced he didn't want to hear from agents during trial, desiring no input "from the peanut gallery," me, especially. Per Craig, he and Greg would do and say what they wanted, when they wanted, with *our* case.

I ignored him. I knew Greg didn't feel this way. This was an FBI case—*my* case. Craig was just along for the ride, whining all the way.

Neither Greg nor Craig appeared interested in the jury selection process, something I found fascinating. Changing someone's mind can prove very difficult, so better to pick someone already disposed to believe in you and your cause. The defense team believed this, given the effort they'd invested, proposing a large jury pool and questionnaires. The defense proposed including questions seeking any possible juror links to law enforcement. I proposed questions to ferret out defense sympathies and anti–law enforcement bias. Judge Carney selected the final questions, dropping many of those proposed as too complicated, peripheral, or best left for the voir dire portion of juror questioning.[4] He decided upon twenty questions to pose. Greg and Craig's continuing disinterest in jurors' answers to these questions puzzled me. I didn't want to miss this opportunity to peer into potential jurors' minds, so I asked Greg if I could review their eighty-plus juror questionnaire answers that night. He agreed. Craig would have said "No."

I channeled my soccer coach player-drafting skills, ranking each one per my own system.[5] I scored jurors by their answers to key questions, assigning each a color: green for "Good," red for "Bad," yellow for "Toss-up." The most illuminating answers came from questions about a juror's:

1. Favorite movie, TV show, and book;

2. Hobbies;

3. Marital status and children;

4. City of residence;

5. Employment;

6. Prior jury experience and verdicts reached;

7. Daily news sources; and

8. Connections or conflicts with law enforcement.

While number 8's importance is obvious, number 7 proved equally relevant. A juror who only read the *Los Angeles Times*, *New York Times*, or *Washington Post*, or watched MSNBC, CNN, or network news exclusively, were tagged red, due to the hard left, anti-police tilt of those outlets. If they read the *Orange County Register* (then a respectable libertarian

---

4. *Voir dire* is an old French term meaning "to speak truly or speak the truth."
5. My daughters, Lauren and Kristen, know this attention to detail landed us some good teams!

newspaper), *Wall Street Journal, New York Post,* or *Washington Examiner,* watched Fox News, listened to talk radio, or consumed a balance of left and right media, I tagged them green. Regarding question number 1, one potential juror was tagged red because his favorite movie was *Twelve Angry Men,* a dishonest depiction of jury deliberations with a "lone heroic juror" holding out for a "not guilty" verdict against fellow racist jurors screaming "Guilty!" We didn't want *that!* Anyone listing pro-police or US military movies or books as favorites usually got a green tab.

The next morning, I returned the juror questionnaires with my rankings. Craig being Craig, he dismissed it outright as "useless," yet he kept my ranking system while changing the colors he pronounced as "too obvious." Once more, he took a simple, workable system and hopelessly overcomplicated it. Greg accepted and used them as presented, with thanks. I then asked him about one potential juror whose favorite book had a Spanish title. When he saw the book title, his stoic face went wide-eyed with alarm, and he told me to mark that person a "hard no." It seems Greg had read that book, authored by a hard-core Argentinian communist. He told me anyone calling it their favorite book had no business on our jury.

Throughout the Chi Mak and Greg Chung years, Greg and I maintained an enjoyable left–right political debate. I always respected Greg's ability to put his politics aside while he pursued justice. As we selected the jury over the next few days, Greg repeatedly bemoaned, tongue in cheek, that he was forced to "kick my people off" the jury in order to impanel "Jim's people." Due to hard-won trial experience, Greg usually tried to exclude postal workers, public school teachers, municipal employees, engineers, and "thugs," whenever possible.

Jury selection was this trial's opening act. First, Judge Carney weeded out hardship cases.[6] The first batch of sixteen potential jurors, twelve with four alternates, were called up. Each side had a limited number of challenges requiring no justification, with the defense having more. We saved our challenges for the worst cases, those people we were *really* uncomfortable with. I was thankful for our Orange County venue, given

---

6. Those who couldn't miss work or lose pay; were full-time caretakers; had prepaid, nonrefundable vacation plans; or had medical conditions or critical medical appointments.

what NSD-9, and the O. J. Simpson prosecution, had dealt with in Los Angeles. Most jurors initially seated were to our liking, but the defense whittled them down and few survived this culling.[7] Sometimes the defense kicked off someone we also didn't want. We accepted this gift with silent thanks. Overall, the jury looked good for us and included a Boeing employee and a US Navy employee's spouse.

We were down to one last juror. He was a scruffy, heavily tattooed Santa Ana municipal worker. Most government workers tend to favor the defense.[8] We'd seen this man and his friend sitting in the back of the courtroom loudly joking, appearing to hold the whole process in contempt. Kevin Moberly reported overhearing them making antigovernment jokes. So, we used our last free challenge to dismiss this man. *However*, the next randomly selected juror to take his seat was his equally scruffy friend, who was probably now ticked off at us. This new guy wore ratty jeans and was tatted up, with long tangled hair, a partially braided full black beard, and a dismissive look. As he sauntered to the jury box and plopped down in the juror seat, Craig turned to me in despair and said, "We just lost the case!"[9]

While I didn't appreciate Craig's panic, I shared his concern. This guy's appearance screamed "antigovernment." But I was also tired of Craig's obsessive doom and gloom. The defense apparently shared Craig's assessment, quickly accepting the juror with broad smiles. Greg posed a few queries, learning this man was from Anaheim, married with a son, and worked for the railroad. He had no favorite books, but loved the film *The Good, the Bad and the Ugly*. Greg accepted him. "Tattooed Love Dog," as squad agents Jessie and Lisa dubbed him, completed our impaneled jury. This wouldn't be the last time he made an impression on us.

The trial would begin the following morning, Wednesday, March 28, 2007.

Here we go, I thought.

---

7. It was an interesting process, analyzing people and their motivations, and one I think my older daughter Kristen would love. She always enjoyed taking and examining personality test results for herself and others.

8. Law enforcement personnel tend to be the exception. They witness human depravity every day, so know people aren't "naturally good."

9. *Now* he talks to me, and *this* is what he chooses to say?

PART III
PROSECUTE

CHAPTER 28

Traitor or "Victim"?

THE MOMENT HAD COME TO PUBLICLY DEBATE CHI'S BEHAVIOR. AFTER the lawyers introduced themselves, Chi Mak, and me, Craig read the indictment and charges to the jury: One, Conspiracy to Export Defense Articles; two and three, Attempted Export of Defense Articles; four, Acting as an Unregistered Agent of the PRC; and five, Material False Statement to the FBI.

Greg explained why we were all there:

October 28, 2005, on a Friday night, a few hours before midnight, a man and a woman were passing through security at LAX. They were on their way to board a midnight flight to China. They never got on the plane. The reason they do not get on the plane is this. [Holding up a CD holder] This was found in the luggage of the man and the woman. What is in this book is what broke this case. And what is in this book is why the defendant is now on trial.

Two words defined the importance of the stolen data: "Kill Chain . . . If you are able to determine the acoustic signature of a submarine, you can find it. And if you can find it, you can kill it." Greg rattled off the numerous lies Chi told us after his arrest, and then read the tasking lists.

I noticed Tattooed Love Dog lean forward, grip the railing tightly, and stare at Chi, ready to leap over and wring his neck. *Love Dog might be a criminal*, I thought, *but dammit, he was an* American *criminal. He got it!* Chi's betrayals equaled dead Americans.

Greg covered the code word sheets and Chi's wartime tracking of US warships in Hong Kong before reading the damning Gu Wei Hao letters aloud. He explained the role PRCIS handlers had played, including their deferential treatment of the Maks in exchange for their services.[1] He ended his ninety-minute opening by previewing an impressive list of government experts who would support our evidence, ending with this conclusion before a rapt jury. "We are confident you will find him guilty of being an agent of the government of the People's Republic of China without giving notice to the United States. You will find him guilty of conspiracy and attempting to export export-controlled documents. And you will find him guilty of making false statements to the FBI. Thank you."

Marilyn Bednarski responded with a dump-truck load of meaningless sentimentality to obscure the facts:

> *I want to start by asking you to think back to a year and a half ago*
> *. . . and maybe get yourselves settled in thinking about a weekend*
> *night and wondering what you might be doing late in the evening on*
> *a weekend night. [For Chi], that night, what happened was he was*
> *sleeping in his sleeping clothes when suddenly the FBI came to his*
> *door, banged on the door, crashed in, and arrested him.[2] He got out*
> *of bed in his sleeping clothes. . . . What a shocking evening.*

Thereafter, Bednarski tossed out lies and contradictions she had no intention of proving, hoping something would stick enough to confuse even one juror. One minute FBI agents were Keystone Kops who couldn't find their rear ends with a flashlight; the next, they were brilliant, racist, Machiavellian puppeteers, manipulating all those around them. On the other hand, Chi Mak was a hardworking, loyal, neighborly immigrant who helped the US Navy and paid his taxes. But because he was Chinese, the government had framed him as a PRC spy. Chi had his employer's permission to do what he did—share unrestricted, publicly available

---

1. Greg then made one gaffe, which we, especially Jessie Murray, ribbed him about later. He called the encryption software author a "China . . . man," before quickly self-correcting himself with "Chinese man."
2. Mostly lies. Chi was awake, Downey PD rang his doorbell, and Chi opened the door.

technology with the world, some of whom just happened to be Chinese. Tasking lists? Generic and meant for others. Code word sheets? A Chinese niece's silly game. Damaging intercepts? Misunderstood and mistranslated. Encryption? More like compressed files. Tracking US military ship movements? A hobby. Mr. Pu? Family friend. Confession? Ambitious NCIS agent lies.[3]

This is about intrusion in Mr. Chi Mak's home and life. This is about alarmist military reaction to technology they don't understand.[4] This is about misperception and prejudice. . . . We expect to ask you folks to return verdicts of not guilty on all the counts charged; that he was not an agent of a foreign government; that he did not intend to send export control material; and that he did not lie to the FBI. I thank you for your attention.

While the jury broke for lunch, Judge Carney confirmed Bednarski had mischaracterized ITAR law, but noted a jury instruction would clear it up. The defense said nothing. It was their strategy to misstate the law to the jury.

Our first witness was Gene Dotson, former president and CEO of Power Paragon, and Chi's friend for nearly twenty years. He traced Power Paragon's history of providing electrical systems for hundreds of USN warships, then identified the sensitive work Chi did and concerns regarding the damage he could do. Ron Kaye's cross-examination took three times as long to air bogus generic claims about the technologies—like, EMALS technology was similar to a roller coaster. Greg's redirect sarcastically knocked down such claims like targets in a shooting gallery. It was a thing of beauty!

Greg: Running an amusement park "roller coaster" is nothing like launching a 70,000-pound F-14 aircraft off a carrier deck using EMALS, is it?

Dotson: No.

---

3. By the end we would prove defense attorneys and Chi were the liars.
4. Let me get this straight: The US government doesn't understand its *own* technology?

Then came Fred Witham, director of Facilities Environmental Health and Safety and Security for Power Paragon, to establish that Power Paragon adequately protected its sensitive US data, countering defense claims. Fred's testimony going into the second day confirmed Chi had no authority to publish Power Paragon's QED and Solid-State Switch documents.

Fred's cross-examination was tense. It was clear he held Kaye in contempt as he shut down Kaye's desperate charges of company neglect, including that "rats" were eating sensitive documents. Kaye also implied Chi was set up, and Power Paragon was "hiding the truth" to protect its USN contracts.[5] Greg's redirect buried Kaye's claims in mockery.

Greg: Does Power Paragon have a problem with rats eating its papers?

Fred: No.

Greg: Do you know if rats happen to enjoy eating naval technical documents over other things?

Fred: No. [courtroom laughter]

Finally, my time had come! I was *so* ready. My testimony would be direct and straightforward. If I didn't know the answer, I would say so, while appearing helpful and earnest. If in doubt, I would qualify my answer, and respect defense counsel's ability to control the questioning. And *always*, I would hide my contempt for the defense attorneys and their client. I began by describing my background and FBI career, before explaining evidence collection, investigative techniques, case agent duties, surveillance methods, minimization procedures, translation protocols, and privacy considerations. Then we broke for lunch and tackled administrative issues.[6]

---

5. Ironically, L-3's East Coast compliance officials would later lie during testimony to undermine the prosecution in an attempt to protect those very contracts.
6. Bednarski requested that government intercepts of Chi and Rebecca Mak praising communism and leaders Mao, Lenin, and Stalin be stricken. I thought they were *very* relevant, but the defense won that argument.

Next came boring but necessary hours of testimony as I read into evidence our *many* microphone, telephone, and automotive intercepts and verified that each was collected, translated, and court-certified. I tried to keep the listeners' interest in mind as I did my readings.[7] Greg had prepared simple outlines for witness questioning. Mine, titled "GAYLORD DIRECT," was a forty-two-page summary of topics and evidence in large, bold capital letters, organized to establish the order, context, topic, exhibit number, date, description, court certification, and formal admission of evidence. Below is a partial example.

IS DEFENDANT TAI MAK'S OLDER BROTHER

CAI—CHOI

NOTEBOOK—IBM—FOUND DURING SEARCH ON TAI HOUSE

EX 111 10/21/05

WHAT IS IT

WHAT PHONE

TRANSLATED

CERT

ADMIT

HIGHLIGHT

[ALSO GO TO CHINA—CM—YOU BETTER GO—I'LL HAVE SOMETHING FOR YOU]

EX 123 10/23/05

WHAT IS IT

WHAT PHONE

---

7. Keeping people awake right after lunch is never an easy task.

I also identified items recovered from Tai, Fuk, and Luo Zhi Xiong at LAX and the Mak homes, zeroing in on the more consequential items, like the code word sheets; encryption laptop and diskettes; Tai's 1971 PLA photographs; trashed tasking lists; the Gu Wei Hao letters;[8] the dozens of locations Pu's 2332 cellphone number popped up; and photographs of Chi and Rebecca with PRC officials. That day ended with a discussion of Chi's wartime tracking of US warships in Hong Kong harbor, plans to retire there soon, and his China travel and discussions with Shouling about how best to avoid a PRC stamp in his US passport.

The next day began with Greg's request to question NCIS intelligence specialist Erin Abernathy out of order, to allow her to fly home that afternoon. Carney took the opportunity to note how long the defense cross-examinations had been taking.[9] Kaye joked, "I'm getting quite sensitive here. There's an implication I'm taking too long, and people might hate me." Yes, and yes! Erin discussed her review of the 926 USN-related documents in Chi's possession and his Hong Kong ship tracking list. When Erin finished, I stepped back up and confirmed that Chi had no documented navy- or ship-related hobbies, shooting down their lame rationale for his ship ledger. I also verified that we'd found the Maks' "go bag," filled with cash and travel documents, before telling stories of how frugal they were.

After confirming that PRCIS intelligence officer Pu Pei Liang shared his 2332 cellphone number with fellow officers Cai Hu and Yan Feng, I had my one moment of sweat. Greg had reorganized my evidence exhibit book in the order of his planned questions, but then changed that order, leaving me with a useless evidence exhibit book with no reference point. I looked like an idiot up there as I flailed around, looking for exhibits everyone else easily found in their logically numbered original versions. Finally, Greg took pity upon me, giving me an original version, and I was back on track.

---

8. I enjoyed reading these devastating letters implicating Chi, Rebecca, and Chung directly into the court record.
9. Unfortunately, it would continue to be a three-to-one defense-to-prosecution ratio for the remainder of the trial.

I introduced Chi's handwritten family tree,[10] Billy's "orangish-yellow health book" that carried Pu's tasking lists, DD(x) data Chi delivered to China in 2004, and the three conference discs he gave to Tai. After Judge Carney complimented Greg's efficiency, Greg responded, "Now I feel pressured!" to laughter. His self-depreciating humor and timing served him well with judge and jury. In contrast, Kaye seemed shrill and humorless; his few attempts at humor fell flat. It was obvious juror Tattooed Love Dog liked Greg, and despised Chi, Kaye, and Bednarski.

I continued dumping evidence on the jurors, imagining myself a truck backing up—*beep, beep, beep*—to drop another load: PRC officials' business cards—*beep*—sensitive USN documents—*beep*—PRCIS officer contact information—*beep*—Tai and Fuk discussing "Uncle Pu"—*beep*. I then read the transcript where Fuk told Billy to get Pu's help while in China:

> *Don't worry about Uncle Pu's side. Whatever you want to do, you can ask him to do it. There is no problem about it. You father had helped them a lot before in every aspect. Work. In every aspect. Work. He had never charged them. So, owing him 100 to 200,000, therefore you, therefore, he, he, he could, he had said that if there is anything, just tell them to do it at any time and they would do it.[11]*

Pu's favors included cars, drivers, money, airline tickets, medical services, and immigration documents. It was his encryption laptop and "group" that was charged with caring for Fuk's mother. After detailing Chi and Rebecca's lengthy conversation about retirement and transferring money to China, I concluded with DOJ's certification that the Maks were not registered agents of China.

Bednarski was again my inquisitor.[12] She quickly attacked, objecting to my "go bag" terminology and claims that Chi wasn't a ship hobbyist.

---

10. It demonstrated that Chi had lied on US immigration papers claiming he had no relatives in China. Three siblings remained there.

11. As I read transcripts into the record, the frequent "unintelligible" markings reminded me of how poor the quality of our microphones had been.

12. I wanted Kaye, whom I particularly disliked.

PRCIS officer Pu Pei Liang AUTHOR'S COLLECTION

She became testier with each of my qualifications to her poorly worded questions, trying to bait me by attacking my pride and posing obscure questions and faulty declarations. I quite enjoyed politely correcting her "confusion," demonstrating to the jury my efforts to cooperate as she became frustrated. Claiming I wasn't interested in the truth, she demanded to know why I hadn't interviewed witnesses in China.

Gaylord:	We're prohibited by treaty from doing that.
Bednarski:	So the answer would be "no"?
Gaylord:	The answer would be "no."

After I demonstrated that her claims that *South China Morning Post*'s reports of USN ship movements were wrong, whereas Chi's log entries were highly accurate, she used a "How dare you!" tone to bluff me into believing I needed to recant earlier statements.[13]

---

13. A tactic very familiar to me from decades of debate with my older sister Susan.

Bednarski: Now, what's intervened between January 20th of last year and now is you've learned about the *South China Morning Post*'s publication at the time of the comings and goings of all those ships?

Gaylord: I'm not sure what you mean by "intervene." I don't believe my answer has changed. Apparently, you think it has.

Her bluff called, she moved on to other unsupported defense "truths," line by line, boring our courtroom audience and frustrating herself before Judge Carney dismissed the jury, telling them:

I think I told you earlier that the first week is a little slow, tedious, cumbersome. Counsel have informed me that the agent's testimony is going to be the longest testimony of them all, so I don't want to scare you; "Oh, my gosh. What am I in for the next couple weeks?" But this is laying some of the foundation of the evidence that you're going to hear from other people. So, I appreciate you bearing with us.

Afterwards, Carney advised Kaye and Bednarski, "[W]ith all due respect, I think we're putting some of the jurors to sleep. They couldn't wait to get out of here."

On day four, Bednarski depicted Chi as an all-American immigrant who paid his taxes and didn't kick stray dogs, putting everyone to sleep yet again. Judge Carney suggested a break.[14] Upon return, Bednarski's silly, unfocused wordsmithing reached new heights. Finally, Greg asked in exasperation, "Your Honor, is there a question here?"

The courtroom chuckled in agreement. Judge Carney smiled and told Bednarski, "It's your examination, but we do need a question to which the agent can say 'yes' or 'no.'"

Unfazed, Bednarski continued droning on for hours. Judge Carney called for a lunch break and told Bednarski, "I think the jury needs a break. I sense they're not taking as many notes, and some are sleepy eyes."

---

14. I noticed Greg was always the first to suggest a break during his questioning—another skill the defense lacked.

After lunch I was replaced on the stand by retired two-star admiral Eric McVadon, for travel reasons.[15] He discussed Communist China's political and military policies and movements, providing a fascinating crash course on Chinese history.[16] When US war games were staged, he played the part of China—"Head Red." He and Greg discussed the Cultural Revolution and how college-educated intellectuals in Shanghai, like Chi and Rebecca, weren't allowed to leave China,[17] as trained engineers were desperately needed and forced to remain. McVadon confirmed that all Chinese defense companies served the state by stealing Western military secrets. He once gave a speech at the Center for Asian Pacific Studies (CAPS) and was pressured to reveal sensitive data. He didn't. He had been warned that CAPS was linked to the PLA.

Bednarski used a laughable backdrop kumbaya philosophy of "living together peaceably in our global world," sharing technology. It fell apart under Greg's crisp redirect: QED, EMALS, and DD(x) were *not* "dual use" technologies; 1960s PRC citizens could *not* leave for medical treatments; and unemployed PRC engineers did *not* exist there in the 1960s.[18] Bednarski's re-cross again compared EMALS to roller coasters.[19]

With me back on the stand, Judge Carney asked Bednarski how much longer her cross would be, stating "I am just anxious to finish the agent's testimony. He has been on and off the stand for several days. We are in agreement he will be finished tomorrow?"

Greg agreed. The defense did not.

Day five opened with Bednarski testifying in the form of posing accusatory questions. It provided a welcome contrast of demeanors as her frustration grew with each question. As the pot calling the kettle black, she accused *me* of mischaracterizing evidence to inflame passions. I wasn't biting. The cross ended with her in a very bad mood.

---

15. We wanted him to be able to fly home that evening.
16. The week previous, he had testified before Congress on China, Taiwan, and US relations.
17. Especially if they had foreign banking connections like Chi, whose father was a Hong Kong banker.
18. We knew Chi and Rebecca had received PRCIS training during their claimed periods of unemployment.
19. Defense attorneys really *will* say anything to win, truth be damned.

CAPS brochure PUBLIC DOCUMENT

Greg breezily conducted a stellar redirect, crisply demolishing each Bednarski assertion. To stop the bleeding, she began registering desperate, unsuccessful objections. We discussed the damning Gu Wei Hao letters. Bednarski's agitation increased. We covered Chi's sabotage of his handwriting sample. Angrier, louder objections. As Greg immediately and calmly rephrased a question she had objected to, we locked eyes in recognition: Bednarski was about to blow. Then Vesuvius roared forth. Bednarski charged up to Greg's left side, pointed her finger just inches from his ear, and shouted, "I object!"

Everyone held their breath. You could have heard a pin drop. Greg didn't flinch, turn, or say a word, calmly fixing his grinning eyes on mine.

Judge Carney reacted. "All right! Why don't we take a break. Ladies and gentlemen, could you give us about ten minutes, please?"

As the jury awkwardly filed out, Greg and I stared at each other, trying not to smirk. I wondered if Greg also had an older sister.

Judge Carney said, "Ms. Bednarski, I'm going to have to ask you not to be so dramatic. State your objections. A lot of your questions were inappropriate, too. And I just don't think it's helping either side for you to be as dramatic as you were."

I had to disagree with Judge Carney, as her hysterics definitely helped our side.

Greg explained that the defense had opened the door on these issues, not us. Bednarski offered no explanation.

When the jury returned, Greg continued his questioning, proving everything we wanted. I even explained how our people had helped defense linguists improve the quality of their work.[20] Greg then switched to a line of questioning I had suggested during pretrial planning to address outrageous defense claims we were targeting ethnic Chinese Americans. We had the perfect squad to counterattack against this slanderous tactic. Unlike other AUSAs, Greg listened to agents.[21] He ran with my idea, adding his unique comedic flair and timing to score big. Strangely, trial transcripts omit portions of this questioning, so I have herein supplemented it.[22]

Greg:	Agent Gaylord, do you have any bias against the defendant because he is Chinese?
Gaylord:	No.
Greg:	Can you give us evidence as to why that is true?
Gaylord:	Well, my co-case agent is Chinese American, and several other agents on my squad are Chinese American or Asian American.
Greg:	Okay. Anything else?
Gaylord:	In addition, several other agents on my squad are married to Asian Americans.
Greg:	Do you have any bias against the Chinese in general?
Gaylord:	No.

---

20. We had showed the defense linguists that headphones were superior to their earbuds, and how to improve equipment performance.
21. If I passed a note to Greg during trial, he read it and we discussed it. If Craig got the note first, he rolled his eyes, shot me a *You dunce* look, wadded it up, tossed it aside, and ordered, "Don't do that again!" I kept doing it. The arrogance!
22. I discovered other parts of trial transcripts that also inexplicably dropped portions of testimony.

Greg:	Why is that?
Gaylord:	I don't think I have any bias against any group, but if you want more specific examples, my wife is foreign-born and three-quarters Chinese.
Greg:	And you have two daughters who are nearly half Chinese, is that right?
Gaylord:	Yes.
Greg:	And does that mean all your in-laws are Chinese?
Gaylord:	Yes.
Greg:	Other than the fact that they're your in-laws, you don't have problems with Chinese in general? [courtroom laughter]
Gaylord:	I may have problems with an individual in-law, but that is *not* because they are Chinese. [more laughter, including from the defense table, judge, and jury]

With that "mic drop" moment—one of my proudest—we had won the jury and forever destroyed this detestable defense that the FBI, American society, and "the system," ad nauseam, is racist.

Before this point, prosecutors had followed the losing strategy of putting their heads down and hoping such charges would go away. Greg didn't. Years later, during a University of California at Irvine Law School evidence course Judge Carney taught, he told his students, "You could feel the air go out of the defense's sails, as they had been banking on this racism claim from the beginning."[23] This evil defense didn't surface again in that trial, Greg Chung's prosecution, or other similar ones. The FBI was far too diverse to level that racist charge. It also proved a turning point in the trial. Their foundational "racism!" defense pillar was pulverized in spectacular fashion. Bednarski's re-cross was halfhearted, asking me engineering questions that I was completely unqualified to answer. We broke for lunch. I was done, and boy was I hungry!

---

23. Greg and I were there to discuss our case and teach future lawyers to know their facts before making wild claims.

Our next witness was ICE Special Agent Josh Barnett, who introduced and authenticated the Maks' immigration files. I wanted Josh on and off the stand quickly.[24] Ron Kaye's explanation for Chi's lies on his immigration forms was flimsy: Chi Mak didn't lie; he just ran out of room on the forms to tell the truth.[25] Craig's redirect effectively mocked Kaye's claims, and client.

Next came linguist Len Pi. Because his answers tended to provide more answer than requested, Craig struggled to keep Len on track.[26] Len discussed the translating, publishing, and certification of verbatim translations and their extensive quality-control process, noting that he'd never seen a case with as many challenges as ours, given the switching between Cantonese, Shanghainese, and Mandarin dialects. To explain the many verbatim reviews he had done, Len declared, "I *am* the linguist."[27]

Testimony turned to Tai's call with Pu about visiting China. All FBI linguists had agreed that Tai told Pu he was with "Red Flower of North America." It was the only reasonable translation for the word "Hong Hua." Bednarski struggled with Len's indirect, long answers, so when he digressed to Emperor Chin's standardized written language of characters over two thousand years ago, and that China was named after him, she asked Judge Carney for help. I chuckled, knowing her plight. But her bigger problem was selling Len her "theory" that Tai had said linguistically different and nonsensical phrases that she claimed meant "Wang Prosperity." Len knew his own language.

When Bednarski's visible frustration grew, Carney called for a break and told Len, "Try to be as directly responsive to the question that's asked as possible. I understand you don't like her questions. I can understand you might think her questions are misleading, her questions are incomplete."[28] He assured Len the prosecution would get the chance to correct any misperceptions. Len apologized.

---

24. ICE mishandled the DD(x) evidence, losing us a charge on the one technology we could prove Chi Mak had succeeded in directly transferring to the PRC.

25. Yet he found room to list in-laws in China, about whom *no* information was sought.

26. Len was atypical of most of our Chinese linguists in one respect: He enjoyed talking about his accomplishments.

27. From that moment on, our squad referred to Len as "The Linguist." He loved it!

28. I loved Len's moxie! He didn't want to participate in the lie he saw Bednarski trying to construct.

After that, Len addressed Bednarski as "ma'am," but kept challenging her questions. She closed by implying I was influencing Len's translations, but he and Craig dismantled that deception.[29] Len explained the Standard Telegraphic Code (STC), which uses four numbers to definitively identify each Chinese character, thereby defeating the confusion the defense wished to create in jurors' minds. Mak and Mai might sound different in Cantonese and Mandarin, but they were the same word, character, and STC numerical designation. "Television" means one thing. Separated into "tele" and "vision," they mean very different things. The Chinese word for "Red Flower" was the same. Separation of the consonants rendered it meaningless. This explanation blew Bednarski's premise out of the water, making her look manipulative and deceptive. Len stepped down triumphant and happy.

Last that day was Power Paragon's facility security officer, Bob Miller, who covered Chi's training, which dictated that "Classified and NOFORN material shall not be removed from the confines of the company except on approved official business and the authorization of the security officer." Chi neither sought nor received any such authorizations. Miller also witnessed Chi's one moment of access to the classified conference materials *after* the Philadelphia symposium.[30] Chi had no opportunity to copy them, period. Greg asked, "If you knew Mr. Mak was going to send this information to China, would you have been concerned?"[31] Miller said "Yes!"

Another strong finish for the prosecution as we headed into the weekend.

---

29. With Craig still having to tap Len's brakes on occasion.
30. They came from an ONR conference titled, "Third Naval Symposium on Electric Machines" and were stored in Bob Miller's work safe.
31. This became a standard type of question that would be repeated throughout the trial, with devastating effect.

CHAPTER 29

"MIT Has No Keg Parties?"

RON KAYE BEGAN THE NEXT WEEK BY CALLING BOB MILLER A LIAR, without producing any proof. But Miller proved the opposite, having documented everything. So, Kaye turned into a frustrated, condescending jackass, and the jury didn't like it. His cross ended on a sour note. Greg's redirect mocked Kaye and reaffirmed Miller.

Then came Power Paragon's king and queen of compliance, Vice President Mike Benthale, a former export compliance official, and Cindy Baleno, the current export control coordinator. They confirmed that *all* of Chi's work was covered by compliance export-control laws, which required authorization before anything was released. That message was reinforced "through posters, pictures hanging on every wall, every machine, every door, every exit, every entrance."[1] Chi never sought authority to release the papers or their data and repeatedly lied to Cindy in emails concerning his intentions.

Greg's redirect cut to the chase: "Can an engineer create a public domain exception by preparing a paper at a conference without approval and thereafter saying, 'Well, it's out in the open now so I can do what I want with it?'" "No!" Benthale declared. For extra points, Greg played a training video Chi had watched of an engineer arrested at a US airport customs station for trying to export a defense article.[2] It was beautiful! Cindy had won the day.[3]

---

1. We showed the jury photographs Omar had taken of all these posted reinforcement messages.
2. We loved this video. Someone suggested we should pass out popcorn to the jurors when they watched it.
3. She was one of this trial's heroes.

Bob Gerrity, head of the China Naval Forces Division in the Strategic, Assessment and Warning Department of the Office of Naval Intelligence, then took the stand. He spoke quickly, so Greg joked, "We know that Washington has a lot of fast talkers, so just for our benefit, slow down." The jury laughed. Gerrity smiled, and proceeded to share his knowledge of China's naval abilities.[4] He provided a fascinating tutorial on the needs and goals of the People's Liberation Army Navy (PLAN). Using a map we set up, Gerrity stepped off the stand to lecture the judge, jury, and defense attorneys in a classroom setting with him as instructor, lending him a certain gravitas.

PLAN's main goal was to overcome US intervention and conquer Taiwan. Its best, most modern weaponry was stationed across from Taiwan, and its troops were trained for amphibious landings. China's ambitions also sought to dominate the waters of the "First Island Chain"—western Japan, Taiwan, the Philippines, and Indonesia—then the "Second Island Chain"—eastern Japan, the Marianas, Micronesia, and beyond. Its only real opposition was the US Seventh Fleet, with its most powerful weapon, aircraft carriers.[5] China's answer was its "Assassin's Mace" program to build weapons to slow and/or sink them, like "carrier killer" ICBMs, quiet diesel submarines, and smart mines.

China's most-needed technologies matched Chi's collection, and its breakthroughs matched Chi's access to each. In reality, Chi worked for PLAN and America footed the R&D bills. Gerrity ridiculed defense claims that the Russian aircraft carrier that China had bought, the *Varyag*, would become a floating casino. And Kaye's suggestion that PLAN was building its navy for humanitarian purposes was devastatingly mocked by Greg.[6]

Greg: As someone who studies naval ships, are you aware of any need for ships responding to, say, a tsunami to have Quiet Electric Drive?

---

4. To avoid messy classification challenges, we had asked Gerrity to base all his judgments upon open-source reporting.
5. The Nimitz-class aircraft carrier carries between 5,000 and 5,200 sailors and airmen.
6. Years later, this "casino" was renamed the *Liaoning* and hit international waters as China's first aircraft carrier.

Gerrity: No.

Greg: There is no need for them to sneak up on the victims?

Gerrity: Correct.

Greg: Are you aware of submarines being used in humanitarian efforts?

Gerrity: I couldn't imagine it.

Greg: You couldn't beach them on the shore?

Gerrity: You can . . . once. [courtroom laughter]

Greg: Even though you are not an engineer, would you recognize there is a substantial difference between flinging a fighter jet into the air on a very short, short deck of an aircraft carrier versus sending a train down a stationary line?

Gerrity: Tremendous difference.

Greg: So you would probably also agree that a roller coaster isn't much like an aircraft carrier?

Gerrity: I would agree.

Greg: Have you ever seen an F-14 launched from a roller coaster?

Gerrity: No.

The jury's continuing laughter, tittering, knowing smirks, nods, and smiles made it clear they enjoyed Greg's effortless filleting of Kaye.

After Gerrity was Mal Zerden, defense controls analyst for the Directorate of Defense Trade Controls, DOS. When he left DC for California, he took off having one role; due to DOJ treachery, he landed with another. Greg and Craig had recently preserved challenged precedent dictating that DOS was the finder of fact regarding what technologies were on the US Munitions List (USML). But days before trial, DOJ/CES issued an unsolicited reversal of its own position, now declaring that the USML question should be decided by a jury. This arbitrary and capricious decision endangered our most serious ITAR charges. What was wrong with these people? Whose side were they on?[7] Zerden had

---

7. Again, remember the warning Los Angeles USAO attorneys gave me about DOJ/CES.

to pivot from being the decider to the influencer. Thankfully, he did a fine job, outlining USML categories and functions.[8] He also confirmed "a standing arms embargo on the PRC" ever since its 1989 Tiananmen Square massacre. Kaye's cross was ineffective.

Up next was our second linguist, Rick Yoo, who confirmed the only possible translation for the word Tai spoke, "Hong Hua," was "Red Flower." On cross, Bednarski claimed Tai spoke the made-up word, "Hong Fa," supposedly meaning "Wang's Prosperity," and accused Rick of being my puppet.[9]

On redirect, Craig demonstrated Rick's integrity by discussing a different intercept's translation where he changed Rebecca's statement from "This is illegal" to an "unintelligible" notation, out of caution and fairness. Months earlier, this had pleased the defense and frustrated us, but it was the right thing to do. Now, it demonstrated Rick's integrity.[10]

Stinging from Craig's rebuttal, Bednarski went into attack mode:

Bednarski: You agree, don't you, that a linguist listening can be influenced by what somebody else says they heard, right?

Rick: When we work, we do not work simultaneously on conversation.

Bednarski: Your Honor, I'd just ask that the question be answered.

Rick: (excitedly and loudly) Your question is loaded! [courtroom laughter]

Craig: (smiling) I'll object on those grounds.

That day, Rick displayed more integrity than Chi's entire defense team, and finished victorious.

Gunnar Newquist then took the stand. His NCIS training and experience were impressive, having done criminal and CI work in the United

---

8. It didn't stop me from cursing DOJ/CES. Were they corrupt or incompetent? My answer? "Yes and Yes!"

9. It was defense attorneys who were dictating translations to their linguists. Exhibit A: Fantasy word "Hong Fa."

10. That's how you make lemons into lemonade!

States, at sea on USN warships, and for "three wonderful years," in Naples, Italy.[11] Gunnar was now one of NCIS's most experienced agents, although you wouldn't know it from his humble testimony. And he was *still* making nice with Chi, identifying him in court with a compliment, "Mr. Mak is wearing a nice blue tie." To close out the day, Gunnar confirmed this was a CI case until Chi copied discs, countering defense claims that we prolonged our CI investigation to exploit supposedly laxer standards.[12]

This next day was all Gunnar's. First, he discussed Chi's initial four-and-a-half-hour interview and introduced its videotape with closed captioning, which proved how well Chi was treated.[13] It also proved how dishonest Chi was throughout and why Gunnar used a generic QED document to question him about the LAX disc.

Then he discussed Chi's third interview on Sunday, October 30, which had included Omar.[14] It was cordial because "Mr. Mak loves to talk about technology," and they let him, in order to build goodwill. Chi eventually became embarrassed by his many obvious lies, so he began issuing corrections: His discs were meant for Pu Pei Liang within the PRC government's "Science and Technology community"; Chi had been carrying restricted data to the PRC since 1983, including EMALS, AEGIS SPY-1 radar power schematics, QED, and other technologies; Chi and Rebecca were recruited by the PLA in college;[15] Tai joined the PLA as a propaganda officer;[16] and via Billy, Pu sent trashed tasking lists to Chi, which he tore up and threw away.

---

11. I learned Gunnar began his CI career at NPS in Monterey, protecting student and civilian professors, at the same time I was studying Vietnamese at the US Army Defense Language Institute in Monterey.

12. The idea that CI investigations have looser rules is preposterous. Criminal cases are much easier to make.

13. Craig always worried Gunnar's aggressive end-of-interview stance would hurt us. I didn't. Anyone viewing the interview saw how absurdly obtuse and insulting Chi's answers became. Besides, the jury clearly liked Gunnar.

14. Our second short interview of Chi on October 29 was inconsequential, with no relevant information exchanged.

15. Shanghai Jiao Tong University.

16. This was before we or Chi knew we had recovered Tai's photographs as a propaganda officer in the search of Tai's home.

Next came Kaye's cross-examination. I was a little concerned because Gunnar is an affable guy and had been on friendly terms with Kaye, a snake who would stroke your ego one minute, and sink a dagger into your back the next. I worried Gunnar would let down his guard. I needn't have.

Kaye began by calling Gunnar a liar who was hell-bent on obtaining a confession. Gunnar countered, "The goal was to learn the truth." But Kaye's narrative was painting Gunnar as an unethical careerist. Big mistake! Gunnar's ire got up and stayed there. The cross became a row as Judge Carney repeatedly sustained Greg's "argumentative" objections. Then Kaye introduced the Wen Ho Lee case, *again*. At a sidebar, Carney sustained Greg's objections of irrelevance.[17] Kaye disingenuously referred to the equally unrelated Katrina Leung case, charging it "fell apart before you interviewed my client," implying undue FBI pressure because of that previous failed case.[18]

Greg objected to the defense's repeated referrals to both trials: "Those cases are notorious, but they have nothing to do with this case. There is no basis in the evidence to believe there's any similarity between this case and those cases." Judge Carney advised he was "privy to" the Leung case, that sensitive sources were involved, and Kaye shouldn't believe what he read in the papers. Translation: Evidence of Leung's guilt had been suppressed to protect sensitive sources and national security.[19] Kaye's questions "crossed the line from fair to unfair to suggest that that was a botched prosecution and they realized they had no case and then they withdrew the charges." Carney would halt questioning if it went overboard, warning Kaye that witness badgering must stop.

When the jury returned, Carney reminded them that witness answers were evidence; lawyer questions were not. Kaye resumed his cross to allege that Gunnar had "credibility" issues. Gunnar responded by pointing out Kaye's deceptive transcript citations. Kaye was losing the jury to Gunnar.

---

17. Ironically, we did have some telephone number links between the two cases but never used them as evidence.

18. He was right about pressure but wrong about its direction and purpose. The Leung case proved an obstacle to our investigation. Its demons had to be exorcised before we could succeed.

19. He was right. Leung prosecutors would have won but for the wackadoodle leftist judge they were saddled with.

Kaye: I'm just saying the accusation for a sixty-five-year-old man who's brought down in handcuffs in the middle of the night, that when you start accusing him of passing technical documents to the Chinese, that it would be a particularly alarming event?

Gunnar: Especially if you have been doing it since 1983.

Kaye: Do you think it would be less alarming, Mr. Newquist, to have two agents, one from the Federal Bureau of Investigation, one from NCIS, both around six feet tall, both, as we saw, ultimately yelling and laughing and taunting, don't you believe that even if an individual didn't pass any documents, don't you think it would have a kind of an alarming effect on them?

Gunnar: Again, if you are telling the truth, you have nothing to fear.

Kaye's questions became so meandering that at one point Carney had to rephrase his questions and point out Kaye's unproductive lines of questioning. Finally, Carney called for a break, telling the jury, "I would like to talk to the lawyers; see if we can pick it up a little bit."

Carney: Mr. Kaye, I'm worried we're losing the jury. . . . And it's not proper for me to tell you how to try your case. I'm hoping you can do it quicker.

Kaye: . . . I'm doing the best I can.

Carney: . . . You are taking more time with him [Gunnar] on cross than his own direct examination. Just as a matter of fairness, you know, I'm not going to let the government take Mr. Mak's witnesses and take twice as long. I don't think that's fair. And I just think the points you are making; you've got to make them quicker. And again, except for maybe one or two jurors, no one is taking notes and they're not even looking at the witness. They're not looking at you, and that concerns me.

Kaye: I'm doing the best I can. That's all I can say, Your Honor.
         I think that this is one of the most critical cross-examina-
         tions, and I think it's effective, and my partner thinks it's
         effective, and we're doing the best we can.[20]

The Ron Kaye Show was receiving terrible ratings, but clueless Kaye
ignored the judge's free legal advice, continuing Gunnar's re-cross until
he had flailed the final ounce of flesh from this long dead filly.

The following morning on redirect, Greg punctured every false trial
balloon Kaye had launched. You could figuratively hear a *pop!* as he
pricked each one.[21] Kaye's re-cross accomplished nothing. Did he still
believe he was doing his best? Even though Gunnar had clearly tri-
umphed that day, Kaye told the press, his willing co-conspirators, that he
had nailed Gunnar for lying on the stand. The media had witnessed otherwise, yet reported Kaye's lies as fact.[22] We'd won every witness on the
stand, yet media reports parroting defense claims misled everyone outside
the courtroom to believe we were losing, and badly. Sal and I constantly
fielded panicked calls from FBIHQ and FBILA asking why our case was
tanking. The defense was gasping, yet we were being pressured to accept
a plea bargain. All because USAO policy prohibited public discussions
of the trial, which produced a one-sided, warped public narrative. To win
such future cases, especially the close ones, this must change.[23]

After Gunnar came our parade of SMEs. First was Nick Mikus,
NCIS investigative computer specialist, to describe the PRCIS encryption
on Tai and Billy's laptop.[24] In a nice bit of show-and-tell, Craig opened
the disc on a laptop and projected it on a screen for the whole courtroom

---

20. I was half expecting Kaye to whine, "But my mom loves me and thinks I'm doing a great job!"
21. I marveled at how Greg could ask clarifying questions that mocked defense arguments as
moronic, without saying so. His rapid-fire redirect and cross questions riddled the body of defense
arguments with verbal bullets.
22. The worst press offender by far was *Los Angeles Times* reporter H. G. Reza, who wrote whatever
drivel Kaye spouted, no matter how contrary to the facts. He and Kaye were clearly trying to influence jury and public opinion.
23. The DOJ and USAO must drop this restriction. At least the prosecuting agency, i.e., FBI, should
publicly refute false defense claims. Yet, the defense constantly accuses *us* of trying to influence the
jury and public.
24. We were very fortunate to find Nick after FBI CEAU supervisors and agents completely
chickened out!

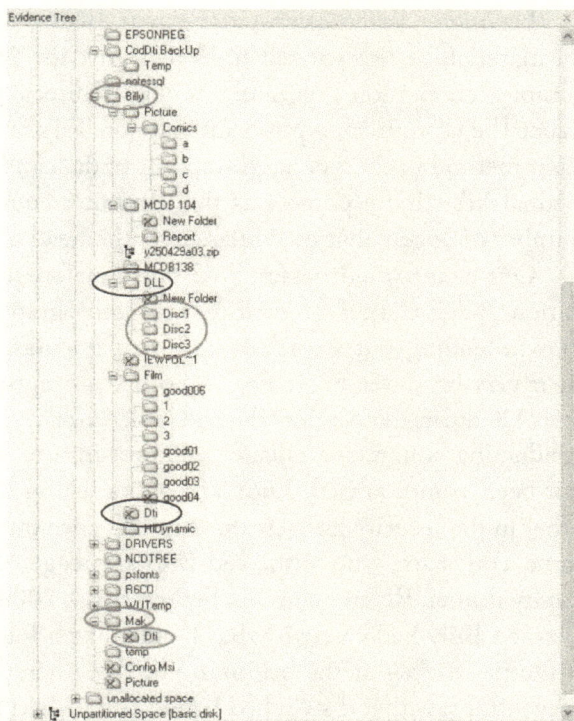

Billy Mak's encryption
decision tree on the
Pu Pei Liang laptop
TRIAL EXHIBIT 25

to see each file. Billy's UCLA biology work and music files opened up, no problem. But the folder Billy deceptively renamed "DLL," containing Chi's technical data, would not.[25] Billy named it "DLL" to disguise it as a "Dynamic Link Library," a drivers file that also looks like gibberish. Mikus explained the encryption program's two files of "Code" and "Decode," "block ciphers," Tai's diskette encryption keys, and how adding a "compression layer" triggered a complex algorithm scrambling the data. He walked us through Billy's encryption steps and the decryption process that revealed the previously deleted 2004 encrypted DD(x) files within the laptop. Mikus closed with the declaration that cracking this code without the diskette encryption keys would be nearly impossible because the number of code combinations were "16 to the 255th power."

---

25. The PRCIS creator had originally named it "DTI" to mimic a commercially available encryption program.

Having no defense computer expert, Bednarski had no proper rebuttal material, so she winged it. Why didn't the Maks use an even *more*
complex encryption program?[26] Craig's redirect quickly dispatched that
issue: The custom encryption software on Tai's laptop was the most efficient method to encrypt large amounts of data and make it unbreakable.[27]
Bednarski's silly response was the computer equivalent of counting the
number of angels that could dance on the head of a pin.[28]

Our next two witnesses, SSG personnel, required special accommodation. Judge Carney ordered that no photographs be taken or sketches
drawn, lending our witnesses an air of gravitas. First up, representing
their very best, was Scott Frye, who had surreptitiously filmed Mr. Luo
at LAX during and after Tai and Fuk's arrest. Scott believed Luo was
conducting countersurveillance and "vetting" to verify Tai and Fuk had
not been compromised. Luo's and Fuk's faking unfamiliarity with each
other in the security line screamed intelligence training. Next to the stand
came Tom Kim, who witnessed Billy's passage of materials to Chi at a
family dinner. Referencing his September 4, 2004, surveillance log, Kim
testified Billy had carried "what looked like a folded-up newspaper in a
white plastic bag at the beginning of the lunch. And after lunch, when
they left, I saw that it switched hands. [Chi Mak] took that package out."
His log report stated:

> *12:10 p.m.   Surveillance observed the twosome walking toward the
> above-mentioned location. At this time, surveillance also observed
> Mak's brother Tai Wang Mak, and his family, meeting up with Chi
> Mak and Rebecca Mak. Surveillance also observed Tai Mak's son
> carrying a package wrapped in plastic, possibly a newspaper, inside
> the restaurant.*

---

26. Why use a code that takes a hundred years to break when you can find one that takes a thousand?
27. This custom program was placed on Pu's laptop just before he gave it to Tai to take with him
to America.
28. She compared "impossible to crack" encryption programs with those "even more impossible to
crack"!

1:08 p.m. Surveillance observed the entire group exit restaurant and talking outside the restaurant. Surveillance observed Chi Mak now carrying the above-mentioned package that Tai Mak's son originally had.

Chi mentioned this exchange later during his call with Tai, and then to Gunnar and Omar, describing receiving an "orangish-yellow health book" carrying Pu's tasking lists, which Chi angrily tore up and tossed. Kaye's cross couldn't touch either of these witnesses.

Then came our last linguist, Henry Dean, with impeccable credentials. In 2004, he traveled to China as FBI Director Mueller's interpreter. Henry was humble and definitive, stating, "The word used by Mr. Mak is Hong Hua. In Mandarin it means Red Flower. . . . If you investigate

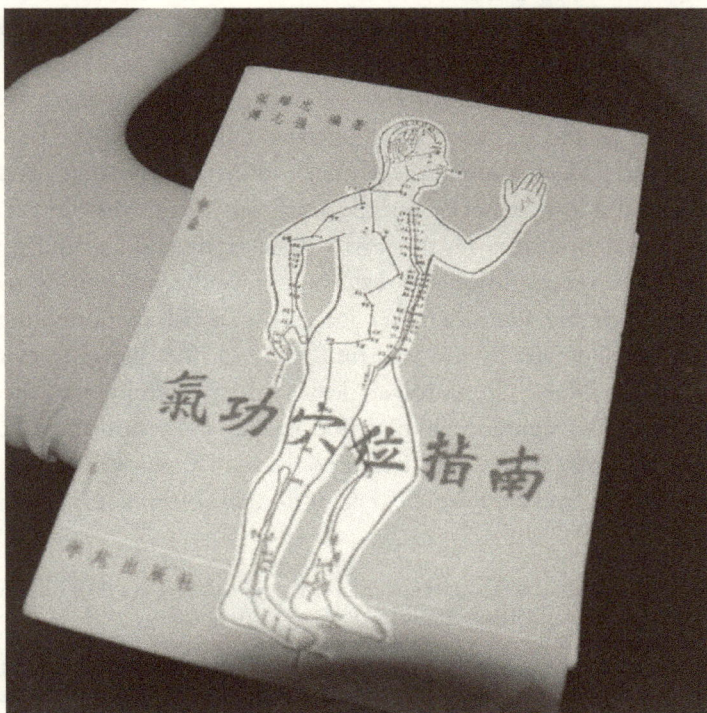

"Health book" that carried Pu Pei Liang's taskings for Chi Mak TRIAL EXHIBIT 54

the dictionary, there is only one entry for this compound word, H-o-n-g H-u-a, and the only meaning is 'Red Flower.'"

Bednarski's clumsy cross initially addressed him as "Mr. Henry." And in a strangely helpful manner, she dug into Henry's impressive résumé.[29] Then she implied his translations were improperly influenced by Len, prosecutors, and me. Bednarski was very poor at reading the room. Henry appeared the most honorable of men. Then she debated him over the pronunciation of Chinese words, again regarding "Red Flower." Her badgering went so far astray that Henry asked the judge, "Do I have to answer this question? Because it's not related to the part that I listened to." Craig's redirect took Henry through other damning intercepts, visibly upsetting Bednarski, whose continued badgering of likable Henry had only damaged her cause.[30]

Greg then called Colleen McKay to the stand.[31] She recounted her twenty-five years as an FBI CI Special Agent and her advanced education in Asian Studies.[32] I was so blessed she was our case analyst. We'd made a formidable team for thirteen years, accomplishing many firsts in the Vietnamese and Chinese CI programs, and both relished sticking thumbs in the PRC regime's eyes. Colleen knew exactly what needed to be done, and did it, whether or not the work was "sexy." She did the hard, small stuff that produces results when done right and faithfully, never receiving the full recognition she deserved. Now she was getting some.

Colleen humbly identified her job as "to assist in evaluating evidence." What she actually did was find and link the disparate evidence that proved the Maks' China travel, despite their attempts to conceal it, through secondary evidence like airline stubs, sticky notes, credit card and hotel receipts, itineraries, frequent-flyer-mile reports, dated photos, train, movie, and laundry tickets, and email references. Our squad

---

29. It seemed like bad defense tactics. Henry had interpreted Mueller's meetings with the PRC ministers of foreign affairs, public security, and state security, among others.
30. Greg's nickname for Bednarski was that used for a particularly famous NFL linebacker.
31. Regarding Colleen's testimony, Judge Carney declared, "We anticipate she'll take a half hour on direct and then cross an hour. . . . That was my attempt to be funny." His not-so-subtle message to the verbose defense went right over their heads.
32. Prior to the Bureau, Colleen had also been a highly respected police officer in the State of Washington.

vacuum cleaner approach, paired with her insightful analysis, produced indisputable travel summaries. Carrying in two banker boxes full of this evidence, Colleen identified nine Chi-and-Rebecca trips to Mainland China between 1980 and 2004, some of which were doubly damning—Hong Kong hotel receipts billed the Maks for calls to Pu Pei Liang's 2332 number; and photographs of Chi and Rebecca with PRC nuclear navy official Ma Fu Bang and wife at their Beijing home in 2000. Colleen had found the critical Gu Wei Hao letters, the original code word sheet, previous US passports, *and* Shouling's tasking list.

Bednarski's cross proved an interesting contrast between the older and younger professional women. One dedicated to truth, the other, not so much. Bednarski claimed the Maks didn't hide their China travel. So why didn't they ever fly there directly?[33] Chi's intercepted conversations with Shouling confirmed their deceptive purposes.[34]

Bednarski's cross closed with a whimper.

Adding insult to injury, Greg's brisk redirect emphasized Bednarski's failure, driving it home by establishing that a "Griffith Park Observatory" photo Bednarski had earlier referred to depicted Chi Mak with Gu Wei Hao.

Although we'd met this SME in person only the night before, it was immediately apparent Rudy Guerin and Greg Staples were *muy simpático*. Both were witty, hard-drinking, irreverent, skeptical men. Rudy was a recently retired FBI section chief of East Asian CI and acting assistant director of CI Division Operations, a Special Agent for thirty years. He'd worked a virtual Who's Who of US spy investigations, including the "Larry" Wu-Tai Chin case, the only previous, large PRC espionage case concluding with a conviction.[35] During Rudy's five-hour interview of Chin at his home, he had confessed to betraying the United States since the Korean War![36] Rudy testified that upcoming defense witness

---

33. They always flew through other Asian cities first, like Tokyo, Manila, Seoul, Taipei, and Singapore.
34. Sensitive reporting indicated Chi was told to conceal his China trips to avoid US intelligence scrutiny.
35. It had been a drought since then. Chin killed himself before sentencing by tying a garbage bag over his head.
36. A CIA employee, Chin wasn't identified as a PRC double agent until *after* his retirement.

I. C. Smith did *not* play the substantive role he'd publicly claimed in the Chin investigation. Rudy had also worked elements of the Aldrich Ames investigation, the case of a traitorous CIA officer responsible for at least nine covert US agents' deaths in the Soviet Union. He'd also worked investigations of Robert Hanssen and Earl Pitts, FBI agents working for the Soviets. Rudy was even awarded designation as CIA National HUMINT Collector of the Year.[37]

During his testimony, Rudy described stages of the typical espionage interview, from initial denial to slow, painstaking admissions and confessions. And the Mak case perfectly fit the PRCIS model: agent selection, family involvement, PRC meetings, handler duties, data encryption, and technologies targeted to tasking lists. Greg knew how to ask, and Rudy knew how to answer. It proved a seamless triumph, burying Chi's claims of innocence and being a "good immigrant." Greg and Rudy were clearly in their element, enjoying a triumphant performance that alarmed the defense. They continued hammering nails in Chi's coffin: The Guangzhou address Chi Mak had "stayed at" during one trip belonged to the Ministries of Public Security and State Security;[38] and the Maks' post-arrest lies were classic, practiced "cover stories." As Greg concluded his direct, I *almost* pitied Kaye.

Kaye opened with the idea of "a little bit of Chinese history just for introduction": the Four Modernizations, Premier Deng Xiaoping, Chinese immigration to the United States, and academic sharing and exchange. Rudy countered: "I don't see a lot of sharing going on. It seems to be a one-way street," a line I had always wanted to say. Kaye was in over his head! When he cited the US Congress Cox Report as authoritative, Rudy responded, "Okay. How many cases did [the members of Congress] work? I bet they didn't work a single case." Courtroom laughter ensued.

Kaye tried to distinguish between PRC government and commercial efforts to obtain technology.[39] Rudy shot back, "[M]ost of the Chinese

---

37. This award goes to those who have handled a human asset of high value to great effect for America's benefit.
38. Roughly the communist totalitarian government's equivalent of our FBI and CIA.
39. Did Kaye understand that "PRC" meant *People's* Republic of China, a Communist Party totalitarian dictatorship?

commercial is state owned, so it would be government anyway. . . . The commercial section is allowed to use the intelligence services to get whatever they want." Kaye foolishly posited scenarios of PRC officials bribing, cajoling, and blackmailing Americans in China to provide information.[40] Then he overgeneralized, claiming "All ethnic Chinese engineers and scientists in the US receive tasking lists from China."[41] Rudy replied, "No, I wouldn't go that far. You are making it sound more dastardly than I am!" The courtroom burst out laughing.

Getting nowhere, Kaye changed tack, falsely declaring that Rudy had falsely accused an innocent man in the Hanssen spy case. But Rudy had actually exonerated that man. Exasperated, Kaye started to crack. After one especially convoluted Kaye query, Greg objected, "The question is incomprehensible!" The entire courtroom broke into open, knowing laughter, having heard too many nonsensical Kaye questions. Judge Carney ruled "Sustained!"

Kaye now descended into childishness. "Not everyone who left China to live in Hong Kong for a while, later coming to the US, was a spy, right?" And when he began mixing up the facts of past spy cases, Rudy had to correct him.

Kaye's next rabbit hole claimed all engineers, Chinese or otherwise, are quiet and solitary; therefore, Chi's life "under the radar" was not suspicious. Rudy replied, "If you are saying because they are scientists, they lead a quiet life—I have a brother who is an engineer. He doesn't lead a quiet life." Kaye countered that "nerds" and "tech geeks" stay at home and "don't go out and party with the keg . . . in college." Astonished, Rudy replied, "MIT has no keg parties? I'm not going there [loud courtroom laughter]. I'm not going to stereotype people because of their high IQ that they're nerds or they don't party." Rudy had turned Kaye into a joke, and everyone but Kaye was in on it.

Kaye retorted, "Chinese people who lead quiet lives are not necessarily spies, are they?" Rudy answered, "No." I'm sure Kaye dimly considered that a win, but he had run into a brick wall of his own making. When

---

40. Reminding the jury that China was an aggressive technology collector seemed like poor defense strategy to me.
41. Just imagine the furor if the US government ever made such a claim.

he asserted PRC border customs was tough, Rudy answered, "No. . . . I just walked right through. They stamped my passport, and that was it. Nobody asked me a question."[42] Rudy mocked Kaye's stereotyping of Chinese, during which Kaye had implied that people with foreign accents were suspect. The Greg-and-Rudy redirect show proved a tour de force, shredding Kaye's credibility in a blitzkrieg of wit and common sense, even using the Cox Report against him: "The political, governmental, military and commercial activities of the PRC are controlled by the overlapping bureaucracies [of the] CCP, the State and the People's Liberation Army."[43]

The next witness, Chris Pluhar, our FBI Computer Analysis and Response Team (CART) Special Agent, described his role: "Preserve and process digital evidence for the purpose of supporting investigations ongoing in the FBI." He explained how digital evidence was seized, preserved, and copied, the latter process being called "hashing," in order to maintain evidence in its original form. He detailed his examination of all digital evidence, from the encryption program placed on Tai's computer in China on April 9, 2001, prior to his immigration to the United States, to the encryption of the LAX disc on October 25, 2005, and all digital actions in between, including the DD(x) data. When printed out, the DD(x) data filled a large, four-inch-thick binder, sobering evidence of all the sensitive information Chi had delivered to China on the 2004 trip.[44] Chris also confirmed that Tai could *not* have accessed the disc's data in Hong Kong to help him "buy QED books" for Chi. Bednarski's cross again proved impotent.

The jury was dismissed while we stayed to discuss trial scheduling for the remaining four Mak defendants. Greg said we were ready, declaring, "We're a well-oiled machine." We also recommended, and Judge Carney agreed, that defense SME Thomas Lipo should be warned against self-incrimination before his testimony the next day because of evidence

---

42. Kaye's argument was that the data encryption was done to sneak Chi's stolen technologies *past* PRC authorities. Hilarious.

43. Per the Cox Report.

44. Again, the USAO should have charged Chi with stealing and transporting *each* DD(x) article to China. Sensitive reporting indicated that Chi had reveled in the praise the PRCIS heaped upon him for that "patriotic work."

we'd uncovered that he'd also wrongly published and released ITAR-restricted QED materials. Kaye should have sought a reasonable plea bargain. We were burying them. But he didn't, and wouldn't. Why? Because he didn't have Chi's best interests at heart. His primary agenda was two-fold: forward their far-left anti–law enforcement political agenda; and increase business. They wanted to represent more than just drug dealers. I'm glad, because the skittish USAO/DOJ would have jumped at any opportunity for a plea deal. Chi Mak, who was paying for every hour of this charade, now became their victim. Of course, I felt no pity for him, just disgust for his attorneys.

CHAPTER 30

Closing Bang, Opening Whimper

As the third week began, Judge Carney allowed all FBI personnel who had testified to watch the trial. I was happy they could see the results of their years of hard work. CI agents from FBILA and surrounding Resident Agencies were already watching. Sal and I also wanted the jury to see all these FBI employees showing up in support. Defense SME Professor Lipo of the University of Wisconsin at Madison took the stand after Judge Carney informed him of his Fifth Amendment rights.[1] Once again, our impeachment research would pay off.

Lipo's résumé was impressive: professor of electrical and computer engineering; author of over 450 papers and 3 books; sponsor of over 50 graduating PhD students (including 6 from China!); winner of 35 awards; and holder of 35 patents. He testified that he and his students performed "generic research" and "directed research" for the National Surface Warfare Center and Office of Naval Research (ONR), including EMALS and QED, with no security clearances required. He'd never even heard the term "NOFORN." He also claimed academic freedom to publish anything he discovered from this work, including QED. It sounded very damaging to our cause. He was the defense witness who worried me most. I didn't envy Greg, believing Lipo's expertise and engineering jargon would make cross-examination difficult and complicated.[2]

---

1. Lipo took the stand out of order due to defense scheduling conflicts.
2. During trial strategy discussions, if Greg nixed one of my ideas, it was usually based upon his reasoning, "If it confuses the jury, we lose. If it's not clear and easily understandable, the defense wins."

But Lipo had a weakness, and Greg possessed a brilliant cross strategy to sink him, which I named "Show me the money!" Chi had handled all of Lipo's government contracts. No Chi, no dough. It also came out that Lipo's work was largely "within the civilian sector"; his work never addressed warships or military applications, and he was totally ignorant of export-control laws.[3] When Lipo claimed his USN work had no value, Greg lowered the boom.

Greg: So when you get a request from ONR for assistance, it's for a military purpose, is it not?

Lipo: Yes . . .

Greg: Sir, the United States Navy is not paying you to engage in purely academic exercises, are they?

Lipo: No.

Greg: And you understand that the United States Navy wants quiet submarines. That's not a big mystery to you, is it?

Lipo: No.

Greg: So [QED] Phase One does have value?

Lipo: Oh, yes.

Professor Lipo then admitted his compartmentalized QED research was meant "to reduce structure borne noise" in submarines, completely contradicting his earlier declarations. He'd never even seen the classified Chi Mak paper he was defending. Lipo's testimony matched a defense witness pattern: Reversals came once they saw *all* the evidence. Kaye and Bednarski fed their witnesses incomplete information in order to tailor testimony to the defense narrative. Greg ended with a demonstration that Lipo had published a paper containing American Superconductor Corporation export-controlled information without authorization, and three telling questions.

---

3. Greg: "Now, you have published a paper with export-controlled information in it?" Lipo: "I don't think that's relevant since I don't understand export control. I don't think that's a good question."

Greg: The question is that the work that you do for the navy, it has value as well?

Lipo: I would assume so. They wouldn't give me money if they didn't.

Greg: In fact, they gave you $80,000, or gave your university for your work on QED. Is that correct?

Lipo: That sounds about right. . . .

Greg: So to end on a cordial note, sir. You agree and I agree that the work that . . . was being done by you and Power Paragon for the navy on Quiet Electric Drive, the navy was not paying you for that so it could be turned over to the Chinese government for free?

Lipo: No.

Kaye wordsmithed his redirect questions to mitigate the damage, but Lipo's ignorance—and his arrogant claim that he could publish anything he liked under "academic freedom"—killed his credibility. His snobbery leaked out under Greg's re-cross when he sniffed that USN conference papers weren't up to the standards of academic conferences, being nothing more than "application engineering papers [for] naval engineers who know literally nothing about the subject." Taking advantage, Greg pointed out the different approaches and interests of naval engineers.

Greg: That's because it's nuts and bolts? . . . And nuts and bolts are what they use to put ships together?

Lipo: That's for sure.

After Greg's roasting, Lipo got his one courtroom laugh with his exhausted and relieved "Thank you!" when Greg dismissed him. If egos were visible, Lipo's would have been covered with grill marks.

As Lipo stepped down, ONR program officer Steve Schreppler stepped up. He managed over $100 million in contracts, working twenty-plus years on stealth technologies for four submarine classes—Ohio, Los Angeles, Seawolf, and Virginia. He mocked defense claims that "stealth" and "ship survivability" were commercial priorities. Cruise ships did not require stealth or QED. Under Craig's questioning, Steve destroyed "a couple of points that Professor Lipo raised when he was testifying," then lowered the boom regarding QED. Lipo's unauthorized published papers *did* contain sensitive, export-restricted data that contributed to "a quiet submarine propulsion system." Lipo had known from meetings he'd attended and government contracts he'd signed that "low acoustical noise generation" and a "capability to control noise signature"—stealth—were the goals.

I then passed out binders containing classified data to each juror, Judge Carney, and defense attorneys for reference during Steve's discussion of Chi's classified 5-MegaWatt paper. Whenever Steve's testimony required a classified answer, Steve referred the jury to labeled portions within their binders providing it, thereby keeping courtroom observers in the dark. For example, Steve stated, "The 5-MegaWatt document talks explicitly about using the 'patent technology in the form of A,' in this case, a submarine propulsion motor drive. . . . It says in the first paragraph, 'The intended purpose of the technology is for a submarine quieting application.'" The jury looked up tab "A" within their binder to see the classified data or phrase to which Steve was referring.

After reviewing "over 95,000 individual [technology] documents" recovered from Chi, Steve listed all those meeting the trashed tasking list requirements. Steve's testimony was a tremendous blow to the defense because it put a face on the depth of Chi's betrayal. The jury hung on Steve's every word. Then he mentioned something that made the defense's blood boil: "The Kill Chain Sequence." Why? Because it highlighted the ultimate cost of Chi's treachery, destruction of US submarines and their crews, from "Detection" to "Targeting," which successful stealth defeats, on down the chain to "Killing" the sub. Steve testified submarine acoustics are classified *above* Top Secret, because "[P]ictures of the inside of the engine room of a US submarine [are *never* released. A] submarine's greatest vulnerability is an adversary that knows what the signatures are of the submarine." Chi's QED data addressed "controlling the noise a submarine makes." Steve thrived on the stand.

Bednarski's cross attempted "graymail," threatening release of classified data to force the prosecution to drop a charge.[4] She failed. Most of her questions were at the splitting-hairs level, which she ineffectively conducted until Judge Carney mercifully called it a day.

The next morning, Bednarski continued her droning line-by-line cross. It became clear that Steve wasn't testifying, Bednarski was, and badly. He even corrected her when she mixed up submarine movies *Run Silent, Run Deep* with *The Hunt for Red October*, produced decades apart.[5] Bednarski's droning resumed, beating her dead horse into unrecognizable pulp. Finally, Carney called for a break and provided Bednarski the same advice he had given Kaye:

> *Counsel, I need to give you a report from the jury. And I—the last thing I want to do is start imposing time limitations, but we're moving too slow. Three of the jurors have suggested we're moving too slow, and they want to speed it up. . . . I just feel, with this witness, we're bogged down. Some of the questions and the answers I think are more appropriate for Mr. Lee or Mr. Mak if he decides to testify. And we have got to get through these witnesses. It's just moving way too slow. So, I'm going to overrule [Craig Missakian's] last objection, but, Ms. Bednarski, I'm going to really have to ask you to wrap it up. You indicated when we broke you were going to need about thirty-five minutes, and you have been at it an hour and fifteen minutes now. So, try to wrap it up in the next ten minutes if you could.*

When the jury returned, Bednarski blew right through Carney's ten-minute request, asking Steve questions about search warrants he had no connection with. Even Steve began advising her, "That would be a more appropriate question for the investigators." Carney let her continue, because defense attorneys receive incredible leeway. Craig's objections became pleas—"Can we have a proffer on the relevance of this line of

---

4. "Graymail" is legal extortion, i.e., defense attorneys threatening to expose classified information. Real patriots!
5. I sat up straight, being a big submarine warfare book and movie fan, and knowing how ignorant her question was.

questioning?" Carney overruled his objection, while voicing wishful thinking: "I think she's wrapping it up soon." She wasn't.

Going under fifteen minutes, Craig's eventual redirect demonstrated how questioning should be done, short and sweet, while he established five points:

1. Chi's tasking lists were meant for power electronics experts, like him;

2. He was in the middle of America's efforts to develop an "*all* Electric Navy";

3. All QED contracts and programs Chi wrote or signed were export controlled;

4. Bob Lee's patent information didn't include Chi's classified QED paper's data regarding stealthy subs; and

5. Developing QED cost millions, and its compromise would save China the same.

Steve had been magnificent, was now done, and had our gratitude!

Rear Admiral William Hilarides now took the stand. He held US Naval Academy graduate degrees in physics and engineering management and had served on attack and ballistic missile submarines as junior, executive, and commanding officer for eleven years. He was now program executive acquisitions officer for all submarine procurements. His testimony mesmerized the courtroom. "We think of [stealth] as the crown jewel. That is your ultimate protection. And the SSBN, the ballistic missile submarine, relies on that stealth as its principal protection.[6] . . . Stealth also helped our subs hunt enemy ships and covertly collect vital intelligence. QED was developed to maintain this stealthy submarine lead."[7] Hilarides discussed deterring Communist China from its plans to force Taiwan's "reunification":

---

6. "SS" denotes submarine, "B" denotes ballistic missile, and "N" identifies a submarine as nuclear-powered.

7. Regarding the complexity of our newest submarine class, Virginia, Hilarides said, "We make the space shuttle pale in comparison."

My personal goal would be every morning to have China open the window and look out and see aircraft carriers and quiet nuclear submarines and go, "Not today," and shut the window again, and go on trading with us and modernizing their country and everything else. So that requires strength, and it requires the advanced capabilities that we built into our submarines, certainly. . . . [T]he actual signature of the ship is one of the most highly classified pieces of information that there is.

Kaye's cross made it clear he hoped Hilarides would testify that Schreppler had overclassified Chi's paper. He didn't.

As soon as you say this can influence the acoustic signature and this is part of the weaving of the technologies of how you would reduce that signature, then I would not say he is dead wrong; that he is dead right. And that even if I choose not to use it, it's part of that fabric that forms the basis of our platforms and forms that crown jewel, and it needs to be protected. . . . Any relation at all to the application on a navy platform puts it in that realm of it needs to be protected because it forms the essence of the capability of all the ship.

Kaye was disappointed. *Every* Kaye question produced Hilarides answers helpful to the prosecution, such as "Everything to do with power and motors and pumps is about stealth." Kaye surrendered.

After lunch came NAVSEA/Naval Reactors (NR) engineer Ed Chabay. NR designs, develops, manufactures, tests, trains, maintains, and repairs USN warship nuclear power propulsion plants.[8] Ed confirmed the technology Chi sent China involved "[r]eal submarines, real sailors, doing real missions," while giving the jury a tutorial on how subs worked, from primary plant to reactor to propeller. He testified that many of Chi's documents revealed acoustic signature data and how to quiet *and* speed

---

8. NR is a DC political powerhouse famously founded in 1948 by Captain—later Admiral—Hyman Rickover, "Father of the Nuclear Navy." While visiting NR's then-leader, four-star admiral Donald Kirkland, we saw Rickover's legendary low, off-balance chair, which he utilized to put his visitors ill at ease.

up circuit breakers and switches.[9] The classified documents Chi copied and sent to China "related to, you know, the stealth performance of the power conversion equipment ... techniques for how to control either the harmonic distortion or the vibration of imperfect machines." Ed agreed that the stealth submarine technologies Chi took were "our crown jewels."

After more "attorney as witness" questions, Bednarski launched into silly, irrelevant, loaded queries Ed could only answer with a version of "I don't know that." Bednarski proved ignorant of the facts many times, asking Ed for help in naming, remembering, and locating evidence. One ignorant question helpfully elicited his very useful answer that a quarter of the documents Chi collected concerned "quieting or stealth." Thanks, Marilyn![10]

Next came NCIS Special Agent Omar Lopez, whose career included "force protection" matters on the Point Mugu USN base and Iraq's Sunni Triangle; service as a US Navy Staff and Judge Advocate General (JAG); and as a lieutenant commander in the Navy Reserve for the Naval Special Warfare Command Operational Support Team One at Pearl Harbor, Navy Seals Command.[11] Omar's training and background were impressive. He was also an essential team member.[12] He and I graduated from the same law school, Loyola, but Omar definitely had the greater interest in practicing law.

While everyone expected his testimony to go smoothly, initially, it didn't, to our surprise and Greg's vexation. It has become a funny tale Greg likes to act out, but back then, there were some tense moments when we all wondered whose side Omar was on. His answers were terse, cryptic, and downright unhelpful. Had Omar and Greg fought recently? Friendly attorneys' direct questions usually elicit easy, useful answers. Omar's responses more resembled those of a hostile witness.

---

9. If power switches are too slow, systems reboots leave a ship dead in the water and at the enemy's mercy.

10. After Steve came Thomas Calvert, who chaired the classified session of the Naval Symposium on Electric Machine Technology that Chi attended in Philadelphia in January 2004, one month before traveling to China. His testimony indicated that Chi Mak likely copied the classified articles at the symposium. Kaye's cross was ineffective and brief.

11. Special Agent Omar Lopez later became the director of the NCIS.

12. The times we all worked and traveled together were some of the best in my thirty-two-plus-year FBI career. We were focused, professional, motivated, and effective, and we liked and respected (and mocked) one another to no end!

Greg: Now in addition to interviewing sources in Iraq, were people also interviewed that might be considered hostile?

Omar: Sometimes.

Greg: And were you given training on how to interview hostile potential sources of information?

Omar: We received training on that.

Greg: . . . Have you received training in regards to your current assignment as a naval officer down in San Diego?

Omar: Yes. [At this point, Greg has said he was thinking *What the &%*! is he doing? Whose side is he on?* We all had similar thoughts.]

Greg: (sarcastic) Not a particularly fruitful answer. [courtroom laughter] Can you talk about it?

Omar: Some of it.

Omar later told us his strategy was to appear distant from the prosecution and therefore more objective to the jury. He also thought it best not to forewarn Greg of his plans—a horrible idea! Fortunately, Omar settled down to accomplish his purpose, but his "idea" and its execution live on in case lore and Greg's memories.

Greg then tackled defense claims. First up were the two classified Philadelphia symposium papers Chi had copied, stored, and carried to China, titled "Dynamic Analysis with Motor with Auxiliary Windings" and "Algorithms for Reduced-Scale Permanent Magnet Synchronous Machine." Using PowerPoint, Omar ended testimony that day by demonstrating that Chi had made at least two copies of each article, with one set likely now in China.[13]

Judge Carney then proposed extending court hours. "[The jury is] very anxious to get the case. And it's my job to help them keep an open mind." Greg promised, "[B]arring a humongous cross, we expect to rest tomorrow."[14]

---

13. Judging by criticisms PRCIS officers had leveled, Chi had given Fuk and Tai "incomplete" "books" that were missing pages. Those pages missing constituted the middle classified article.

14. An obvious shot at the defense's now infamous long-winded cross-examinations.

Kaye claimed his witnesses would require eight days:

Kaye: If Mr. Mak should testify . . . we definitely made that
         commitment in the opening statement . . . Mr. Mak has a
         lot to say. Agent Gaylord put in hundreds of exhibits that
         are going to be reviewed closely . . . many of them have to
         be discussed . . . We'll be done with all of our witnesses
         by that point.[15] . . . [W]e have been criticized about being
         a little long on our cross-examination.

Carney: [Y]ou have put a substantial part of your case through
         the government witnesses.

Greg: [Assuring Judge Carney that Chi's cross would be quick,
         he added a disclaimer.] Frankly, we don't think it's our
         fault that it's taken as long as it has. These crosses have
         doubled or tripled the length of our directs. I have never
         had that happen in any trial I have ever done. I can
         assure the Court we have no intention of doing that. . . .
         I do not feel comfortable having watched what they do
         on cross to imagine what they're possibly going to do
         on direct. And I think May 4th [Carney's target date]
         is even far out. I mean, the Court has discretion, as you
         know, to run its calendar, and, you know, speaking can-
         didly, allowing the defense to play rope-a-dope with the
         jury. If they want to do it and sink their case, I should be
         fine and let them do it, but it's just not getting anywhere.

While clearly suggesting Judge Carney had indulged the defense,
Greg promised only one or two rebuttal witnesses, but warned Kaye
might put crazy, cranky codger Bob Lee back on the stand. "[A]nd for
what? To pound in [the jury's] skulls for the 90th time? I think the Court
is correct. I don't know how much of their case they have. They tried to
ram their case down the throat of every one of our witnesses regardless
of the fact that they had no foundation on these documents." This exasperated side of Greg was refreshing. He had been the bigger, patient,

---

15. I *fervently* prayed Chi Mak took the stand. I knew his huge ego demanded it. Would Kaye
dissuade him?

reasonable attorney in this court, but he'd reached his limit. (I'd reached mine at the first detention hearing!) Greg's words gave Carney pause; he obviously respected Greg. Kaye proved clueless as ever.

> *Whatever people perceive about our case—we have been getting comments that we have been very effective. And we feel like we're doing a good job. We have tried hundreds of cases between each other, and we think we're serving our client well. Ultimately time will tell if it bears fruit, but we're doing the best we can. . . . We think we have been effective. So be it.*[16]

Kaye was painfully obtuse. I adjourned happy. Another banner day for the prosecution.

Omar continued on the stand the next day, explaining Tai and Fuk's illegal 2001 travel to China via Vancouver, using PRC and British passports, and our home microphone intercepts of Chi and Rebecca. Greg tried to manage juror expectations: Hollywood depictions of FBI technical prowess shamed our Keystone Kops product. While CCTV footage of Chi and Rebecca in the house on Sunday, October 23, 2005, played, Omar read aloud the subtitle captions. Greg joked, "Just for the record, this is what is known as a high-tech production," eliciting courtroom laughter at the absurdly poor quality. Omar summarized what the jury had just witnessed: Chi and Rebecca copying, creating, and packaging three CDs; Rebecca mentioning this data was for "Little Pu" and that "Customs" would not find it; and Chi labeling the discs "Reconfig" (Reconfiguration) and "Prop" (Propulsion).

Omar then narrated polecam footage of the Maks' departure from home to deliver the data discs to Tai Mak. Greg made him pay for his overly spartan narration:

Greg: Agent, if you could point out what is occurring.

Omar: That's Mr. Mak walking to the car, and then a few seconds later, it's Ms. Mak.

---

16. Time did tell. They sucked!

Greg: That's her walking out now?

Omar: Yes.

Greg: They're getting in the car and backing out?

Omar: Yes.

Greg: Doing a great job on the description there, Agent. Thanks."
        [courtroom laughter]

Omar: Sorry.

During Chi and Rebecca's return home, their car microphone recorded them saying that Tai would encrypt the data. Omar noted the CDs contained sensitive, restricted ONR and DARPA technical data.[17] Omar also explained the meanings of the code word sheets in both Mak homes and verified Chi's US warship list log was extremely accurate, and *not* based upon faulty Hong Kong newspapers as the defense had alleged.

The next topic was Omar's interview of Fuk and the many lies she, Tai, and Rebecca each told.[18] The eclectic nature of Omar's later topics, after covering his core duties, was because he had been assigned the job of "utility cleanup witness" for the team, entering evidence into the record that had been put aside, overlooked, or had surfaced since Gunnar and I testified.

Finally, Omar addressed Chi's confession on October 30. His time with Chi was cordial, especially after he and Gunnar told Chi they represented the US Navy, *not* the FBI. Once Chi admitted his cover story lies, other admissions cascaded forth. In fact, Chi wanted to keep talking—like the first two times—when they ended the interview.

Kaye's cross claimed Omar was being sensationalist, before raising his own racist stereotyping, implying all conference attendees with Chinese surnames were first loyal to China. Kaye also reasoned that a United States serious about protecting sensitive data would prohibit ethnic Chinese from attending such sensitive conferences. That was pure, unadulterated racism, and par for the course with Kaye.[19] *That* was what

---

17. DARPA is a Department of Defense agency that develops "over the horizon" military technologies.
18. Tai even denied having a brother in the United States.
19. Again, the government would have been *roasted*, and rightfully so, if it had made such claims.

Chi and his racist PRC masters believed—that the first loyalty of every ethnic Chinese must be to China, no matter their country of birth or citizenship. Greg objected and Judge Carney sustained.

Kaye then kept incorrectly quoting Omar's FD-302 interview report for Chi, and Omar corrected him: "That's not really what was written. I can read it, or I can tell you what it says." Hypocritically, Kaye kept relying upon Gunnar's report, which he had previously charged was fantasy. Now, Kaye was subtly acknowledging Chi *had* made those admissions!

Now his questions began bouncing all over the place, from conference security to Fuk's ailing mother to Omar's "interrogation" history. Gunnar had been depicted as Chi's bully, and Omar was now portrayed as Fuk's. Kaye was desperately flailing, and everyone knew it. During all of this, Omar gave only one incorrect answer.[20] In response to Greg's objections over Kaye wasting time, Judge Carney urged Kaye to speed things up. Finally, Kaye's absurd questions petered out. Judge Carney asked, "Mr. Staples, how long do you think your redirect is going to be, sir?" Reading the room, Greg answered "Zero seconds. Hold your applause, please [courtroom laughter]. We have no questions. The witness can be dismissed." Greg had once again signaled to the jury his disdain for Kaye.

Our last witness took the stand, Captain Kevin Eyer. An engaging, likable man, Eyer had been a surface warfare officer, then served as naval aide to the Fifth Fleet Admiral before extensive training on AEGIS technology and assignment to AEGIS cruisers as weapons and combat systems officer, executive officer, and captain. He also held a master's in law and diplomacy, served at the Pentagon, and had been operations officer of the USS *Abraham Lincoln* Carrier Strike Group.

Eyer explained, "[AEGIS] is without question the most significant change that has occurred in naval science and defense of the battle group as far as I know, ever."[21] He compared the old radar—a two-dimensional monochrome radar circle system with rotating radius line identifying

---

20. He claimed I went home that Sunday as he and Gunnar left to interview Chi. I actually stayed in the office to catch up on work.
21. China developed its AEGIS capability, "Magic Shield," twenty years ahead of time, while Chi Mak was working on US AEGIS power systems. Chi told Omar and Gunnar that he gave AEGIS data to the PRC.

blips every five seconds, with an unwieldy, easily jammed firing process—with AEGIS, continuously tracking an infinite number of targets 360 degrees in all directions, and immediately prioritizing and firing on all potential targets. Its broad frequency band usage makes AEGIS extremely difficult to jam; it even detects targets in planetary orbit! It also controls independent firing modules, which easily load and switch out as needed. Eyer's enthusiasm for AEGIS was infectious, declaring it "can pick up a bee, a bumblebee at ten miles." His tutorial on modern US Navy warfare tactics was fascinating as he explained the United States would *never* share AEGIS with China because we needed to maintain our ten-year lead.

> [T]his technological edge is what is going to keep me out of the water in the next war. . . . [Losing it means] unlimited numbers of American boys and girls coming home in body bags. . . . I am a true believer in AEGIS. Sometimes I don't love the navy, but I do love AEGIS! [courtroom laughter] . . . It is impossible for me to overstate the dramatic leap that AEGIS was to the United States Navy. . . . It's AEGIS that allows us to even talk about shooting down ballistic missiles. . . . [American] AEGIS technology would be at the very top of any country's wish list.

Kaye declined to cross, knowing his questions would only help the prosecution. Greg declared, "Your Honor, the government rests." We had closed with a *bang!*

The defense opened with a whimper. Its first two witnesses, Mr. Saba Saba and Mr. Udomchoke Bhavilai, hadn't worked with Chi Mak in over twenty years and could only state that Chi was a hard worker who'd said he was from Hong Kong. Carney stepped in to give Kaye more advice: To make an impact, Chi Mak should be his next witness.

Carney: You are not entitled to a perfect trial. You are entitled to a fair trial. . . . We have a very anxious jury. . . . They want this case, and I have to fight them, tell them, keep an open mind; you haven't heard all the evidence. . . . I want

you sensitive to that. . . . [S]ix hours for direct examination for a trial is a long time. They have the fundamen-
tals. They know all the evidence. I don't think you want
to take Mr. Mak through the details of that.

Kaye: I have never had a direct examination this expansive.

We were dismissed, but our long day wasn't over. Kaye told us two
L-3 WashOps witnesses were arriving that night for testimony the following day.[22] We interviewed them that evening at their motel. Fortunately, Fred Witham, Cindy Baleno, and Valerie Hampton had warned
us about these two—Nancy Hindman and Ken Shelly—and provided
us invaluable email exchanges demonstrating that Hindman had tried
to force employees to reverse their position on Chi's stolen technologies.
They jeopardized their own jobs to tell the truth. Heroes all!

Hindman was worried L-3 would lose USN contracts if Chi was
convicted and the navy blamed L-3 for losing USN secrets. In truth,
Power Paragon employees saved their company by warning us about
Hindman's intentions. If her corrupt gambit had succeeded, Gunnar and
I would have signed off on L-3's debarment, halting *all* US/L-3 contracts.
Instead, we supported Power Paragon when the USN later asked us about
it. We had Shelly and Hindman by the short hairs, which they, and the
defense, never saw coming. That's what lies get you. And the employees
were right: Hindman was an imperious, egotistical, condescending witch!
Craig added "angry, unhappy schoolmarm" to the description.

The next day, Craig objected to Hindman's and Shelly's testimony,
but Carney ruled they could testify about Chi Mak's state of mind concerning what technologies were on the US Munitions List (USML),
even though they'd never met him.

First came Hindman, internal special compliance official for Wash-
Ops, part of L-3's New York City corporate office, but based in DC. After
high school, she spent over twenty years in the US State Department,
the Department of the Navy Chief Licensing Office, and the Defense
Technical Security Administration. She then became a private-sector
bureaucrat, processing export-control licensing concerns for L-3. Once

---

22. This late notice violated discovery requirements, but that was par for the course for the defense.

on the stand, Hindman discussed the USML, exports, and ITAR matters, but *never* addressed Chi's "state of mind." Kaye read ITAR's statutory definition of "technical data": "Information other than software as defined in 12104 which is required for the *design, development, production, manufacture, assembly, operation, repair, testing, maintenance or modification* of defense articles [emphasis added]."

Hindman declared Chi's papers didn't fit the "technical data" definition, "because you cannot use it to do any of these synonyms."[23] Hindman admitted that she had "corrected" Cindy Baleno [export control officer at L-3] and others because "Initially they indicated that it was technical data, and through an exchange of emails we got them to understand that it was not." Hindman denied conflict with Power Paragon compliance personnel, saying she was only giving them guidance after receiving Baleno's erroneous email on July 24, 2006. "[Cindy Baleno] was in error on that. She was not focusing on the ITAR when she said that. . . . They had not followed L-3 policy." Hindman told the State Department that Chi's data did *not* fit ITAR definitions. Kaye was smug as he concluded, thinking he had blown a hole in the side of the prosecution's ship. How could we prosecute Chi Mak for acting on what his employer believed?

Craig stood and conducted his most effective and consequential cross of the trial, establishing that Hindman had never communicated with Chi Mak, proving she had no "effect whatsoever on his state of mind." Hindman confirmed Chi "ignored L-3 procedures" regarding publishing conference papers and reporting international travel, and that the Department of State had final authority over what was "technical data."[24]

Craig deftly then moved to her faxes and emails. Power Paragon personnel had told her Chi's papers constituted "technical data," and refused to recant, despite Hindman's pressure to do so. Hindman claimed she "changed their focus," through gentle, reasoned persuasion. Craig brought out bigger guns—her emails, which *ordered* them to change their answers. Hindman had earlier denied writing such change orders and was caught in that lie.

---

23. In ignorance, they had just stepped on a land mine for which the prosecution would make them pay dearly.
24. She also declared something no other defense witness would: giving this data to China didn't threaten national security!

Craig:	When you said a moment ago that they came up with that on their own, that was not true, was it? You gave them the language?
Hindman:	Yes.

Hindman's troubles piled up when Craig cornered her for lying about when she researched topics and issued orders regarding ITAR communications. She also claimed higher company backing where there was none. The wheels flew off with Craig's coup de grâce, placing the "technical data" definition on the screen and reading aloud all the "related synonyms" which Hindman had claimed only meant "manufacture."[25]

Craig:	Let's talk briefly about the definition of "technical data." [Reading off each definition word] Design?
Hindman:	Closely related.
Craig:	Engineering?
Hindman:	Yes.
Craig:	(voice rising in astonishment with each Hindman caveat) Repair?
Hindman:	They are related.

And so on, making Hindman look more rigid, inflexible, and blind to the obvious with each answer. These "synonyms" neatly fit ITAR's definition of "technical data" and what Chi had provided China. Craig's questions revealed Hindman's verbal gymnastics were done to avoid possible fines and sanctions against, and debarment of, L-3. Thus, the force-fed "findings." If Chi's data was "not on the USML," there would be "no technical data" finding, thus guaranteeing no US government punishments.

Alarmed, Kaye objected to the questioning. Judge Carney called for a break, telling the jury, "Let me have a little time to go over this with the lawyers."

After the jury filed out, Carney shocked us all.

---

25. Hindman would only use the word "manufacture," claiming all the others were "related synonyms."

I'm going to instruct the jury that this is technical data, this being the 5-MegaWatt document. . . . I don't see how you can say that this document is not related to the "design" and "development" of a defense article. . . . Everyone has asked that question and she dances around it and says it is related to the manufacture, production, blah blah blah. I don't see how this is not related to the design and development which is specifically in this regulation. . . . I think the jury needs to understand why she is wrong specifically. . . . The law is what the law is and this is technical data. . . . And you can bring in a million experts with whatever degrees but they're not going to be able to change the law. . . . If it's an independent expert who is going to come in and say that this is not related to the design and development, I'm not going to allow that. . . . I'm going to give a pretty strong instruction [to the jury] . . . . In fairness to the jury, in fairness to the witness, in fairness to both sides, they need to understand why the witness is wrong.

Hindman had repeatedly lied, and Judge Carney could no longer ignore it. Her testimony completely discredited her and defense counsel. QED was "technical data," period. I'd never seen a defense witness's testimony interrupted by a judge, labeled a lie, and excluded from further consideration. Her testimony was done. Yet years later Hindman was bragging about her role in the trial.[26] Shame on her, and on L-3 for not firing her. Amazingly, Kaye then called Hindman's assistant, Ken Shelly, to the stand. He fared little better. *None* of the testimony that morning had actually addressed Chi's state of mind. It was all a defense lie.

Next came a defense witness I eagerly anticipated, Tai's boss, Wu Xiaoyong, CEO of Phoenix Satellite TV USA. Wu, publicly identified as a former officer of the PRC Ministry of State Security, was taking the stand in a US courtroom, thus subjecting himself to perjury laws. I wanted Greg to trap him in a perjurious lie (hey, a US counterintelligence agent can dream, can't he?). Wu testified Phoenix was a joint venture under controlling partner Liu Chang Le in Hong Kong, with US offices in Irwindale (Tai's workplace), New York, and Washington, DC. Wu

---

26. Fred Witham told me years later that Hindman bragged to fellow L-3 employees that she had been a hero in the Chi Mak case. He, Cindy Baleno, and I were astounded she still had a job.

claimed Phoenix's PRC-owned partner, Asia Television (ATV) hired Tai in 2001, and swore Tai had *not* returned to Asia once since then. Colleen's records, her testimony, and Chi's and Fuk's own words said otherwise.

Mocking Bednarski's claims of Tai's prodigious talents, Greg asked, "Was one of his qualifications his ability to carry encrypted defense information out of this country to China?" Wu deadpanned, "No." Greg, only interested in winning our case, ignored most of Wu's lies as irrelevant in order to keep his cross brief. He did get Wu to grudgingly agree the PRC "struggled" against "intellectuals" and "bankers" during the Cultural Revolution, forcing them into slave labor on remote farms. They certainly did *not* allow them to leave the country, as Chi and Rebecca claimed, without ulterior motives.

Greg then pushed on Phoenix's PRC government connections. Wu denied CEO Liu Chang Le's public affiliations with the PLA, and the PRC regime loans he received and used to start his past and current companies. Closer questioning revealed Wu's own probable PRC intelligence education, followed by extensive advanced Western courses and degrees from specialized journalism schools at Harvard and the University of Missouri.[27] In response to Wu's sob stories of personal government persecution, Greg pointed out his PRC privileges: Wu's father was a member of the Central Committee of the Communist Party of China and former PRC foreign minister and vice premier, while his boss, Liu Chang Le, served as a high-level officer in the PLA.

Greg: Now, you're aware that your CEO, Mr. [Liu], has connections with the intelligence branch of the PLA?

Wu: Mr. Liu doesn't have any connection with the intelligence community.

Greg: You're not aware that he got assistance from the intelligence department of the PLA to start up an oil company?

Wu: No.

Greg: You understand that's been reported? . . . [Y]ou're aware that Liu received $2 million from the National Security Bureau to start [your] company?

---

27. Aren't we generous to subsidize the education of China's intelligence officers for them?

Wu: No. That's ridiculous. I did the fund-raising.

Greg: And in fact, Mr. Liu was a colonel by the time he left the People's Liberation Army. Is that correct?

Wu: That could be, yes. . . .

Greg: Now, Mr. Liu was, about two years ago, appointed to the 10th Committee of the Chinese People's Political [Consul-tative] Conference. Are you aware of that?

Wu: Yes.

In Bednarski's redirect, Wu claimed Phoenix and ATV made no cash payments to Tai, despite Tai/Fuk intercepts saying otherwise.[28] Wu ended his testimony swearing, "I do my best to present all the truth I have to my best knowledge." To my frustration, Greg declined re-cross.

The next defense witness was crotchety Bob Lee, once a brilliant engineer, but now just a naive Chi Mak friend, willing to say anything. He didn't worry us. Kaye's direct covered Lee's career, stretching back to pre–World War II. He claimed Chi's stolen technologies were public knowledge on the internet.[29] Lee claimed he had patented it all (he hadn't), and that Professor Lipo openly taught it at his university (he didn't).[30] After Lee declared that *none* of the QED research was paid for by the US Navy, Carney called it a day.

The next morning, Lee declared that Chi's 5-MegaWatt paper's "schematics were identical" to Lee's work and patents, and that his con-cept wouldn't even work.[31] Then he attacked witness Gene Dotson's memory regarding Chi's AEGIS work before recanting his own previous faulty testimony that he and Chi had never had anything to do with AEGIS: "[W]e were never invited into the radar system beyond building the power supply. . . . And from there on, it was all a black hole." It was a "black hole" to Lee because he lacked the security clearance Chi had to

---

28. This normal PRC underreporting trick cuts down on taxes paid to the United States and their salaries paid to US-based employees.

29. The defense never provided evidence of this because it didn't exist.

30. If true, that would make Chi and Lipo frauds and plagiarists.

31. Strange, given the fact they kept accepting money for it and publicly presenting it as viable, valuable work!

perform further work. Lee was testifying about things he knew nothing about, so Carney sustained Greg's multiple objections of "No foundation." Lee then painted the government as evil and racist, again out of ignorance.[32] His direct examination ended.[33]

Greg's efficient cross produced many befuddled Lee responses. If Lee and Chi's QED work was useless, why did the Maks hide, encrypt, and lie about it? If the QED data was on the internet, why not just refer friends in China to it? Lee looked foolish, ignorant, and deceptive. He had *no* export-control or classified-materials training, and his stated degree of friendship with Chi kept changing.[34] Defense counsel had kept Lee ignorant of case facts to sculpt their narrative, so his QED timeline was comically incorrect and self-serving. And since Lee was paid for QED work he labeled "worthless," he was either incompetent or dishonest. But this re-cross was not without its humorous moments:

Greg: Isaac Newton, three hundred years ago, invented calculus, didn't he?

Lee: He and another guy from France.

Greg: I can't pronounce his name, so I left him out. [courtroom laughter]

When Lee stepped down, Greg good-naturedly commented that he would miss talking with him, and shook his hand, as he did with all defense witnesses.

I had looked forward to the next defense SME who would discuss the history and politics of the PRC. He reminded Colleen and me of the many old Communist Party USA members we'd encountered in our careers. He had the same background and smarmy, condescending, willfully ignorant attitude. Any facts or events that interfered with their beliefs were ignored or dismissed as capitalist lies and propaganda. Considering communism's horrific, bloody track record of tens of millions of imprisoned, tortured, and murdered souls, inflicting starvation, disease,

---

32. Lee had declared Chi, and Wen Ho Lee, were victims of a racial prosecution. He would pay for this during cross.

33. Rigoberto Saenz, a video store owner, took ten minutes to testify about processing some Mak intercepted conversations. Just another irrelevant defense witness.

34. From "close" to "social" to "work associate."

and economic devastation upon every nation it touched, it's amazing any believers remain.[35] I looked forward to seeing Greg disassemble this guy.

Up stepped Stanley Rosen, political science professor and director of the East Asian Study Center at the University of Southern California (USC), with offices in Hong Kong and Shanghai. Rosen had recently dined with the mayor of Beijing to celebrate their new US-China Institute in China. USC even had a joint program with Shanghai's Chao Tung University—Chi and Rebecca's spy recruiting alma mater. Rosen also received federal funding.[36] His specialty was the Cultural Revolution and Red Guard Movement. Rosen had lived in Hong Kong from 1973 to 1976, studied Mandarin, interviewed former Red Guards and Cultural Revolution survivors, published books on those subjects, and traveled to China at least twice a year while regularly hosting "intellectual exchanges."[37]

Rosen: You just tell them what they're seeing and how to understand what they're seeing. I work liaison with the Chinese, on the Chinese side, to arrange the program.

Kaye: I see. And that's directly with the Chinese government?

Rosen: Well, it's directly—it's either—sometimes it's Ministry of Education. . . .

The PRC State Administration of Radio, Film, and TV considered Rosen a Chinese film industry expert, inviting him to give talks in Beijing. He had written seven books and sixty articles on China and served as a Ford Foundation consultant.[38] All of Rosen's previous trial testimony experiences had benefited China, including its double agent, Katrina Leung. He had repeatedly refused to testify for the US government, yet claimed, "I have no ideological bias."[39] I had no doubt he was an expert on modern China and the CCP, *and* that he was a PRC mouthpiece. So was Mao Tse-tung! That didn't make him correct or credible.

Rosen's testimony consistently downplayed or skirted horrific PRC policies, punishments, atrocities, censorship, corruption, and oppression

---

35. One hundred million deaths and counting.
36. Your tax dollars at work, undermining American interests around the world.
37. Sounds eerily familiar, doesn't it?
38. Anti-communist owner and founder Henry Ford be damned!
39. I *never* would have authorized such an offer; I knew *who* and *what* Rosen was.

by using euphemisms that hid ugly realities. People weren't murdered, they "simply dropped out." He actually claimed Mao launched the "Hundred Flowers" Movement to consider dissenting opinions.[40] A man who could soft-pedal the greatest mass murderer in history was certainly capable of explaining away Chi's behaviors. So, his warped narrative became that Chi's Hong Kong–based banker father did *not* present a problem. In fact, such people were "encouraged" by the Communist government during the Cultural Revolution. In truth, that murderous regime targeted such "capitalist running dog imperialists" and their families for greater suffering, and death. Rosen produced an excuse for each suspicious Mak activity. The photo of Tai in a PLA propaganda officer's uniform? "Everyone wore military uniforms." Rosen said China's custom of "guanxi" explained Mak family behavior.[41] This wasn't ignorance; it was dishonest apologetics. With Kaye *way* over his witness time estimate, Judge Carney requested a status report.

Kaye:	We're doing good, Your Honor. I think I'm trying to fly here. I think my speed has moved and with Professor Rosen I think we'll be done in twenty minutes, I hope.
Carney:	How about ten? You've been going about two hours and fifteen minutes.
Kaye:	Yes, sir. I understand.
Carney:	Try to get it in ten.

I watched the jury during this exchange. They obviously agreed with the judge.

This glacial farce hit a snag when Rosen was given questions about the Center for Asian Pacific Studies (CAPS), which Kaye had asked him to research. But wait, that meant Rosen was *not* an expert on CAPS. And from whom did this "research" come? The answer: colleagues *in* China at CAPS who declared CAPS was legitimate. Naturally![42] Greg called for a sidebar.

---

40. In truth, it had the opposite purpose—to weed out dissent, meaning jailing and murder of dissidents.
41. Per defense definition, it was a corrupt, illegal version of "You scratch my back, I scratch yours."
42. Of course, if these Chinese professors did *not* parrot the CCP line, they would never be seen again.

Greg: This is an outrage. They're having an expert testify not based on his expertise, but on research that he has done in preparation for this case. Admiral McVadon did not do that. [He] offered opinions based solely on his experience. . . . We'd ask that last testimony be stricken.

Craig: Outrageous . . . This witness . . . [has] gotten on the phone . . . spoken to people directly about the issues in this case . . . taken the information given . . . taken their opinions and now he wants to give that information to the jury. It's gross hearsay and it's absolutely an outrageous abuse of the expert witness. . . . It just can't be done. It's never been done.

Kaye: (whining while offering no legal defense) They don't want to allow us to present our case!

I half expected Kaye to throw himself on the floor, screaming and flailing, evidentiary rules be damned. Greg pointed out that Rosen was unqualified to discuss CAPS and other topics as an SME because he had no personal experience there. Admiral McVadon had testified about his actual "preexisting knowledge and experience [at CAPS]. What you cannot do is bring a witness in and after the fact say, go get expertise on this for me by calling a few people. That's entirely improper and should be excluded." Clueless Kaye claimed Rosen's CAPS answers came from "hours researching this, talking to colleagues, looking on the internet. He is not presenting something that is hogwash."[43]

But Judge Carney also wasn't getting it. He just wanted questions rephrased. Craig countered that Rosen was testifying as to what others had *told* him. "It's rank hearsay. . . . We cannot cross-examine the people that he's spoken to." And Rosen had done this with other issues, citing phone conversations with PRC citizens, *not* his own experiences. Kaye retorted that government agents had done the same thing. Greg snapped, "[T]hey're not testifying as experts. Don't you get the difference?! . . . [Rosen's] not an investigator. He is not a fact witness."

---

43. Riiiiiight . . . . and professors under the thumb of a totalitarian state always tell the truth.

Rosen arrogantly and obtusely interjected, "I couldn't conceive . . . that a center in such an important university that is trying to get overseas funding and working with the Ford Foundation and the Council on Foreign Relations would allow the PLA to use them that way." (Sure! A totalitarian state's university could prevent its government from using it as a cover for intelligence activities. Really, Professor? How stupid or dishonest are you? And how dumb do you think we are?)

Carney: [Ruling] That's improper hearsay, to be relying on it.

Kaye: So perhaps if [Professor Rosen] can't speak about this, then we should strike Admiral McVadon's testimony on this issue.

Greg: That's absurd. Admiral McVadon was speaking from experience. He did not go out and research that issue before he came to testify.

Carney: (agreeing) The difference is the admiral [discussed CAPS] in his capacity, his military capacity, on his own. He didn't do it in connection with this case.

Kaye: Why does that differ?

Carney: (impatiently) That's a huge difference, sir. It's hearsay. . . . If you are acquiring [knowledge] just for purposes of this litigation, you are nothing more than a hired gun, and I can use some more colorful descriptions, and I wouldn't want to impugn the professor because I know that's not what he did. But you are setting him up for giving improper testimony.[44]

Carney: [to Greg] How long will your cross be?

Greg: Twenty minutes, thirty at the most. Not a long one.

Carney: It would be nice to finish this witness.

Greg: I agree.

I didn't! Why limit us when Kaye was wasting hours on repetitive, dishonest, improper questions? We couldn't possibly cover all of Rosen's

---

44. As we'd seen, Kaye didn't care two figs about encouraging "improper testimony," and never would.

bogus testimony in that time. This smug, deceiving "useful idiot" of an SME required ridicule. I'm sure Greg had his reasons for keeping his cross short, but I didn't see them. Kaye continued with a few CAPS issues Rosen claimed *personal* knowledge of, before ending the direct of this PRC sock puppet and shill for communism.

Greg's cross quickly established that Rosen was *not* an expert on "Chinese foreign intelligence." Also, eighty thousand intellectuals' homes were looted in a two-week period in Chi and Rebecca's hometown of Shanghai, with many publicly humiliated, tortured, forced into suicide, or beaten to death.[45] The PLA *did* enlist college students, and only its agents cared about USN warships in Hong Kong harbor. Finally, it was the rare PRC citizen who survived a 1965 escape to Hong Kong, which was always perilous. As if to say the "Bamboo Curtain" wasn't real, Rosen blamed England—"The British side was really the obstacle." He was shameless.

Greg had been uncharacteristically deferential to Rosen, who deserved utter derision, despite having thoroughly researched PRC political history and reading several histories, including one authored by Rosen.[46] He repeatedly and uncharacteristically let Rosen off the hook. We didn't "lose" this witness, but neither did we win, as we had all others. It was a draw, not because Rosen was brilliant—he was a hack—but because Greg held back. I've never understood why. Did Greg believe the jury saw this and, paired with Carney's push to finish Rosen, decided a quick cross was the best course? As he stepped down, Rosen said, "I think it's a good day." I imagine he was relieved Greg had not dissected him like the other defense SMEs. I was disappointed.

But then came a glimmer at the end of that week's tunnel. Carney asked Kaye, "Will Chi Mak be testifying next week?" I prayed the answer was "Yes!"

---

45. Hardly the cakewalk Rebecca had portrayed.
46. Greg often skillfully coined Maoist phrases as jokes. We often called him "Chairman Staples" and "Our Great Helmsman."

CHAPTER 31

"Lies, Lies, Lies, Yea-ah"

MONDAY MORNING, DEFENSE WITNESS YURI KHERSONSKY TOOK THE stand, then quickly invoked his Fifth Amendment right against self-incrimination. Carney dismissed him and Bednarski falsely charged we had intimidated him. The remaining defense witnesses were puzzling, seeming extremely tangential to the case. First was Mohammad Zahzah, a Power Paragon engineer and manager who confirmed Chi was a competent, helpful coworker interested in "the science of things." Greg's cross confirmed that engineering cubicles were downsized in April 2005, Zahzah *never* stored documents at home, and DD(x) data was restricted and should never leave the workplace, once again turning a defense witness into a prosecution asset.

Next came Maryanne Deem, Chi and Rebecca's neighbor across the street. She and her husband met the Maks when they moved into the neighborhood in 1980. After that, she told one lie after another about their "friendly [Mak] neighbors," doing each other favors, exchanging fruit, etc. "I know I could always call on Chi Mak or Rebecca if I needed them. They would gladly come help us. . . . They're always friendly. They're outgoing. They always have smiles on their faces."[1] It was *all* a lie. Rebecca couldn't put two English words together and Deem didn't speak a lick of Chinese.

Like Professor Rosen, this was another witness with an agenda. Greg pointed out Deem told the FBI she *never* entered the Maks' home

---

1. What Mak family was Deem talking about?

in twenty-seven years, had only seen two visitors there, and had no idea where the Maks went on their trips. Like Rosen, this dishonest publicity hound wasn't served the humiliation she deserved, despite having lied to the media about these "good immigrants," the bigoted "FBI persecution," and her "close" relationship with the Maks. Greg also didn't address her hatred for the FBI due to the conviction of her brother, the traitorous former FBI Special Agent R. W. Miller. Maybe Greg thought she wasn't important enough to bother with.

Suresh Gupta, an engineering consultant, then took the stand. He'd worked with Chi and Bob Lee years earlier at Teledyne and confirmed Chi was an excellent engineer. But Greg's cross exposed glaring gaps in Gupta's knowledge: He worked from home and never handled military, government, restricted, or classified data. Therefore, Gupta became a government weapon in Greg's hands.

Greg: If you would have been caught sending [your work] documents to India, would you have lied about why you sent it?

Gupta: Why should I lie?

Greg: I agree.

The day's last witness was linguist Eddie Yip. He stated the defense had purchased a sound-filtering device to listen to the Mak intercepts and claimed their equipment was superior to ours.[2] Eddie then declared Tai spoke their invented phrase, "Hong Fa" ("Wang Prosperity"), not "Hong Hua" ("Red Flower"), and played their doctored recordings as evidence, but no one could hear the sounds they were selling. Eddie also testified that none of the Maks ever used the word "encrypt." Craig objected and Judge Carney sustained because the defense never produced alternate transcripts for these conversations.

Craig's cross established that no one checked the Yip brothers' work and that they falsely listed their credentials as "Certified Chinese Court Interpreters"; they were *not* listed on the State of California website as

---

2. "No good deed goes unpunished." We had showed them how inferior their earbuds were, and *told* them what headgear and computer language programs to buy.

certified, registered interpreters; and they had misused Federal District Court forms to imply their work was independently reviewed. Also, Eddie had previously applied for an FBI linguist position and been turned down.[3] Craig's questions demonstrated defense linguist translations were determined by defense attorney positions established well before the linguists were even retained, raising questions of integrity.[4]

After the jury departed, Kaye informed the Court that Chi Mak would testify (hallelujah). Carney advised Kaye, *again*, "You owe it to Mr. Mak to try to present it in the most interesting way. I sound like a broken record, but the jury are anxious to get this case. And I just don't think you are going to be doing yourself or Mr. Mak a favor if you get bogged down in documents. . . . I just don't think you are advancing the ball or advancing his interests if you are going to be getting down into technical information."[5] Judge Carney noted that the jury was "tired and getting cranky."

The next defense SME was one I had anticipated more than any other, a former FBI Special Agent in Charge (SAC) with a huge ego and exaggerated sense of importance—standard fare for many FBI executives. Before trial, Kaye had recruited him with repeated flattery and pleas that he was Chi Mak's only hope, appealing to his ego while hiding critical case facts. His name was I. C. Smith, author of a self-serving book with himself as the hero.[6]

I purchased a used copy of Smith's book for $5 and highlighted his every ridiculous claim of counterintelligence expertise before presenting it to Greg. Like most FBI executive blue flamers, Smith had changed positions every couple of years, climbing up the ladder and taking credit for others' accomplishments, all while not truly understanding the work. He was a poser, selling ignorant testimony against fellow agents to feed his ego.

On direct, Smith claimed to lecture and write about his expertise, the "Larry" Wu-Tai Chin espionage case, and PRC espionage in gen-

---

3. More successful impeachment research from our squad, which we gave our AUSAs to put to good use. Our idea.

4. Turns out, earlier defense accusations of influenced government linguists were only projections of defense behaviors.

5. Judge Carney regularly offered advice to the defense, and they regularly rejected it.

6. *Inside: A Top G-Man Exposes Spies, Lies, and Bureaucrat Bungling Inside the FBI.*

eral. Kaye used Smith and his book to dismiss Rudy Guerin's testimony and draw faulty parallels between the Chin and Mak cases. After the Washington Field Office, Smith's career path flitted from one administrative rung to the next until he landed as SAC of the Little Rock Field Office.[7] He had never directed a major CI case, Chinese or otherwise, but claimed he'd received sporadic case "updates." He made up answers as he went, and butchered straightforward Asian proverbs like, "The emperor's law stops at the village gate." He threw out generalities without substance to support whatever foolish argument Kaye presented:

1. The PRCIS would never use agents with relatives in Hong Kong;

2. Family groups don't collect intelligence;

3. Spies don't commit other crimes;

4. Finding evidence connecting agents and handlers was impossible;

5. Spies never store technological data in their home; and

6. The PRCIS would never task spies to report enemy ship deployments, etc.

Smith had little CI knowledge and Kaye had little regard for the truth. A match made in heaven.

This time, Greg's cross proved appropriately aggressive and dismissive, forcing many damaging admissions from Smith. As a bonus, each time Smith spoke an untruth, Greg used Smith's own words to contradict him, reading a portion from his book and asking, "Do you agree with what you wrote?" Smith kept mixing up "code names" with "code words." Greg revealed that Smith hadn't worked a "source"—informant—in over twenty years, and that his claims about the Chin investigation, the only major Chinese intelligence case to which he was tangentially connected, were false. Smith was *not* its primary investigator, and he couldn't remember major case details.

---

7. Hardly a hot spot of Chinese intelligence activities.

Smith frequently asked Greg to remind him what his own book said. When Greg replied, "I'll have my agent find it," I did so gladly, wanting Smith to eat every deceptive word. Greg was inflicting such massive damage that Kaye requested a sidebar. Carney declined, noting Kaye's earlier spoon-fed questions to Smith: "So as far as I'm concerned, the door is wide open. [turning to Greg] You can do whatever you want to do." Smith claimed the PRCIS did *not* use tasking lists because they were "silly" and "useless."[8] So, Greg directed him to read Chi's trashed tasking list out loud. He then told Smith to turn the list over and recite it from memory. He failed miserably!

> Greg: So you would agree that a tasking list is particularly useful when you are trying to collect technology, wouldn't you?
>
> Smith: Well, of course, yes.

Smith's book said, "If counterintelligence is for long-distance runners, then Chinese counterintelligence is for the ultra-marathon runner." Greg asked, "Well, in fact, your career working Chinese intelligence was more like a fifty-yard dash, wasn't it?" Greg then summarized Smith's career of less than six years of sporadic work on some intelligence matters, which had ended in 1985, twenty years earlier. Greg continued to pummel Smith with his own words, proving he knew nothing about Chinese counterintelligence, including recent cases like Katrina Leung.[9] This was their China expert! It was a pathetic performance by a small man who had missed feeling important and relevant.

When Smith claimed Greg was being misleading, Greg shot back, "They're your words!" To salvage his sense of expertise, Smith insisted he was recently briefed on cases.[10] When Smith compared himself to Rudy Guerin, Greg bit down hard:

---

8. Wait—hadn't the defense earlier, and repeatedly, claimed that *all* ethnic Chinese received tasking lists from China?

9. In an FBI interview years earlier, Smith stated, "The only thing I know about [Katrina Leung] is what was referenced in the newspaper."

10. Classic FBI executive hubris, thinking a drive-by, 30,000-foot summary of something equals expertise!

Greg:	[Guerin] has spent his entire career on the operational side of the FBI; correct?
Smith:	Well, I'm not sure that you would call—as I recall, he went over to the CIA, the Office of—
Greg:	That's classified!
Smith:	I think . . .
Greg:	I would move to strike that, Your Honor.
Carney:	Stricken. Granted.

Smith was so out of touch that Greg had to prevent him from spouting classified information! Greg piled on, pointing out that Smith's exalted claims of handling the Chin case were false, having left the case a year before Chin's arrest. Defeated, Smith admitted, "I wasn't the case agent, that's correct." Then Greg drove the humiliating dagger home.

Greg:	So there were two supervisors after you then?
Smith:	Sure.
Greg:	And Schiffer was the supervisor when Chin was arrested?
Smith:	That's correct.
Greg:	Did Ken Schiffer write a book claiming he handled the investigation?
Smith:	No.
Greg:	Did Tom Carson, the case agent, write a book saying he handled it?
Smith:	No.
Greg:	[quoting Smith again] "The database for determining [the PRCIS's] modus operandi is pretty thin. We don't have that many cases to draw on." But here you are today opining on what the modus operandi is of Chinese intelligence; isn't that right? What changed? How many counterintelligence cases have you worked since you gave that [*New York Sun* news] interview to where you came to testify as an expert today?
Smith:	I haven't worked any. I have been retired.

You could have heard a pin drop!

Greg kept going, quoting Smith's additional declaration to the *Sun* that without his help, Chi Mak would be railroaded. Smith's own book also said US warship movements were valuable intelligence, the opposite of what he now testified.[11] When Greg posited that an engineer is more useful in obtaining nuclear secrets than a farmer, a frustrated Smith flippantly replied that it depended upon the farmer's access.

Greg snapped, "I'm not talking about a farmer who might have a nuclear missile silo on his farm. . . . In your experience, have you seen a lot of Chinese farmers over here digging up defense technology?"

Smith meekly responded, "No." Humbled temporarily, he conceded that Hong Kong was infested with PRCIS spies who are also sent around the globe. Finally, Smith agreed that the PRC is "a very oppressive, despicable regime."[12] Greg stopped the bloodletting and closed his cross.

The truth was, Kaye had recruited Smith by appealing to his vanity, interested only in his SAC title, not his expertise.[13] Greg declined re-cross after this merciless trampling. Happily, either my disdain for Smith had rubbed off on Greg or he wanted to send the jury a message—or both. When Smith stepped down and passed our table, Greg did *not* shake his hand, something he had done with every other defense witness. The jury must have noticed. I was happy, hungry, and ready for lunch!

After lunch, Kaye called another irrelevant witness, his private investigator, John White, whose one small contribution was made moot by Craig's effective cross.

Finally, it was time for Chi Mak. I still couldn't believe it. As likable and charming as Chi could be, even Houdini couldn't escape the web of lies he had spun. Judge Carney dismissed the jury for a short break to discuss "handling of exhibits." In reality, the US marshal didn't want Chi taking the stand unescorted, but Kaye worried about the "message" an armed escort might convey. A compromise was struck: Chi would be

11. Ironically, the defense's Hong Kong shipping registry exhibit listed the wrong dates for the USS *Henderson's* visit, Smith's own ship of service. But Chi's ship ledger nailed it!
12. When Greg agreed, Smith got his one courtroom laugh, saying, "Glad we agree on something, counselor!"
13. Kaye called Smith more than ten times that year to convince him to testify, wearing him down through appeals to his ego, claiming Smith was Chi's only chance to fight a government frame job.

escorted to the stand outside the jury's view. I thought if the jurors always saw Chi seated on the stand, but never his arrival or departure, it would raise more eyebrows and questions, but no one asked me.

The jury entered and watched Chi stand to swear to tell the truth. I quietly rejoiced, "This is really happening!" Kaye dove right into their three main claims:

1. Chi believed the disc data could be exported because he published it at conferences;

2. He gave the discs to Tai to encourage technical exchanges of "Power Electronics" and "Motor Drive Technology," *not* to pass sensitive US technology to the Chinese government;[14] and

3. The data was meant for *three* individuals: Professor C. C. Chan of Hong Kong University; Chi's close friend M. F. Chan at Hong Kong Electric Company; *and* "family friend" Pu Pei Liang in Shanghai's "private sector technology community."

Then came Chi's background as victim and hopeless romantic. While growing up, his family moved constantly for his father's bank accountant job, and to escape communism.[15] His father in Hong Kong supported his Mainland family with no repercussions, and Chi's "cousin" Ma Fu Bang told Chi to study electrical engineering at Chao Tung University. That's where he met Rebecca around 1960. After graduating, while working at a power plant, Chi developed rheumatism from poor nutrition, spending almost six months in the hospital. For better health and employment, Chi moved to Hong Kong with Red China's blessing.[16] Rebecca moved in with Chi's mother in Guangzhou, later emigrating to Macau in 1967. This was a love story! Kaye claimed Chi visited Rebecca weekly in Macau via hydrofoil. Then he teed Chi up, asking if Rebecca was a beautiful woman. But Chi whiffed it, testifying that *Macau* was beautiful.

---

14. He had since jettisoned the lie that he wanted Tai to consult the discs and buy him QED books in Hong Kong.
15. Yet Chi's family later returned to Communist China from free British Hong Kong.
16. Who knew Mao Tse-tung's regime was so compassionate?

That's about as romantic as Chi Mak got![17] Soon after, Rebecca moved to Hong Kong to join him, where they married in December 1968. But in this tale of woe, they couldn't produce children, disappointing Chi's father. The vast majority of Kaye's tale was irrelevant and unsubstantiated; Greg objected, but Carney allowed it.

The epic continued, with Chi spinning the tale as best he could. He was working three jobs, yet he had time for a hobby—tracking USN warship deployments in Hong Kong harbor—all while landing three more jobs. It was there he met Professors C. C. Chan and M. F. Chan. Chi claimed he moved to the United States in 1978 because the US General Consulate in Hong Kong kept inviting him, and Chi found America's "higher power system" interesting. He didn't list *all* of his siblings on the immigration form because he, Rebecca, and Shouling decided they shouldn't, so as to avoid "negative effects." Clear as mud! And why lie? "I don't hurt anything, except me. But I don't think anything else." Figure that one out. After a series of jobs in Southern California, a Teledyne headhunter gave him a job addressing power distribution issues occurring within the US Navy's AEGIS SPY-1 radar system.

Chi declared that we FBI and NCIS interviewers had misunderstood him due to his poor English skills.[18] Chi never worked on AEGIS and never passed sensitive data to China. He was a hard worker, and that was the reason Chi emailed QED and DD(x) work home. That also explained the thousands of printed pages of restricted data there. Chi declared he never sent any of it to "a Chinese person."[19] Desperate to move things along, Greg stipulated to the admission of all of Kaye's exhibits. It didn't help much. Carney dismissed the jury for the day.

When Kaye confirmed Chi's direct examination would consume the whole next day, Greg expressed concern over the massive list of things the defense might address. Judge Carney counseled Kaye yet again:

---

17. Having watched these two for years, I can attest to this. There wasn't a single spark of affection between them.
18. Everything that had ever gone wrong was always someone else's fault—a common Chi complaint.
19. Yet he'd admitted sending the LAX disc data to three friends in China in 2005.

Carney: Remember the big picture. You are going to lose your impact, Mr. Kaye, with all due respect, and my comment is to try to protect you and Mr. Mak as much as to try to keep the case going. You fire so many missiles out to the ocean, if they don't hit something, you haven't made your point.

Kaye: (whining) The comments from my crew have been things have been going well.

I left court that day energized. I outlined for Greg each lie Chi had said under oath. The next few days were going to be fun.

I was psyched Wednesday morning, so I inserted a CD, cranked up the volume, and sang along to the Thompson Twins song, "Lies," and its chorus, "Lies, Lies, Yea-ah!" during my commute. I *loved* that Chi Mak was on the stand, lying for all the world to see, especially the jury. A reckoning was coming. Chi had a unique way of answering every question ambiguously, ending with implied qualifications and caveats that always left lots of wiggle room. Chi's defense was a house of cards. Greg's cross would be a typhoon!

But my enthusiasm was temporarily dimmed upon seeing two government attorneys in court—never a good sign. They represented Professor Robert Ashton, who the defense had subpoenaed to testify. It was an unwelcome interruption of Chi's testimony. The defense had kept our AUSAs in the dark, but Greg had no objections once I told him Ashton was good for us.[20] He specialized in power electronics and had authored the missing second "Secret" article within the classified Philadelphia symposium booklet from 2000.[21] He also worked with Chi, Bob Lee, and Professor Lipo on QED matters. More importantly, Chi had called him in 2005 requesting a copy of that article. Ashton declined, telling Chi to go through proper channels. By asking Ashton to confirm

20. What was Kaye thinking? Our previous interview of Ashton indicated all positives for the prosecution.
21. The article was titled "Algorithms for Reduced Scale Permanent Magnet Synchronous Machine Propulsion Drive" and was presented at the Third Annual Symposium on Electric Machines.

Chi Mak was cleared to view that QED paper—never in dispute—the defense invited the government fox into their flimsy henhouse.

Craig's cross highlighted Chi's strange request for a classified document, something Ashton had never experienced before. Chi could have reviewed it in Power Paragon's vault, but he didn't. Why? Because he needed a *copy* of it for China. Craig finished, and Kaye had no redirect. This defense move has always mystified me. Nothing Ashton said helped Chi, while much of it hurt him. Judge Carney declared a five-minute break, saying he needed to "go over an evidentiary logistical thing with counsel." It was time to cover up Chi's escorted trip to the stand again. I found this repeated, obvious subterfuge distasteful and beneath the justice system.

The jury returned, again finding Chi magically on the stand. Chi admitted presenting his QED and Solid-State Switch papers at the 2004 and 2005 ASNE conferences, but he denied attending them to obey trashed tasking list directives. Chi declared his QED paper was flawed and unusable, then claimed ignorance of export-control requirements and a lack of training. He portrayed himself as a "lifelong student" with an "interest in technology" who had innocently shared QED and EMALS with the world.[22] Chi's explanation for the trashed tasking lists? "I have *Sea Technology* [magazine]. I subscribe. If you read those magazines even monthly you will find all these names, the so-called task list is already there."[23]

Chi Mak did admit to a "technological exchange" with C. C. Chan, M. F. Chan, and Pu Pei Liang, with him receiving a 1979 book titled *Electric Machine Handbook*, covered with a brown paper bag book jacket much like American schoolchildren put on their textbooks. What did the PRC get? Contemporary, sensitive US Navy research on QED, EMALS, AEGIS, and other vital defense technologies. This was their straight-faced definition of a "technological exchange"!

---

22. "I'd like to buy the world a home / And furnish it with love / Grow apple trees and honeybees / And snow-white turtle doves. It's the Real Thing" (1971 commercial kumbaya "Hilltop" song, "I'd Like to Buy the World a Coke").
23. I dare anyone to explain this response.

Chi first met Pu in Guangzhou in 2000, when he began caring for Fuk's mother.[24] He never explained *why* Pu helped Fuk's mother, but he did admit to sending Pu technical data while claiming Pu "had some linking to some technical [*sic*] in Shanghai . . . Pu asked me if anything interesting technology or especially from the conference. I said let me see. If I have, I will send to you." Chi also sent testing standards to Pu through Fuk and 2003 magazine articles on linear motors. He vaguely explained that Pu had "some connection to the electronic equipment manufacturer in China," and that the dozens of places we found Pu's number in his home reflected Chi's concern for Fuk's mother's health.[25] Chi's testimony claimed more concern for Fuk's mother's health than even Fuk and Tai had expressed.[26]

Next, Chi selectively denied elements of his confession to Gunnar and Omar, while admitting others, continuing his vague rope-a-dope strategy: deny, but offer no reasonable explanation. This highly educated, fluent speaker of *three* Chinese dialects also denied knowing the Chinese word for "encrypt"! When Chi was asked why his "cousin" Cai Hu and "tour guide" Yan Feng shared Pu's 2332 telephone number, he responded, "No idea. I never compare them. If I knew them, I don't need to write so many out. Just one phone number."

Then they discussed Gu Wei Hao, who Chi claimed was Rebecca's "cousin-type uncle from Shanghai." Chi claimed irritation with Gu's 1987 letters to the Chungs, indignantly declaring, "It shows that he tried to make me like a messenger or carry something for Gu Wei Hao from Chung. Looks like that is the case. . . . I don't want to be messenger." Chi claimed he passed on Gu's respects, his business card, and a present to Chung, but *not* the letter. A 1988 Gu letter in Chung's home had described Chi as "a safe way of passing documents," while another one hoped Chi and Rebecca would act as Chung's couriers. Chi claimed all of this angered him, so he told Rebecca "No," and refused to serve as Gu's messenger. He did meet Gu in Los Angeles once, but ignored his 1990

24. Remember, Chi repeatedly denied knowing Pu during his videotaped interview.
25. Pu told the Maks to *never* call him from the United States. Strange rule, given the mother's care was such a high priority.
26. Yet Chi claimed to have spoken with Pu only twice on the telephone and once in person.

letter requesting contacts in Orlando, Florida.[27] Chi admitted that Gu was trying to obtain technology.

Another "cousin" came up, Ma Fu Bang of the China National Nuclear Corporation. Chi met Bang at his Beijing home and confessed that Colleen's testimony had forced him to acknowledge his extensive China travel, which he said was done to visit relatives.[28] (Chi never mentioned the multiple lectures he gave to academics, manufacturers, and government officials over the course of many years, which he never reported.[29]) This portion of testimony produced a lighter moment when Bednarski quietly repositioned Kaye's chair, unbeknownst to him. When Kaye tried to sit, he plopped down on the floor, rear first. Painful for him, hilarious for us.

While Kaye recovered, Chi denied DD(x) or other data went to China in 2004 and claimed the code word sheets were the idea of an unidentified niece attending a Hong Kong family reunion dinner. It was her way to communicate regarding Fuk's mother. Chi said he told her it was silly, but he went along with it and even rewrote a version for brother Tai.

Kaye: But you took it. You took it from her, did you?

Chi: Yes. This is same thing as the one she wrote it. But I correct something I think the English wrong or something. I correct it.[30]

The nonsensical explanations continued with claims the police school dormitory address he wrote on his PRC visa as his destination was just for show, to impress PRC officials. He didn't stay there. Chi continually demonstrated that lying to gain an advantage came naturally to him.

For the next phase of denial, this time about QED, Kaye regurgitated irrelevant minutiae to obscure the five-hundred-pound gorilla in the room: Chi's numerous ties to PRC officials. But humor was never too far

---

27. Maybe Gu just wanted someone to show him Walt Disney World's EMALS/roller-coaster technology.

28. If true, why lie about them to Gunnar and me, saying he had none left in the PRC?

29. Confirmed by sensitive source reporting we had to protect and therefore couldn't use in court.

30. Chi told Gunnar and Omar he removed two phrases from the code word sheet due to redundancy.

away. When they began discussing the Solid-State Switch paper, Judge Carney asked if this was a good time to break for lunch. Kaye said, "Sure," then began asking Chi another question. The whole courtroom laughed. Carney said, "I felt like we were in a different room!" More laughter ensued as Kaye looked around, confused, until Carney explained it all to him. Kaye apologized, saying it had been a long day, eliciting more laughter. Everyone knew Kaye was the reason the day was going long.

After lunch, the testimonial death march continued, as they spun every intercepted conversation.[31] Chi gave vague, convoluted, incomprehensible explanations for each redundant question Kaye asked. Greg's continuing stipulations to enter irrelevant defense exhibits helped little as Kaye marched us all into wonderland: Tai copied the DD(x) proposal on his laptop because Chi's computers couldn't, and Chi never requested the data be encrypted. Questions multiplied: Why not use his "manager's" DD(x) disc? What happened to the copy Tai/Billy made? Why didn't Chi return the "manager's" copy? Why didn't the defense call Chi's 2004 manager as a witness? The Chi/Kaye vaudeville act even claimed Tai "tricked" Chi, encrypting and sending DD(x) data to China without Chi's knowledge. Now that's chutzpah!

Then Chi called Bob Miller a liar, saying he allowed Chi to make copies of the Philadelphia articles that he put into a three-hole binder. Yet Chi couldn't produce the binder, or the extra copies.[32] The lies kept flowing: Chi requested the classified article from Professor Ashton for work, forgetting he already had a copy;[33] Chi received a tasking list from an unknown Chinese visitor to Power Paragon in 1988, which he placed in Shouling's empty envelope ("I just keep it there. I don't know. I don't do anything, but since somebody gave it to me during this visit, I just keep it there. I forget it."). Of course, he had reported none of this to

---

31. Another bit of humor arose. After Kaye asked Chi if there were "international people at the Future of Power Electronics Conference," Greg objected "as to what 'International People' means." Kaye cheerfully commented, "That's a good objection." The courtroom laughed and Judge Carney said, "You don't need me. You guys can just work it out," eliciting more laughter.
32. This from a man who *never* threw any technical documents away, including those from the 1950s. We all knew those binder copies were now in China.
33. We never found *any* copies of that middle article.

either employer or authorities. Once again, clear as mud from the Yellow River!

But Kaye found it all perfectly reasonable. Chi now admitted finding tasking lists in the "health book" from Pu and Billy and destroying and tossing them. "First I feel a little scared. How can this kind of thing come to my books? Second, I'm upset because I feel somebody tried to tell me to do something which I would not do, number two. Number three, I feel a little I laugh, because those titles so common, you can open the internet or many magazines, they all there. Just only the name."[34] Chi's lies were absolutely stunning in their stupidity and arrogance, an insult to the listener. Kaye's questions didn't dare touch the printed tasking list, given Chi's utter subservience to those instructions.

Next came trolling for sympathy, depicting poor, cold, confused, abused, and frightened Chi and Rebecca Mak the night of their arrest. The interview videos told a different story.[35] Kaye emphasized Chi's emotions: "How did you feel about that? . . . How did you feel then? . . . How did you feel? . . . Did you feel a little nervous?" As if Chi's feelings trumped facts. But facts don't care about feelings.[36] Chi's lie that Tai carried the disc to help him purchase QED books for Chi had been patently absurd, so it mutated into a new one: The data was meant for C. C. Chan, M. F. Chan, and Pu Pei Liang. Yet Chi admitted his truthfulness depended on his own cost-benefit analysis: 1) Deny knowing Pu—otherwise, "[t]hat mean you go to deeper into China. . . . He [Gunnar or myself] already said this passing things to China so I try keep a distance"; and 2) Say Tai was buying QED books—"You can say it's not true because without anybody's instructions, he probably can't select for me. But my intention still want some book back." For Chi, a lie was a fluid, justifiable self-help tool, and he could justify each one.

---

34. Once again, Chi's testimony confirmed the veracity of Chi's confession as recorded by Gunnar and Omar, which the defense had earlier charged they invented to further their careers. We're still waiting for Chi's and Kaye's apologies.

35. Chi and Rebecca were treated deferentially. Those arrested in China for espionage should only be so lucky!

36. Shout out to Ben Shapiro.

Chi: Yes, I downplayed this number because I feel they suspect me. Frequent travel must be a problem. I suspected that case.

Kaye: You didn't tell the truth?

Chi: Not true.

Kaye: Why didn't you tell the truth?

Chi: Later on I tell the truth.

[and later]

Kaye: Did you have relatives in China?

Chi: Many. Many. . . . I don't lie usually, I don't, but that night push me so hard, and I feel scared.

Kaye: Are you lying today?

Chi: No.

Kaye: Why not today?

Chi: I don't have such a pressure. I believe that justice [*sic*].[37]

Judge Carney suggested a jury break. Greg said Chi's cross would take two hours, so he requested it begin the next morning. Kaye boasted he'd drastically reduced Chi's questions, estimating thirty more minutes, and closing arguments taking two hours. "We don't think the jury has any loose ends. We're pretty confident." Once again, Kaye was removed from reality.

Kaye returned to his nauseating "Feelings, nothing more than feelings" line of questioning, asking Chi about his "hopes and dreams." Then he addressed Chi's second and third interviews. About the former, Chi actually told the truth: "That was very short time talking. Mainly Mr. Gaylord, he focus on two questions. One is, who trained you; second is, what is a code. I said nobody trained me and no code." Then he returned to lying about the NCIS Sunday interview, denying his confession, after confirming nearly every detail Gunnar and Omar had reported from it. He then made bizarre new allegations that Omar told him: 1) Ignore the advice of his future defense attorneys; and 2) The US Navy would hire defense attorneys for each Mak family member charged.

---

37. Chi is on trial for his life, yet *now* he feels no pressure to lie?

Kaye ended with a strange choice, playing the videotape we seized from Mr. Luo at LAX, unaccompanied by testimony.[38] The video depicted Luo's family life in China and his countersurveillance of Chinese university delegation visits to Harvard and MIT, before his covert filming of Fuk and Tai at LAX. This was baffling, as it helped *our* case proving PRCIS activity.

After Carney dismissed the jurors, Bednarski again charged the prosecution with intimidating its witnesses Lipo and Khersonsky with threats of prosecution. Judge Carney agreed with Greg that he had a legal duty to notify the Court of any witness about to incriminate themselves on the stand, saying, "That's why we hold our government to a higher standard."[39]

I ended up in Greg's office as he considered Chi's cross and voiced frustration over balancing the size, variety, and number of topics to address with the commitment to brevity he'd made with Judge Carney. He needed a common, organizing theme.

My advice that afternoon was simple and straightforward: "If Chi is so innocent, why all the lies?" Chi was *always* lying, while claiming everyone else was lying, or that they had simply "misunderstood" him. Everything was always someone else's fault. Chi was the eternal victim. This was true *long* before the FBI entered Chi's life. He lied to British and US immigration authorities and federal background investigators and employers long before he lied to the FBI, NCIS, and jurors.[40] Chi Mak was a congenital liar. To his great credit, Greg listened to me, a lowly case agent. I left that evening feeling confident he would properly and effectively barbecue Chi Mak the next day, and slept well that evening. Greg had this. Tomorrow would be a hoot!

---

38. Judge Carney had ruled that any Kaye commentary would allow the government to respond. As we readied the video, Carney told the jury they would receive free meals during deliberations. Greg asked, "When do we talk about our breakfast tomorrow?," drawing laughter.

39. A straightforward court admission that defense counsel is held to a lower standard, and boy, was that obvious with this bunch. Sometimes it seemed the defense was competing to see how low it could go without suffering repercussions.

40. I'd previously provided Greg an extensive list of Chi's lies, with proof of each, including intercepts, witness statements, surveillance reports, immigration and travel records, work history, etc.

I again rocked out to my Thompson Twins' Chi Mak theme song on my morning drive to court. *This* was the day Greg would lay bare Chi's deceptions. Rarely had I anticipated an event with such relish!

Once more, to continue the charade that Chi was not a prisoner, he took the stand before the jury entered.[41] Greg took off like a shot. No "Good morning" or other pleasantry. To my delight, and the courtroom audience's shock, Greg barked his first words to Chi: "Mr. Mak, you are a liar, aren't you?" (Hallelujah!) Everyone sat up, leaned forward, and strained to hear. Taken aback, Chi belatedly stammered, "N-n-n-no." With that answer, Greg was off to the races:

Greg: Well, two days ago in court you told this jury you lied on your immigration application. Do you recall that?

Chi: Which area? I don't recall.

Greg: About not disclosing your family members in China in 1978?

Chi: I don't call this is lie.

Greg: You said in court it was a lie. You admit it wasn't true; correct?

Chi: I explain the reason already.

Greg: My question to you is, it wasn't true, was it?

Chi: It was not complete, but not a lie.

Greg: Well, you knew it wasn't complete when you filed it, didn't you?

Chi: I knew that.

Greg: You knew it wasn't true when you filed it?

Chi: I don't know the difference between a not true or not complete.

Chi's evasive answering techniques were on full display, and the morning's template took shape: Greg asks Chi about his lie; Chi denies knowing what Greg means; Greg is more specific; Chi denies lying; Greg

---

41. Surely the jury must have seen through this defense PR farce by now.

applies pressure; Chi gradually retreats by obscuring Greg's question and meaning by claiming he was misunderstood; Chi minimizes the lie's effect before admitting he wasn't *entirely* truthful, and then blames someone else as an excuse.

It became clear that Chi lied whenever it suited him, using nearly thirty phrases justifying lying: "I did not tell the full truth"; "Not complete true, I agree"; "At that time, I don't distinguish this"; "I have several options"; "I just shortened it. I minimized the time"; "This accuracy I don't think is anything important"; "Different conditions"; "Depends on definition"; "I want to keep consistent"; "This is what I thought, not what I agree"; "I don't know if it is true or not."

> Greg: And "Not complete true" you said twenty-three times during the interview [with Gaylord and Newquist], didn't you?
>
> Chi: I did not count how many times.
>
> Greg: You said it a lot, didn't you?
>
> Chi: Several area, yes.
>
> Greg: Do you have a problem with saying the word "lie," sir?
>
> Chi: Can I explain? I have a problem.

Chi didn't lie only when "under pressure." He easily and readily lied about everything when it benefited him, no pressure required. On the stand, Chi became the Little Dutch Boy, stretching to plug his leaking lies in his testimonial dike. There were so many:

- The disc's data was for Tai / Pu / C. C. Chan / M. F. Chan;
- Chi's immigration document swearing he knew no one in China;[42]
- Tasking lists "came from magazines," Chinese strangers, Billy or Pu;

---

42. At one point Chi said, regarding his immigration paperwork, "I did not even mention my sisters!" Greg retorted, "Just makes it a bigger lie, doesn't it?"

- Chi sent no data to China;[43]
- Tai wasn't supposed to encrypt the DD(x) disc;
- A "niece" created the code word sheet to help Fuk's mother;
- Yan Feng was a tour guide and Cai Hu a cousin;
- No authorization was needed to publish sensitive technologies; and
- QED's Phase One research stage didn't relate to submarines.

Greg replayed interview videos, forcing Chi to slowly give ground. It was like pulling teeth from a flailing dental patient. Then he asked about Chi's huge lie to the jury days earlier:

Greg: You stated in court that you wanted your brother to give those discs to C. C. Chan. Do you recall that?

Chi: Correct.

Greg: During the interview on October 28 you told the agents you didn't want those discs to go to C. C. Chan, didn't you?

Chi: I don't recall I say that. [He did, several times, on videotape.]

Chi had no problem lying to government agents decades ago, years ago, or to the jury days or even minutes ago, even when under oath. He admitted that prior to the last three Mak trips to China, sensitive US defense technology was copied and encrypted before contact with Pu Pei Liang, then quickly added, "But no relationship!" Chi claimed the tasking lists and Gu Wei Hao's letters upset him, yet he never reported them to authorities. Chi told the Court he was poor, yet he owned his home and cars free and clear, with over $900,000 in savings.

Greg's cross often took a mocking tone. Concerning Chi's claim that the code word sheet was about Fuk's mother, Greg asked, " 'Good Material' . . . Is Fuk Li's mother a comedian? . . . She doesn't write good material like comedians do? . . . Is [she] a seamstress? Doesn't work with

---

43. Citing Tai/Fuk intercepts to the contrary, Greg asked, "Are your brother and sister-in-law in the habit of lying and making things up when they're talking to each other?"

bolts of material? . . . That's referring to technical documents; correct?" Chi replied, "No. I don't think she mean that. . . . [It was] meaningless . . . whole thing is ridiculous." Yet Chi edited and handwrote a copy for Tai and kept the original. The list only made sense when applied to Chi's life as a spy: "Cinema = Retirement"; "We = Tai"; "I = Chi"; and "Weather Uncomfortable = Come back here for work." Greg's dissection of Chi's silly lies was supremely entertaining!

Greg: Now, you say that your brother was supposed to be taking this disc or discs to C. C. Chan and M. F. Chan; correct?

Chi: Yes.

Greg: How were they going to decrypt the discs?

Chi: I never expected it.

Greg: Well, is your brother an idiot?

Kaye: Objection. Argumentative."

Carney: Overruled.

Greg: Is your brother stupid? [courtroom laughter]

Chi: No.

Greg: Why would your brother take three discs from you and encrypt them?

Chi: I don't using the word "encrypt." I don't understand, but I cannot explain.

Tai couldn't decrypt the data, and carried no contact information for either Chan. Was he a drooling moron? Greg also highlighted Chi's own company emails. He pointed out an email from Cindy Baleno to Chi: "It's necessary to get clearance from L-3 Corporate prior to presenting any technical paper," and Chi's emails to coworkers: "[F]or the international meeting, I think we need approval, especially the QED type application." One Chi email even stated QED Phase One was for submarines. Chi had lied under oath in the past twenty-four hours.

Then there was the law of averages.

Greg: You are a great mathematician. What do you say the odds are that your cousin [Cai Hu], your tour guide [engineer Yan Feng], and Mr. Pu [technology acquaintance], out of all the millions of people in China, would have the same phone number [2332]?

Chi: I have no surprise. Yan Feng and [Cai], the same phone number because Yan Feng work as a tour guide. Actually, is not real tour guide. Just lead us to show us somewhere. He is recommended by [Cai]. Pu same phone number, I have no idea.

As he often did, Greg let Chi's incoherent, nonsensical answers hang there as rotting, stinking reminders of how insultingly stupid Chi thought the jury was. Greg also mocked the imbalance of Chi's "technological exchange," pointing out that Chi gave China cutting-edge US Navy research and "all we get in return for it is this moldy old book," while holding up the 1979 engineering text Chi claimed C. C. Chan had given him.[44] In a defensive, hurt tone, Chi squeaked back, "It's *not* moldy!" I fought the temptation to smile. The extreme imbalance of this "exchange" didn't bother Chi, just criticism of the condition of his book.

Changing gears, Greg contrasted Gunnar and Omar's honesty with Chi's history of unforced lies, such as those Chi wrote on his application for a "Secret" clearance, claiming he had no relatives in China.

Greg: You wanted to lie so you can get secret clearance, didn't you?

Chi: The same reason [as immigration form], because they have no relationship with my work.

Greg: You telling me that you are getting a secret clearance to work on classified documents and you don't think that having relatives in China has any bearing on it; is that correct?

Chi: I don't think any bearing myself.

---

44. Espionage defendants and their supporters often criticize law enforcement for interfering with the "free academic exchange of ideas." The problem? This "exchange" always and only flows in one direction: *out* of the United States and *into* China, Russia, Iran, Cuba, North Korea, etc. Nothing valuable ever flows our way.

Greg: That's not the only lie you told on it?

Chi: I just keep consistent with my immigration records. . . . This
        was Yuri push me to go for that direction [security clear-
        ance]. I have no reason to really lie, no.

Greg: You had no reason to lie, so you lied for the heck of it?

Chi: I just keep consistent with whatever things.

Greg: Keep consistent with your previous lies; is that right?

Chi: No, I don't. I explain a little bit before. I don't consider it a
        lie.

Greg set Chi up for another perjurious lie, asking him whether he
took prohibited materials home due to an April 2005 company rule limiting engineer storage spaces, as Chi had previously claimed.

Greg: Did you take the article on the "50% Reduction in
        Virginia-Class Submarines [home]"?

Chi: Yes, I did.

Greg: And you had that *in your office* prior to [April 2005]?

Chi: Yes.

Greg: Nothing further, Your Honor. Thank you.

Greg plopped down in his chair, physically and mentally drained, and
whispered, "*That* was unpleasant!" I, however, found it *very* pleasant! We
dismissed for lunch.

When we returned, Kaye came out flailing away while avoiding
Greg's damaging strikes, setting up straw-man issues to knock down
instead. Chi's lies were simply semantic errors.[45] But Kaye couldn't produce one coherent explanation for Chi's code word sheets, finishing his
redirect with two weak declarations: Chi did *not* 1) give the discs to Tai
for China; or 2) believe that export of the discs' data was prohibited.

---

45. Chi Mak, who spoke and read English for decades at work, had misunderstood? Absurd. Chi's
English only became subpar when he was on the stand. It was all an act by this fluent English
speaker.

Greg's re-cross contrasted sharply with Chi's conflicting answers from that morning.

Chi explained he had changed his mind. Now Chi agreed that Rebecca had said Tai still needed to work on the discs.

Greg: What was [Tai] going to do?

Chi: I have no idea.

Greg: Did your wife frequently make nonsensical statements to you? [courtroom laughter]

Chi: I didn't say that.

When the questions got too hard, Chi refused to answer. He agreed his conduct had matched the printed tasking list's instructions, but he couldn't explain why. Chi could be absolutely exasperating.

Greg: But my question is: Did you not ask anybody in the jail, a guard or anybody else, if you could use a phone to call a lawyer? Did you?

Chi: The guard will not help me.

Greg: (frustrated) You're not helping me either. I just want you to answer my question. [entire courtroom laughed, including defense counsel]

Judge Carney called a recess to again support Chi's "free man" fiction as the jury left. Bednarski stood and challenged our three proposed rebuttal witnesses—Steve Schreppler, Jim Edmund of Power Paragon, and FBI co-case agent Sheldon Fung. They didn't like Steve, and wanted me on the stand rather than Sheldon.[46] Carney also wanted me to testify. Greg and Craig explained that my testimony would open a door for the defense to challenge the classified reporting on each covert entry, since I'd authored all those reports, whereas Sheldon had not, yet could also rebut Chi's testimony about storage of Electric Boat's "50% Reduction in Virginia-Class Submarines" NOFORN article in his workspace only

---

46. I agreed with the defense. I wanted to take the stand, *one more time!*

after the April 2005 workspace reduction.[47] That was enough for Carney. Sheldon was in.

The jury returned.[48] Kaye announced that the defense rested. Greg then stood and announced, "Your Honor, in rebuttal, our first witness is Jim Edmund of Power Paragon." He was Chi's product engineering manager. Greg gave him a defense exhibit and asked, "Could you just look over those last two pages quickly for us?" Edmund's review actually took a while, so Greg used the awkward silence to get another laugh, quipping, "Think I should know better than to ask an engineer to look at something quickly." Edmund's testimony thereafter sunk Chi's claim that Edmund had approved Chi's request to publish the Solid-State Switch article. Edmund didn't even have that authority. He also confirmed Chi's QED paper was restricted.

Kaye's cross opened with accusations that Edmund and Power Paragon had not cooperated with the defense, spinning irrational, conspiracy theories of collusion between Fred Witham, Gunnar, and me, before moving on to Chi's irrelevant positive employee performance evaluations. Greg had one question on redirect: "Why did you refuse to talk to the defense?" Edmund explained that he had spoken with the defense team before last year's detention hearing and had heard Kaye completely twist Edmund's words to Judge Carney.[49] Edmund said he would never trust Kaye again. I was delighted the jury heard a witness discuss defense deceptions.

During the break, Judge Carney relayed the jury's request to "complete the case today. They want a day off, and they really would greatly appreciate it if you'd just keep to the points that are really important, that they feel they understand the issues." Craig pledged, "Your Honor, I will do my absolute best." Kaye remained mute, and clueless.[50]

---

47. I had asked Greg to nail Chi down on this because Chi would lie, and we could prove it. So, Greg's respect for agents paid off again, as we'd seen and photographed this document in Chi's home in September 2004.

48. But Kaye hadn't, so Judge Carney joked he would greet Kaye's return by mimicking the judge in *My Cousin Vinny.* Just then Kaye walked in with a surprised, goofy expression, looked around, and said, "Nice to see everybody," getting a big laugh that he didn't understand.

49. Par for the course!

50. Again, everyone but Kaye knew he was the problem.

Craig called Steve Schreppler back to the stand.[51] I again passed out classified folders for the jurors to refer to, using a graph and keyword list Steve had created. Steve described "dirty power" versus "clean power" in a shipboard system, referring to "phrase F or phrase G resulting in phrase D and phrase E." Each phrase would be an engineering term with a classified meaning within the context of building a quieter submarine. Steve then proceeded to surgically excise each errant claim Bob Lee had made. The courtroom's mood lightened considerably during Craig's attempt to discuss submarine propulsion acoustic signatures with Steve.

Craig: Can you describe in more of a non-technical sense what each one of these little jags [referring to lines on a graph] would do to the shaft?

Steve: Well, without using a code list . . .

Craig: Would you agree with the characterization that if you have dirty power, each one of those little jags or pulses would be like taking a hammer and whacking that shaft?

Steve: It would be what we call an impulsive load on the propulsion system, yes.

Craig: So it would be like whacking it with a hammer?

Steve: Whacking—okay. [courtroom laughter] That's your characterization. Yes. Whacking it with a hammer.

Craig: I'm trying. [courtroom laughter continues] So the shaft, if it gets whacked with a hammer, something like a tuning fork, it's going to start to vibrate, correct?

Steve: Phrase G. [laughter]

Craig: Check. [laughter] If you have phrase G, you have phrase F . . . H, after you had that whacking with the hammer. [laughter]

Steve: That is correct.

Craig: And that vibration is going to go off into the air or the water?

Steve: It creates phrase D and E.

---

51. This was Steve's third visit. I loved him being on the stand, and like me, he loved being there.

Craig: Check. [laughter] And phrase D and phrase E would be picked up in the water if there was a sensor?

Steve: Otherwise known as phrase B. [laughter]

Craig was a good sport through all of this, endearing him to the jury somewhat, something he had been lacking. The jury already loved Steve.

The courtroom became Steve's classroom once more as he, pointer in hand, educated his student jurors on US Navy canceling harmonics used to quiet submarines. The defense objected to Steve's effective tutorial, so Judge Carney called an extended "sidebar," inviting the attorneys, courtroom reporter, and secretary into the enclosed hallway behind the judge's bench.[52] This left Chi alone at the defense table, Steve on the witness stand, me at the prosecution table just feet from the jury, and the courtroom audience, including many of Chi's adult nephews and nieces—Shouling's children.

As time stretched on, an uncomfortable, tricky, and sensitive situation developed. Jury members, sensing the trial's end was near, were in a jovial mood. Some of them began asking Steve about his plans for returning home, back east, and his eagerness to see his kids. Meanwhile, Gunnar and Omar came over to discuss matters with me. I became concerned that the jury's friendly, personal questions to Steve were becoming too familiar, including more laughter. No trial issues were mentioned, and Steve was *not* initiating the interactions, but still, it didn't look good.

Other jurors began asking similar questions of Gunnar, Omar, and myself. They liked us as well, even me, the straight man of the group. Meanwhile, the Mak relatives glowered at us. I worried they would report a twisted version of this situation to win a new trial. And there was no objective third party in the room I could trust to tell it straight. I began imagining future Kaye histrionics, shouted charges of "Jury tampering!" and "Undue influence!" But I didn't want to tell jurors to stop talking to us, which might engender hard feelings. The trial had gone too well to let this trip us up.

---

52. The official court record misreported and omitted these events. The jury was *not* dismissed but remained in their seats throughout this sidebar.

I whispered to Gunnar and Omar to find an excuse to leave the courtroom or converse with agents or linguists in the back. I then walked up to Steve on the stand, folder in hand, interrupting his conversation with jurors to "ask" him something. I whispered my concerns to Steve. It worked! As we continued our quiet "conversation," the jurors turned to talk with each other. Finally, the judge and attorneys reentered the courtroom, to my great relief.[53] Upon reentry, Judge Carney dismissed the jurors for the day.

The jury knew who to blame for their lost day off. Judge Carney warned the defense:

Carney: I'm worried that the jury is having the impression it's the defense's fault that we're not getting through this.[54]

Kaye: We'll take whatever they want to—whatever they impute to us. We're ready for it.

Carney: I'm telling you they're getting angry, okay?

During a break I warned Greg of the "sidebar" situation, fearing Chi's relatives might complain to Kaye. Greg assured me it was no big deal; I had handled it correctly. And *that* is why I didn't tell such things to Craig. He would have hyperventilated and blamed me. After the break, we discussed and dismissed a report that a courtroom observer was seen handling "classified" material.[55]

We then discussed jury instructions, Judge Carney finding both sides' ITAR suggestions confusing: "My point being is jury instructions get trial courts in more trouble than anything else. . . . Just give them the Yes/No question." This began a lengthy debate over "public domain" instructions between Craig, defense counsel, and Judge Carney. Greg's question—"One request. Can we leave?"—was ignored. Judge Carney

---

53. I later learned the sidebar had been a debate over Craig's intended line of questioning for Steve.
54. Any objective, sentient being would come to the same conclusion.
55. Turned out it was an attorney representing Greg Chung, taking notes to prepare for his upcoming trial. Carney reviewed her documents, declared them unclassified, and allowed her to go. She left hopping mad!

then ruled each side would be given two hours to make closing arguments in this order: Prosecution, Defense, Prosecution.

The next day would end all testimony. Steve continued his devastating testimony, demonstrating Chi's QED and Solid-State Switch papers were *not* in the public domain. Craig closed his direct and Bednarski began her typical aggressive, dismissive, condescending cross, mocking Steve's animated graphics demonstration as "your computer show." In turn, Steve continued to aggravate her with qualified, caveated answers requesting clarification or correction of her questions.[56] She tried to force him into being an expert in commercial shipping, but he resisted, saying "I do not follow commercial shipbuilding practice closely." When she criticized Steve's analysis, citing Bob Lee, Steve responded, "Mr. Lee should have done his own analysis and brought it in the Court and proved that. I disagree with any type of conjecture he made on the stand because there was no proof offered."

Bednarski was becoming unhinged and desperate. She retreated to the initial improper charges USAO and DOJ executives had foisted upon us. "You are aware that at the time of the arrest, the day after the letter [in question] was written, that Mr. Chi Mak was charged with theft of government property?"[57] Craig's redirect solidified Steve's jury credibility. Since Bednarski had nothing further, Steve was excused for a third time.

Our last witness was co-case agent Sheldon Fung.

Greg got right to the point. Sheldon had been inside Chi's home during surreptitious searches in September 2004, during which he saw the thick Electric Boat NOFORN proprietary presentation rather verbosely titled "Concepts for Achieving 50% Cost/Displacement Reductions While Retaining VA Class Capability and Providing New Capabilities," authored by Jack Chapman.[58] It addressed many other sensitive platforms, in addition to our new Virginia-class submarine.

---

56. My favorites: "[I]f you are referring to a boat as a submarine . . ."; "I don't agree with that complete statement"; "I think I would like to revisit my testimony in the correct context"; "I think I just said that, yes"; "I disagree with your question"; and "I think that's well-plowed ground."

57. Even at this late hour, another reminder of the damage feckless DOJ/USAO executives had visited upon our case years earlier.

58. We called this the "Chapman Brief."

Advanced Power Systems

NOFORN and Dist D
ELECTRIC BOAT PROPRIETARY

**Concepts for Achieving 50% Cost/Displacement
Reductions While Retaining VA Class Capability
and Providing New Capabilities**

Prepared by:

Jack Chapman, *Principal Engineer*

*Advanced Power Systems, Concepts
& Programs*

April 17, 2003

GENERAL DYNAMICS
Electric Boat   Copyrighted 2002 ©

NOFORN and Dist D
ELECTRIC BOAT PROPRIETARY

Chapman Brief TRIAL EXHIBITS 114 AND 185

Sheldon's testimony proved once more that Chi had recently lied under oath to the jury when he claimed he only stored this document prepared by Jack Chapman and other sensitive data in his house because of Power Paragon's April 2005 storage space limitations. Sheldon displayed two large volumes of covert September 2004 FBI photographs depicting the Chapman Brief in Chi's home, and testified none of our pole camera footage, surveillance reporting, or intercepts depicted Chi Mak bringing these or any other such large documents home in 2005.

Bednarski's cross tried to trick Sheldon with false "facts" she implied others had testified to. But Sheldon denied Bednarski each important straw she grasped at, until she surrendered. He had proven Chi's final lie, under oath, to the jury. Pleased as punch, Greg stood and proclaimed, "I ask for no applause, but we passed the finish line. We rest."

Judge Carney dismissed the jury, requesting they return Monday morning, and admonished them not to discuss the case with anyone, nor do any independent investigation, form opinions, or read or listen to reports on the case.

The courtroom stood and the jury filed out.

Administrative matters remained. The parties agreed on the verdict form, then negotiated jury instructions and closing argument formats. Craig then started another argument with Judge Carney over ITAR jury instructions, not knowing when to quit while ahead. Although I agreed with him in principle, he had a poor track record with Carney. *Finally*, Craig relented, curtly stating, "Thank you, Your Honor. Submitted."

Crisis averted. Monday seemed a long way off.

Our team discussed next steps over lunch, then I grabbed some time alone with Greg to discuss his closing argument. Craig would go first, laying out case facts, relevant evidence, and testimony in ninety minutes. Kaye would then have two hours, after which Greg would have thirty minutes to rebut Kaye's arguments. Once again, I advised he keep it simple, emphasizing lies Chi had told over decades, not just those to FBI and NCIS agents. Chi and Kaye never provided a credible rationale for the number, size, and variety of lies Chi had told. We had a great, plausible explanation for Chi's behavior, and could emphasize those lies Chi told the jury under oath. This was an extremely intuitive, commonsense argument every juror would understand.

We parted company for the weekend feeling good about the case and what we had accomplished. Monday morning, the entire focus would be on the individual efforts of Craig Missakian, Ron Kaye, and Greg Staples. Ours was the far superior team, with the law, facts, and common sense solidly on our side. I was confident, but I also knew individual jurors remained the greatest variable. The defense only needed one to buy into their nonsense. Was there a juror who would? Who knew? As they sing in *Les Misérables*, "One day more!"

CHAPTER 32

"Our Pal, Mr. Honesty"

AFTER A WEEKEND OF WAITING, WE GATHERED MONDAY MORNING AND watched Judge Carney issue jury instructions.

Then up came Craig. He opened by describing our country with many "rooms," occupied by people like Admiral Hilarides, Captain Eyer, Steve Schreppler, and Ed Chabay, all working tirelessly behind closed doors to keep the United States safe. Admiral Hilarides dreamed of the PRC opening its window each morning, looking out over the Taiwan Strait, seeing a prepared, intimidating US 7th Fleet, and saying, "Not today." Our technological superiority preventing war resided in places like "the engine room of a submarine. . . . Silence is a submarine's only armor. Silence is a submarine's only shield. If Chi Mak gets his way, PRC officials will open that window . . . [and] say, 'Okay, today.'"

Chi's crimes included two counts of 22 USC. § 2278(b)(2)—International Traffic in Arms Regulations (ITAR) for his 5-MegaWatt and Solid-State Switch papers, and one count of 22 C.F.R. § 127.1—Conspiracy. He conspired with others to send this data to China, knowing he was breaking the law.

> *[Chi Mak] got up and took an oath and looked you straight in the eye and said, "No, it was just a mistake." Just a mistake. Well, we know that he had lied before he got on that stand. He lied before, there is a chance he'll lie again. In fact, while on the stand, he got caught telling a real whopper, and I'll get to that in a little bit.*

Chi had years of export-control training. Even his own emails proved he knew his acts were illegal. Chi's own witnesses, lacking proper training themselves, knew it. His efforts to hide his actions demonstrated guilty knowledge. Chi and his co-conspirators told coordinated lies, like about the data disc's "music" being for Tai to listen to. And if the technology was actually faulty or harmless, why encrypt it? Why not email, fax, FedEx, or mail it to China? It was neither in the public domain nor a legitimate subject of "exchange." Chi published and sent this critical US military data in obedience to his PRC masters.

Chi Mak was also facing one count of 18 USC. § 951—Acting as an Agent of a Foreign Government and one count of 18 USC. § 1001—Making a False Material Statement. He committed numerous illegal acts to spy for the PRC and lied about each of them. We chose one lie—that the NOFORN Chapman Brief was in his home only *after* new April 2005 storage rules. Craig continued:

> *That's the "whopper" I'm talking about. He looked you straight in the eye and he lied. That's the whopper he got caught with because you heard from the FBI. They had been in his house the September before, and that document was already there. . . . You know that when this man retires to China, every NOFORN document in his house, every bit of classified information in his head, crosses right into China with him.*

Chi collected technology his PRC handlers demanded, then copied, encrypted, and carried it to China. Who received it? "It doesn't matter!" Craig explained. "He could have been sending it to M. F. Chan, or C. C. Chan, or Jackie Chan, for that matter. . . . It just can't leave the country!" The night of his arrest, Chi denied the disc went to *anyone*. Days later, he admitted it was for Pu Pei Liang, a PRC "Science and Technology" expert. Now he's added the Chans to the list.

And where were all these defense witnesses? Surely the Chans, Pu Pei Liang, Cousin Cai Hu, and his niece, the author of the code word sheet, could clarify things. From his college recruitment, facilitated travel to and jobs in Hong Kong, intelligence reporting on US Navy ships and personnel, to emigration to America, all were backstopped by lies.

"Everything he does, he hides, he hides, he hides. . . . This story [of the niece creating the code word sheet] sort of reminded me of an onion. The more you peel it back, the worse it starts to smell."

Craig turned to address Chi:

Mr. Mak, your country is the United States. It was that country in 1978 that you lied to on this form when you said you had no relatives in China. It was to that country in 1996, Mr. Mak, that you lied to get your SECRET clearance. And Mr. Mak, it was that country in 1996 you signed this document, an agreement between Chi Mak and the United States. And it was this document, sir, that you violated.

Craig had spoken for ninety minutes.

After a break, defense counsel Kaye stood and thanked the jury for their patience (as well he should!). He then made a proclamation:

The truth is, ladies and gentlemen, that Mr. Chi Mak is not an agent of the People's Republic of China. He did not violate export-control laws with information that was in the public domain, that he had no idea he was not allowed to send to China. He didn't make a false statement. Chi Mak . . . was engaging in a technological exchange.

Chi Mak was "a loyal American. . . . A good man, an innocent man, a man who has been defamed by this government." (I knew then that we had them! The evidence screamed otherwise. Ours was not a fevered law enforcement wet dream.)

I prayed that Kaye would continue this thread, and he didn't disappoint. He misrepresented everything, vomiting up the same old unsupported, unsubstantiated, unbelievable, disproven lies. The government fabricated a "confession" because their case was actually weak. Strong cases don't seek confessions (news to me!). Besides, Gunnar was "not trustworthy," and Omar was "a trained attorney . . . a wolf in sheep's clothing."[1] (This was Kaye projecting.) Kaye's diatribe finished with a

---

1. This "wolf's" argument was so absurd and contradictory as to be both amusing and enraging at the same time.

promise of more to follow: "I'm going to explain to you who is this man Chi Mak, that the government would not even bring to your attention." With that weak tease, we broke for a much-needed lunch. Listening to this manipulative weasel spin bald-faced, shameless lies was exhausting.

Kaye's second hour was spent introducing "This man, Chi Mak. The actual man. The man the government was unwilling to look at. The man who the government has been hiding from you this entire case." Thus began Ron Kaye's epic Hallmark tearjerker about a studious young man who is accepted to the best Chinese university, excels, works hard, and loves his job. He visits libraries to better himself and learns of superior Western power technologies, spurring him to move to Hong Kong, leaving his fiancée behind to hold down multiple jobs while sending her money as she cares for his mother.

To fill his lonely days and nights, this young man takes up a hobby—tracking US Navy warship movements. His beloved fiancée leaves China for Macau. This young man, a hopeless romantic, perilously travels on weekends via hydrofoil to steal precious moments with his beloved. Once she reaches Hong Kong, they marry and live with his father.

But young Chi still dreams of working with "big amounts of [Western] power," so this man of ambition moves to America, the engineering land of opportunity, marred only by minor, unintentional errors within his immigration papers, due to well-meaning but errant advice from his older sister. Thereafter, this model immigrant couple of destiny lives the American Dream in the promised land, while moving up the engineering ladder.[2] But what about the lies?

"He's not a liar. I mean, he lied. But put yourself in his position. He's got two six-foot men [questioning him] . . . and he starts to lie. He knows something is up. He knows that he is in trouble for something . . . [and the agents] never accepted a word he said anyway." Chi Mak was actually a *victim* of Western prejudice. A tragic story indeed.

---

2. My alternate version? "Well, the first thing you know, ol' Chi's an engineer. The kinfolk said, 'Chi move away from there!' Said 'Californy is the place you oughta be.' So they loaded up the bags and they moved to Dow-Ney—LA, that is. Classified—Defense Tech [cue banjo solo]." Apologies to *The Beverly Hillbillies*.

Kaye tried to justify each Chi lie, saying FBI and NCIS agents ignored all evidence of Chi's innocence. "This is not someone involved in spycraft. [Agent Newquist] beat up and bullied" poor, innocent Chi, confusing him. "I mean, a spy wouldn't talk to somebody, period. . . . They are trained." Chi Mak ignored Gu Wei Hao and his letters, never delivering them.[3] The trashed tasking lists? They could have been for anyone.[4] China sends these tasking lists to *all* ethnic Chinese.[5] Kaye continued,

> *The fact of the matter is, ladies and gentlemen, he doesn't have the qualities at all of someone who would be engaged in spy-like behavior. He doesn't. . . . [T]hink about how his mind works. . . . He uses his discretion. . . . He knew in his mind that the Chinese already had it. . . . Why should I not send it to China? . . . It doesn't mean anything. . . . Why can't I engage in this technological exchange with C. C. Chan and M. F. Chan and Mr. Pu Pei Liang?*

Kaye's rationalizations ended in a nonsensical crescendo: "The jury instruction protects human beings, because we got laws in this country!"[6] And this fool wasn't done, stating, "We are not hiding from [Chi] making some lies, during his October 28th interrogation. I brought that up first, if you recall. Mr. Chi Mak admitted he lied because of the pressure he was receiving. . . . This was not material to the case."

Kaye said the government and jury misunderstood Chi because they didn't understand Chinese culture. Chi's actions made sense to enlightened audiences. Kaye asked the jury to consider something:

> *[W]hat my response would be to Mr. Staples. You think about how I would respond to some of his arguments. . . . If Mr. Staples, as Mr. Missakian did, pushes this patriotic flag and says that we need to*

---

3. We proved Chi and Rebecca delivered gifts, business cards, verbal greetings, and letters to Chung. We even displayed photographs of the Maks and Gu together in China and America. Chi did *not* spurn Gu.
4. What were the odds the listed taskings matched the same electrical engineering projects Chi had access to?
5. Now *that's* some serious racial profiling!
6. That's right, dadgummit!

protect our defense . . . you just think about what I would say. Because remember our country and this constitution is not about fearing foreigners. [Chi Mak is] a fine, fine human being. [He planned on retirement and a quiet life], and then, ladies and gentlemen, this nightmare happened. . . . I ask you, ladies and gentlemen, to send this innocent man home.

Kaye was done. We all took another well-earned break.

I thought of all Greg's preparations for his closing. I'd provided him with two lists: "Chi's Lies Under Oath" (over eighteen of them), and another one containing *all* of his lies. Next to each I identified when and where the lie was told, and the evidence we had proving it was a lie. I'd also given him a ten-page outline entitled "Closing Rebuttal Points—The Sum Total Is Greater Than Its Parts."[7] I'd suggested Greg argue that Chi's strategy was always to lie, and to recruit others to lie for him, and then blame anyone and everyone else for his predicament, including Tai, Rebecca, and Shouling. Chi as perpetual victim.

Defense counsel had also manufactured lies to support their strategies: "compressed" vs. "encrypted"; "generic" tasking lists for all Chinese vs. specific lists for Chi; and inaccurate Hong Kong newspaper clippings vs. Chi's hyper-accurate ship log. And how about all the times they called us "liars" for claims they later admitted were true? Bottom line: They couldn't explain away the *hundreds* of documents, videotapes, photographs, intercepts, admissions, interviews, and other interlocking evidence weaving a seamless picture of Chi's work for the PRC since the 1970s. I didn't know if Greg would take any of my suggestions, but I hoped he would at least channel my disgust for Kaye's and Chi's lies.

All eyes turned to Greg as he stood for rebuttal. I was nervous, praying Greg would slam the door on Chi Mak, as his cross the other day had done. My concerns vanished with Greg's first short sentence:

A lot of lies! If there was a particle of truth in what you just heard, if there was an ounce of intellectual honesty, or even a shred of common

---

7. Craig would have tossed it back in my face or into the nearest trash can.

sense to everything you just heard, then why lie? If for four hours you have an innocent explanation like they claim the defendant had, tell it! They just told you the defendant spent four hours fighting to try to get the agents to understand what he is talking about. I think we need another dictionary out here to look up the meaning of the word "fighting," because apparently it now includes lying constantly. Chi Mak lied twenty-three times about Tai picking him out books, then admitted on the stand, "Yes, that's a lie."... Scratch off the false statement count, ladies and gentlemen, because he admitted it on the stand under oath.... "Not a material statement." That's a joke!... You don't have to understand "cascade topology" or "inverters." All you need to understand is human nature.[8]

Greg summarized his main points. Agents Newquist and Gaylord treated Chi with respect, but "he paid them back with lies. . . . Lies, lies, lies.[9] Is this how you fight to tell the truth?" If the data was already on the internet, why didn't Chi ever tell us where? Because it wasn't, and he knew it. During the interview, he denied what he now claims—that the data was going to C. C. Chan.

Why lie? [Regarding this] great technological exchange, he is sending them information on propulsion drives for navy nuclear submarines. And what do we get back? Nothing but a 1979 engineering book. There is no technology exchange here. . . . [If there was,] they would have brought to you something more than a thirty-year-old book to show for it. . . . It is a one-way trip to Beijing with restricted material.

Supporting our conspiracy charge, Greg pointed out that all the defendants told the same lie—that the disc's music was for Tai. The same lies for the same purpose. "That's proof of a conspiracy. . . . Conspiracy is an agreement to commit a crime. . . . You find an agreement from conduct." Chi and Rebecca created and delivered three discs to Tai. Billy compressed, encrypted, and hid them on one disc. Tai and Fuk hid and

---

8. Greg's entire closing should be required reading for future prosecutors.
9. My Thompson Twins song! "Lies, Lies, Lies . . . Yea-ah!"

carried it, headed to China. Greg then switched to dripping sarcasm. "I want to talk to you about credibility. . . . We have been with the defendant long enough now to stop calling him a defendant. We should give him a name, so I'm going to call him 'Mr. Honesty.' Given his track record, that will be his name."

The defense claimed *every* prosecution witness had lied—company personnel, analysts, experts, and agents.

> *Malarkey! They are not the ones who lied on immigration applications . . . to get SECRET clearances [or] gave military information to family members to take to China. . . . [Only] "Mr. Honesty" is accusing these good people of lying. . . . Most offensive for me, personally, is the attack on the agents in this case; specifically, Omar Lopez and Gunnar Newquist.[10]*

Greg referenced Jack Nicholson's famous *A Few Good Men* courtroom speech about US military men manning walls to protect society. Gunnar and Omar were *not* "glory seekers, though that's what [the defense] despicably try to impugn to them. They work in places like Iraq and ships at sea. They spend a long time away from their families to do their job, but their name never gets anywhere. . . . And yet, they are attacked? . . . Who is the proven liar in this case? It's not Agent Newquist and it's not Agent Lopez. It's 'Mr. Honesty' back there who lied."

Greg then highlighted Chi's lie to the jury under oath regarding his home storage of the Chapman Brief. Sheldon Fung's testimony, and dated FBI photographs, proved it. With quiet anger, Greg whispered to the jurors,

> *[Chi] sat there. He looked you in the eye. He lied to you. . . . The people who have been misrepresenting to you are over there [pointing to the defense table]. They said Chi didn't lie to the FBI, yet he admitted on the stand that he did. They claimed a technological exchange.*

---

10. I had urged Greg to make this argument, especially since both agents appeared to be well liked by the jury.

Nope! And they couldn't produce a single engineer who took and kept NOFORN data home. But "Mr. Honesty" did!

Even defense experts with no export-control training knew they couldn't send it to China. "They know that and [Chi] doesn't know that?! This is where your common sense comes in. You don't need to understand the technology to realize that's a bunch of baloney."

Then Greg's sarcasm skewered Kaye's claims that *all* Chinese receive tasking lists.

Let's look into a common Chinese household in Southern California— "Did you pick up the mail, dear? Yes, I did. Anything interesting? Oh, just some bills, a Penny Saver, and those pesky Chinese with another tasking list." That's absurd! Those are not generic lists. They don't mail them out. I forgot to ask Mr. Mak, "Does China get a bulk rate on its tasking lists when it sends it in the US, since they send so many?" . . . Let's stop and think where we heard those words [like EMALS, DD(x), QED, and AEGIS from the tasking list] before. Oh, I know. That's what he does! Generic? I don't think so.

And if the data was innocent, why did Tai, Fuk, and Billy hide it?

Why would [Chi's] brother go out and encrypt it? Is he a prankster? Is he just stupid? He's none of those. He did it because he was part of a conspiracy. There was no other reasonable explanation. [Chi] now blames his brother. . . . The finger of blame from "Mr. Honesty" points in every direction except one. It never points at himself. Everyone else is to blame.

Then Greg reminded us of all the broken defense promises of the "truth" they would prove. He reminded the jurors, "Our witnesses held up our end of the story."

Next, Greg shredded the despicable "racism!" charge.

The ugly specter of prejudice was raised both in their opening and their close. We, the government, are out to prosecute Chinese people. This is nonsense. . . . Can they point to a single document or a statement saying that this case came about solely because he was Chinese? No. This came about because his brother was at the airport with a disc with encrypted defense information. The case agent, who is married to a Chinese woman, he has got Chinese in-laws, Sheldon Fung is Chinese. Where is this great anti-China conspiracy? It's not there. It's not in the record. It's just rhetoric and argument from the defense with nothing to support it.

Mockingly, Greg read Gu Wei Hao's description of Chi as "dependable and totally trustworthy" and asked, "What's going on? Is it one of 'Mr. Honesty's' academic trade fairs where we all swap term papers? . . . This is not contested. Their interpreters looked at this. They are not denying that this is what it says. It says, 'As usual, you can also pass information to me through Mr. Mak. This channel is much safer than others.'"

Greg's masterpiece ended with a humorous, effective dig at Kaye and Bednarski of the defense—a reminder for the jury:

We have come a long way and we are done. I would like to say that when you leave us and you reach a point in life where you think it's going by too fast, think back to your days with us and realize you can crawl. Painfully, slowly, you can crawl [laughter]. We thank you for your service. We are confident that when you consider the evidence in this case, you are going to find the defendant guilty of conspiracy. You will find him guilty of attempting to export defense technology, and you will find him guilty of acting as an agent for the People's Republic of China, and you will find him guilty of making a false statement to the FBI. Thank you very much.

We were done. Chi Mak was now in the hands of the jury.

I was elated. Greg had knocked it out of the park!

Kaye moved for case dismissal, claiming we had produced insufficient evidence to convict Chi Mak. Judge Carney's immediate ruling and explanation was very encouraging:

> *[T]he government I believe presented substantial evidence during its case in chief regarding, among other matters, encryption, code lists, tasking lists, documents at Mr. Mak's home, copying classified documents, the letters from Mr. Gu, allegedly lying on security clearance applications, allegedly lying to the FBI. They presented evidence regarding the recorded conversations, particularly relating to the words "Red Flower" and encryption, the alleged confession to the Naval Intelligence Agents, the technical data contained in the QED document and the technical data contained in the Solid–State [Switch] document. I believe that evidence is sufficient.*

This should have served as clear notice to the defense of things to come, but as usual, they remained clueless.

Judge Carney told us to be within thirty minutes of the courtroom at all times during jury deliberations, then remarked:

> *I really feel that both sides did a great job. Mr. Mak got a very aggressive, zealous representation. So, no matter what happens, he had a fair day in court. And from the government's standpoint, this wasn't an easy case on some of the charges, certainly. It was difficult, and you guys did a great job. Some people can get bogged down in the technology and the documentation, but I thought both parties were very, very well served. It's a good case.*[11]

True to form, Greg made a joke of it all, commenting he was unhappy and wanted another try at the whole thing. I wasn't, and didn't.

Now we waited, and wondered. *What would win the day?* I was confident we'd get convictions, but how many? Everyone but Craig expected victory, yet ITAR charges could confuse a jury. Were we expecting too much of this one?

The first day of deliberations, Tuesday, May 8, remained quiet. I used it to prepare for the other Mak trials, this time organizing the trial exhibit books to be logical and efficient, grouping evidence by location found

---

11. As usual, Carney was being overly generous with the defense.

and type. Because exhibit numbers would change, I cross-referenced them with Chi's trial's exhibit numbers for easy reference.[12] I removed all the evidence that only applied to Chi and added that which applied to the other defendants. The number of exhibits increased to nearly four hundred because we'd quadrupled the number of defendants and defense attorneys. This would be a *long* trial, and summer.[13]

Next, I reviewed *all* of my testimony, knowing four new defense attorneys would review it and try to claim "errors" and "discrepancies." Tai's John Early and Rebecca's Stan Greenberg, both former AUSAs, would lead that charge, but I was confident I could frustrate them all as much as I had Bednarski.

Day two of deliberations brought a court summons to discuss a jury inquiry. Judge Carney notified us the jury had requested a copy of the entire ITAR statute. This fed our fears that they would become bogged down by its one-foot-thick stack of paper. Thankfully, Carney denied their request, afraid it would only confuse and delay them. Greg agreed; Kaye didn't. The defense sought any doubt, while we needed to prove things beyond a reasonable doubt, requiring simplicity and clarity. Carney told the jury they had everything they needed to continue deliberations. I was concerned ITAR might prove too complicated. "Espionage" would have been a clear, easy conviction, like "Agent of a Foreign Power."

That third morning was quiet. Speculation began of a split jury or verdict. I considered what great variables human beings represent. After lunch we received another court summons. The jury requested a portion of State Department expert Mal Zerden's testimony be read to them. As we stood for the jury's entrance, I realized our roles had reversed. *They* were now the show, and *we* the audience. I studied each face for clues but got nothing. The court reporter then read a specific portion of Zerden's testimony. With the prosecution's backs just feet away from the jury, we couldn't watch their reactions like the rest of the courtroom, but we could hear any sounds that they made.

---

12. When I delivered the final product to Greg, he *loved* it, thanking me for the time obviously invested.
13. Even without the droning meanderings of Kaye and Bednarski.

This portion of Zerden's testimony was great stuff for us, saying how Chi's data sent to China was ITAR-protected. My thoughts swerved to a Gunnarism: "It's all good!" After five minutes of reading, I heard a juror whisper to her foreperson, "He got it. He got it. You can stop." The foreperson stood and said, "Your Honor, we have heard enough. We are ready to go back and continue deliberations." Judge Carney thanked and excused the jury.

While he spoke, I broke protocol and turned around, curious to see what I was hearing. I saw the foreperson standing to leave. Next to her was the whisperer. I made eye contact and smiled.[14] Next to her was our old friend, Tattooed Love Dog. His face had always been an open book of contempt for Chi and his attorneys, and kinship with Greg. He locked eyes with me, smiled, shook his head in frustration, and shrugged his shoulders in resignation to indicate, "What's a guy to do?" He then motioned with his right thumb toward the jury's back left side and rolled his eyes as if to say, "Someone back there is being difficult."[15]

This was good news! Jurors re-heard damning government expert ITAR testimony. Yet the defense seemed even happier, laughing among themselves like this was a good sign for them. Was I missing something? Zerden's testimony clearly declared Chi's guilt. The jury hadn't requested any defense witness rebuttal testimony. They were confirming something, not deciding between two choices. When we returned to Greg's office, I informed the team of Tattooed Love Dog's behavior.

Within the hour we were called back—the jury had reached a verdict! I was optimistic and notified Sal and my squad. They invited CI agents from FBILA and neighboring Resident Agencies to come.[16] I

---

14. It doesn't hurt to maintain a friendly demeanor with jury members.

15. Years later I learned who. After giving a Chi Mak industrial espionage briefing to a group of Boeing employees, a woman approached me, identifying herself as an alternate juror on the case. I remembered her. My notes had identified her as a divorced mother of three, living in Yorba Linda and working twenty-one years for Boeing as an accountant. She told me she laughed during my briefing, knowing exactly to whom Love Dog was referring, an exacting juror—a technical engineer—who made everyone's life difficult with his constant pursuit of minutiae, the proverbial fly in the ointment. (Greg had always tried to exclude engineers, teachers, and postal workers from the jury, apparently for good reason!) We each gained insights into trial deliberations that day. I'd love to hear more!

16. West Covina, Long Beach, and Riverside.

watched the gallery fill with fellow agents and members of the press. The defense entered wearing big smiles, more upbeat and energetic than ever, and joking with Chi. It was disconcerting. What did they know?

Judge Carney entered and brought in the jury. Once more I searched their faces and came away with nothing, other than some anxiety. Who would they disappoint today? I prayed it wasn't me.

The foreperson confirmed the jury had reached a decision and passed their verdict form to the court secretary and judge for review. Carney stoically read it silently, then passed it back, asking the foreperson to read the verdict aloud for each count. In preparation for this moment, Sal and I had instructed our squad that there was to be no verbal or physical demonstration of emotion, no matter the verdict. We expected a win, but either way, we didn't want any "Yes!" or "No!" shouts, fist pumps, or angry gestures, desiring to appear consummate professionals, no matter what.[17]

Now came the moment we had worked and waited for, for more than three years, logging long hours and traversing years of ulcer-inducing obstacles. I placed my hands flat on the table, stared at them, and prayed.

The foreperson read: "As to Count One, the Jury finds defendant Chi Mak *guilty* of conspiracy to violate export control laws in violation of Title 22, United States Code, Section 2778(b)(2) and (c), and Title 22, Code of Federal Register, Sections 127.1(a)(3) and 127.3."

I held my breath and kept my head down. I didn't dare look at Chi or anyone else, afraid to break the momentum of the moment.

"As to Count Two, the Jury finds defendant Chi Mak *guilty* of attempting to violate export control laws in violation of . . . As to Count Three, the Jury finds defendant Chi Mak *guilty* of attempting to violate export control laws . . ."

My urge was to jump and shout—we'd won the most serious charges! But I wanted a clean sweep, all counts, especially a judgment that Chi was a PRC spy.

"As to Count Six, the Jury finds defendant Chi Mak *guilty* of acting as an agent of the Peoples Republic of China. . . . As to Count Eleven, the Jury finds defendant Chi Mak *guilty* of making a false statement as to a

---

17. And we did. My squad was magnificent throughout the trial and its conclusion. I was extremely proud of them.

matter occurring within the jurisdiction of the Federal Bureau of Investigation in violation of Title 18, United States Code, Section 1001."[18]

The courtroom was deathly quiet, but inside my head I was screaming *We did it!* We'd broken the curse, buried the "racism!" charge, and created the model for successfully prosecuting PRC spies! Guilty on *all* charges. Chi is a spy for China. The defense can't credibly spin *this* verdict, and we've badly embarrassed that wicked regime.

I let out a long, slow sigh of relief and looked up. I smiled and nodded at the beaming faces of Sal, Colleen, Gunnar, Omar, and other colleagues, quietly thanking them for all their hard work. Kevin Moberly smiled broadly at me and winked. He was happy for me *and* himself. His own PRC espionage case against Greg Chung had just gotten stronger. Our years of enduring immense pressures and unrelenting battles had paid off. We'd also defeated the low expectations of, and sabotage from, elements of the FBI, NCIS, CIA, USAO, and DOJ. Defense attorneys were now on notice. The lazy racism defense would no longer work.

I began hearing murmurs of "No!" among Chi's relatives.[19] I was happy to see the smug smiles wiped off the defense attorneys' faces, replaced by confusion. They were *so* clueless. They'd let their radical anti-government agenda obscure their client's best interests. Yet to this day, I doubt they see that. They never requested or offered a plea bargain. I was glad, knowing that cowardly USAO and DOJ executives would have jumped at any offer.

At that moment, they began to console Chi. His unrealistic expectation of victory that they had encouraged had now burst, and he appeared to be crying. Kaye stood and requested the jury be individually polled. Knowing how fickle people can be, I held my breath again and listened as twelve "Guilty" verdicts were confirmed. Judge Carney dismissed the jury, with thanks. We all stood as they left, and I smiled slightly and nodded in thanks to each. A few female jurors had tears in their eyes, I presumed

---

18. Because of poor USAO charging practices, and ICE mistakes, we had to drop all charges involving Chi, Tai, and Billy's theft, encryption, and transport of DD(x) data to China, creating the nonsequential charge counts.
19. Shouling's children. Tai and Billy were in jail, and the out-on-bail wives and Shirley never attended a single day of court.

in sympathy for Chi Mak, or recognition of the gravity of their decision and its consequences.

Now defense counsel bitterly moved to strike the verdicts for "insufficiency of the evidence," "mistaken interpretations of the law," ad nauseam. Judge Carney overruled each, before referring the matter to the "Probation Office for Investigation & Report," scheduling sentencing for September 10, 2007, and setting a June 11 deadline for post-trial motions.

We stood and watched as Chi was consoled by defense counsel and led out by US marshals. We then spilled out into the hallway, muting our reactions while some jurors and Mak relatives remained in the area. As they left, our celebratory mood and volume grew to big smiles, handshakes, laughter, hugs, and back-slapping. Agents and linguists from other CI squads congratulated us, declaring we'd paved the way for their efforts as well. Greg told me to invite my team upstairs to the AUSA offices before heading off.

When I entered the AUSA space and approached Greg's corner office, I saw him standing with a big cat-that-ate-the-canary smile. Greg brushed my extended hand of congratulations aside and grabbed me in a bear hug, lifting me in the air and yelling "We did it!" This was an extraordinary display from a normally stoic, cynical man. He put me down, shook my shoulders, and turned to open a small off-the-books fridge he and other AUSAs used to store spirits, offering everyone a beer. Despite standing DOJ, FBI, NCIS, and USAO prohibitions, many took him up on it.[20] All you could hear was shouting, laughter, and tall tales.

Hearing the noise, and the news, many AUSAs came over to congratulate us and have a drink. I didn't know most of them, but more than one told us they'd heard that the level of investigative and prosecutive support we'd provided Greg and Craig was unprecedented and becoming legendary. Never had investigators produced such regular, reliable, and immediate responses to prosecutor requests. I was proud to hear that, since I was determined from the start that nobody could credibly blame our squad for a court loss or setback. I was grateful for the AUSA comments but under no illusion that they or their executives would have

---

20. I demurred and waited for someone to offer an ice-cold Mountain Dew, my drink of choice.

apologized or hesitated to throw us under the bus if the case had failed, with Cardona and Craig leading the charge.

Amid this revelry, Greg was told that reporters downstairs wanted a statement from him.

"Shit! I've got a few beers in me!" he said, and asked us if he smelled of it. We said "No" and urged him to go down, but not to get *too* close to reporters, "just in case." I accompanied him in support. Finally, the prosecutor would be able to weigh in!

On the steps of the federal building, Greg gave a succinct, generous statement to CNN reporter Casey Wian of the *Lou Dobbs Tonight* show:[21] "We won this conviction because of the professional work of the FBI, . . . Naval Criminal Investigative Services, and the Department of Homeland Security. They did a fantastic job of investigating this case. The evidence was there. We just had to put it on."[22]

When Wian requested defense attorney comments, Kaye reverted to his oily, inflammatory, prissy form: "[Chi Mak] has committed his life to advancing engineering, and to advancing the defense of the United States of America, and we believe to hold this man accountable for insecurities and fear of the government is a travesty."

Once safely back upstairs, we celebrated some more, and I called my wife Melody with the good news. Gunnar, Omar, Sheldon, and I then went to our SARA-4 space to celebrate with the whole team.[23] We also called FBILA and FBIHQ leadership to break the news.

That night was one of the most content of my life. The burden was lifted and nothing could diminish its enjoyment. Melody made my favorite meal in celebration. I would now continue preparations to ensure the same result for the remaining four Mak defendants, whose trial was less than three weeks away. Chi's trial and conviction had shown the way. Life was good and looked to get even better!

---

21. Casey Wian and Lou Dobbs provided the only fair, accurate, and objective reporting we saw throughout the case. No left-wing agenda. Their only error was mentioning USAO spokesman Thom Mrozek's lies about an absence of classified documents as the reason espionage charges were never brought.

22. Greg had to pause to mentally work out NCIS's long name. And whether from relief, good mood, or the beer, he was overly generous regarding the DHS role.

23. Years later, during the appeals process, the RA changed locations and names from the Santa Ana Resident Agency (SARA) to the Orange County Resident Agency (OCRA).

CHAPTER 33

Et tu, Brute?

In the days following the verdict, we continued prepping for the fast-approaching second trial. While these defense attorneys were completely unprepared for trial on Tuesday, June 5, we were, so this would be a cakewalk. For all Kaye and company's faults, at least they had prepared for trial. This group had no SMEs, no witness lists, no linguists, so requests for plea deals were expected.

The only fly in this ointment was Craig, who continuously whined about his long commute and its effect on his beloved Porsche. He kept reenacting his "All is lost!" routine, voicing anxieties over his career and reputation. FBIHQ sources told me Craig was lobbying USAO to remove him from the case or force plea bargains. I welcomed the former, being done with his prissy complaints and disdain for me and my people. I told Greg of these plea deal rumors. He promised no plea agreement without my input. I was encouraged that Greg welcomed the upcoming Mak and Chung trials. Craig's efforts would fail, and Fuk, Billy, and Tai would get jail time. Rebecca wanted to fight, but her attorney Stan Greenberg had no stomach for it and was ridiculously unprepared.

Friday morning, June 1, I was driving to work when Pete, my newest FBIHQ China Desk supervisor, called to ask about the plea bargain with Tai Mak. I assured him it must only be a defense proposal since I'd heard nothing from Greg. Pete was adamant it was a done deal. I called Greg and he confirmed a deal with a ten-year imprisonment cap! Dumbfounded, I reminded him of our recent agreement, told him I rejected this

298

deal, and would see him soon. I was furious—with Craig, yes, but also with the USAO, DOJ, and even Greg.

I arrived ten minutes later, livid. I greeted my linguists, who we'd loaned out to help Greg and Craig. I entered Greg's office and closed the door. He was taciturn. I again reminded him of our prior agreement. What was going on?

Greg explained that his management had instructed him to propose Tai's ten-year maximum sentence offer.[1] He had offered it to Tai's attorney, John Early, that morning, and was waiting to hear back. Early was Greg's friend, a former AUSA who had recently left the USAO.[2] I told Greg I understood following orders, but *not* breaking promises. He had agreed to advise me first, so to honor it, he needed to withdraw the offer until the FBI had weighed in.

Greg refused, saying the deed was done. He must await Early's response. It was now a matter of his honor and reputation. I was angry. What about his honor and reputation over breaking his promise to me? Also, I had seen AUSAs, including Greg, nonchalantly instruct agents to reverse or withdraw commitments agents had made. So, only the words and reputations of AUSAs concerning agreements with defense attorneys were sacrosanct? The integrity of the average Special Agent towers above that of most AUSAs.

I knew Early would be crazy to reject Greg's overly generous offer. I needed to line up FBILA and FBIHQ opposition quickly. Greg then gave me the other barrel: He had also proposed plea bargains to Rebecca, Fuk, and Billy. Rebecca's attorney Greenberg had already refused, but Fuk's and Billy's attorneys had jumped on the offers. Greg's morning had been busy, breaking four promises to me in minutes. Fuk and Billy would get time served (no prison time!) for a guilty plea to a minor crime. My head was spinning. This was outright betrayal! To mitigate my anger, Greg explained that Billy and Fuk's deals required truthful admissions about their activities during a "proffer." Billy was coming this afternoon

---

1. I never did ask Greg *who* ordered him to make this proffer. I wish I had. My money is on Cardona.
2. This is what most AUSAs do: Get experience as a prosecutor, then strike out in private practice as a defense attorney for the bigger paycheck. Early seemed a very capable defense attorney, although a lazy one.

to do just that. If he lied, the deal was off, and we'd go to trial. Same for Fuk, who would come tomorrow morning. Greg asked me to attend, along with Gunnar and Omar. I promised we'd be there, knowing Billy and Fuk were inveterate liars, and therefore would sabotage their own deals. Then we could go back to planning their trials.

I saw two acceptable paths forward: One, they would lie, and we could go to trial. The other, they answered truthfully, and we gained a lot of actionable intelligence about PRCIS operations, methodologies, and personnel, here and in China. I discussed the situation with Sal, Gunnar, and Omar, asking the latter two to prepare questions to ask Billy and Fuk. Sal was upset with Greg and the USAO and contacted FBI Los Angeles management, which, to its credit, was outraged and complained to the Acting USA.[3] I told my superiors the rationale Greg had shared with me for the plea deals: DOJ and USAO executives "were elated and relieved by the Chi Mak verdict. They don't want to chance diluting its effect, which 'Not Guilty' verdicts concerning the underlings might bring."[4]

That was foolishness. Chi Mak, the leader, had been convicted. Any verdicts for underlings would come months later. Also, our strong case would come before the *same* judge and jury pool, using the *same* attorneys, agents, witnesses, and evidence! Greg added, "Besides, these are low-level co-conspirators, much like a drug dealer's mules, of little consequence." It was an absurd comparison. Rebecca and Tai were major players and military intelligence officers. I argued, "How many failed mule convictions have tainted the dealer's conviction?" FBI management disagreed with the USAO, but acquiesced, citing the foolish words of former FBI director and US Attorney Robert Mueller, "Let the agents investigate. Let the prosecutors prosecute." Hogwash. If I'd followed that advice from the start, Chi Mak would *not* have been charged or convicted. Agents do 95 percent of the work. Sal also warned me that nothing good comes from prosecutors cutting deals and sweetening the pot with promises of truthful proffers.

---

3. They dug in, claiming "an AUSA's reputation" was at stake, and offering no apology for breaking promises to the FBI.
4. As I've said, USAO management has always been composed of a bunch of cowardly fools.

That afternoon, Gunnar, Omar, and I sat in the AUSA's conference room, ready for Billy's proffer. When Craig showed up to conduct it, alarm bells went off in my head. He would do *anything* to keep this deal. Billy's attorney, Thomas Wolfsen, was there. He seemed an honorable and honest defense attorney.[5] But his client Billy was another matter, an ungrateful, sneering punk.

Craig lobbed softball questions regarding Billy's background and other trivial matters, dancing around the important issues, and asking nothing about PRCIS operations. I intervened with some basic questions to test Billy's honesty. He failed them all. Craig knew it but didn't care. Billy's attorney Wolfsen *did* care, knowing it could sink the plea deal, so he kept reminding Billy he must tell the truth to get the deal. Greg had said he wanted us to get valuable information, but since Craig didn't want that, the fix was in. He didn't challenge Billy even once. What did bother him were the pointed questions Gunnar, Omar, and I asked to test Billy's veracity. Craig needed this plea deal with Billy to happen, so he was becoming angry, not with Billy, but with us.

One of our questions lit up Billy's lies like a Christmas tree. Craig curtly called for a recess to speak with the agents outside, his face twisted in fury. We walked to an adjacent open space, near Greg's office doors. But Craig wasn't interested in conversation. He stopped, spun around, and shrieked at me, "Stop asking questions!" *He* was running this proffer and would let me know if *he* wanted my assistance, which he most certainly did not! He spoke as an English lord, dressing down his serfs. Craig declared I was purposefully sabotaging Billy's proffer.

Although taken aback by his shrill, unprofessional tone and volume, I was already loaded for bear, and gave him both barrels, shouting that I was still waiting for real questions. I shouted that Craig's inquiries' only purpose was to close this deal. He didn't care whether Billy lied, which he most certainly had, repeatedly. Craig screeched back that I had no say in this proffer. I'd had it with this spineless, self-important little worm of a man, so I bellowed "I am the *case agent*!" and would *not* let his sniveling cowardice destroy our work.

---

5. Admittedly not a high bar. Maybe it was because he had sons in the US Marines of whom he was very proud.

As we shouted at each other, a linguist Wolfsen had hired to sit in on the proffer session gingerly walked between us on his way to the bathroom, glancing back and forth as if he feared assault. I no longer cared. Craig's shrill squawking already guaranteed Billy, Wolfsen, and the entire office of AUSAs could hear this row. Rarely have I been that angry. Craig was suborning Billy's lies yet was blaming *me*? I came as close as I ever have to sucker-punching someone, which this weasel well deserved.

Gunnar and Omar also weighed in, more calmly telling Craig that Billy was obviously lying. Greg could no longer ignore this commotion and came out calling for calm and an explanation. Craig angrily repeated his silly charges, saying Billy had been truthful, and accused me of lying to sink this agreement. I repeated my charges that Craig was overlooking Billy's lies to close the deal, then reminded Greg he had stated that only the truth was acceptable. Craig interrupted me, crying, "Agents aren't allowed to run things!" I reminded Greg of his promise of either truth or trial. He considered this, then announced *he* himself would conduct this proffer session while we observed.

We reentered the conference room. Greg calmly explained to Billy and Wolfsen that "my agents" had proof Billy was lying. If Billy wanted this deal, he had to tell the truth. Greg would be the judge. He began his inquiry, but unlike Craig, he included follow-up and clarifying questions. Billy told the same lies, confirming my account and discrediting Craig's. Greg stopped the proffer to inform Billy and Wolfsen he wished to speak with his team alone.

I was confident of the outcome. Greg was obviously uncomfortable. After a long pause, he said, "Billy is lying . . . but we are going through with the plea deal." What?! We were vindicated and Craig humiliated, revealed as the gutless wonder that he was, but it meant nothing.[6] Greg explained that Billy was "a little lying shit," but he had USAO orders to close these cases no matter what. Once again, Greg's promises made hours earlier meant nothing. We had been manipulated. His "honest proffer" pledge was the only reason I had *not* declared war over the Tai Mak betrayal and had continued to cooperate.

---

6. Craig didn't say another word. Greg's words had confirmed Craig's cravenness. Craig and I never spoke again.

Greg claimed his hands were tied. I pointed out the obvious—that we would now also never get a straight answer from Rebecca or Fuk. I had no more words and left, crestfallen, while Greg called Billy and Wolfsen back in to finalize the plea deal agreement. Billy would plead guilty to "aiding and abetting an attempted illegal export"; all other charges would be dropped; and he would receive "time served," meaning immediate release from the Santa Ana jail once Judge Carney signed off on the deal.

Morose, I couldn't go to my office that day, so I called Sal to tell him what had happened, and that I would revisit it with Greg the next morning, Saturday. I didn't think I could ever work with Greg or the USAO again. Sal was supportive, saying he understood, and didn't try to convince me otherwise. He proved himself a savvy supervisor that day, and I was sincerely grateful. I went home and answered no work calls. I informed my wife Melody of the situation. She worried that I might develop an ulcer.

I went to bed early and woke up the next morning, Saturday, with new resolve. I drove straight to Greg's office, not wishing to speak with anyone else. Upon arrival, I greeted Len Pi and our other linguists who were there to aid Fuk's proffer session. I told Gunnar to "stand by" as I headed in to see Greg. I could hear Fuk's rat-like attorney Tom McDonald whining loudly about some perceived injustice or slight he believed he'd suffered, even though we'd provided a linguist for his client's proffer because he was too lazy and cheap to hire one. It was never enough.

I entered and sat in Greg's office and asked him to outline each plea bargain offer he was committed to, since truthful proffers were no longer required. I learned that Tai would receive no more than ten years, probably less; Billy and Fuk would get time served; and Rebecca had now been offered a maximum of three years. It was all now clear to me: Every lie I was told was designed to continue my cooperation.

I pointed out that we would be at the defense attorneys' mercy, even though none of them had made even the most basic preparations for trial and were in no position to bargain. We had held *all* the cards. Trial would be like shooting fish in a barrel. The USAO's actions were insane! Greg stuck to his previous excuse: His hands were tied.

That was no longer good enough. He had repeatedly broken his word, yet I was supposed to smile, leave his office, endure McDonald's crap, and ask my colleagues to work on a Saturday to aid a plea deal we loathed?[7] I wouldn't do it. I couldn't! And I couldn't ask colleagues to either. I'd worked 24/7, doing whatever justice required. This was *not* justice. I was done being manipulated.

My voice broke in rage and frustration as I quietly told Greg, "Other agents may not have the testicles to stand up for anything, or themselves, but I'm not one of them. You guys think you can make all the decisions and we just have to take it. But you're wrong. I'm not helping anymore, and neither is my team. You think you can do it without us? Fine. Go ahead. Do it."

Greg said nothing.

I stood up and left. Stopping at the conference room, where Fuk and McDonald were sitting, I leaned in and told Len, "We're leaving. You can go home. We are not helping them anymore." I ignored McDonald's protests. I was done putting up with this idiot. A confused Len stood up and joined me, asking questions as I pulled him along to another room containing Gunnar and our other linguists. I told them the same thing. They would be paid for their time spent to this point, plus their commute home, but nothing more. They should leave immediately.

Clearly distressed, Gunnar asked to discuss this in a side room. He understood my reasons but was concerned that our wonderful partnership with Greg, whom we both considered a friend, would break. Wasn't there another way? We both got quite emotional, flooded with frustration, but we remained on the same side, as always.[8] I told him I didn't know what would happen Monday regarding plea agreement finalizations, but I was done cooperating with Greg or his office and added that I considered Gunnar free to remain in San Diego that day.

I felt absolutely enraged and impotent as I left. How could things change so quickly, so drastically? I stopped at a nearby Carl's Jr. restaurant

---

7. FBI Special Agents are salaried. We don't get overtime or *any* other compensation for off hours or weekends.
8. Gunnar's support and friendship during our long-term partnership in this herculean task had proven invaluable.

to sit and think. I didn't answer calls from Sal, Gunnar, Sheldon, and others, suspecting someone would try to justify Greg's or the USAO's actions with the same old crap: "It's their call"; "We have no say"; "We *have* to work with them," blah, blah, blah. That was unacceptable. The one call I would have taken, Greg's, never came.

Hours later, I did take a call from Sal. He wanted to talk in person. I agreed to meet him at a nearby Taco Bell. He listened to my whole story. Wisely, he didn't try to convince me, order me, or excuse their conduct.[9] I appreciated this and said I needed to be alone to consider my options. I wouldn't let this stand but was unsure of next steps, other than refusal to help Greg or the USAO. I would not be walked on or stepped over. Sal understood and simply requested that next time he called, I answer. I agreed. Sal assured me of his support no matter my decision and encouraged me to try to enjoy the rest of my weekend. He was a gem.

I went home, thought it over, and discussed options with Melody. For over two years we'd defeated naysayers, saboteurs, friendly fire, and insulting defense claims to bury spy Chi Mak and his accomplices under a mountain of evidence. We'd demonstrated to the FBI, USAO, and DOJ how to successfully prosecute PRC spies. We'd also instilled newfound pride in the CI agent community. Yet weak, stupid, and political USAO and DOJ elements, which had handicapped us for years, were once again cutting us off at the knees in the eleventh hour, forcing moronic settlements rather than pursuing guaranteed convictions. My resolve was rock-solid by Monday, and I was at peace. Chi Mak's conviction was a fait accompli, yet the USAO was now forcing corrupt follow-up settlements, devoid of any "justice."

Predictably, Rebecca, that crusty old Maoist battle-ax, refused to settle, despite the generous terms offered. Her attorney, Greenberg, as disagreeable as McDonald, would continue pushing the envelope. That meant I still had leverage. With Rebecca's trial still scheduled for Tuesday, the USAO/DOJ needed FBI personnel for evidence exhibit book prep, witness scheduling, testimony, etc. I needed to quickly and publicly telegraph refusal to cooperate, meaning Rebecca's case would collapse.

---

9. I would have refused any such order and resigned. I already had twenty years in.

Monday morning, Tai's and Billy's plea bargains were formalized. Defendants and their attorneys sat at the defense table, and Greg and Craig at the prosecution table. No case agent! I sat in the back of the courtroom with my colleagues. Carney accepted Tai's plea to conspiracy and a sentence cap of ten years. His attorney, Early, expressed the expectation that it would actually be much shorter. Tai "waived" his right to appeal.[10] It was done. Greg, Craig, and the USAO had given their friend John Early a substantial gift for very little work done. They also confirmed Billy's plea bargain and immediate release.

I exited to the hallway intending to leave, but Sal asked me to stay. Other agents were subdued, unsure of what to do. An unhappy Greg exited the courtroom, saw us and our icy reception, and curtly asked, "What's the deal? You aren't going to help now?" I stared back in disgust. Apparently, Saturday's events meant nothing, or he had assumed it would blow over, like it always did, with FBI agents swallowing the bitter pill served them and moving on.

But this wasn't one of the thousands of white-collar criminals, drug dealers, and bank robbers who routinely cut deals. Espionage trials are rare—once-in-a-lifetime stuff—and *extremely* difficult to prosecute. We'd sent a message with Chi's verdict. It was now being frittered away. Chi's conviction required a perfect storm of talent and circumstances to succeed: highly skilled, complementary, experienced investigators fanatically working and sacrificing to obtain overwhelming evidence; an all-star AUSA; an excellent, fair judge; *and* Orange County's wonderful conservative jury pool. Greg had forgotten that Success = FBI + AUSA. I needed to remind him, the USAO, and DOJ how essential *agents* were to their efforts.[11] We weren't mere footnotes to their victories.

I walked away from Greg, voicing my answer: "Do it yourself." I took an early break to cool off, again alone, and pulled out the brown bag lunch Melody had prepared. Inside, I found the beautiful note of encouragement she'd written:

---

10. About as good as an AUSA's promise. Tai later appealed his eventual sentence.
11. Something FBI directors should do but stopped doing long ago.

My darling Jim,
I've been praying, reading Scripture, and crying for a while. No "this
is what you should do" answer has come—one of those situations God
in His Sovereignty wants you (us) to wrestle through, I guess. The one
conviction that has solidified during this time is that God's approval,
His honor, and working for His values (truth, justice, righteousness,
holiness, love, etc.) are tantamount, as they always are. I am praying
for discernment and clarity for you as to how to apply that to this
situation, and strength to follow through. If the trial goes forward,
I think the conviction of Rebecca will bring satisfaction in the long
term, but I know there are other principles to weigh in the short term.
My heart aches for you, but it is also overflowing with sooooo much
love and pride. You are quite a man and you are mine!
All my love always,
Melody

At the office, people didn't know what to do. Should they help prepare for Rebecca's trial the following day? I told them I would support
whatever they decided. As for me, I was done helping the AUSAs.

Hours later, Sal invited me into his office to say he had stayed
behind at the courthouse that morning and spoken at length with Greg,
reproaching him for betraying me. I don't know the conversation's par-
ticulars, but I *do* know that Sal doesn't pull punches. He is loyal to his
agents, a much rarer quality in FBI managers than it should be. I have
never met another supervisor who had the guts and loyalty to do all the
things he did. Most would have ordered me to "suck it up and do whatever the AUSA wants," and they would have failed. Then and there, my
absolute trust in Sal Valdez was cemented for life. We'd gone through
the gauntlet together, facing treacherous bureaucrats over the years,
having each other's backs, but this topped them all. Sal's managerial star
shone brightest in the FBI after Chi's conviction, yet he risked tarnish-
ing it now to go to the mat for me, no matter the executive criticisms
that *would* come.

With my twenty-plus years in the Bureau, I would have resigned rather than submit to this.[12] It was a matter of high principle to which too many agents surrender. I was indispensable to Rebecca's case and important to Chung's future prosecution. The USAO needed me more than I needed it. But whatever Sal told Greg worked, because Greg indicated he wanted to talk. Tai's, Billy's, and Fuk's deals were settled, but Rebecca's was not.

That afternoon I went to visit Greg. On the way, I ran across Craig and just glared at him. I still wanted to wring his scrawny neck. He looked down and walked away.

I entered Greg's office, shut the door, and sat down in silence. Greg began by acknowledging our squad's essential work in convicting Chi. He said he now needed help to convict Rebecca and Greg Chung. He didn't apologize for the forced settlements, again blaming USAO management. I countered that Sal and I fought our management repeatedly, oftentimes to obtain authority or funding needed to accomplish tasks Greg had requested. I simply expected reciprocal loyalty and support from Greg. Orders, I understood, but *not* promises broken in the dark.

Greg admitted to breaking his promises and asked how he could regain trust and cooperation for Rebecca's, and especially Chung's, trials. He confirmed Tai's, Billy's, and Fuk's deals were irrevocable, while admitting the latter two were inexcusably weak.

"What about Rebecca?" I asked. Turned out it was a ridiculous offer: three-year sentence cap in exchange for pleading guilty to conspiracy, with no proffer of truth required. I'd always assumed prosecutors with strong cases offered tough plea bargains with short acceptance deadlines, and even harsher terms if deadlines passed. Not so.[13] The USAO's offers were always painfully weak, with no response deadlines or incentives to settle quickly.[14] This was absolutely unacceptable. Rebecca, like Tai, was a highly culpable defendant. I insisted his offer *had* to have a very short

---

12. More senior agents should have done so when directors Comey and Wray turned the FBI into a partisan political weapon.
13. These weak terms proved this was no *Law and Order* episode.
14. Whenever I had suggested a deadline and escalation during past plea deal offers, Greg and Craig had ignored me.

deadline. If Rebecca didn't accept it by beginning of jury selection on Tuesday morning, it must be replaced with harsher terms: three *full* years' imprisonment, Rebecca's written confession to acting as an unregistered agent of the People's Republic of China (no spy for China had ever admitted this in writing), surrender of her US citizenship (notoriously difficult to revoke), and uncontested deportation to China, *after* serving her sentence. In addition, Greg must fight for Tai's full ten-year imprisonment at his sentencing hearing.[15]

I also told him I would no longer tolerate Craig Missakian's disdainful, dismissive behavior directed toward me or my agents. After Rebecca's case was concluded, we would never work with him again, including the Chung trial. Greg agreed to all conditions.[16] With that, we agreed to rebuild our relationship and partnership. I didn't respect, and in fact *hated*, what Greg had done, but I had to weigh his behavior over the last four days against his earlier stellar work and the great relationship, mutual trust, respect, and success we'd built over the previous two years. That afternoon, evening, and the next morning, I prayed Rebecca and Greenberg would reject the original plea bargain offer. I needed to test Greg's latest promise.

On Tuesday morning, I confirmed with Greg that Greenberg had not yet contacted him. My proposed deal was now the only offer! This didn't make sitting through Fuk's plea bargain approval any easier, however.[17] "Time served" for this criminal liar meant only a few days, since the USAO had blocked detaining Fuk because she was a woman. Fuk had used her freedom to "entertain" multiple men while husband Tai and son Billy sat in jail. Her equally unsavory attorney, Tom McDonald, strutted like a rooster, despite having done *nothing* to cause this result. Fuk had the USAO to thank for that. Comically, the hearing revealed that Fuk continued to lie, this time to the probation officer, claiming to be an only child (she had at least one brother in China). This sham prof-

---

15. If we had gone to trial on all charges, Tai likely would have received fifteen to twenty years' imprisonment.
16. I knew Craig wouldn't be a problem. He wanted off of these cases almost as much as I wanted him gone.
17. In hindsight, I shouldn't have attended. This bargain had been made over my and the FBI's objections and was unjust.

fer and deal demonstrated Fuk's, McDonald's, and the USAO's absolute contempt for the justice system.[18]

We now began jury selection for Rebecca, which proved surprisingly entertaining. Where Chi had appeared friendly and cheerful, Rebecca proved surly, suspicious, and aggressive, like a cornered rattlesnake. Chi had social skills. Rebecca demonstrated none, sitting there and glowering at everyone. Having a linguist sit next to her to translate didn't help. Judge Carney outlined the basics for the jury pool: a six- to eight-week trial, the charges, etc. After weeding out those jurors with hardships, Carney sat the first sixteen potential jurors in the jury box and asked them to declare any reasons they might not be impartial. Half raised their hands. Now came the fun!

The judge called on a middle-aged white woman for her explanation. She asked how long Rebecca had lived in the United States. Carney answered, "Nearly thirty years." She replied, "That's what I thought. I have a real problem with someone who comes and lives here that long and yet doesn't know how to speak English." Judge Carney dismissed her "for cause." A young Hispanic woman next to her then gave the same reason. Carney dismissed her too. Next, an older white woman in the front row explained her husband was a hydroelectric dam engineer in China when the United States had accidentally bombed a PRC embassy during Yugoslavia's disintegration. PRC authorities arrested and charged him with being a US spy. Many months later, he was released without apology and expelled. This woman was dismissed.

Then came a middle-aged Asian male in the back. He worked technology sales for a private aircraft supply company, so he regularly staffed company booths at international conventions. He and colleagues had noticed that PRC nationals visited company displays and "vacuumed up" handout materials and models, asked numerous, detailed questions, and took photographs of displays. The next year, those same PRC competitors sold "knock-offs" of their products at lower prices. He said China was notorious for stealing and copying Western technology. Judge Carney dismissed him. This comedic scene played itself out for quite a while. I

18. At least Billy's attorney, Wolfsen, had had the decency to be uncomfortable with his client's lies and undeserved deal.

loved it, and Orange County. Each dismissal was for something prejudicial to the defendant. And the rest of the jury pool in the courtroom was hearing all this. Our message was already being disseminated.

Then, a small, wrinkled hand was raised, front and center, belonging to an elderly Asian woman. In broken English she asked Judge Carney, "Do I understand, that woman [pointing at Rebecca] is from Mainland China?" Carney said, "That's right, ma'am." The woman responded deliberately, "Well, I am from Taiwan, and [pointing and looking intensely at Rebecca] *she* is my enemy!" I suppressed a smile. While Judge Carney dismissed her, I leaned over to Greg and joked, "*Boy*, I wish we'd been able to keep her." Her replacement proved acceptable to all parties, so the jury was now set. This had been much easier than with Chi, and loads more fun.

As we broke for lunch, Greenberg approached Greg to counter-offer probation rather than a jail sentence.[19] The old USAO regime would have jumped on it. Per our agreement, Greg declined, adding that the offer had expired. He outlined the new, tougher terms. Greenberg was shocked, unacquainted with this new accountability. He harrumphed, hemmed, and hawed, saying he would discuss it with his client but doubted she would accept. I knew she would, or Greenberg would force her to. He was completely unprepared for trial, having banked on a lax plea deal. We and our newly selected jury were ready. Greenberg was not. Unlike Chi, Rebecca was an unsympathetic defendant, and Greenberg knew she didn't have a dissident's chance in China!

After lunch, Greenberg returned, grousing and demanding a lighter sentence. Greg declined. In a very gratifying moment for me, Greenberg accepted our terms.[20] It was an important, hard-won victory. My refusal had produced three years of prison and an *extra* dose of justice: Rebecca's expulsion from the United States and return to her beloved national prison of China; and forfeiture of her US citizenship.[21] In the PRC, she

---

19. Greenberg knew this jury would give Rebecca the death penalty, if allowed.
20. This was one of my proudest moments. I had forced this change. At least Rebecca would receive some justice.
21. Any person convicted of betraying this country should serve their sentence, then be deported to the hellhole they were helping. It's only fair. They shouldn't continue to enjoy the freedoms and privileges this nation affords.

would *not* be lauded as a hero. China despises spies who are caught, much less publicly convicted, considering them an embarrassment, *especially* those who publicly admit to being their spy. Her leper status there was secure, being the first Red China spy in history to admit it in writing.[22] Thankfully, convictions and PRC banishments would also taint Tai, Fuk, and Billy. Ironically, US citizen and convicted main spy Chi could not be deported when his long sentence ended. But he couldn't further harm this nation, since he would be in his eighties, unemployable, and filled with knowledge only of old technology, *if* he survived prison. If he did return to his socialist paradise, he would lead the drab existence of a disgraced, convicted spy, a scenario that gave me great comfort.

Informed of our agreement, Judge Carney dismissed the jury and scheduled Rebecca's sentencing hearing. As probation agents formed their sentencing recommendations, we built our own while working toward our next big goal: the prosecution of PRC spy Greg Dongfan Chung.

---

22. I was also *very* proud of that.

CHAPTER 34

Closing the Mak Door

On October 29, 2007, Judge Carney officially found "Time Served" as adequate for Billy's and Fuk's sentences. It wasn't, of course, but that horse had long since left the barn. Even so, US Probation officers got it. They recommended *at least* three years' imprisonment for Billy and Fuk, based upon sentencing guidelines for the one low count each pled to.[1] The other charged counts weren't considered, including Fuk's marriage fraud business, demonstrating how Probation's whole process is whitewashed by the time it reaches the public. An outside observer would never know the truth. Note this deceptive report line: "According to [prosecutors], Billy Mak and Fuk Li received favorable binding plea agreements based not only on their lesser culpability in the offense, but also because of the litigation risk associated with prosecuting close family members, which was effectively eliminated when Tai Mak agreed to plead guilty." What "risk"? And if Tai's deal eliminated it, why the cozy deals with Billy and Fuk *afterwards*?

I didn't want them to enjoy an extra second of freedom in this great country, so I enlisted ICE agents to take Billy and Fuk into custody at the end of these hearings, to be held until deportation. Unfortunately for those two, but fortunately for justice, that meant they would remain detained for another seventeen months. The best part? The delay was due to China's reluctance to take them back, dragging its feet in issuing return visas. So, each received nearly an extra year and a half of incarceration because their Communist masters were ashamed of them. *That* is ironic justice.

---

1. This, despite the absolutely byzantine, ridiculous, and lax sentencing guidelines.

Billy Mak mug shot FBI RELEASED

Fuk Li mug shot FBI RELEASED

Fuk and Billy await deportation flight at LAX AUTHOR'S COLLECTION

I had wanted to see them off at LAX when they were deported, ask a few questions, and take some photos for closure, but I missed them, due to erroneous US Marshals' Office flight information. I did, however, speak later with the marshals who escorted them. They said PRC authorities were notified but never showed for the handoff, and that Hong Kong airport authorities refused to cooperate. As the marshals left to catch their own return flights, Fuk whined they had no money, relatives, friends, or place to go. With a more gullible heart than mine, one marshal gave Fuk $20 from his own wallet and wished them well (I would have told them to call "Uncle" Pu Pei Liang). Hopefully, that was the last US citizen Fuk ever conned.[2] I still get warm and fuzzy thinking about the rejection by their masters. On November 12, 2008, the FBI's *Congressional Notice* reported the "Deportation of Fuk Li and Billy Mak." That's the last I heard about either of them.

Tai Mak mug shot FBI RELEASED

2. Billy had close friends in Hong Kong and nearby Guangzhou.

After nine months of defense delays, Tai's sentencing hearing arrived. His attorney John Early expected considerably less than the ten-year sentence cap Greg's plea deal had guaranteed. Probation recommended five to six years, despite Tai being Judge Carney's "second most culpable" defendant. John Early challenged our evidence and Tai's level of culpability.[3] He claimed Rebecca—limited to a three-year sentence—had more guilt, and that Chinese hierarchical family relationships and "Guanxi" were to blame for Tai's deeds. It was the old "My older brother and Chinese culture made me do it" defense. After providing Carney plenty of evidence of Tai's guilt, Greg's filing concluded, "[Tai's] seeming ambivalence in the face of betraying this country warrants the maximum sentence of ten years. . . . Defendant repaid this country by sending its military secrets to the PRC."

Once again, Judge Carney proved he got it, better than DOJ and the USAO ever could, sentencing Tai to the full ten years. His opinion declared, "The offense pled to does not fully reflect the gravity of this case. This was not a simple exportation case." Carney cited risks to national security and our armed forces, including the lost DD(x) data that was not charged, and he pointed out Probation had not seen all the evidence he had. If the USAO hadn't capped his jail sentence at ten years, Tai would have gotten much more.[4] This was a great rebuke to DOJ and the USAO's weak charges and settlements. Early was *not* a happy camper, but I was. Once more my instincts were proven correct, over *all* the government attorneys. Early notified the Court he was stepping down as Tai's counsel. No appeals for him. He'd milked this case for all the easy money he was going to get.

Next up came Chi's sentencing hearing. Although the USAO prohibits it, since it sees agents as plebes, Greg showed me the US Probation Presentence Investigation Report and Sentence Recommendation for Chi Mak. They recommended nineteen years and a $50,000 fine, less than Chi deserved or sentencing guidelines called for. I gave Greg my two-page outline titled "Chi Mak Sentencing Factors—30 Years," attached to the sentencing guidelines and my long list of Chi's criminal

---

3. Why is this even allowed once they've admitted guilt in exchange for a guaranteed lower sentence?
4. Hear *that*, USAO and DOJ? Boy, did this judge get it. Cormac Carney for US Attorney General!

Chi Mak mug shot FBI RELEASED

acts and betrayals. Judge Carney had indicated Chi was the key to all of this, being the only person with access. Without him, this case wouldn't exist. He also had taken the stand and perjured himself before judge and jury. As the indispensable defendant, he faced a maximum possible sentence of forty-five years and a $3,500,000 fine.

Greg made compelling arguments. Chi was not only a spy but also a traitor to the country that took him in. His wife Rebecca had already admitted in writing that she and Chi came to the United States as PRC agents to steal our nation's military secrets. As usual, defense arguments both fascinated and repulsed me. After every maudlin and conflicting argument, they added reference letters from relatives and clueless "friends" saying he was an honest immigrant. The attorneys claimed the jurors had not believed Chi's NCIS confession (wait, what?); Chi was charged only with "administrative offenses" (hardly!); and that he'd suffered enough. Kaye's conclusion? "A very good man has been convicted.

... He will be an old man any way you look at it. ... He deserves more."
He certainly did, but not in the way Kaye meant. Chi Mak then gave
a brief speech as if the trial hadn't yet concluded: "[E]ngineering is my
life. [I] never intended to violate any law. [There is] nothing wrong with
knowledge exchange. ... I still am hopeful for justice."

After hearing Probation's recommendation, Judge Cormac Carney
published his twelve-page "Statement of Reasons," affirming our whole
case *and* the reality of Chi's confession to Gunnar and Omar.

> *Mak served as a covert agent for the PRC, [passing] sensitive naval
> technology to the PRC ... Mr. Mak betrayed the United States. ...
> Mr. Mak lied to avoid prosecution and conviction. We will never
> know the full extent of the damage that Mr. Mak has done to our
> national security. [A long sentence] will provide a strong deterrent to
> the PRC not to send its agents here to steal American military secrets,
> and it will ensure that Mr. Mak will never attempt to pass any of our
> military secrets to the PRC again.*

Aggravating behaviors called "enhancements" lengthened Chi's sentence:
He was the leader, had abused his employer's and nation's trust, and told
rampant lies to obstruct justice. Carney stated:

> *When [Chi Mak] told these lies to the jury, his testimony was certain,
> not faltering, and he did not appear confused, mistaken, or as if he
> were suffering from a faulty memory. Mr. Mak's lies during the trial
> were demonstrable, material, and willful. ... In fact, Mr. Mak's
> untruths are so pervasive they can fairly be characterized as a "trail of
> lies" used to carry out and then cover up his scheme.*

Man, Judge Carney was good.[5] He outlined Chi's "pattern of deceit,"
then sentenced him to 293 months in prison—over twenty-four years—
because of the grave harm he had caused our nation's security. Carney
hoped that "should Mr. Mak outlive his prison term, any military defense

---

5. He also had picked up on the "Lies, Lies, Lies, Yea-ah" theme. Innocent people don't lie to the
authorities.

information that he has retained will be outdated and obsolete."[6] He wished to deter others from betraying this country and rejected Chi's "upstanding citizen" claims.

> *The Court finds that Mr. Mak's lack of criminal history, good reputation in the community and professional accomplishments contributed to his ability to carry out and conceal his crimes over an extended period of time. Were Mr. Mak not such a well-regarded engineer and previously upstanding citizen, the government and his employer never would have entrusted him with and given him access to sensitive naval technology. But for his good reputation and covert behavior, Mr. Mak never could have committed his crimes against the United States.*

The sentencing guidelines recommended a range of 235 to 293 months, so I was happy with Carney's maximum, along with a $50,000 fine. His ruling finally hit home with Chi, who wiped his eyes. He would serve his sentence at the minimum-security federal correctional institution (FCI) in Lompoc, California. Kaye then announced he would *not* handle Chi's appeals, getting out while the getting was good. Appeals attorney work was hard, an uphill battle, and didn't produce the publicity and pay Kaye and company craved.

That didn't end the challenges, however.

A year later, Judge Carney denied "Defendant's Motion to Vacate the Conviction and for New Trial" after Chi's new attorneys alleged a "Brady violation." More fabricated nonsense arrived with Greenberg's "Hail Mary" pass, alleging "egregious government misconduct." In truth, Bill Gertz of the *Washington Times* had printed a story quoting "senior Justice Department officials," most of which was wrong.[7] Some deeply buried government apparatchik back east had leaked bad information, and Greenberg hoped to taint us with this.

Judge Carney "ordered the government to submit a status report on the investigation it has undertaken to determine whether any government

---

6. Judge Carney clearly understood the gravity of Chi's crimes.
7. Just some tidbits of reported information were true.

official had improper communications with Mr. Gertz." The yearlong FBI investigation by WFO agents interviewed over five hundred people and pointed to *two* leakers, an NCIS analyst and a DOJ official. Judge Carney ordered Gertz to appear on June 13, 2008, to identify his source. We all believed Gertz would claim First Amendment rights of the press.

The morning of the hearing, the WFO agent was both angry and apologetic. DOJ attorneys had just arrived with new marching orders. When Carney brought Gertz to the stand, in a complete reversal, they announced they were withdrawing their subpoena for Gertz and *opposing* his questioning. Carney, nearly speechless, said, "I feel like a prom date left waiting on the curb." Greenberg was apoplectic, not far off from his usual demeanor. This one time, he was justified. Once again, a last-minute DOJ betrayal, *after* agents had invested a year and thousands of hours in hundreds of interviews. DOJ hadn't even forewarned Greg ("Watch out for CES—they'll screw you every time."). Their arrogance was breathtaking but no mystery. They were protecting their own, the DOJ leaker. That fact had doomed the WFO investigation.

Rebecca's scheduled September 2008 plea deal formalization was delayed once again, to October, after Greenberg arrived late to request it. He told Greg, "I think [Rebecca] is getting very bad advice from someone in the Chinese community." It would eventually prove worth the wait and even more entertaining than Rebecca's jury selection. Greg and I sat at the prosecution table—Craig was thankfully long gone—as Judge Carney went over the sentencing guidelines, with each phrase painstakingly translated into Mandarin for Rebecca. Carney was "comfortable that a three-year sentence as stipulated by the parties . . . is a fair and appropriate sentence in this case."[8] Carney agreed to Greenberg's request that Rebecca's citizenship revocation be delayed until after her sentence concluded, to prevent deportation delays.[9] It was now time for Rebecca to make her statement before final sentencing. Greenberg hesitated. Carney probed, "Does she wish to make a statement?" Greenberg replied, "I don't

---

8. Greenberg had lobbied Carney for a lesser sentence. Whatever happened to honoring your agreements?
9. Deliciously, Greenberg's request guaranteed Rebecca an extended ICE detention thanks to deportation delays courtesy of PRC reluctance to issue her a visa and accept her return to the motherland.

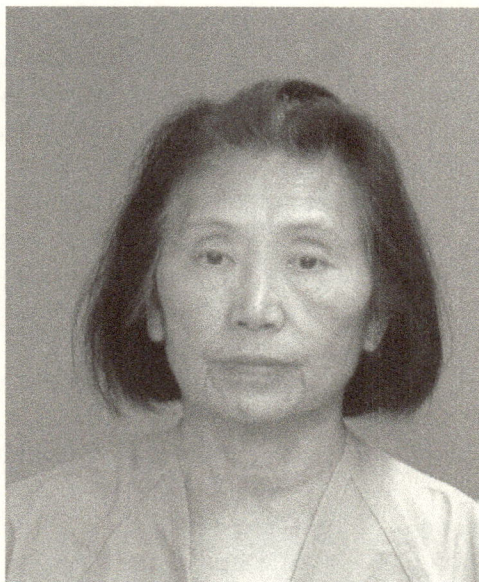

Rebecca Chiu mug shot FBI RELEASED

think it will be very helpful, but yes, she wants to make a statement." As he walked back to his table, Greenberg whispered to Greg, "This is the part that makes me nervous."

Rebecca stood, took out notes, and calmly began reading in broken English, "Consideration for imprisonment in home last three years" (she was requesting credit for the time she was free on bail during the Mak prosecutions). Her mitigation claims continued: "arrested in bed," "not shown a warrant," and spending "twelve days in jail." Rebecca also declared she was a victim of "visa fraud," illegal telephone taps *after* the arrests, "bank account theft," "ID theft," and "great physical and psychological suffering," predicting she "may get sick from stress." She declared it was "not a crime to know about or like" electrical engineering, and vowed, "Love this country. Didn't hurt or betray it. Didn't violate any law. Fulfilled obligation as citizen."

Throughout all this, Greenberg interrupted her repeatedly to take her aside. Everyone could hear him loudly and emphatically whisper, "This is *exactly* what I said you *couldn't* say! You have put the judge in a very difficult position. Don't say it again!" But Rebecca kept at it as Greenberg kept apologizing for Rebecca's words and behavior, requesting Judge Carney's understanding. It was a joy to behold. When Rebecca's statements continued to veer into dangerous territory, Greenberg nudged her. She stopped, looked at him, and he snapped, "You're done!" Rebecca began to speak, but he repeated emphatically, "You're done!" He leaned into her ear and whispered loudly in frustration, "We discussed this already! You can't say those sorts of things. You said that you would agree and sign this!" Rebecca stopped talking. Greenberg turned to Carney and said, "I believe she is finished. Thank you. She's done."

Carney asked for Greg's input. Greg said, "These agents, many of whom are here in Court, the Court has seen before, are really the finest I have worked with in my career and are a real credit to the government, and I'm confident none of them had anything to do with [Rebecca's claims of victimization]." Greg added that her claim, "I did not breach the law," had to be withdrawn, since it contradicted her guilty plea. Otherwise, we should go to trial, and "if we went to trial, we would win."

My heart jumped. I still wanted a crack at lengthening Rebecca's sentence, maybe to fifteen years. If Rebecca's statements were left as is, she was guaranteed an automatic appeal. Carney declared Rebecca's guilt was "proven beyond a reasonable doubt at [Chi Mak's] trial." He clarified that she must admit guilt to get this plea deal. Carney asked her, "Were you an agent of the PRC as you previously represented to me?"

Greenberg requested a ten-minute recess to "explain" the question to his client, beginning a long, torturous process of bargaining and threatening that was loads of fun to witness, especially since it was murder for Greenberg. Finally, he shoehorned her into verbally agreeing to plead guilty and sign the admission. Carney asked her his question again. She hesitated, looked over at a glaring Greenberg, and weakly answered "Yes." Carney commented that had this been a different case, Rebecca's behavior would have made him nervous. But he had seen the "extensive record of Mrs. Chiu's guilt. . . . Over a six-week trial I saw overwhelming evidence of her guilt." He assured Rebecca that she had faced major jail time and was very fortunate to get this sentence.[10]

---

10. Tell me about it! My instincts and our results repeatedly proved how wrong the USAO/DOJ got *everything*.

But Rebecca wasn't done yet. She jumped in to say, "I merely want to say, as a citizen, I fulfilled my obligation as a citizen. That I'm willing to obey the law. I'm finished."[11]

Judge Carney then gently addressed Rebecca's various ridiculous claims and reiterated that she "got an incredible deal."[12] Greenberg, panicking that the plea deal was collapsing, did his best to explain away Rebecca's "confused" statements before asking, "Can I just interrupt again? I just need a moment with my client." This was more than I could have hoped for.

Greg stepped in to extend a humbled, sweating Greenberg some mercy by indicating that the government was satisfied. Judge Carney accepted the plea and ordered Rebecca to surrender to "the Bureau of Prisons on or before 12:00 noon on November 27, 2008 (Thanksgiving Day!)," to serve three years at the Dublin women's prison in Northern California.

When Carney then advised Rebecca of her limited right of appeal, her eyes lit up as she asked, "I still appeal?" I had to stifle a laugh. It reminded me of the *Dumb and Dumber* scene where the girl tells Jim Carrey's character his chances with her are one in a million, and his face lights up as he triumphantly exclaims, "So you're saying there's a chance!" Carney tried to tamp down her enthusiasm by stressing the limited scope of her appeal. Undeterred, she asked, "So, if I want to appeal now, do I say it now?" Carney tiredly responded, "No. You have ten days." He then accepted Greg's motion to dismiss all other counts against Rebecca and closed the proceedings. A relieved Greenberg said, "Welcome to my world. Thank you, Your Honor."[13] All the Maks were now convicted: two deported, and three shipped off to prison, with future deportation for two of those.

Still, related events kept popping up. We'd had an acceptable working relationship with Melissa, our primary contact at Langley during the

---

11. Greenberg, a difficult personality, fully deserved Rebecca, an equally difficult personality.
12. Rebecca's complaints about being free on bail made me wish yet again that the USAO had allowed us to detain her and Fuk as I had wanted. Then she *really* would have had something to complain about.
13. No sympathy here. Cry me a river.

case, with little of the usual CIA snobbery.[14] But when the CIA began blackmailing our tradecraft SME nominees to force their withdrawal, I'd prohibited any further CIA contact. Now Melissa's colleague Auburn asked to meet with us, acting hurt and confused over our shunning, and claiming ignorance of CIA actions, which she attributed to a different unit. Her "left hand doesn't know what the right hand is doing" explanation was rehearsed and familiar. I expected the CIA to lie to enemies, not friends. They changed nothing with this approach.

With all Mak proceedings finished, Greg told me to save anything we wanted that was stored within the AUSA meeting space before it was destroyed the following Monday, to make room for their next big trial.[15] It had been our "war room" for three years and was a well-stocked, efficient thing of beauty.[16] Since most of its contents held historic significance and might still be needed for appeals, I told Greg I wanted to save core materials like original evidence, motions, transcripts, and other important documentation. He agreed. I personally spent days sifting through the room's contents and transporting items to our secure OCRA space.[17]

During my team's transition back to a normal FBI counterintelligence squad, interesting, related events continued to surface. As I had predicted, the Mak case kept returning to life. Despite Rebecca's plea deal's waiver of rights, in keeping with her personality and our system's weaknesses, she was granted seven extension requests to hire an attorney to appeal the terms of the agreements she had signed. The Court finally and mercifully dismissed her eighth request as she neared the end of her sentence.[18]

Rebecca's attorney, Stan Greenberg, had requested she retain her US citizenship until her prison release, hoping she would slip through the cracks and remain a citizen in the United States. Left up to ICE, he would have succeeded.[19] But Greenberg didn't know me. That would only

---

14. Although one CIA officer had told me FBI agents were "nothing more than flatfoots [cops]."
15. Thus, continuing this "great circle of trial life," to misquote *The Lion King*.
16. We mostly stocked it with AUSA office supplies because they always had better stuff. Lawyers, right?
17. This is one reason for all the specific details I've been able to give in my account here.
18. Of course, taxpayers footed the bill for all of this Rebecca foolishness.
19. She left prison with no ICE detainer filed, free to roam the United States.

happen with my untimely death![20] I waited patiently, watching for the Bureau of Prisons (BOP) notification of imminent release, which should trigger the ICE detainer in place. I didn't want her to spend another free minute in our country! ICE had dropped the ball before with me, once allowing a Chinese intelligence officer to remain in the States and gain US citizenship. So, I kept bugging BOP authorities, who resisted keeping me, a fellow federal law enforcement officer, apprised. Meanwhile, ICE officers repeatedly assured me they were on top of it. Yet Rebecca's release day came and went in silence, without notice, and my BOP and ICE inquiries produced conflicting reports.

Finally, I received word that Rebecca had been released, *weeks earlier*, on her own recognizance. All my reminders, and they *still* managed to screw this up. I re-sent them all the Court documentation verifying their duty to immediately detain and deport Rebecca. ICE acknowledged their duty but wouldn't commit to prioritizing her arrest and detention. I literally had to reopen Rebecca's FBI investigation to gain authority for the investigative techniques necessary to locate her myself, learning that she'd rented an apartment in Alhambra.

I got on the telephone and threatened ICE superiors that if they didn't do their jobs, *now*, I would notify Judge Carney. That motivated them. A week later, they picked Rebecca up and began the paperwork to revoke her US citizenship and deport her. She spent another *two* years under ICE detention while China slow-walked its issuance of her return visa.[21] Justice had reacquired Rebecca. Her three-year sentence was much more satisfying now that it had been stretched to five. Where was Stan Greenberg? Long gone, on to other clients and bigger paydays, never wondering about Rebecca Chiu.

While Rebecca was under ICE detention, I interviewed her twice to see if she would provide any useful information. I even offered her the chance to stay in the United States until Chi was released. Then she could visit him in prison. But her position, and personality, had only hardened. She wanted to stay, but denied all guilt, despite the facts and her earlier signed admission. And now she also was claiming "racism!"—criminals

---

20. Life experience had taught me ICE had a short memory and its notifications were unreliable.
21. That's another happy part of this story. More ironic justice.

learn quickly—and a US government conspiracy. Her stone-faced countenance only cracked once, when I explained her intransigence meant she would be deported to China and likely never see or talk to Chi Mak again—he would be eighty-six when released, she eighty-three, *if* they both survived. Rebecca momentarily blanched, before recovering her stoic, angry demeanor. The last time we met, she was waiting to board her deportation flight at LAX in September 2012, accompanied by two US marshals. She said she hoped to live with relatives. I was pleased she would spend her final days in her beloved PRC prison state and pitied the relatives condemned to live with her.

Rebecca Chiu awaits deportation flight at LAX
AUTHOR'S COLLECTION

Tai also appealed his plea bargain. Apparently "surrendering your right of appeal" to get a favorable sentence doesn't mean what it used to. As guardian of all Mak trial records, I assisted Greg as he wrote his answering arguments. Tai's petition for a writ of certiorari was denied by the Supreme Court of the United States in October 2009, finally putting another conviction to rest. Only then could I interview Tai in prison.

He was being held in a privately contracted facility in Post, Texas, about forty minutes southeast of Lubbock. I hoped his prison life there would be so boring—with few Chinese speakers—that anything would seem an improvement, even speaking with the agent who put him there.

After jumping through many BOP hoops and recruiting Janette, an FBI linguist from Dallas, the interview was on.[22] The first thing Tai asked me was, "Has the Chinese government contacted you about me?" I answered "No," to Tai's shock and disappointment. He explained that Jimmy Carter and other US officials had gone to North Korea to retrieve imprisoned Americans, and that the United States and Russia regularly exchanged political prisoners and spies. Tai was hurt China wasn't seeking his release, especially since his and his family's lives had been destroyed by his efforts to help China and elder brother Chi. The least they could do was trade for his freedom. The first interview went slowly, interrupted by facility security considerations, mealtimes, and other administrative requirements, but we left it on good terms. I needed to learn more.

Over a year later, Janette and I returned. It took some doing, since I was now a supervisor, not an investigator. But time was running short. Tai would soon be released and deported. He told me the first thing he would do was lodge a complaint with the PRC government over how they treated him and his family. *Good luck with that!* I thought. *I hope the reeducation camp they send you to is in a temperate climate.*

In any case, his cooperation provided useful information, which I passed along to FBIHQ and appropriate partner agencies. Tai never admitted to *all* of his activities for China, but he did reveal a number of valuable things. I also thought him the most honorable of the Maks. He genuinely loved his children, and even Fuk, though it was obvious he suspected her infidelities. Tai had no contact with relatives, other than his daughter Shirley, and was starving for news. He was very proud of his "princess," who called him every two months. Tai bragged she was attending the University of California at Berkeley and getting straight As. I said nothing. Why burst his bubble?[23] She remained a foul-mouthed

---

22. FBILA wouldn't pay for linguist travel. Classic! Janette proved a real trouper though, driving over nine hours to Post and back, in addition to performing the exhausting interview interpreter work.
23. The only family member not charged, Shirley was definitely Fuk's daughter: She never visited her father in jail and repeatedly lied to him.

party girl living with her boyfriend in Southern California, a community college dropout who never spent a day as a Cal Bear.

Tai complained that he'd assisted elder brother Chi out of filial duty and helped China out of patriotism yet was repaid by both with treachery. He recounted how Chi's attorney had even accused him in court of "tricking" Chi. Tai insisted Chi and Shouling, along with the PRC government, had tricked and abused Tai and his family. I often wonder what happened to Tai. Did he lodge his complaint with the PRC? Was he punished? Did he walk in on Fuk with another man? Did he ever learn the truth about his "princess," Shirley? Most likely, Tai moved in with his son Billy in Hong Kong, helped him with his automobile lighting business, visited a few relatives, and eventually learned the truth about both Mak women.[24] I had requested BOP and ICE authorities begin the visa process early with the PRC government so Tai could be deported within a reasonable time frame. I owed him that much, at least, for his cooperation.[25] When Tai was released, his detention and deportation went smoothly and quickly. No attorneys required.

Fittingly, I suppose, the biggest Mak fish took the longest to clean and put in the freezer. Chi Mak appealed his conviction for years.[26] Greg handled these appeals and frequently called upon me for documented verification. Chi's enormous appeal challenged the constitutionality of ITAR itself, sufficiency of the jury instructions, and claimed denial of a proper defense (What, Kaye and company did a poor job?). Greg had to seek permission "to file an oversized brief"—17,691 words—to counter the defense's gargantuan brief of 23,845 words. Arguments were made and filed by June 2012.

I enjoyed reading the Court's decision, particularly its declarative sentences like, "[T]here was overwhelming evidence that [Chi Mak] knew his actions were illegal." Best of all was its conclusion: "For the foregoing reasons, we AFFIRM Mak's conviction." Greg had defeated all defense claims before the Ninth Circuit Court of Appeals, known to law

---

24. Tai was the only Mak I felt sorry for. He had *some* integrity, having loved, and sacrificed for, his family.

25. In contrast to non-cooperating Rebecca, Billy, and Fuk's well-deserved extended detentions.

26. If convicted of spying in his beloved, totalitarian PRC, there would have been no appeals available.

enforcement as "The Ninth Circus" for its convoluted logic in support of its far-left decisions to free criminals. Within the year, Chi's US Supreme Court appeal was also denied.

I was happy for several reasons: First, Chi's conviction didn't feel final until *every* appeal was exhausted. Second, I wanted to interview Chi, but I had to wait for appeals to conclude to defeat any later charges of violating his right to counsel.

So, I contacted Gunnar, now Special Agent in Charge of the NCIS Southwest Field Office in San Diego. It seemed only fitting we should interview Chi Mak together. Plus, Chi liked him.[27] I scheduled the interview for an October 2014 afternoon at Chi's prison, FCI Lompoc, near Vandenberg Air Force Base. Gunnar drove two hours to Orange County, and then I drove the remaining four hours. It proved a long, relaxing drive up some beautiful coastline, giving us time to catch up and discuss interview strategy.

Upon arrival, we met a guard who knew Chi well and reported he was a "model prisoner" (sound familiar?), teaching math and English (!) to other prisoners. Chi seemed content with his life in prison.[28]

The guard ushered us into a small rec room where, minutes later, a very friendly Chi entered, grinning from ear to ear as we all shook hands. He hadn't aged a day and reported doing well and enjoying teaching the other inmates. We then inquired after facts of his case and posed questions to fill in some of the blanks.

His replies surprised us. Not only did Chi Mak continue to deny the obvious facts and jury conclusions, he was more recalcitrant than ever, denying his videotaped statements and even testimony from years earlier. He now claimed, with a smile, that we'd planted the trashed tasking lists. He was "innocent" of all charges, declaring we had targeted him from the outset because he was Chinese and it helped our narrative about PRC espionage. All of this was said very politely, even though he was accusing us of framing "an innocent man." Chi softened his charges by saying it wasn't our fault, and that he held no animosity toward us. We were just believing what we wanted to believe (?!). It was a strange, calm,

---

27. Gunnar would end up being the only person present for every Chi Mak interview.
28. Something I'm sure no one would ever say of a PRC prison.

remarkable conversation. All attempts to persuade Chi otherwise failed. We applied no pressure, agreeing to disagree. Chi was convicted, in prison and going nowhere. In short, Chi showed no remorse and declared he had done nothing wrong.[29]

Chi's guard eventually came in, notified him dinner would soon be served, and asked what sandwich he would prefer as the alternative. Chi's eyes lit up, remembering it was "Pizza Night," which he didn't want to miss. We ended the interview and said our good-byes, again, on good terms.

Gunnar and I stopped for dinner on the way home and laughed about "Pizza Night," recalling Chi's earlier recorded jailhouse calls wherein he marveled to Rebecca of the high quality and quantity of fried chicken it provided. Apparently, it was a vast improvement over their Maoist home diet. We discussed in amazement Chi's positions, posited theories on why he maintained the deceptions, and reminded ourselves we had imprisoned a trained, polished, egotistical intelligence agent who would never admit defeat.

The next day, I wrote my FD-302 interview report, which would later prove invaluable for Chi's continued incarceration. A year later, I received a handwritten note from Chi, returning a form I'd sent to aid his request for return of items.[30]

Dear Jim,

Enclosed is the claim-form I return to you with my signiture [sic]. I could not use your postage-paid envelop [sic] because the prison officer took it away (I guess the rule is not allow anything related to money, and the postage is money—a very funny rule).

Thanks for your help and I am looking forward to receiving my property.

Best Regards and happy Thanksgiving holiday.

Chi

11/18/2015

---

29. I was ready to promise efforts to shorten his time in prison if he cooperated. Given Chi's stance, I never brought it up. Remorse or contrition had to be present, yet Chi was calling us ambition-driven racists.
30. I don't know whether he ever got back the property he sought.

Dear Jim,

Enclosed is the claim-form I return to you with my signature. I could not use your postage-paid envelop because the prison officer took it away (I guess the rule is not allow anything related to money, and the postage is money — a very funny rule).

Thanks for your help and I am looking forward to receiving my property.

Best Regards and happy Thanksgiving holiday.

Chi

11/18/2015.

Chi Mak note to Special Agent Gaylord, November 18, 2015 AUTHOR'S COLLECTION

I retired from the FBI in March 2017, though I've kept in contact with some members of my old team. I attended Gunnar's retirement ceremony as SAC of the NCIS San Diego office and later Sal's from the FBI. We formed a lasting bond over this case, which I believed had finally ended. But then in May 2020, Greg Staples called to say Chi Mak had filed for early release from prison, citing his elderly status and COVID-19 concerns. Greg wanted my opinion.

I adamantly opposed it, informing him that Chi's only known medical conditions were rheumatism and an old bout with shingles. Besides the COVID-19 danger, Chi's attorney claimed he was a changed man, had admitted his guilt, and was remorseful. "No, he most certainly has not, and is not!" I replied, telling Greg about Chi's 2014 prison interview. Greg asked me to write a declaration for the Court containing that information, which I did, reporting every Chi misstatement, opinion, and denial, ending with my assurance that "At no time did Chi Mak express any remorse or apology for his actions or role which resulted in his incarceration, and emphatically and repeatedly denied that he was in any way guilty of, or responsible for, any illegal acts." I signed and dated this declaration that June and sent it to Greg, who later reported that Chi's counsel angrily accused me of speaking to Chi without legal counsel.

And here I had thought that the Chi Mak case was done giving me joy. I was still making defense attorneys angry. That made my month! Greg also stated Chi's counsel had threatened to call me as a witness at their motion hearing. "Anytime, anyplace," I replied. I truly hoped I would get another opportunity to look at Chi Mak as I testified against him. I wanted him to see that the guy he continued to lie to and call a racist would *never* go away and continually ensure he served his *full* term. Is that weird? The hearing never happened, and Chi lost his motion, remaining in prison, *getting* COVID, and surviving it just fine. Incredibly, months later he filed another COVID-based motion and lost again.[31]

In the summer of 2023, I was watching a rerun of an episode from the CNN show *Declassified*, titled "Red Storm Rising," about the Chi Mak investigation.[32] It had originally aired in August 2016, but an ending coda had since been added: "Chi Mak died in prison, October 2022." I was shocked. No one had notified me. I checked the Bureau of Prisons website and confirmed Chi's death on Halloween, 2022. I made inquiries into the exact cause of death but never heard back. I must admit to a sense of satisfaction. After the damage this spy for the totalitarian PRC state had intentionally inflicted upon this free nation, which generously took him in and extended an open hand, and his repeated lies, accusations, and denials, Chi didn't deserve a single day of freedom. And he didn't get one. His had appropriately been a death sentence.

---

31. This was Chi Mak's "last gasp," figuratively speaking. We are *much* too good to foreign spies and criminals in general. Those convicted should serve their full sentences, whether ill or not. Does illness reverse their crime? Does it compensate the victim? They need to pay the full price for their deeds. Society and their victims certainly have!
32. Season one, episode seven.

Part IV
After Mak

CHAPTER 35

China Spy II?

WITH CHI AND HIS FAMILY MEMBERS HANDLED, WE MOVED ON TO THE next spy family, the Chungs, in pursuit of a historic one-two punch. Their story began quietly with our first covert search of Chi's home in September 2004, during which we discovered address books leading to many inquiries and preliminary investigations of listed associates, mainly engineers, government employees, and others with access to sensitive information and officials. After data analysis, most were ruled out as being of no further interest, but some remained. The Chungs topped the short list.

"Greg" Dongfan Chung was born January 20, 1936, and raised in Liaolin, China. Because his father was a member of the Kuomintang (Chinese Nationalist Party), his family fled to Taiwan when the CCP won China's civil war, seizing the Mainland. Greg graduated with a BS in civil engineering from the National Taiwan University in 1960, and the next year he married a beautiful young woman named Ling Jia Wang. It was true love and a match of political equals, her father being an air force pilot for the Nationalist government.

One year later, the Chungs immigrated to the United States, using Greg's F-1 student visa. He graduated from the University of Minnesota in 1963 with an MS degree in civil engineering and went to work in Philadelphia, designing steel and reinforced-concrete buildings. In 1964, he became a stress engineer for Boeing in Ridley Park for the CH-47 helicopter while taking structural engineering courses at Penn State. In 1972, he and Ling Jia obtained US citizenship, and he took a job at McDonnell Douglas as a strength analysis engineer on its DC-10 and

F-15 airframes, later returning to Boeing to work the B-52 Life Extension Program and the A-10 aircraft support structure. Chung finally ended up on the Space Shuttle program, obtaining his "SECRET" clearance in 1973 and working for Rockwell and Boeing in Downey, California.[1]

Boeing eventually closed its Downey facility, moving its employees to its large Huntington Beach campus. The Chungs moved to nearby Irvine, where they prospered and bought investment properties, including a small triplex in Alhambra, commercial real estate in Cypress and Long Beach, and a large plot of land in the hills of Orange, where they designed and built their dream home. They were living the American Dream, while repeatedly visiting the oppressive land and regime their parents had fled for freedom. Engineer Greg Chung had access, association with Chi, and frequent PRC travel. Our interest was definitely piqued.

After the Mak arrests and searches, we began interviewing Chi's associates. On April 24, 2006, squad agents Jessie and Scott interviewed Greg Chung and Ling Jia. They claimed to vaguely know the Maks, mentioned a mysterious "Mr. Gu" in passing, and admitted some tourist trips to China. They were obviously holding back, but a second interview might tip our hand or even make them flee or destroy evidence, so we waited. Our second search of Chi's residence on June 7, 2006, produced more Chung connections than we could have imagined: The Gu Wei Hao letters, an aviation tasking list, photos, business cards, and hand-drawn maps all proved the Chungs had lied to us about their close connections with the Maks and PRC officials. The Chung case changed from some smoke to a five-alarm conflagration. We now had overlapping espionage investigations!

Now what? I was up to my neck in Mak trial preparation and couldn't take my eye off that ball. Winning that case took precedence and our whole squad was dedicated to it. Yet I wasn't going to farm it out to another RA or FBILA. Our squad's proven skill and experience were

---

1. This is when Chung began writing letters to PRC officials offering his expertise. He and Ling Jia wanted ethnic Chinese to look good on the world stage. They also later came to ideologically identify with the socialist motherland. China needed help from Western volunteers like Chung to develop their fledgling space program.

impossible to duplicate, and there were too many interconnections with the Mak case. We *had* to keep this in-house.

I polled SARA-4 for interest. Some senior agents had experience but not the desire, while younger agents were interested but lacked the skills, drive, or work ethic. Sal and I came up with the same candidate—Kevin Moberly. He had recently joined the FBI, was enthusiastic, knew the Mak cases thoroughly, had prior intelligence experience in the US Air Force, *and* had a strong interest in aerospace and outer space. He was intelligent, confident, creative, and energetic, willing to follow our examples and learn from our mistakes, and itching for a larger role. To help, we assigned Tom Grandmain as co-case agent, an experienced, steady, methodical former criminal agent who'd joined our Mak investigation to provide support. Tom's reserve and caution balanced Kevin's kinetic energy and passion, just as Sheldon and I had done for each other. On June 16, 2006, Kevin opened a full investigation of the Chungs, code name "Red Card."[2] He was off to a great start.

Two things made this investigation different. First, the Chungs were forewarned of our interest, which meant they were more cautious and could take mitigating steps. Second, *all* our evidence against them was over ten years old, so it wouldn't get us FISA coverages or criminal searches. Taking a sheet from our playbook, Kevin initiated trash covers and surveillance and recruited NASA as his partner, like NCIS had been for the Mak investigations. This gave Kevin NASA's knowledge and access to the victim company.

The Chung trash cover proved key to the whole case. Surveillance had witnessed peculiar trash disposal behavior. Household and yard waste were put out the night before, but Chung waited until just before leaving for work to roll out the recyclables, looking around the whole time. Trash cover results would explain this behavior. Sifting through the recyclables, Bill, a SARA-4 agent, found stacks of Chinese newspapers. Being fluent himself, he browsed through them and found inserted within their pages sensitive, restricted Boeing, Rockwell, and NASA documents, including test results, system data diagrams, schematics, and technical readouts.

---

2. This name reflected Kevin's, Gunnar's, and my interest in soccer, *and* the political system of our adversary.

Five weeks of trash collection produced hundreds of restricted, sensitive documents. This was what we needed to freshen our probable cause! Our old evidence demonstrated Chung collected for China in the past. This new trash proved he still possessed prohibited data, paving the way for a search warrant.

To prepare for a second Chung interview, Kevin discreetly interviewed Chung's supervisor, Bill Novak, and other Boeing officials. Then he and AUSA Greg Staples wrote a criminal search warrant for Chung's spacious home and property at 7412 East Grovewood Lane, Orange, California. It was based upon Title 18 USC. § 951, Acting as an Agent of a Foreign Government, using hard-won experience from USAO Mak charging screw-ups. It wove a tale of Chung's work history, access, training, Chi's Gu Wei Hao letters, aerospace tasking lists, photographs, the Chungs' mentions of Gu, PRC travel, and the fact that their trash's technical paper contents matched Gu's letters' and Shouling's tasking list requests. US Magistrate Judge Block, a notoriously tough sell when it came to search warrants, quickly signed off on it, giving Kevin a broad

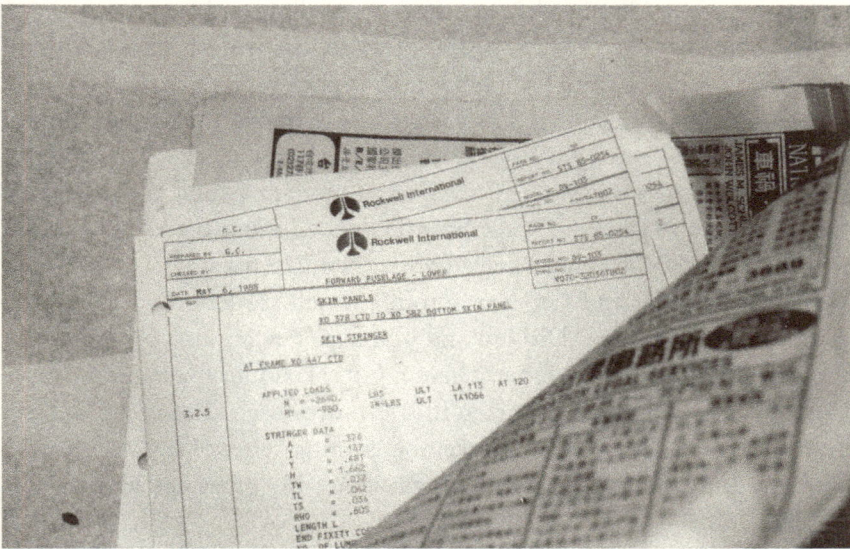

Greg Chung trash concealing technical documents TRIAL EXHIBITS 168–173

mandate. SARA-4 already excelled at espionage searches. To this "A" team we now added NASA investigators.

The operational plan for the interviews and search, and SARA-4's execution, was flawless. We approached the home with two teams of two, seeking interviews of both Chungs. We didn't mention the search warrants we had. Kevin and Gunnar handled Greg Chung upstairs while Colleen McKay and I took Ling Jia downstairs.[3] We interviewed Ling Jia in her "showroom," their garage, filled with canvases of her abstract art covering the floor. As expected, Ling Jia lied throughout the interview. I documented each lie in my FD-302 interview report. Like Rebecca and Fuk, Ling Jia proved a superior liar to her husband. No matter the proof, she denied or downplayed it. Her lies became more blatant and damaging with each increasingly damning Gu letter we showed her. As her lies grew, her "cooperation" shrank. Eventually, we ended the interview.

Upstairs, Greg Chung proved more fruitful. He eventually reversed his initial lies, declaring he first met Chi and Gu during a 1980 Los Angeles meeting of one hundred "expatriate professionals from China" (Chinese American engineers), hosted by the "China/American Friendship Association." Since then, the Chungs and Maks had met at least once a year, yet Chung claimed they never discussed work, China, or travel there—in over twenty years. He also claimed to know nothing about Gu's work, despite Gu's request for Space Shuttle data.

They met Gu again in 1985 when the Chungs took their teenage sons to Beijing University one summer for eight weeks of Mandarin study. While the boys studied, the parents toured China and met with Gu, who kept requesting Space Shuttle data. Gu and the Chungs again met in the 1990s, when he stayed with them on his way to Las Vegas. When asked if he and Gu ever communicated via letters or third persons, Chung said, "No." Did Gu and Chi have a relationship? "No." They showed Chung the 1990 letter wherein Gu asked Chi for referrals in the United States. Chung minimized it as Gu overreach. Then they showed him Gu's 1988 letter to the Maks, mentioning letters Gu wrote to the Chungs, and asking the Maks to pass along his greetings and request

---

3. Colleen and I had been jointly interviewing people for over a decade. This would be the last time we got to do so.

that the Chungs visit him in China. Similar Chung response. Finally, they read him the 1987 Gu letter addressed to the Chungs and delivered by Chi Mak, outlining all that Greg and Chi had *already* done for China and the tradecraft utilized to maintain that technology pipeline.

This straw broke Chung's back. He began recanting his lies, accusing Chi of first identifying Chung to Gu and then bragging about providing his own data to Gu by using a route to Hong Kong and Guangzhou that left no evidence of PRC travel. Chung confirmed "Gu is a PRC government official," and acknowledged traveling to China to meet with university students, while denying other known facts.[4] As for the technical documents hidden in his trash, they were attempts to "hide" and destroy them, so people wouldn't know he possessed prohibited data. He assured Kevin and Gunnar that only a "few" restricted documents remained in his home.[5]

Before our search, we sought the Chungs' consent to do so, not telling them of our search warrant and army of search personnel waiting outside.[6] We treated them both with great respect, to encourage their cooperation. The age-old adage is as true in investigations as in life: "You catch more flies with honey than with vinegar." Given the chance to "cooperate," we believed the Chungs would prove more amenable to answering questions during the search, as they tried to talk their way out of trouble. They signed the consent.[7]

Kevin whipped out his walkie-talkie and before you could say "Mao Tse-tung," we'd opened the doors and waved dozens of personnel in, carrying boxes, tape, labels, gloves, and portable tables. Even if the Chungs got buyers' remorse and revoked their consent, we still had our warrant. But they didn't. Allowing them this illusion of cooperation got us more answers. The home's huge size and utter disarray, the sheer volume of evidence seized, and the heat from a very hot day, made this a search for the ages.

---

4. Such as giving China/Taiwan "reunification" speeches in the PRC, which were documented by internet articles identifying him and Ling Jia as doing exactly that.
5. This proved the understatement of the century.
6. It was a hot day, and those outside had been cooked to "well done" by then.
7. They probably assumed just the four of us would conduct a hopeless search of their palatial home.

Chung residence crawl space contents TRIAL EXHIBITS 34, 181, AND 182

After the interviews, Gunnar, Colleen, and I had no search assignments, so we filled in where needed. SARA-4 members Sal, Kevin, Tom, Jessie, Scott, Lisa, Doug, Bill, Tanya, Sean, Len, Harriet, and others tackled their assignments like the well-oiled machines they were. Sal helped document the event through photographs and diagrams, while Tanya and Jessie were the evidence gatekeepers, efficiently processing everything collected. When especially interesting items were found, Sheldon and Kevin would ask the Chungs for an explanation.[8] The Chungs liked Sheldon, no doubt because he was young and Chinese, likely reminding them of their sons.

Because this huge home was built on a steep hill, it held many enclosed crawl spaces underneath. That's where I went first. We found racks of Boeing and Rockwell binders and boxes.[9] This proved an incredible find! I then hit rooms within the home, and a separate guesthouse. The day's extra challenge? The main home was absolutely filthy, often

---

8. For example, the Chungs described how different gifts (medals, tie clips) came from PRC defense companies like CATIC (China National Aero-Technology Import & Export Corporation), CAE, and Xian Aircraft, as thanks for presentations Greg Chung gave to their executives and engineers.
9. Along with various dead animals—mice, rats, and rabbits.

worse than the crawl spaces. In my whole career, I encountered only one home that was worse.[10] The problem was a mix of hoarding behavior—intermixed stacks of paper, clothing, and trash—and the hair, urine, and feces of old, sickly pet dogs allowed free rein within the home. *Every* space on *every* level, inside and out, contained this toxic mix, even bathtubs and showers.

While Chi Mak's home had been incredibly dusty, it didn't have this level of filth. At one point, our great linguist Harriet came up to me and said, "Oh Jim, pleeeeease don't think all Chinese are so messy!" She feared the unkempt Mak and Chung households would leave this impression. I laughed and reminded her, "Harriet. Remember, my wife is also ethnic Chinese, and she is an immaculate housekeeper." Harriet's concern reminded me how PRC officials twist such a desire for pride to their advantage, recruiting ethnic Chinese to "help China so that Chinese people look successful to the world." Personally, I don't want communists, Chinese or otherwise, to "look good" or prosper![11]

As the day advanced, the Chungs "revised" many of their earlier statements, admitting travel to China over the decades to give presentations at PRC universities about the US Space Shuttle and manufacturing processes, using Boeing slides. They also now reported a 2001 approach in their Shanghai hotel room by a "Mr. Chen," asking about the Space Shuttle's composite structure. Another unknown man during a later trip approached them in another Shanghai hotel room requesting similar data. They said this visit occurred while they were traveling with Cal State University Long Beach professor Hsien Yeh and his wife. To explain the racks of sensitive Boeing and Rockwell materials under their home, Greg Chung claimed Boeing had planned to destroy them, so his boss offered the documents to him for use in writing a future book about the Space Shuttle program. No such book existed.[12]

---

10. Home of the Hells Angels Minneapolis Motorcycle Club chapter president, with human DNA spread throughout.
11. Individuals are responsible for their own conduct, not for that of members of their race or ethnicity. Cannibal Jeffery Dahmer, spy Aldrich Ames, or ancient US and European slave masters don't reflect on me.
12. Evidence of an intention to write such a book never surfaced. Also, Chung's boss made no such offer, and Chung never requested those materials, nor was he given permission to possess them.

As the day ended, we were exhausted and filthy, and didn't dare put our dirty hands anywhere near our faces. As the sun set, we overloaded SARA's old blue "pervert" panel van, named for its poor condition, lack of windows, and disreputable appearance, with sixty moving boxes containing nearly 300,000 pages. We should have charged the Chungs for cleaning services. Besides removal, our search had methodically moved, arranged, and stacked materials left behind, leaving *every* area neater, cleaner, and roomier. Our "before and after" search pictures, always taken to protect us from phony damage claims, proved as much. This was the first case where a searched premises looked demonstrably better *after* our search.

Just before departure, Kevin served the Chungs with our search warrant and provided a receipt for the items seized. This would discourage any claims that consent was required or never granted. Searchers bade each other weary farewells, content in knowing we had sealed the Chungs' fate. I arrived home, walked *around* the house to my backyard, hands elevated like a surgeon, and jumped into my chlorinated pool, clothes and all, to scrub myself from head to toe. I'm no germophobe, but I left my clothes in the pool to soak, threw in more chlorine, and showered before I touched anyone or anything.

In the following weeks and months, we analyzed our mountain of damning evidence, including dozens of letters between PRC military, government, and university officials and the Chungs regarding Chung's provision of sensitive US aerospace technologies under the familiar moniker of "technological exchange." These detailed letters discussed the Space Shuttle and various US aircraft—fighters, bombers, helicopters, and experimentals. Chung had even quietly acted as a go-between to help China acquire Boeing planes.

Because he wanted his correspondence to be perfect, Greg Chung often wrote several drafts (which he kept) before sending his final version. That habit ensured us possession of *both* sides of this correspondence. Topics included B-1 bomber manuals Chung had sent to a PRC consul in San Francisco for shipment to China.[13] Chung also kept personal journals documenting PRC trips, briefings, and meetings with Gu Wei Hao and other PRC consuls, officials, aerospace executives, companies,

---

13. A diplomatic pouch wasn't large enough; the volume demanded a diplomatic crate!

Chung and Yeh technical presentation in China TRIAL EXHIBIT 22

universities, and academics. Chung documented VIP treatment—limos, hotels, banquets, etc.—that he and Ling Jia received in China, including one year as honored guests at the Great Hall for National Day.[14]

Chung painstakingly translated dozens of Boeing technology slides into Chinese for his detailed briefings in Beijing, Nanchang, Xi'an, and Shanghai regarding the Space Shuttle, US helicopter designs, and finite element modeling programs. He kept a collection of business cards for PRC officials, academics, "businessmen," and aerospace company executives, a tasking list, volumes of CCP propaganda, and reams of newspaper articles extolling PRC accomplishments.[15] We also found photos of the Chungs meeting with PRC officials at homes and universities in China and the United States.[16] Other pictures showed the Chungs at a Beijing University presentation, accompanied by Professor Yeh and his wife.

---

14. Like a formal Fourth of July. People who received this treatment had already proven their worth to the motherland.

15. Propaganda included dozens of Mao Tse-tung's Little Red Books, as well as stuff going back to World War II.

16. US locations included the Chung home, Disneyland, and "The Wedge," Newport Beach's world-famous bodysurfing location. At Disneyland and the beach, officials stuck out like sore thumbs, dressed in bad suits and ties.

Chung had also printed out thousands of pages of sensitive Boeing technical data, stacked within his home and inserted within newspapers intended for the trash.[17] Telephone bills confirmed calls between Chung and nearby PRC consulate officials. We could now prove Chung provided sensitive data to China about the USAF C-17, F-15, CH-46/47 Chinook helicopter, NASA/DARPA X-37 Space Plane, the Space Shuttle, and Boeing's Delta IV heavy-lift rocket, and we shared the evidence with our NASA partners. Soon thereafter, Boeing fired Greg Chung to prevent any further damage.

We were often later asked, "How did Chung get hundreds of thousands of technical documents home?" The answer? Chung worked at the Rockwell International, and later, the Boeing, facility in Downey.[18] When it closed, Boeing moved its personnel, including Chung, to its Huntington Beach campus. Engineers destroyed duplicate documents on-site and shipped the rest in "Iron Mountain" boxes. Over many months, Chung transported documents in those same boxes to his home in Orange on his way to Huntington Beach.

Fortunately, Kevin and Tom had the time to consolidate and organize this evidence, with Boeing's and NASA's help, to conduct interviews, and to select subject matter expert (SME) witnesses. Our newly discovered pile of evidence and history of success instantaneously created a prosecutable case, cutting out much of the PR groundwork the Mak investigation had required. FISA coverage was never needed, meaning linguists only needed to translate documents. Thankfully, most of the resources the Chung investigation required came *after* the Maks were tried and safely locked away. After the Maks, everyone but Kevin and Tom returned to regular case work. I joined the team as a co-case agent to aid trial preparations. My presence also helped to keep professional Mak skeptics within FBILA, DOJ, USAO, and FBIHQ at bay. I was the blocker, reminding critics just how good our squad was, and how wrong they had been about us. I was happy to make them eat crow whenever necessary.

---

17. We found evidence in the ashes of the Chungs' fireplace that they had also burned these materials there.
18. Coincidentally (?), the same city where Chi and Rebecca Mak resided.

With the Maks, we tried to coordinate with the CIA. With the Chungs, it was the National Security Agency, which desperately tried to prevent being mentioned in this book. Bear in mind, it didn't try to stop another FBI agent writing a case study book two years earlier from mentioning it frequently, because that book praised the NSA. My account doesn't. I won't allow it to be "No Such Agency," as FBI personnel jokingly refer to it. The CIA and NSA both made the sharing of intelligence very difficult, insisting we share, while they wouldn't. We provided them reams of intelligence on PRCIS tradecraft but got nothing in return.

We knew Mr. Luo's personal digital assistant, which we seized at LAX during the Mak arrests, would be a treasure trove for the NSA, so Sal, Kevin, and I planned a trip to Maryland. Then we learned that they possessed a conversation between PRCIS officers during which Greg Chung was possibly discussed as a PRCIS operative. We wanted access to that conversation, but the NSA refused us, despite admitting its linguists didn't understand some of the Chinese words being spoken. We wanted our linguist Len Pi to listen to it. The NSA refused, with the same snobbery we got from the CIA, claiming their people were more cleared, skilled, professional, experienced, vetted, yadda yadda yadda. Sal countered with his usual, effective negotiation tactics, "No Len. No FBI trip. No FBI information." The NSA relented, so the four of us hopped on a plane.[19]

Once at Fort Meade, we sat down in a large conference room across from an NSA officer and his two linguists. The officer requested our data discs. Savvy Sal said, "First Len listens to the conversation." The officer refused, explaining he had lied, never intending to let Len listen to it. It was the CIA all over again. And their reasons were just as indefensible. The dumbest one was the claim that their two lily-white Ivy League–educated linguists were more proficient in Chinese. Therefore, Len, our native-speaking engineer, "would add no value." Anyone who speaks a foreign language knows this is a lie. The level of NSA arrogance was staggering.

---

19. FBI agents can carry weapons on US aircraft, so I also transported Len's comb-over VO5 hairspray, per his request.

I deeply resented this treatment, but the patriot in me still wanted them to have our data, for the good of the country. But Sal had a better approach. Becoming our "blunt instrument" again, he said, "No Len. No FBI information." I cringed and held my breath. Sounding hurt, the NSA officer whined, "You mean you won't give us any of your data?" Sal confirmed his meaning, again demonstrating courage and wisdom few FBI supervisors would. He knew that if we accepted their terms, we would have returned with nothing except false follow-up NSA charges that we'd been rude, unprofessional, and uncooperative.

After a pregnant pause, the officer surrendered, and we waited while Len was escorted elsewhere to review the NSA's holdings. When Len returned, he looked like the Cheshire cat, trailed by the two very sheep-ish-looking NSA linguists. Len cheerfully confirmed their discussion *did* identify Chung as a Chinese intelligence operative. How did he know? The "Chinese words" these two PhD Ivy League linguist snobs couldn't identify included the very American name "Boeing," Chung's employer. Boy, did Sal make them eat crow. Only then did I hand over our Luo data disc, while extracting a promise from their officer that he would let me know of any results they gained from it. To no one's surprise, I never heard from them again. Not so much as a "thank you"![20]

In spring 2007, AUSA Greg Staples wrote a "Government's Trial Brief," two years before Chung's scheduled trial date, and ran it by us to check for accuracy and begin marshaling evidence. Its fifteen counts included conspiracy to commit Economic Espionage (EE) in aid of a foreign country, acting as an agent of the PRC, obstructing justice, making false statements to the FBI, and criminal forfeiture of Chung's home in Orange. This fifty-six-page document was a breathtaking indictment covering Chung's entire adult life. Greg's narrative included Chung's enthusiastic pledges of PRC allegiance and truckloads of technical data sent to his "Socialist Motherland," beginning in the 1970s. He quoted one NASA expert who said Chung's home archive of Space Shuttle data was second only to NASA's. Greg also noted that among the billions of Chinese the world over, only one thousand people attended the PRC

---

20. Imagine what could be accomplished if the CIA and NSA actually treated the FBI as a full and equal partner!

National Day celebrations in Beijing, including the Chungs. And some documents recovered from the Maks' homes included names and numbers for "Yeh" and the Chungs, next to PRCIS officer Pu Pei Liang's. Greg also noted that although the EE law had been passed decades earlier, only six such cases had been charged, and none had gone to trial.[21]

Then Greg submitted his first Prosecutive Memorandum (PM) to the current USA, our old obstructionist nemesis George Cardona, and to DOJ's John Dion, requesting EE charges against Chung.[22] Authorization was received in October 2007, but only because Chi's case had succeeded, and we had been shaming the USAO and DOJ, with Greg's help. The USAO had refused EE charges for Chi Mak, instead promising us EE charges "next time." They tried to renege regarding Chung, but we forced them to honor their promises through an aggressive PR campaign we ran inside the FBI, DOJ, and NASA.

Kevin and NASA Special Agent Zachary Schwartz testified before the grand jury and received a "True Bill" for the charges. Unbelievably, we *still* had to battle to include foreign agent and false statements charges, both of which perfectly demonstrate the defendant's intent—*mens rea* ("guilty mind"). Cardona's USAO resisted both, despite the number of times we had already proven him/it wrong. I pushed aggressively, and Greg reminded Cardona of this pressure in a PM footnote: "The FBI would like an added count for a violation of 18 USC. § 951, acting as an agent of the PRC government without registering. . . . Because the FBI believes the foreign agent charge would have significant benefits for deterrence, we will continue to assess the 951 charge." Not only did it deter, it simplified and sank defense claims and spin that the defendant was simply confused by complex ITAR and EE laws, thereby proving they were PRC agents. I salute Greg for fighting for these charges. We also had more aggressive support from FBILA executive management willing to confront Cardona and other USAO/DOJ roadblocks, allowing us to later add those false statements as well as acting as an agent of a foreign government charges. Mak case precedents got us these.

---

21. If I know my USAs, it's because they all were settled in sweetheart defense deals.

22. Greg had run it by us first, a commonsense check other AUSAs disdained. We answered Greg's questions, noted needed corrections, and filled in areas left blank for our input.

Meanwhile, we continued to solidify our case. On September 7, 2007, Kevin and I interviewed Cal State University Long Beach (CSULB) engineering professor Hsien Yeh at his home. He insisted his wife Ching be present, and they immediately opened with the old "racism!" charge. Despite our counterpoint that the Chungs had referred us to him, Yeh declared he didn't know Chung well, a demonstrable lie. He and Ching lied about every important issue. They had traveled to China with the Chungs and given technology lectures to, and socialized with, PRC officials. When asked about Chung's Shanghai Hotel mystery visitor, asking Space Shuttle questions, Yeh angrily shouted, "A trick question!" He declared it never happened.[23] Yeh denied participating in PRC politics and consulate functions, denouncing our questions based upon Chung's journal entries as errors or FBI lies. He repeatedly and desperately shouted, "No! Trick! Not true!" He did admit one thing, however—extensive contacts with the Office for Taiwan Affairs of the Communist Party of China to further its "reunification" with the PRC. Lastly, although Yeh

---

23. Yet Chung had volunteered that it had.

FBI agents enter Chung residence to conduct search and arrest TRIAL EXHIBITS 181 AND 182

had worked at CSULB since before 1994, he denied knowing Chi Mak, who taught engineering courses there at the same time.

On February 6, 2008, Chung was indicted under seal in preparation for arrest. We were ordered to postpone it because FBI director Robert Mueller was in China. We would delay our takedown until he left the PRC and also synchronize it with an investigation back east, which Sandy Kable had labeled "Chi Mak on steroids." We coordinated simultaneous arrests and searches, which ended up making a big news splash during a joint press conference by opposite coast USAs concerning our arrests of PRC spies.

Sal again took pictures to document our second Chung home search and his arrest. I was so proud of this team, which had served my case, and now Kevin's, so well. Upon entry, we learned the Chungs were babysitting their toddler grandson. As we conducted the search, we witnessed this child walking about the house, sitting and lying down in its dog hair and feces filth and picking up things and putting them in his mouth! Those among us who were parents especially had to fight our natural instincts to grab and carry him away from all this. It was a nauseating sight. The Chungs finally called their son to pick up the boy, to our great relief.

Before Greg Chung called his son, Shane, Kevin told him that he wished to speak with both his sons about the family trips to China, so Chung was not to discuss such topics with either until later. Chung agreed. Kevin called Shane and left a message requesting an interview. Shortly thereafter, Shane called his dad to ask about Kevin's message. With agents around him, Chung told Shane in Mandarin that FBI agents were at the home conducting a search and wanted to speak with Shane when he came by to pick up his son. Chung then whispered to Shane, "[A]bout the Beijing trip. Say you've forgotten." But Jessie Murray, a fluent Mandarin speaker, overheard this. It later served as the basis for an obstruction charge against Chung.

When Kevin interviewed Shane soon after, he followed his father's instructions, claiming to remember nothing about his time in Beijing. When confronted with his father's overheard instructions, Shane acknowledged them but insisted he couldn't independently remember the trip. As the second search concluded, Kevin arrested and handcuffed

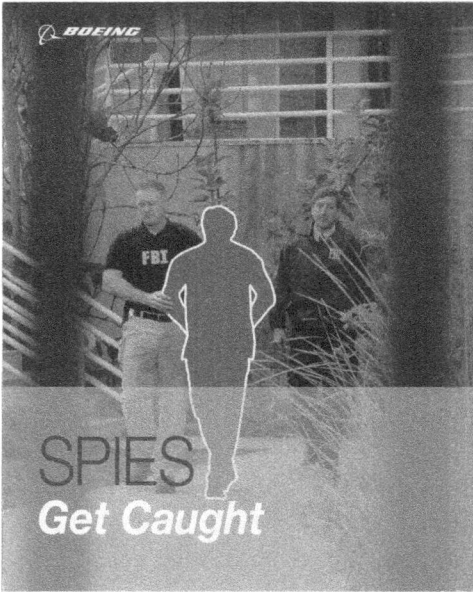

Boeing security poster (Special Agent Gaylord on right) AUTHOR'S COLLECTION

Chung. As they left, Shane told Sal, "I'm sorry about my dad. He has always hung his heart out way too far for China. I will talk to him about that." I appreciated the sentiment, but this time, late was *not* better than never. Shane's father had betrayed his country, been charged, and arrested. No one anticipated how heavy a price Chung's family would end up paying for his treachery.

Kevin asked me to help escort Chung to his car. As we did, Sal snapped some pictures. I was caught off guard, having never done a "perp walk" before, and it showed. This photograph became famous at Boeing because they turned it into a security awareness poster and campaign entitled "Spies Get Caught." Kevin and I were pictured in FBI raid jackets, escorting the outline of Chung away in handcuffs. Kevin was a natural as the determined, steely-eyed young FBI agent, accompanied by an ill-at-ease, tired, even haggard-looking older agent. Despite my appearance, it proved an effective poster. The headline and message were unmistakable: Don't do it, or you'll be spending your golden years in prison!

Chung received bail at his initial appearance, conditioned upon staying at home with an ankle bracelet (a nearly useless device), surrendering his US passport, and promising to stay away from international borders, transit centers, and PRC diplomatic establishments. I opposed bail or release, but I was only a co-case agent. If I were Chung, given the overwhelming evidence, I would have bolted to China via Mexico. Absconding was the only way he would ever see his grandchildren again.

Greg Chung under arrest FBI RELEASED

Thankfully, he stayed put, possibly believing the promises of his attorney Tom Bienert, by whom Chung would be ill served in every way possible. Add in Chung's huge ego and strong Chinese racial pride, and the result was some very poor decision-making.

Between Chung's arrest and his trial, our squad lost many good agents to transfers and career decisions. Jessie Murray moved to a criminal squad, while Scott moved to a specialized surveillance unit. But as we lost veterans, we gained great new agents from our FBI Academy and other field offices. Fortunately, Kevin and Tom remained, as did Colleen McKay and linguists Len Pi and Harriet Hao, all of whom continued working the Chung case. Sadly, Gunnar and Omar moved on to new NCIS duties and locales, but we gained NASA Special Agent Zach Schwartz, who worked closely with Kevin and Tom. Although I certainly helped as a co-case agent, my role became more advisory, and I was assigned outside cases and assets. I also mentored our new agents, who worked Mak and Chung spin-off cases, and became a relief supervisor for Sal.

With all the bridges Sal and I had burned and angry battles we'd fought with upper management, we both figured he would climb no further. A ton of mud had been slung on us from all directions, and it didn't wash off easily. But a funny thing happened: Chi's case success made all the unfounded criticisms vanish. Sal and I suddenly became hot properties, but we both refused to consider DC assignments.[24] Management eventually made exceptions for us both. Sal was appointed an Assistant Special Agent in Charge (ASAC) at FBILA. I wasn't seeking anything, but I was now viewed as experienced, successful, and promotable. I was happy where I was and pleased that Sal was finally being recognized for his outstanding leadership, bravery, and loyalty. This time doing the right thing paid off.

With Sal's promotion, we received a new supervisor, Chris Nicholas. He was relatively new to the Bureau but not law enforcement, having previously served as a Georgia state trooper. He came from the New York Field Office, which has a lot of CI work, so I was hopeful. Chris settled in nicely, and he and I developed a great working relationship and friendship, especially after I became his primary relief supervisor.[25]

With changing circumstances and freshly mandated Bureau priorities, we settled into new squad routines. Local industry preventative outreach and relationship development were now a priority under our "Domain" program. We were positioned perfectly. Our Mak PowerPoint, previously developed to garner case support, was now a brief for company employee and executive presentations. It was current and fascinating, given its "insider threat" subject, local connections, true-crime-drama feel, and successful outcome. These briefings became very popular and took me and other squad members across the country and around the world. As a result, our "Domain" metrics went through the roof and

---

24. This promotion policy stops *many* talented agents from ever seeking management positions.
25. He had a few difficult agents to deal with, but those great, outrageous stories are for another time and place, and best told by Chris.

produced case referrals from companies. Unfortunately, these "Domain" efforts took away from other FBIHQ-mandated metrics, like number of cases opened, investigated, and closed, which was something Chris was evaluated on. With *two* agents, Kevin and Tom, and some support personnel dedicated 100 percent to the Chung prosecution, those metrics were suffering. One day Chris pointed this out and mentioned to me thoughts of assigning Kevin and Tom additional case work. Alarmed, though understanding his concerns, I said:

> *You don't want to do that. No one will ever remember whether SARA-4 met its "Cases Investigated" metric this quarter. Everyone will always remember if we lose the Greg Chung case. Our reputation is tied to this case. We cannot risk losing because we strove to meet some artificial, bureaucratic, and ultimately meaningless FBIHQ metric. You, and we, would regret it for the rest of our lives!*

While this might sound overly dramatic, my experiences during Chi Mak, surrounded by critics, made every word true. Chris deserves complete credit for listening that day, leaving Kevin and Tom free to fully pursue Greg Chung's prosecution.

As the trial date approached, Greg requested another PowerPoint dog-and-pony show, this time for Tom Bienert, Chung's attorney, another former AUSA who had jumped ship for private "pieces of eight." I now knew better. These free shows were fruitless for us, yet they provided defense counsel clues about our prosecutive strategy. But Kevin Moberly, an intelligent and enthusiastic case agent, certainly couldn't be faulted for listening to Greg. So, he created and showed a PowerPoint presentation chock-full of damning evidence, including Chung's own written words. Greg offered Chung a deal *if* he testified against Chi. But like the other attorneys, Bienert didn't care about his client's best interests. We learned later from other AUSAs that Bienert normally held out until the last minute, to better drain his client's bank account, before pushing for settlement. The deeper his client's pockets, the longer he spent emptying them. And Chung's pockets were deep. This seemed to me a form of legal malpractice.

Our extraordinary new team of supporting agents for trial proved perfect for the job, working well with the remaining veterans, building a case even stronger than the one against Chi.[26] The longest, strongest nail in Chung's coffin was the *number* and *nature* of uncensored, smug, clear, handwritten correspondence between Chung and his PRC masters. But for Bienert's greed, it wouldn't have gone to trial. USAO cowards would have jumped on any plea bargain, had he offered. But Bienert's practices led to missed defense opportunities, and when Chung grew tired of the delays and rising costs, he cut off Bienert's money train, insisting his poorly prepared counsel go to trial. As a cost-cutting measure, Chung requested a bench trial, which is typically shorter and cheaper. It also means no jury, with the judge as the trier of fact. But this was Judge Cormac Carney, who had already proven he understood government espionage cases. Carney also knew the relevant Mak trial evidence that would be inadmissible in this case. We were happy. Carney would *not* be distracted or confused by specious defense arguments, as a jury might.

The only thing that could stop our juggernaut was poor prosecutorial decisions. My previous clash and reconciliation with Greg Staples over USAO and DOJ interference convinced me that wouldn't happen again. Still, they tried to weasel out of the EE charges. We made many more trips to FBILA, the USAO, and Washington, DC, to emphasize we had the same squad, prosecutor, judge, and jury pool as Chi, with even stronger facts. I said, "If not EE now, then when?" We won that argument, but sadly lost another. They refused to prosecute Chung's wife, Ling Jia, still spouting the same sexist, nonsensical claim that it would look like blackmail. We had a truckload of evidence to charge her with conspiracy, acting as an agent of a foreign government, and false statements. But I wasn't the case agent, and Kevin and Tom didn't feel as strongly about this. They were just relieved we would be getting the EE charges. So, the USAO's twisted chivalry and incompetence would continue. Ling Jia Chung would escape formal justice, despite approving, encouraging, enabling, and facilitating everything her husband did for the PRCIS. Informal justice, however, would prove a bitch!

---

26. They included Casey, Jo-Lein, Adam, Rafik, Clem, Alex, and Sean, future FBI all-stars all!

To prepare for testimony, Greg's second chair, AUSA Ivy Wang, fresh from Harvard Law School, prepped me for my opening testimony by covering the case's Chi Mak origins. I sat down in her office, and she began asking questions about Chi's case, with which she was unfamiliar. I noticed a picture nearby of Ivy standing with President Barack Obama. I wasn't surprised but made a mental note nonetheless.[27] Ivy's questions began.

Ivy: So, I understand that you had FISA coverage in the Mak case?

Gaylord: Yes.

Ivy: What kind of coverages?

Gaylord: Well, we had wiretaps on their phones and—

Ivy: (surprised) On their phones?!

Gaylord: Yes, and microphones in their cars and—

Ivy: (irritated) In their cars? [By now, I knew how this was going to go and enjoyed every subsequent answer and escalating response.]

Gaylord: And microphones in their office and home—

Ivy: (spluttering) In their home?

Gaylord: As well as cameras.

Ivy: (enraged) You had cameras in their home? Did you have a warrant for that?

Gaylord: Of course I did. [I was tempted to innocently answer, "No. Why? Were we supposed to?" so I could watch her head explode.]

This was a Harvard-educated attorney who knew Chi Mak's FISA coverages had survived legal scrutiny, yet I nonetheless received this knee-jerk leftist outrage. She eventually calmed down and began asking me unimaginative, unproductive, disorganized, and confusing questions about the Chi Mak evidence I would be introducing. I had to keep

---

27. Most AUSAs are left-wing and work as prosecutors for a short period to learn the ropes before switching sides for more lucrative positions as private defense attorneys. Thereafter, they manipulate younger AUSAs and the USAO for their own financial gain, and society's loss. I find this practice despicable. Greg and Deirdre were two great exceptions to this rule.

requesting question clarification, as if she were a defense attorney trying to trip me up. Some of her queries were literally unintelligible. I left her office discouraged and worried over her role on the prosecution team. Craig had been a deceptive coward and a snob, but at least he knew how to frame a series of questions leading to a useful conclusion.

After me came returning tradecraft expert Rudy Guerin, waiting just outside. We exchanged skeptical, worried glances as I made a beeline for Greg's office. I warned him of Ivy's initial anger and incompetent, incoherent questions. Greg's stoic demeanor betrayed some concern. I then predicted that if she took the same approach with Rudy, he would soon exit her office swearing a blue streak and threatening to leave. And that's just what he did, making the same beeline to Greg's office. His critique shook Greg's walls, escaping into the surrounding offices, as he shouted, "She doesn't know up from down or what the hell she is doing. You better get someone who has their shit together. I will not be questioned by her again. She's a f——ing disaster!"[28]

I later gave Kevin a heads-up and said that although it was Greg's call, he should urge Ivy be removed from the case, and if Greg kept her, he should promise to keep her on a very short leash. Greg did keep her, explaining to Kevin and me that he would mentor, monitor, and restrict her to a few tasks, assuring me she would be properly prepared to question me at trial. I was dubious. He did, however, change the plan regarding Rudy, who he decided to question himself. I suspect Rudy's strong reaction, and colorful description of her skill set, or lack thereof, made the difference.

The government's considerable evidence list grew to 25 pages, containing nearly 350 exhibits. Len and Harriet did a marvelous job translating the massive number of Chinese-language documents. Our witnesses came from the FBI, Boeing, Chung's family, and four SMEs from NASA, the Defense Intelligence Agency (DIA), US State Department, and the FBI's former executive Rudy Guerin. All were locked and loaded. Chung's defense, led by an ill-prepared Tom Bienert, requested another trial delay. This last one Greg opposed and won. The trial was on!

---

28. I've actually cleaned these sentences up somewhat for the reader.

CHAPTER 36

China Spy II!

GREG CHUNG'S TRIAL BEGAN ON JUNE 2, 2009, AND AFTER OPENING statements, I was called as the first, eager witness. I spent the next hour explaining the Chung case's Chi Mak origins with AUSA Ivy Wang doing a better job of posing questions this time around. Defense co-counsel Ken Miller's cross-examination impotently claimed Chi and Chung were barely acquainted and the Mak evidence only implicated Chi. I was soon done, pleased to apply the first layer of evidentiary foundation. It was easy duty compared to my Chi Mak trial responsibilities.

As case agent, Kevin Moberly would now do the heavy lifting—introducing the background narrative and cache of damning evidence from Chung's home. I was surprised Ivy also conducted Kevin's direct, since he was the key prosecution witness. He spent days on that stand, one on direct, and two more under cross-examination. The defense had to break Kevin, or the evidence. They didn't. On day two, he discussed the B-1 manuals Chung had sent to China via its San Francisco consul and Space Shuttle briefings he'd delivered to PRC officials and engineers. The more documents Kevin entered, the more tired, bored, and monotone Ivy became. Kevin became visibly frustrated with her increasingly unfocused questioning, often rescuing her bad questions with good answers. I was glad this was a bench trial. They also discussed the tasking lists tailored to Chung's access, which the defense repeatedly moved to exclude, unsuccessfully.

Miller's cross-examination falsely claimed we'd made "just plain silly" mistakes: The documents were not trade secrets, restricted, or even wanted; Chung's PRC awards were exaggerated; Chung only gave a few PRC presentations; his tasking lists were more like "requests"; and Chung's huge home collection was sloppy and "cluttered," not sinister. Their semantics offensive became comical. Sensitive documents were not "secreted" within the newspapers, just "put in between" the pages. "[C]rawl spaces" didn't require crawling.[1] Miller's re-cross proved short and ineffective. Kevin did well, giving the defense nothing.

Linguist Len Pi then took the stand to identify documents he'd translated. His short cross by defense co-counsel Ariana Hawbecker accomplished nothing.[2] How could it? The defense didn't hire its own translator. But then, Chung was fluent in Chinese and English. He knew our translations were accurate.

The next day brought Boeing witnesses, starting with Clifford Barnett, engineer, manager, and Delta IV rocket expert. He'd worked the Apollo program since 1962.[3] Greg Staples turned Barnett into our courtroom professor, using an easel to illustrate Boeing's unique Delta IV launching technology. Bienert made his first appearance, conducting an aggressive, bullying cross that reminded me of option three of a trial lawyer's "Last Resort Rules . . . hammer the table."[4] He claimed Barnett was ignorant and obsolete, and overreacting to distract us from past Boeing scandals. Again, no offer of proof. Bienert forgot he was arguing before an experienced judge, not a naive jury.

Steven Carbaugh, a Boeing rotor integrated product team leader, confirmed that Chung's CH-46 and CH-47 Chinook helicopter data remained sensitive and valuable before Greg called aerospace engineer Bill Novak. He had worked on the Space Shuttle since 1973 and supervised Chung's forward fuselage structural analysis work. Novak confirmed that Chung should not have taken his work home, the data was strictly protected, and it must never go to China. Chung, who experienced no "language barrier," never mentioned writing a book, yet he had

---

1. They often did!

2. Lead attorney Bienert's absence was the rule rather than the exception. Just how much was Chung paying him?

3. What an amazing career and era for an engineer.

4. "If you have the facts on your side, hammer the facts. If you have the law on your side, hammer the law. If you have neither the facts nor the law, hammer the table."

downloaded vast amounts of data after receiving his Boeing layoff notice. Miller declared Chung's Space Shuttle work "unrestricted" and charged that Novak was colluding with the FBI to frame Chung.

Bienert moved the next day to throw out Chung's statements to agents, claiming a "Brady violation," specifically that Kevin and Gunnar "selectively interviewed" Chung regarding Boeing materials.[5] He also requested *all* Boeing analysis of Chung's documents, names of agents who met with Boeing officials, and all agent notes about Boeing personnel. Defense attorneys had found *one* sentence within a Boeing summary of Chung's briefing materials by Novak and a second engineer which said, "No classified or Boeing proprietary data was found in either binder." Bienert claimed "agent wrongdoing."

Thankfully, Greg replied, "I'm slow to anger, but I am not going to sit here and have the integrity of my agents impugned. The suggestion that they colored their investigation is outrageous. . . . That is a scurrilous accusation." We'd never seen this Boeing comment. The defense received these materials through *their* subpoenas to Boeing for its records. We had interviewed that second engineer, obtained that same opinion from him, and provided it to the defense. They were never in the dark, yet they preferred to lie. Judge Carney found no Brady violation but granted Bienert's request for all Boeing analysis and a list of agents who met with its officials.

Boeing policy, employee expectations, and valuations of sensitive stolen data were addressed by Gary Lee Graber, who ran F-15 technology integration for forty years. Senior Boeing engineer Emad Farag explained the value of Space Shuttle phased array research and the obligations of departing employees to return all Boeing property.[6] To stress the layers of security protocols protecting Boeing data, and the "Goldilocks" balance between stifling rules and lax security, either of which damages a company's bottom line, we leaned into the Chi Mak trial template, calling upon various Boeing compliance and security personnel. They did

---

5. "Brady" states the government must disclose all evidence gained that materially favors the defendant.
6. We later opened cases against Chung's retired Boeing engineer friends who also did this to help the PRC.

as admirably as their Power Paragon counterparts, demonstrating that Chung had no authority to release Boeing data and never sought it. He even signed a pledge upon his departure that *all* Boeing property had been returned, a dramatic contrast with the hundreds of thousands of pages remaining in his home.[7] Miller's cross was ineffectual and brief, foolishly claiming Boeing's data was "general science" found in school textbooks and the public domain.

Our subject matter expert (SME) parade began with Michael Danis of the Defense Intelligence Agency. He outlined how thousands of the PRC-controlled Aviation Industry and China National Aero-Technology Import & Export corporations, not "private" companies, served China's military and commercial needs. PRC-managed entities sponsored international conferences in China to "steal" visitors' technologies.

After Danis came former FBI agent and crowd favorite Rudy Guerin to discuss PRCIS tradecraft. As with Chi Mak, he linked PRC tradecraft, officers, and Chung case facts, discussing tasking lists, handler behavior, and targeting strategies against Chinese American engineers, using appeals to ego and racial, ethnic, and national pride. Bienert proved no match for Rudy. Using a silly, transparent "searching to understand" approach, Bienert told Rudy, "I want to know what's going on in my client's head." Rudy answered, "Why don't you ask him?" drawing courtroom laughter. When Bienert used a falsely familiar tone to claim, "We're all in the spy game," Rudy replied, "I don't know. Are you?" producing more courtroom laughter, before forcing Bienert to address Chung's journal and PRC letter exchanges. In under five minutes of redirect, Greg crisply destroyed every point Bienert had labored to make.

Next came Wayne Hale, NASA expert on all things Space Shuttle and the space programs of Russia, China, France, India, and Japan. He told an illuminating story of Russia's Space Shuttle program, which failed because they'd stolen everything from us but our secret for applying heat-shielding tiles. His point? Most Space Shuttle technology was

---

7. Great credit goes to Boeing employees Karen Trevett, global trade analyst of Export Compliance; Shelley O'Neil, senior manager for Security and Fire; and Mike Heller, facility security officer (FSO). I was happy that Fred Witham of Power Paragon attended much of the Chung trial, witnessing the fruits of his own previous labors.

public, but *not* the sensitive, crucial stuff. Chung had stolen those missing, restricted pieces, helping China build what Russia couldn't, and leapfrog it to our newer, safer, cheaper rocket technology.[8] The US government was also utilizing the Delta IV rocket as its heavy-lift platform, making it a top PRC target for theft. And Boeing and other US companies were competing directly with China for lucrative commercial launches. Greg followed with Tony Dearth of the US State Department to confirm that the data Chung stole was *not* in the public domain.[9] Once more, the defense proved impotent.

Then came other Boeing employees confirming B-1 bomber, shuttle drawing system (SDS), heat shield, X-37 Space Plane, X-33, and Delta IV rocket data were all proprietary, export-controlled, "need-to-know" technologies, and Chung had no "need."[10] He printed over one thousand SDS documents to take home when he was laid off. There, he used Wite-Out to cover security caveats and his Boeing printer number, before translating, delivering, and briefing them in 2003 to PRC officials. Even his destruction of these materials via burning and trash disposal was illegal. Greg also buried defense claims about Chung's poor English.[11]

Trial day seven, June 11, opened with another Bienert gambit, claiming a Jencks violation.[12] He demanded copies of all emails our SMEs had sent us and objected to our witnesses. Judge Carney overruled both motions. Then FBI Special Agent Chris Pluhar's testimony confirmed his proper handling of Chung's computers and digital media before our squad agent Sean Kim discussed the SDS documents he discovered.[13] Special Agent Jessie Murray came next. First, she discussed Chung's initial FBI interview, then demonstrated her Mandarin fluency, having

---

8. America's Orion project, using singular rockets, not the Space Shuttle, was being built to return us to the moon.

9. The Chung trial's version of Mal Zerden.

10. Paul Benson, Chung's Boeing supervisor; Jack Harrington, direct manager of Safety and Reliability; and Richard Wu all provided fascinating testimony on these subjects. During this testimony I saw Chi Mak's counsel Ron Kaye in the gallery. Why was he there? Regret? Curiosity?

11. Funny how both Mak and Chung defense attorneys thought poor English skills were an espionage defense.

12. Bienert claimed we had failed to produce verbatim statements or reports made by our witnesses.

13. Amazingly, Sean knew Chung's son Shane in high school, where both were on the track and cross-country teams.

Greg Chung CATIC medallion award TRIAL EXHIBIT 18

been raised in a Chinese home.[14] She had overheard Chung tell his son to lie to interviewing agents, thereby obstructing the investigation. Her cross by Miller proved curiously short. This trial was humming along, streamlined by the lack of a jury.

Sheldon Fung then took the stand, coming from the FBI Sacramento Field Office he had recently transferred to. During the September 2006 home search, Sheldon had a friendly daylong conversation with the Chungs, during which they made many claims and admissions. First, Chung had used Boeing overhead transparencies for his Shanghai University presentation. Second, he was awarded medals and issued

---

14. Her last name of Murray came from her husband, a well-known Orange County prosecutor.

invitations as thanks for passing his technological expertise to Chinese university students. Third, the Chungs knew Gu, a PRC official, well, and spent time with him in China and at their home in Orange. They also showed him and Xian Aircraft Company vice president Gao Zhanmin a good time in Southern California. Chung had met Chi Mak and Gu long ago at a Los Angeles event and experienced surprise visits since in his PRC hotel rooms by a "Mr. Chen" and another PRC representative. Both asked for Space Shuttle data. But Chung lied to Sheldon that he was storing Boeing data in his home with his supervisor's permission. Again, our witness testimony was short, sweet, and damning. Miller's weak cross claimed Chung had been confused.

FBI linguist Harriet Hao then took the stand to confirm her translation work, but Ivy had done a poor job preparing her questions. Harriet looked like Rudy Guerin and I felt when Ivy first questioned us, fielding haphazard and unrelated questions. I felt for Harriet, who was always so conscientious.[15] The defense cross-examination was even longer and more disoriented than Ivy's. The defense often couldn't locate the translations they were asking about. Harriet was exhausted and visibly relieved when she finally stepped down.

Ivy re-called Kevin to testify about Shane Chung's interview and the lies his father told him to tell. Miller objected, claiming hearsay, so Carney ruled Shane Chung must testify first. Kevin stepped down and Shane took the stand to say his father told him FBI agents would question him about a trip they took to Beijing, telling him, "You don't know anything." Shane admitted he lied to the FBI when he denied having spoken with his father. It was tense and uncomfortable testimony, and I thought we were too deferential, not challenging his lie that his father's words were reassurance, not orders to "forget." Shane was eighteen during that Beijing visit. Of course he remembered it. It was preposterous to claim otherwise. But I wasn't the case agent, so I said nothing.[16] The defense reinforced Shane's narrative, and Greg didn't redirect, despite knowing Shane's testimony directly challenged our obstruction charge.

The real drama arrived when Shane left the witness stand and walked toward the exit. His mother Ling Jia, who was sitting in the gallery,

---

15. I assured her later it wasn't her fault, but I doubt she believed it.
16. I wish I had, since this soft approach returned to bite us.

stepped out for a hug. Shane refused, briskly walking past her. Like a crack of thunder—I jumped in my seat!—Ling Jia emitted a sudden, ear-splitting primal scream and collapsed onto the ground in a wailing heap. Judge Carney called a recess. In the hallway outside the courtroom, Ling Jia continued her caterwauling as she tried to hug and talk with Shane, who was having none of it. He was clearly ashamed of his parents' betrayal of this country and resented being forced to lie under oath for them. I felt sympathy for Shane and contempt for Ling Jia and her theatrics. For decades she and her hubby had betrayed their children's nation. What did she expect?

I'd seen similar situations while working against the Socialist Republic of Vietnam and its "useful idiots," a Fifth Column of Vietnamese students studying in the United States during the Vietnam War who called themselves American Vietnamese Patriots in the United States. They accepted America's largesse to study here—government grants, scholarships, and loans—yet slandered our troops. These hard-core communists weren't stupid enough, however, to return to live in Vietnam once the war ended, choosing freedom over the oppression they enabled in their "homeland." Their children grew up loving America and despising their parents' hypocrisy. Sadly, I heard years later that Shane had committed suicide.

When we reconvened, Greg unnecessarily apologized, saying "If I thought I could have made our case without calling his son, I would have done so, and did not relish having to do that. For that, I'm sorry, but I just wanted the Court to know." But Chung created this situation by telling his son to lie about his parent's betrayal of America, not Greg, who had nothing to apologize for. Unfortunately, Ling Jia's pity party served its purpose, in that Greg halted all aggressive pursuit of the obstruction charge.

Kevin returned to the stand after Karen Trevett retook it to verify that Chung never requested authority to release information, and Boeing engineer Dong Ngo confirmed Delta IV rocket technology was not publicly available. He had challenged Shane about his lies. Shane then recanted, apologizing to Kevin for lying about the Beijing trip. He then quoted his father's instruction: "Tell them that you don't remember anything about the trip to Beijing in 1985. You don't remember anything. You just can't remember." Clearly, Chung had directed his son to lie to the FBI. On cross, Miller attacked Kevin's FD-302 interview report and his chain of evidence, and recklessly accused him of lying to the grand jury. It was long, tedious, pointless, and ineffective. Carney asked Miller, "[C]an we get to the point?" Miller never did. Due to her disorganization, Ivy's request for Special Agent Sean Kim to retake the stand was withdrawn. That slowed the prosecution's momentum before it rested the government's case.

Miller opened by moving to dismiss all charges. Carney declined.[17] Miller's first witness was the Chungs' younger son Jeff, who described his father as an intellectual who read a lot. He testified his parents' home's crawl spaces were unlocked and remembered little about his family's 1985 Beijing trip. Another teen with amnesia. Afterwards came Boeing mechanical and aerospace Space Shuttle engineer Tian Lai Hu, who declared, without proof, that the public could access the B-1 bomber manuals. Greg's five-minute cross shredded Hu's credibility. The B-1 manuals addressed sensitive nuclear bomber program applications that would aid hostile foreign governments and could *not* be found in *any* library or on the internet. They also were stamped with warnings barring distribution, storage at home, or provision to foreign nations. Presentations on the subject were prohibited. Hu's best answer came when Greg showed him FBI photographs of all the document binders in Chung's crawl spaces: "This should be in Rockwell storage or a warehouse!" Defense attorney Hawbecker's redirect weakened the defense position further: The B-1 program was still producing bombers for our national security. Hu's testimony ended as another plus for us.

Bienert then called his only defense expert, Georgia Tech professor Dr. Stanley. Our impeachment research told us he'd done past work for NASA, universities, and private contractors but knew little about phased array technology and had no experience with the Space Shuttle. He also had a ponytail, which Kevin believed lent him a very nonserious air.[18] Professor Stanley's task was to testify that *all* the information Chung provided China was in the public domain. After highlighting a lot of

---

17. Lead high-profile defense attorney Bienert was again absent. Chung was *not* getting his money's worth.

18. This may have reflected Kevin's Texas roots. However, my California roots also thought it hurt Stanley's credibility, especially when he periodically stopped to adjust or flip it to the side.

public Space Shuttle information, he couldn't prove the technologies we were concerned over had ever become public. They hadn't, because NASA and Boeing still protected them. As a bonus, Stanley came off as haughty and condescending.[19] Due to underhanded defense tactics, Carney ruled Greg's cross must wait until the following week.[20]

Next came Cal State University Long Beach (CSULB) professor Hsien Yeh, whom I had eagerly awaited. Greg advised that Professor Yeh should be apprised of his Fifth Amendment rights against self-incrimination, since he had also made technology presentations in China. Judge Carney agreed. Yeh had also traveled to China with the Chungs, knew PRC officials, and denied knowing Chi Mak, despite common CSULB employments and references to "Yeh" found within the Mak evidence. Yeh came as a character witness for Chung, despite earlier swearing to Kevin and me that he barely knew him. He took the stand and acknowledged also attending the PRC National Day celebrations, an honor he claimed many Chinese American community leaders enjoyed, including the mayor of the local city of Cerritos.[21] He declared he and Chung were trying to help poor Chinese students through Yeh's Chungwah Foundation. Yeh and Chung lectured undergraduate students together at Beijing, Shanghai, and other universities.

When direct questioning concluded, I leaned forward, eager to hear Greg's vigorous cross. "No questions, Your Honor," said Greg (?!). I believed we had just missed a golden opportunity, convinced Yeh was a talent recruiter for China. I wanted his answers, and lies, on the record and under oath for future perjury charges. Instead, Yeh was allowed to slither away without challenge or exposure. I later expressed surprise and disappointment. Greg explained he felt Yeh's testimony was unremarkable, and unhelpful to Chung, so his risk calculation said to do nothing. I believed this thinking was overly restrictive, given the FBI's greater mission.

---

19. Greg made me laugh when he quickly made the crazy sign—finger circling the ear—to Emad Farag, signaling Stanley was all over the map.

20. Without proper notice, defense attorneys added seven topics Stanley would testify to. Judge Carney ruled that rather than strike all of Stanley's testimony, he would give Greg extra time to prepare for the cross-examination.

21. What he *didn't* say was that it was an honor reserved for PRCIS agents and those they wished to recruit!

Bienert re-called Bill Novak to the stand as *their* witness to discuss Boeing's analysis of its documents found in Chung's home. Defense efforts were disorganized and unproductive, at one point requiring Judge Carney's intervention to rephrase a defense question to make it comprehensible. Greg's five-minute cross refuted defense claims: The FBI did *not* hide evidence from the defense, and Chung gave China Boeing's proprietary data. We had won yet another defense witness appearance.

Tuesday, June 16, began with some irrelevant defense testimony.[22] Greg then began his cross-examination of Professor Stanley, immediately establishing him as something of a poser, having designed but never built anything, and a snob concerning blue-collar workers. Although "briefed" on the Space Shuttle, he never worked on it and had far less experience than the government's experts. He even admitted there were sensitive Space Shuttle technologies *not* in the public domain, which negated Stanley's entire purpose for testifying. Stanley also confessed that he knew nothing about economic espionage or PRC intelligence, economic, military, tactical, or strategic goals.

Stanley's examples of "similar" technologies in the public domain were actually *not* similar.[23] In fact, he had ignored evidence, conducted incomplete reviews, and cherry-picked easy but inaccurate technology comparisons, spending an "inordinate amount of time" unsuccessfully trying to prove Chung's stolen Space Shuttle technologies were already in the public domain. Since the internet didn't exist in 1985, when Chung stole and ferried US helicopter technology to China, Stanley's discovery of this data during a 2006 internet search was worse than irrelevant or useless; it was deceptive. This became a classic Greg Staple cross-examination beat-down, destroying Stanley piece by arrogant piece. It made for excellent entertainment.

Greg ended his cross by establishing that Boeing engineers Novak, Benson, and Farag were in a much better position to judge what was Boeing proprietary data. Greg's foot was firmly, mockingly, and figura-

---

22. The name Chen Qinan had surfaced in the trial but was of no consequence to any trial issues.
23. Our incredibly knowledgeable SME Wayne Hale was a great help to Greg in preparing for this cross.

tively planted on Stanley's neck, especially regarding briefings Chung gave in China.

Stanley:	The PowerPoint is usually there just to help you refer back to something. You don't write down everything you are going to say.
Greg:	The rest of it is in your head?
Stanley:	Sure.
Greg:	And you are not a biologist, but when the defendant went to China, his head went with him, didn't it?
Stanley:	Yes, I believe that's the case, sir.[24]

After Stanley's dismissal, Bienert called Boeing general counsel Sean Muntz to the stand regarding the alleged Brady violation. Muntz was clear as mud, not remembering receiving Novak's review report and unable to locate his own notes on it. He couldn't be sure whether a copy of Boeing's review was sent to the FBI or not. Judge Carney ordered Muntz to send him all related notes. This unnecessary drama demonstrated the wisdom of L-3 security managers and executives who throughout the Chi Mak case strove mightily to keep their lawyers out of it. Here, Boeing Legal had aggressively inserted itself into our investigation, and although generally cooperative, their presence had mucked many things up, increasing administrative complexities.

Greg called engineer Emad Farag to the stand to confirm Boeing's proprietary properties and financial interests. Because he was effective, Bienert's cross was aggressive, attempting to confuse Farag by constantly interrupting him. Greg objected and Carney told Bienert, "I'm not going to let you put words into the witness's mouth." Carney's patience was wearing thin. Bienert concluded his cross, then he reversed himself, asking for time to formulate more questions.

Carney:	No.
Bienert:	Can I have five minutes?

---

24. Classic, commonsense Greg Staples humor to make a point. The exchange reminded me of the Supreme Court nominee who couldn't define a woman because she was "not a biologist."

Carney: No . . .

Bienert: Can I have thirty seconds?

Carney: You can have thirty seconds.

Bienert: That's all we have, Your Honor.[25]

The defense called Bill Novak to the stand *again*. Carney commented, "Mr. Novak, third time is the charm; right, sir?" Novak groused, "I hope so!" Bienert questioned Novak about the spreadsheet and notes he created while reviewing Chung's materials. I perked up when Novak said, "I believe I also had a follow-up call from an agent, FBI Agent Gaylord, who wanted to make sure I had received the data and was starting to look at it in preparation for the meeting." Weirdly, I hoped I would be re-called to the stand. Novak clarified that he hadn't told us he had taken notes. Bienert did *not* want to hear that, so he kept pressing, poring over every detail to find some prosecutorial misconduct, in a last gasp to salvage a badly lost case. He found none. On cross, Novak confirmed he'd never shown us his spreadsheet review. He then stepped down.

Kevin stepped up again, this time to introduce his FD-302 report to prove we never had the documents Bienert claimed we withheld, and calmly ignored Bienert's outrageous and condescending "crooked agent" conspiracy goading. Government discovery had provided everything to the defense. Frustrated, Bienert concluded with a 31-page case brief that focused on a few legal trees, but ignored Chung's 300,000-plus-page forest of Boeing proprietary technologies at home. Greg's 47-page brief's answers buried them.

June 24, the tenth and final day of trial, opened with more defense fireworks. Bienert doubled down, claiming the government had committed Brady violations by withholding "exculpatory" information from the defense. It was *so* ridiculous. The defense had learned of this Boeing work product *before* Kevin did, the documents were *not* exculpatory, and the issues were addressed *during* trial. Yet Bienert's feigned "outrage" over "misconduct" continued.[26] Carney asked, "How has the defense been

---

25. Note to defense attorneys: Don't tick off the judge, *especially* when he is the trier of fact in your case.

26. Remember the third admonition of the "Last Resort Rules? . . . Hammer the table!"

prejudiced?" Bienert admitted, "I don't know that we have been prejudiced directly on the issue of those documents." Still, he moved that Carney toss the entire case or strike *all* of Kevin's testimony. It was hard to sit there and listen to this lazy creep. At least Miller and Hawbecker exuded some sense of humility and self-awareness when they spoke.

Judge Carney turned to hear Greg express his outrage:

> *We violated no rule. Agent Moberly violated no rule. The most important weapon that an FBI agent has is not his gun, his training, or his experience; it's his integrity and his reputation for it. . . . I'm not going to sit here and have his integrity assailed when there is no basis for it. There is no Brady violation. . . . Boeing is not the government. I, as a prosecutor, am not responsible for what is in the files at Boeing, especially when I don't know about them, and the same applies to Agent Moberly. . . . But where in the cross of Agent Moberly did it come out that he was anything other than truthful? . . . They admit there is no prejudice. And they want you to strike his testimony? That's absurd. . . . This is upsetting to me. . . . I just want the record to be clear this agent does not color his investigations. He does not withhold information.*

Carney agreed. "I'm going to make a finding that there was no evidence of intentional misconduct or bad faith on the part of Agent Moberly, or anybody associated with the government," he said, and called for closing arguments.

Ivy opened with, "Your Honor, I'm just going to cut to the chase. Defendant is guilty of all counts charged in the indictment," before going over each count and our evidence supporting it. We had proven six counts of Economic Espionage concerning the Delta IV rocket, Space Shuttle, and C-17, as well as Conspiracy, Acting as an Agent of a Foreign Government, and Material False Statements, but the Obstruction of Justice charge had been weakened by the prosecutors' light touch after Ling Jia's courtroom theatrics.[27]

---

27. For instance, Greg did not call Sal Valdez to the stand, even though Sal heard Shane admit that his father told him to lie to the FBI. If *all* the evidence had been forcefully presented, this charge

Bienert opened his closing argument with a claim only hinted at during trial: Chung *was* a spy in the 1980s—twenty years ago—but hadn't been one *lately*. His admissions included: "He did some dumb things"; "Violated Boeing rules"; "Didn't report travel to China"; "Helped China." What changed? Bienert declared Chung became angry over the Tiananmen Square massacre, so he violated "spy protocols" to demonstrate his displeasure, never to return.[28] Chung's collection of Space Shuttle materials? An enthusiast writing a book. His latest trips to China? Purely philanthropic. The Chungs' VIP invitation to celebrate the PRC's National Day at the Great Hall? Any of the over billion Chinese could get one. The sensitivities of the stolen documents? It was all general knowledge, found on the internet (which didn't then exist).

Bienert began phoning it in, forgetting he was arguing before an experienced, knowledgeable judge, not a gullible jury. Carney had seen all of these claims refuted. Bienert continued, saying Chung kept documents because he was a "pack rat," and all government and Boeing witnesses had lied. Chung had suffered enough. Besides, all of Chung's "handlers" had died or retired. Bienert then focused on the obstruction charge, before entering the realm of the absurd, declaring we'd proven nothing. His conclusion mimicked Ron Kaye's: The defendant was only guilty of being intellectually curious, striving to learn and accumulate knowledge.[29] Bienert's closing line stood logic on its head when he declared, "The evidence shows a clear picture of a guy who refused to become a spy for China."

Greg's rebuttal opening was classic: "Truth. I'm happy to hear that word. That's what we are here for is the truth. Regrettably, you heard very little of it in the last two or three hours." Greg was highly skilled at regurgitating and using defense arguments to destroy them with sarcasm. Chung just wanted to legally help China? Then why didn't he tell someone? Why the secrecy? Other employees with presentations got authorization first. "Is [Chung] the only person out of thousands

---

would have also been a slam dunk. And of course, the USAO refused to charge Ling Jia, a knowledgeable, participating, lying co-conspirator regarding every crime Chung committed.

28. *No* evidence was ever presented to support this Bienert fantasy.

29. Does that argument ever work? You'd think they would have learned something from the Chi Mak trial.

of engineers at Rockwell that didn't get that message? Was he out sick that day?" If your documents reflect the public domain, why hide them? Because Chung knew otherwise. Hiding 300,000-plus pages of Boeing and Rockwell documents isn't the behavior of a "pack rat . . . [It's] a pack elephant!" Rockwell employees viewing photographs of Chung's crawl spaces exclaimed they resembled "a Rockwell storage room." Boeing decided when technical data could be released, *not* Chung, who had no plans for a Space Shuttle "book." Gu wanted Space Shuttle information and Chung provided it, simple as that. What about the other materials Chung stole? Was he going to write about the F-15, B-52, and B-1, or was his book going to be an encyclopedia of US technologies? Who in their right mind ships B-1 bomber manuals to China via its San Francisco consulate!

Chung hid *all* of these activities. The Chungs' 2002 National Day invitation was a reward *after* Tiananmen Square and wasn't issued by the United Front Work Department of the Chinese Communist Party to just anybody. "What tourist gets that? None. People who work for China get that," declared Greg. Chung spent thousands of hours preparing detailed, specific technology briefings. "The Chinese got their hands on this Space Shuttle technology through him!" Derisively referencing Professor Stanley, Greg told Judge Carney that "Mr. Google's" testimony was completely inadequate.[30] Boeing's engineers and manufacturers were the real experts. Chung's signed Boeing exit agreement promised that "All Boeing documents have been returned" . . . *except* the 300,000-plus pages he had stashed at home! Defense claims of "Brady" violations were simply red herrings.

In summary, all the proof against Chung came "out of his mouth and out of his pen." He told his PRC masters, "I feel ashamed for not doing more to help the motherland." He did all of this for China. But where was his duty of loyalty to America? Greg closed with, "We believe when the Court considers all of the evidence in this case, there is no doubt that the defendant is guilty on all counts."

Three weeks later, we gathered in Judge Carney's courtroom to hear his verdict. Greg seemed nervous, I suspect because this case sought to

---

30. This echoed Greg's derisive label for Chi Mak, "Mr. Honesty."

set legal precedent. Despite the statute being decades old, no federal court had yet adjudicated Economic Espionage charges. Success would establish the template for future prosecutions; failure would discourage such future prosecutions. Mercifully, Judge Carney got right to the point:

> *One count of being an agent for the PRC, one count of conspiring to violate the Economic Espionage act, six counts of violating the Economic Espionage Act, one count of making a false statement, and one count of obstructing justice. After considering all the evidence and the arguments of counsel, I do find Mr. Chung guilty of all counts except the obstruction of justice. Mr. Chung has been an agent of the People's Republic of China for over thirty years. Under the direction and control of the PRC, Mr. Chung misappropriated sensitive aerospace and military information belonging to his employer, The Boeing Company, to assist the PRC in developing its own programs. . . . [sending it via] mail, sea freight, a Chinese agent named Chi Mak, and even the China consulate.*

He'd "cast aside [Boeing's trust] to serve the PRC, which he proudly proclaimed as his motherland. I now must hold him accountable for his crimes." Carney explained his "not guilty" obstruction finding. Despite finding Jessie's and Kevin's testimonies very credible, he could not be certain of what Shane said to his father before Chung responded, "Tell them you don't know."[31]

Judge Carney then wished to discuss forfeiture of Chung's Orange home, which we'd requested because the Chungs had used it for years to conceal evidence of their crime—the stolen 300,000-plus technology pages. Loss of a million-dollar home would serve as a great deterrent to the many future would-be Maks and Chungs out there. Carney asked that the charge be reconsidered, given the hardship it would impose upon Chung's wife, children, and grandchildren. But the Chungs owned *four* other properties in Southern California—two nice homes and two

---

31. Sal Valdez's testimony would have settled that question. Shane told Sal he understood that his father had told him to lie to us.

commercial rental properties, and their "children" were adults with their own homes and families.[32]

As Judge Carney discussed scheduling a sentencing hearing, a relieved and excited Greg Staples rose. The hair on the back of my neck stood up. I'd seen that look before. Greg was about to make an unnecessary concession in light of this great victory, without consulting Kevin first. Greg announced, "That's fine with the government. And with respect to the Court's comments, I appreciate and understand the Court's position and would move to dismiss the forfeiture allegation at this point." I was tempted to stand up and shout *No!*, to remind Greg and Carney of the truth.[33] Greg didn't have to make that decision then and there, and should have asked his FBI partners first. He had time, but in his enthusiasm, the old AUSA/USAO privilege came to the surface. Carney dropped the charge. Nevertheless, our stupendous achievement ruled the day.

Carney raised the question of bail. Greg held tough there, asking that Chung be remanded until sentencing, given his PRC contacts, age, and the long sentence he faced. Bienert requested release on bond, Chung having "amassed a fair amount of property. . . . [F]ive separate real properties in this country . . . So, there's significant assets; significant wealth that they have accumulated." Carney responded, "I respectfully disagree. These charges are very, very serious and the exercise of trying to reach a decision really forced me to get into the facts and the details. So, I'm going to remand him to the custody of our US Marshals who I see at the back of the courtroom."[34] Carney handed out his fifty-page decision, which verified what a slam-dunk case this had been, cogently reciting the facts, beginning with Chi Mak and concluding "[Chung] was a spy for the PRC."

Bienert responded with motions requesting a new trial and Judge Carney's recusal, alleging "judicial bias . . . because the Court was

---

32. Once again, we were haunted by the USAO's refusal to charge the wife.
33. We also *knew* the PRCIS had paid Chung for his betrayal, and that some of those funds likely went into this property.
34. Did Carney have buyer's remorse upon hearing that forfeiture of Chung's Orange home would in fact *not* be a hardship?

influenced or relied upon facts learned while presiding over a separate criminal trial in the matter of *United States vs. Mak et al.*, . . . and the Court's reliance on extrinsic evidence prejudiced the defendant." The second motion was especially scummy. Bienert knew about Carney's role in the Chi Mak case *well before* trial and could have acted then. Instead, he saved it for reversal purposes should he lose. Dirtbag! Carney denied both motions with one interrelated answer:

> *The declaration is untimely. I think you needed to file such a declaration once the case was assigned to me. . . . I don't think you have shown good cause to excuse not filing it timely. [The] magnitude of documents [Chung] secretly [tried] to destroy . . . sealed the verdict. That, to me, reflected a consciousness of guilt. . . . Coming into this trial I really wanted to find him innocent. . . . I came into this case . . . to be very aggressive and very tough on the government, but what hit me pretty early on when I was hearing the evidence was all those documents that were found in his possession. . . . the evidence concerning Mr. Mak was legally insignificant.*[35]

On Monday, February 8, 2010, the day of sentencing, we *again* endured defense hysterics and a new lie that "Special Agent Gaylord" withheld evidence from the defense about a witness defense was therefore unable to call. They claimed that "Professor Gu," aka, Gu Zhen Luong, one of the PRC official letter writers, made exculpatory remarks about Chung to me that I didn't report, thereby committing another Brady violation.[36] They had since interviewed Professor Gu, who claimed he had said good things about Chung to me, which went unreported. Once again, it was a complete lie. My FD-302 report stated the truth: Gu was uncooperative and refused to discuss Greg Chung.[37] Of note, he also had refused to testify for the defense.

---

35. Quite an extraordinary admission for a judge to make! Judges are supposed to enter a case indifferent to the verdict and the parties involved, not "wanting" one verdict over another, or planning to be harder on one side than another.

36. This individual was also known as Ku Chen Luong.

37. "No good deed goes unpunished." The defense didn't find Professor Gu; *we* did! I interviewed him because he had exchanged damning letters with Chung while working in China at the Harbin

Carney ruled that the defense had made an insufficient showing. Greg responded, "[We are] prepared to address the accusations that Special Agent Gaylord somehow did not include in his 302 what was contained in Mr. Gu's letter; that's absolutely not true. What is in the 302 is what Mr. Gu told Special Agent Gaylord." Once again, I appreciated Greg's confidence in me. Confusing things even more, the defense kept mixing up Professor Gu Zhen Luong of Harbin Institute with PRC aviation official Gu Wei Hao. Official Gu died in China, without being interviewed. Professor Gu was alive and well in the United States and had been interviewed by both sides.[38]

Probation's eleven-page "Government's Sentencing Position" was brief and to the point. Given the offense level, they recommended 168 months, in the middle of the recommended 151- to 188-month range, and a fine of $90,000, based upon Chung's net worth of over $3 million.[39] The prosecution requested an "upward departure/variance," given Chung's intention to "benefit the 'motherland' . . . a country that maintains a hostile military posture towards the United States . . . Given that the defendant has not accepted responsibility for his conduct, a high-end sentence of 235 months is warranted. . . . There are few crimes more serious than espionage." We discussed the military threat China poses to the United States on land, sea, air, and space, and the need for deterrence. Since sixty-seven-year-old Chi Mak had received a sentence of over twenty-four years, a twenty-year sentence for seventy-three-year-old Greg Chung seemed equitable. Kevin had worked hard to get Boeing's evaluation on lost product value and revenue due to Chung's betrayal. Boeing's estimate was $2 billion, most of that representing Chung's compromise of Delta IV rocket technology.

The defense requested a four-year sentence, calling Probation's recommendation "draconian," and citing a Washington, DC, spy case related to Chi Mak which never saw trial because the defendant cooperated

---

Institute. Gu refused to be interviewed until I agreed to do it over the telephone. He was vague, deceptive, and refused to discuss Chung.
38. I do hate the fact that this PRC foot soldier is now living the good life in America. He deserves to be deported.
39. The recommended amount for the fine should have been $3 million.

and pled guilty. But Greg Chung had not cooperated, even though he was given a chance to. The defense also submitted twenty "Sentencing Letters" pleading for leniency, only one of which, from a tenant, didn't have a Chinese surname. Only one letter writer, Chung's elder brother, acknowledged Chung's guilt. Another letter used a "Buy American" defense, depicting Chung as our national salesman, giving technical data to China in order to convince it "to buy our products." At least that one was creative.

Greg Chung submitted his own seven-page "Autobiography," describing himself in glowing terms while acknowledging his failing health, with no admission of guilt, just excuses, like Chi Mak. Chung's wife Ling Jia submitted a three-page typed letter, more about herself than her husband.[40] Same lies. Days before the sentencing, Chung submitted another handwritten letter of denial. "Your Honor, I am not a spy. I am only an ordinary man. I have never been as an agent of PRC. I never accept any order from PRC. I have never asked Chi Mak to send anything for me and I have never given any information to Chi Mak."

Bienert turned this into a theater of the absurd, ignorantly claiming we'd assigned Chung an individual number, like *all* ethnic Chinese we investigated.[41] What we *had* done was translate Chung's full name into the universal Standard Telegraphic Code (STC), to ensure Chinese names are *not* confused. Bienert's crew had failed to understand this, thus their mixing up of professor Gu with official Gu. Bienert then whined to Judge Carney how unfair life was.

Bienert: The problem, of course, is you were part of Chi Mak, Mr. Staples and his agents were part of Chi Mak. The only people who were not part of Chi Mak was us. So we're fighting, not only the phantom of the witnesses we can't get ahold of, but it turns out they knew at least one of them, but we're fighting the phantom of Chi Mak, yet again, when we weren't even part of the trial.[42]

---

40. Both of these people had huge entitlement issues and egos, which explained their actions.
41. Another veiled "racism!" charge.
42. Oh, but they were. They repeatedly sat in on Chi's trial, and we even offered them a deal to testify in said trial.

Greg: Put Agent Gaylord on the stand. They can cross him to their heart's content. There are no other reports on Mr. Gu. . . . This 302 is not Brady. This 302 contains what Professor Gu told Agent Gaylord. We were not obligated to turn it over. . . . And that's that . . . And with that, with the court's indulgence, I'll just call Special Agent Gaylord to the stand.

Carney: I would like to hear Agent Gaylord. I think, in defense to him, he probably wants to be heard, and we'll put him under oath.[43]

On the stand, I described my lead to interview Gu at a Fullerton city address. Professor Gu's daughter was there. She told me he lived in Chicago and gave me his telephone number. On my first call, Gu said he didn't have time to talk. During a second call, Gu said nothing regarding "the public nature of the documents," as defense had claimed. He didn't wish to speak further with me. Greg's direct went mere minutes.

Bienert did his best to shame, rush, confuse, and fluster my testimony, hoping it would blow up into a massive scandal over one small contact. He failed. I said, "To my knowledge, the only information about Mr. Gu is in [my] 302, and what was present at trial, the letters. To my knowledge, that's all that is documented anywhere about Mr. Gu." I then schooled him on how agents conduct interviews, while he tried to sell a threatening *Law & Order*–style interrogation version. I repeatedly corrected Bienert with "As I said" clarifications. His aggressive, clumsy attempts to bully me into making faulty testimony backfired. He looked foolish and desperate.

After I verified for Judge Carney that professor Gu Zhen Luong was a different person than PRC aviation official Gu Wei Hao, Greg asked me about the connections between the Mak and Chung cases, angering Bienert. Professor Gu was the only PRC-based letter writer in the Chi Mak and Greg Chung cases we had found or interviewed in America. Judge Carney was satisfied, and Bienert was out of gas.

---

43. Judge Carney got that right—I wanted to take the stand once more and go toe-to-toe with Bienert, who I'd come to despise.

I left the stand for the last time, considering it an honor to be the first and last witness against Greg Chung. Carney ruled against the defense, citing Professor Gu from my FD-302, "China has been bullied in the past hundred years. We all hope our race can be respected."[44] There it was again, this racial and ethnic obsession that China must attain a favorable public image.

Then came Judge Carney's sentence. He rejected *all* defense arguments. Because Chung gave China national defense information, Carney added time for abuse of trust, while recognizing Chung's advanced age, medical infirmities, and the harm imprisonment would cause his family. But Carney erred in one area. He said that no evidence existed implicating Chung's wife Ling Jia.[45] Chung's other aggravating sentencing factors included decades of theft, lies to employers and the FBI, Boeing's security training, and restrictive markings on documents he possessed and doctored. Mimicking Greg Staples's arguments, Carney said:

> *The law doesn't allow him to make that choice [of what can be publicly released]. . . . [Boeing doesn't] spend millions of dollars of taxpayers' money just to, 'Well, here, you can go ahead and have it, PRC.' . . . [I] view this as a national security case [needing to send a message to China]. Don't be sending your spies to this country. . . . I'm not going to shy away from the Chi Mak case.*

Carney again admitted to having rooted for Chung's innocence, hoping Chi was the exception, and being disappointed when the evidence indicated otherwise.[46] Consideration of Chi Mak's sentence proved "relevant to the analysis . . . 188 months is the appropriate sentence."[47]

Carney asked for Chung's comments. He stood and read a statement:

---

44. Gu's sentiment was very telling, as well as widespread within the Chinese community.

45. Thanks again, USAO—Ling Jia was an addressee on every single PRC letter, was widely traveled and frequently photographed with her husband and PRC officials, knowingly served as Chung's cover for many China trips, and lied about it all.

46. An extraordinary statement: The "objective trier of fact" rooted against us, yet *still* had to rule in our favor.

47. The US Probation Office had recommended a much shorter sentence.

Your Honor, I'm not a spy. I'm only an ordinary man. The documents I saved at home; they were used for my work. And I was planning to write a book. That's a technical, practical book. Those documents were used for my references. When I gave lecture in China, I only discussed the general aircraft design. Those were probably available information in an academic setting. Your Honor, I love this country. My children and grandchildren all live here. I wish this country is the best country so my children and grandchildren can have a better life. Your Honor, I beg your pardon to let me live with my family peacefully. Thank you, Your Honor.

Once again, no expression of guilt or remorse.

Bienert buttered up Carney, declaring how much they respected him, before requesting a five-year sentence and reduced fine. Carney promised no fine that might "impose an undue hardship."[48] Greg Staples pointed out defense attorney misstatements and urged a long sentence for deterrence.

Judge Carney imposed the 188-month sentence (amounting to fifteen years and eight months), with recommendations that Chung be imprisoned at a West Coast facility, which would allow family visits, before remanding Chung to US marshal custody. Carney had just imposed the longest Economic Espionage sentence *ever*, one we all believed was a death sentence. Given Greg Chung's betrayal of his adopted country, it seemed appropriate.

Kevin and the rest of SARA-4, Greg, Ivy, and my father Ed, who was visiting that day, celebrated over lunch at Dave & Buster's. A good time was had by all!

Days later, the defense filed all-encompassing "kitchen sink" appeals to the District Court and Ninth Circuit. The latter was no small threat, given its long history of far-left activism. To our surprise and delight, the Ninth Circuit filed a lengthy decision on September 26, 2011, affirming Chung's convictions. We could now close the book on Greg Chung. Soon afterwards, Kevin Moberly transferred to his "Holy Land" of birth,

---

48. How? Chung was worth over $3 million, including five real estate properties, as documented by his own attorney's court filings.

Texas. Co-case agents Tom Grandmain and I now handled the administrative cleanup.

In January 2011, I became SARA-4's supervisor, and as such, urged Tom to interview Chung in prison, since his appeals were exhausted. Tom resisted, but I ordered it. Chung agreed, likely wanting another opportunity to protest his innocence. The National Reconnaissance Office (NRO) requested case information and a seat at the interview to ask whether Chung had compromised any sensitive Space Shuttle payloads. Although nothing indicated such—NRO's concerns were dubious at best—we granted their request. Unfortunately, Tom allowed two NRO officers first access to Chung, not following us, as I had instructed. They got nothing. More importantly, their questions and demeanor irritated Chung so much that he refused to talk to the FBI thereafter. I was ticked! Our opportunity to learn from Chung, and his chance to improve his situation, were lost forever.

During the COVID-19 pandemic, Chung sought early release, just like Chi Mak. Greg wanted my opinion. I vehemently opposed early release, as I did for Chi. I gave Greg my reasons in bullet-point form, which he incorporated within his winning motion to oppose. Chung remained in prison, and within a year, he had passed away. If I had known the future, I wouldn't have changed a thing. Prisoners shouldn't be released for health concerns. If they did the crime, they should do the time.

The only sympathy I feel is for the Chung family—the sons, and their wives and children—*not* Greg and Ling Jia. They came to this country fleeing communist oppression and were given a new start, world-class educations, and bright futures. In repayment, they spit on the

Greg Chung's first days in America FBI RELEASED

United States and the desires and sacrifices of their parents and grand-parents, who had fought for freedom from Chinese communist oppression and escaped from it. The Maks and Chungs did the opposite, actively and enthusiastically aiding the vicious brutes who run the CCP and its regime, which has murdered millions more of their own citizens than *any* other government in world history. Both couples reveled in accolades received from totalitarian thugs and helped condemn over a billion fellow Chinese to continuing oppression and death. The Chungs just visited China. They weren't stupid enough to live under the brutal regime they worked to enable. I have nothing but contempt for them.

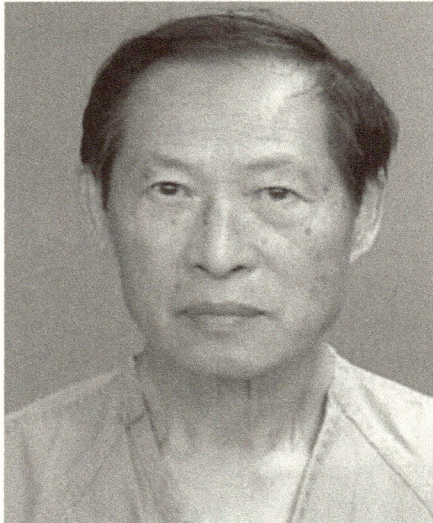

Greg Chung's last days in America FBI
RELEASED

Epilogue: China Spies!

The Mak and Chung prosecutions led to other PRC espionage cases. The most important of those was Sandy Kable's "Chi Mak on steroids" case, focused upon PRC agent and naturalized US citizen Kuo Tai Shen and his two recruits, defense contractors Gregg Bergersen and James Fondren. It spanned three Field Offices—Washington, DC, New Orleans, and Houston.[1] Kuo, a Taiwan native who owned a New Orleans furniture business, moonlighted as a spotter and recruiter for the PRCIS. He was supervised by Lin Hong, another CAPS official who also oversaw Pu Pei Liang, the Maks' handler. Kuo recruited Bergersen and Fondren to provide US foreign policy, defense strategies, and other sensitive information regarding Taiwan's defense. He obtained their classified data under the guise that he represented US-friendly Taiwanese business interests, a classic "false flag" operation.[2]

Since our Mak case was the first trial canary in the PRC espionage coal mine, Sandy and I kept these other case agents informed of our progress through the Weekly Investigative Updates (WIUs) I sent to FBIHQ. I also traveled to our Houston and Washington Field Offices (WFO) to share our trial preparation experiences. At one point, WFO investigators laughingly congratulated me on the aggressive language I used within my WIUs. They got a kick out of how direct I was regarding unmet resource requests and criticisms of FBILA, FBIHQ, USAO, and DOJ managers. While I always used objective, non-emotional language, I found ways to creatively illustrate the ridiculous and incompetent management we struggled against. WFO agents had an easier time getting

---

1. Houston stepped in for New Orleans because of the devastation wrought by Hurricane Katrina.
2. This is the disguising of the intelligence operator's true national allegiance, making the acts of espionage appear more palatable when apparently done on behalf of a friendly nation.

resources but could never get away with such pointed criticisms, being located near so many interfering DC blue flamers. For better and worse, I got fewer resources, and less interference, being on the West Coast, which made me thankful.

WFO and FBIHQ's incestual relationship causes many FBI public relations problems. Blue flamers jump back and forth between these parallel ladders on their climb up, remaining insolated within DC's political bubble, away from real America, just like our politicians. This environment trains this inbred class to choose the cautious, cowardly approach, second-guessing, diverting blame, and seizing credit due others. These managers cause disaster when they run investigation themselves.[3]

Gregg Bergersen held Top Secret clearance as a weapons system policy analyst / director of C4ISR programs at the US Defense Security Cooperation Agency.[4] He provided the Chinese classified US defense data, like planned weapons/technology sales to Taiwan, and was paid thousands in cash, lavish dinners, and Las Vegas gambling trips for it. In an infamous, damning video recorded within his own rental car, and shown on *60 Minutes*, Bergersen is seen driving and talking with Kuo about their "illegal" activities as Kuo stuffs money into Bergersen's shirt pocket, assuring him everything will be fine. It's nauseating.[5]

James Fondren was a former US Air Force lieutenant colonel working as liaison office deputy director for US Pacific Command, also carrying a Top Secret clearance. As its only "client," Kuo paid thousands to Fondren's one-man consulting company. Although each man declared he believed the information he provided was going to private Taiwanese interests, *not* the PRC, neither claim was credible, especially Fondren's. He hosted a PRCIS officer in his home and took a fully paid trip to China, not Taiwan, where he met PRCIS supervisor Lin Hong.

---

3. Consider Case Agent Peter Strzok of Comey, Clinton, and Russiagate fame. Peter was a smug, arrogant political poser, *not* an investigator. He hated my Chi Mak case because he couldn't claim credit for it.

4. C4ISR = Command, Control, Communications, Computers, Intelligence, Surveillance, and Reconnaissance.

5. And for more than one reason. It demonstrates the huge difference between WFO's high-quality audio/video coverage vs. FBILA's within the Mak cars and homes.

Stellar FBI agents produced the goods proving both American traitors deserved the death penalty, yet the defendants received mere slaps on the wrist plea deals, proving even the sale of classified data doesn't guarantee stiff sentences. In March 2008, Bergersen received less than six years' imprisonment; in January 2010, Fondren received three years. A complete farce, especially when compared with USAO public pronouncements that espionage was one of the worst crimes an American citizen could commit.[6] In June 2010, Kuo's sentence of nearly sixteen years was *slashed* to six years, due to "cooperation" and "equity" concerns. Shame on the prosecutors, and shame on the judge! Chi Mak and Greg Chung each received sentences longer than Bergersen, Fondren, and Kuo, combined.

Requests for case briefings began pouring in. Since Kevin and I couldn't do them all, other squad agents took up the slack. I was averaging multiple Chi Mak / Greg Chung presentations per week, locally, nationwide, and overseas, from classrooms taught by federal judges Cormac Carney and David Carter to FBI and other US intelligence community, military, and civilian training facilities, to friendly foreign services, multinational defense contractors, national laboratories, universities, conferences, think tanks, and private security associations. Kevin did the same and proved adept at public relations. Both prosecutions became source material for a number of books—both accurate and inaccurate—and counterintelligence training videos, true crime television series episodes, podcasts, and museum exhibits.[7] They also spawned articles within *The New Yorker* and *New York Times Magazine*.

Throughout all of this we continued working PRC counterintelligence hard. First came two spin-off cases from the Mak and Chung investigations. One was a Boeing engineer I'll call "Mr. Withers," who gave Chung the restricted Delta IV information. By the time of our investigation, Withers was at death's door. We interviewed him and searched his home, finding correspondence from China expressing gratitude for Withers's technical contributions to the motherland, awards for

---

6. Apparently, Los Angeles USAO management hasn't the only collection of weak, lazy, cowardly attorneys.
7. Currently at the International Spy Museum and FBIHQ's Museum, both located in DC.

PRC presentations, and invitations for "honored" Chinese abroad such as himself to attend events in China.[8] Once again, an immigrant and his family enjoying America's largesse were betraying it to support the oppressive communist dictatorship they'd fled. It didn't bother Withers that the wretched PRC regime oppressed fellow Chinese, as long as it stroked his ego. Unfortunately, we lacked enough recent evidence to bring charges.[9] We had to close the case. Withers remained free under our generous system of justice but died shortly thereafter. I shed no tears.

We also investigated another engineer who traveled with Chung to China, aggressively recruited fellow engineers for the PRC, and provided what US technologies he could access. I'll call him "Mr. Smug." This racist considered himself and the Chinese community superior and above our inquiries. We interviewed him and his equally aggressive wife and searched their home under a warrant. Even more so than with Mr. Withers, we found loads of evidence indicating both spouses represented the PRC, provided technical materials, and received letters and awards for their time, efforts, devotion, and aid provided to the motherland. In the home of these "PRC Overseas Chinese Advisory Board" members we found nearly as many Boeing and Rockwell binders as in Greg Chung's house, except these were *empty*. We were too late. The Smugs had learned Chung's lesson, dumping all their incriminating technical materials. Once again, PRC refugees had bitten the hand that fed and sheltered them in order to aid an evil prison state. The Smugs were no better than the Chungs, just another set of ego-driven left-wing posers, soaking up accolades from Red China while safely living free of its oppression.

And then came a case we *could* publicly pursue.[10] It grew from an outreach briefing we had provided to Edwards Lifesciences, a world-leading manufacturer of medical devices in Irvine, California. Edwards contacted us on Wednesday, November 14, 2012, to report a suspicious employee: He repeatedly traveled to China to "visit his mother," but before each trip downloaded large amounts of company product device data. Another trip to visit dear old mom was coming in two days around midnight, Friday,

---

8. Sound familiar?

9. Most violations require criminal activity within the last five years. Otherwise, the statute of limitations kicks in.

10. There were many more we took private, classified action on.

November 16, at LAX.[11] Two of my agents, Jo-Lein and Brooke, took the lead. I hooked them up with Greg Staples to quickly draft arrest and search warrants as we worked with Edwards to identify all past PRC trips, data downloads, and other probable cause. As always, our squad's agents did a magnificent job getting everything ready in two days' time.

That Friday evening, as he boarded his China flight, Jo-Lein and Brooke arrested engineer Wenfeng Lu, forty-six, married, with children. We interviewed him, searched his belongings and Irvine home, and found a treasure trove of thumb drives, laptops, DVD-Rs, and other digital media upon which he'd stored Edwards's proprietary data and his signed contracts with PRC officials. China had agreed that Lu would steal medical device trade secrets from Edwards and two past employers and carry it to China. In exchange, China would provide Lu $328,000 in financing, three years of free laboratory space in a Nanjing technology park, tax breaks, financial incentives, and other aid, all part of a huge PRC program designed to encourage ethnic Chinese to bring stolen Western intellectual property "home" to start their own businesses. With few research and development costs, and low employee wages and overhead, Lu's company could undercut Edwards's prices and corner the China market quickly, before moving on to the world. This time-honored strategy still works well for the PRC today.

We now had proof that Lu had stolen cutting-edge medical device manufacturing data for treatment of cardiac and vascular ailments from his last three employers. We caught him hand-carrying the data, including photographs of crucial equipment, copies of company reports, presentations, emails, and test results. Our arrest prevented Lu from completing his business plan, which was to transfer all that data to China, enriching himself and significantly harming Edwards and other past employers. We indicted Lu on twelve charges of theft of trade secrets—eight from Edwards, and four from another former employer. Following our proven playbook, we worked closely with both victim companies, getting their crucial valuation of anticipated losses and documentation of security measures exercised to protect their intellectual property.[12]

---

11. Eerie reminders of Chi Mak, but with even fewer days' notice before departure.

12. Security measures include limiting log-in privileges to those with a "need to know," sign-in sheets, restricted area escorts, stringent data security training, employee nondisclosure agreements,

Because Greg Staples was too busy to take the case, it was assigned to AUSA Mark Takla, a reputed go-getter. Not so much, it turned out, at least by comparison. And the weak USA at the time, Eileen Decker, made things worse. I'd dealt with her when she was AUSA Decker, during the Mak and Chung cases. She was another naysayer, championing what could *not* be done. Her press release on Lu was big on taking credit and full of empty talk and promises.

Intellectual property (IP) theft poses a grave threat to businesses and the employees who depend on those businesses for their livelihoods. Moreover, when the stolen material is destined for foreign entities seeking to compete with American businesses, as it was in this case, IP theft also threatens the security of our nation. Because of these threats the Department of Justice prosecutes individuals for intellectual property theft out of a National Security Division. Lu is likely to face a lengthy jail term and a substantial fine if found guilty of the charges. Each of the 12 counts carries a maximum prison term of 10 years and a fine of $5 million per count. Lu's trial has been scheduled for June 21, 2016.

Sounds impressive, but to the USAO, these are just pretty-sounding words, crafted for publicity, not reality. There is no intention to make good on these promises.

As we waited on the USAO, I combined elements from the WFO espionage squad and Kevin and Boeing's security campaign to highlight our squad's unprecedented successes, starting a "Spies Get Caught" wall in our squad space within our new Orange County Resident Agency (OCRA) location, having moved from and closed the old SARA facility. On that wall we placed pictures and descriptions of each perpetrator, the charges made, and the dates of their convictions. I bought a frame in anticipation of the Lu conviction, but this time the USAO outlasted me *and* the original prosecuting agents. Jo-Lein and Brooke transferred to other offices, and I ran up against my mandatory retirement age, leaving in 2017.

---

marking trade secrets, requiring employee signatures, and acknowledgments that all products and data produced belong to the employer.

I left Lu's photo, frame, and information for my successor, Jerry, to mount when the time finally arrived. Years passed as the USAO kept pushing back trial dates, over FBI objections. Finally, on Monday, January 28, 2019, over *seven* years since his arrest and indictment, Lu was sentenced on six—not the promised twelve—counts of unauthorized possession and attempted possession of trade secrets under a plea deal. Lu got twenty-seven months in federal prison, not the decade(s) or millions in fines USA Decker had mentioned.[13] Once more, an unreliable, impotent Los Angeles USAO had reduced and removed consequences because it couldn't be bothered to do its job. This time, the immigrant betraying his adopted country wasn't a racist or communist sympathizer, just a greedy bastard. And he didn't care how he got rich, or who he betrayed to do it. I welcomed final closure on this last public case of my Bureau career and was pleasantly surprised the "professional" attorneys had not completely botched it.

The number of espionage prosecutions is climbing rapidly, yet make no mistake about the true number of actual cases. The few that go to trial are a drop in the bucket, a mere handful of the tens of thousands of yearly betrayals of, and thefts from, American companies and military branches. Multiple instances occur every day, increasing exponentially throughout the following weeks, months, and years, directed by and for the People's Republic of China. The threat is real and ever growing, and we are doing too little to stem it.

On July 7, 2020, in an address before the Hudson Institute in Washington, DC, FBI director Christopher Wray declared, "The greatest long-term threat to our nation's information and intellectual property, and to our economic vitality, is the counterintelligence and economic espionage threat from China. It's a threat to our economic security—and by extension, to our national security."[14]

We all pray he is wrong, but I know he is right.

---

13. Revisit and compare the impressive-sounding USAO release quoted above to the actual results.
14. Christopher Wray, "The Threat Posed by the Chinese Government and the Chinese Communist Party to the Economic and National Security of the United States," Federal Bureau of Investigation, July 7, 2020, accessed November 25, 2024, https://www.fbi.gov/news/speeches/the-threat-posed-by-the-chinese-government-and-the-chinese-communist-party-to-the-economic-and-national-security-of-the-united-states.

ACKNOWLEDGMENTS

WRITING THIS BOOK WAS NOT EASY, AND WHILE IT SOMETIMES SEEMED a solitary venture, it certainly wasn't. Because I was never alone, I must acknowledge those whose support proved instrumental in this book ever seeing the light of day.

My parents, Ed and Thelma, both educators, were lovers of the written word and encouraged the same in their children. I was a beneficiary of this love—I even married a librarian!—and strove to instill it within my children and grandchildren. They all love a good book. May it ever be so.

It was during the Chi Mak investigation that Charles H. "Sandy" Kable IV first suggested the idea of a book, at a time such a venture was the furthest thing from my mind. His energy, enthusiasm, and encouragement were inspiring.

To my "Glazed Stone" partners, thank you for your professionalism, hard work, stamina, and good humor. When all the "experts" claimed we were sinking, you steamed ahead to reach port and dropped anchor in spectacular fashion. Very well done.

After the convictions, I met author and historian H. Keith Melton, who became a mentor of sorts, sacrificing time and effort to point my writings toward brevity and relevance.

I am grateful to Jonathan Kurtz at Prometheus for believing in this book and its subject enough to give this first-, and likely last-, time author the opportunity to document this historic case.

My rock and support for over forty years has been my wife, Melody, who has nurtured, advised, and encouraged me through thick and thin. She has always been my joy and inspiration. No one possesses a kinder, gentler heart. In my corner of the world, nobody's thoughts, opinions, and goodwill matter more.

And last and most, my eternal gratitude to my highly intelligent and vastly talented daughter Lauren, my principal editor and advisor, without whom this book would never have succeeded. With thoughtful, diplomatic critiques, she guided me past all of my writing vices—redundancy, beloved idioms, exclamation points, lists, tangents, and ALL CAPS words. Throughout, Lauren displayed the wisdom of Solomon, the patience of Job, and the kindness of Christ. Thankfully, she takes after her mother.

LIST OF ACRONYMS

A/ASAC	Acting Assistant Special Agent in Charge
AD	Assistant Director
ASAC	Assistant Special Agent in Charge
ADIC	Assistant Director in Charge
AOL	America Online
ASNE	American Society of Naval Engineers
AUSA	Assistant US Attorney
CART	Computer Analysis and Response Team
CCP	Chinese Communist Party
CCTV	closed-circuit television
CEAU	Cryptologic and Electronics Analysis Unit
CES	Counterintelligence and Export Control Section
CI	counterintelligence
CT	counterterrorism
DARPA	Defense Advanced Research Projects Agency
DOJ	Department of Justice
DOS	Department of State
DSS	Defense Security Service
EC	Electronic Communication
EE	Economic Espionage
EMALS	Electromagnetic Aircraft Launch Systems
FAVIAU	Forensic Audio, Video, and Image Analysis Unit
FBIHQ	FBI Headquarters
FBILA	FBI Los Angeles Field Office
FCI	federal correctional institution
FISA	Foreign Intelligence Surveillance Act

ICE	Immigration and Customs Enforcement
ITAR	International Traffic in Arms Regulations
MCC	mobile command center
NCIS	Naval Criminal Investigative Service
NOFORN	no foreign dissemination
NR	Naval Reactors
NRO	National Reconnaissance Office
NSD-9	National Security Division 9
OCRA	Orange County Resident Agency
ONR	Office of Naval Research
PLA	People's Liberation Army
PLAN	People's Liberation Army Navy
PM	Prosecutive Memorandum
PRC	People's Republic of China
PRCIS	People's Republic of China intelligence services
QED	Quiet Electric Drive
RA	Resident Agency
SAC	Special Agent in Charge
SARA	Santa Ana Resident Agency
SCIF	Sensitive Compartmented Information Facility
SDR	surveillance detection route
SME	subject matter expert
SRV	Socialist Republic of Vietnam
SSG	Special Surveillance Group
STC	Standard Telegraphic Code
TECS	Treasury Enforcement Communication System
USA	US Attorney (e.g., USA Yang)
USAO	US Attorney's Office
USML	US Munitions List
USN	US Navy
WFO	Washington Field Office

Index

A/ASAC. *See* Acting Assistant Special Agent in Charge
Abernathy, Erin, 197
Abraham Lincoln, USS, 236
Abu Ghraib prison, 136n2
"Acting as an Agent of a Foreign Government": Chi Mak and, 97, 148–49, 148n2, 156, 192, 282; Chung, G., and, 337, 347, 370
Acting Assistant Special Agent in Charge (A/ASAC), 4–5, 20
ADIC. *See* Assistant Director in Charge
AEGIS SPY-1 radar power equipment, 60; Eyer relation to, 236–37; Lee, B., on, 243; "Magic Shield," 236n21; "Science and Technology community" and, 211; Teledyne and, 258
"Aiding and Abetting," 156n21
airtel, 10n5
"Algorithms for Reduced Scale Permanent Magnet Synchronous Machine Propulsion Drive," 232, 259n21
Alhambra residence, *62*, 125, 129, 169
Allain, Alex, 126
American Society of Naval Engineers (ASNE), 60, 260
American Superconductor Corporation, 225

American Vietnamese Patriots in the United States, 364
America Online (AOL), 37
Ames, Aldrich, 341n11
AOL. *See* America Online
Apollo program, 358
appeals, 319; of Chi Mak, 328–29; Chiu relation to, 322–23; of Chung, G., 380; of Tai, 326
Applied Power Electronics Conference, 9n3, 59–60
Arleigh Burke-class destroyer, 144
ASAC. *See* Assistant Special Agent in Charge
Ashton, Robert, 143–44, 259–60, 259n20, 259n21, 263
Asian wife stereotype, 57
Asia Television (ATV), 26, 88, 88n9, 241–42
ASNE. *See* American Society of Naval Engineers
"Assassin's Mace" program, 208
Assistant Director in Charge (ADIC), 30–31
Assistant Special Agent in Charge (ASAC), 352
Assistant US Attorney (AUSA), ix, 97, 307; CI relation to, 84–85; Early relation to, 299n2; executive leadership of, 296–97; plea bargains and, 185, 299–300; "Royal Tourist"

and, 16; SME relation to, 180;
USAO and, 355n27
"Attempted Export of Defense Articles,"
192
ATV. *See* Asia Television
Audi A6, 62
AUSA. *See* Assistant US Attorney
Automated Case Support system, 5, 5n6
aviation, 162–63
Avila, Alejandro, 181, 181n3

B-52 Life Extension Program, 334–35
Baleno, Cindy, 207, 238, 239, 241n26, 270
"Bamboo Curtain," 249
Barnes, "Pancho," 163, 163n4
Barnes, Shouling, 87, 130, 131, 137,
141nn1–2, 152; aviation relation to,
162–63; handwriting samples of,
141; "knock and announce" and, 161;
PRC relation to, 197; Tai relation
to, 328
Barnes, William, 162–63, 163n4
Barnes Aviation, 163
Barnett, Clifford, 358
Barnett, Josh, 205
Bednarski, Marilyn, 138, 193, 195n6;
Carney and, 194, 200, 202–3, 205,
228–29, 266; Chabay and, 231;
computer forensic experts relation
to, 215–16; EMALS relation to,
201; Fung and, 279; on "go bag,"
198; grand jury relation to, 199;
Kaye and, 262; Khersonsky and,
250; Len relation to, 205–6; McKay
and, 219; "Red Flower" and, 217,
218; Schreppler and, 228–29, 278;
submarines and, 228, 228n5; Wu
and, 243; Yoo and, 210
Behavioral Science Unit (BSU), 115–16
Beijing University, 343–44
bench trial, 354

Benson, Paul, 361n10, 367–68
Benthale, Mike, 207
Bereznay, Timothy, 93, 94, 156–58
Bergersen, Gregg, 383, 384–85
Bhavilai, Udomchoke, 237
Bien, 149–50
Bienert, Tom, 351, 356; Barnett, C., and,
358; Brady violation and, 359, 375;
Carney and, 368–70, 375; Chung,
G., and, 358n2, 371, 374; Guerin
and, 360; Jencks violation and,
361, 361n12; Novak and, 367, 369;
Staples and, 353; STC and, 377
Block (Magistrate Judge), 337, 338
blue flamers, 3–5, 3n1, 63n1, 69, 95n15,
384; Bereznay as, 157; at FBIHQ,
63–64; Smith, I. C., as, 252n6;
Smith, J. J., as, 184
Boeing, 334, 341, 371–72; Delta IV
rocket and, 358, 376; Farag on,
359–60; Huntington Beach campus
of, 335, 344; PRC Overseas Chinese
Advisory Board and, 386; PRC
relation to, 342. *See also* Chung, Greg
Dongfan
Boeing security poster, 350, *350*
Bolick, Dan, 104, 105
BOP. *See* Bureau of Prisons
Brady violations, 177, 177n18, 319,
359n5, 372; Bienert and, 359, 375;
Staples and, 378
Brust, Pete, 91, 92, 110; Bereznay and, 94;
Tidwell and, 156–57, 156n24
BSU. *See* Behavioral Science Unit
"Bucar," 170n1
Bureau of Prisons (BOP), 325, 327, 332
Bureau politics, 31
Bush, George W., 41n10

C4ISR. *See* Command, Control,
Communications, Computers,

Intelligence, Surveillance, and
Reconnaissance
C-17, EE and, 370
Cai Hu, 167, 271; Chi Mak relation to,
282; Pu relation to, 197
Cal State University Long Beach
(CSULB), 111, 341, 348, 349, 366
Calvert, Thomas, 231n10
Canada, 41
Canadian Security Intelligence Service
(CSIS), 41, 41n9
canceling harmonics, for submarines, 276
Cantonese, 42–43, 43n3, 74n4
CAPS. See Center for Asian Pacific
Studies
Carbaugh, Steven, 358–59
Cardona, George, 98, 99–100; Missakian
and, 296–97; Staples relation to,
299n1; USAO and, 148, 148n3, 347;
Yang relation to, 158n27
Carney, Cormac, 136–39, 176n15, 385;
Bednarski and, 194, 200, 202–3, 205,
228–29, 266; bench trial relation
to, 354; Bienert and, 368–70, 375;
Brady violation and, 359; Chiu
and, 312; Chung, G., and, 277n55,
372–74, 380; FISA relation to,
174–76; Fung and, 273–74; Gertz
and, 319–20; grand jury relation to,
188, 200, 232, 274n, 293–94, 310–11;
Greenberg and, 320n8, 322; Guerin
and, 221; Hindman and, 241; Kaye
and, 197, 200, 233–34, 236–38, 246,
259, 263, 263n31, 266n38, 274n48;
Khersonsky and, 250; Ling Jia and,
379; Mak, B., and, 303; McKay
and, 218n31; Miller, K., and, 365;
Missakian and, 280; Newquist and,
212, 213–14; plea bargains and, 306;
"Probation Office for Investigation
& Report" and, 296; Rosen and, 248;

sentencing hearing and, 316, 317–19;
Smith, I. C., and, 254; SSG relation
to, 216; Staples relation to, 198,
233–34; Tai and, 316
"carrier killer" ICBMs, 208
Carson, Tom, 255
CART. See Computer Analysis and
Response Team
Carter, David, 385
Carter, Jimmy, 327
CATIC. See China National Aero-
Technology Import & Export
Corporation
CCP. See Chinese Communist Party
CCTV. See closed-circuit television
CDs. See compact discs
CEAU. See Cryptologic and Electronics
Analysis Unit
cellphone, of Pu, 85, 85n6, 131
Center for Asian Pacific Studies (CAPS),
108n18, 182–83, 202; PLA relation
to, 201; Rosen relation to, 245–48
Central Intelligence Agency (CIA), 15,
92n12, 182n6, 346n20; McVadon
relation to, 183; National HUMINT
Collector of the Year, 220, 220n37;
NSA compared to, 345; SME
relation to, 182, 324
CES. See Counterintelligence and Export
Control Section
CH-47 helicopter, 334, 358
Chabay, Ed, 138, 180, 230–31, 281
Chan, C. C., 257, 258, 260, 264, 269–70,
282
Chan, M. F., 257, 258, 260, 264, 270, 282
Chao Tung University, 245, 257
Chapman, Jack, 278, 279
Chapman Brief, 278, 279, 279, 282, 288
Chen Qinan, 367n22
Chen Rong Dong, 129
Chicago FBI Field Office, 45

Chi Mak, *58*, *113*, *117*, *168*, *317*; Chiu and, *12*, *13*, *167*; as "Johnson," *131*. *See also specific topics*

Chi Mak note, *331*

"Chi Mak Sentencing Factors-30 Years," 316, 317

China/American Friendship Association, 338

"China lobby," 179

China National Aero-Technology Import & Export Corporation (CATIC), 340n8, *362*

China National Nuclear Corporation, 132, 262

China Naval Forces Division, 181

Chinese Academy of Engineering, 132

Chinese Americans, 142–43, 155, 203–4

Chinese Communist Party (CCP), 45, 382; Office for Taiwan Affairs, 348; United Front Work Department of, 372

Chinese Counterintelligence Squad, 65

Chinese culture, 285–86

Chinese Nationalist Party (Kuomintang), 334

Chinese Navy, xi, xii

"Chi's Lies Under Oath," 286

Chiu, "Rebecca" Laiwah, 10–11, *12*, *13*, *117*, *167*, *321*; Asian wife stereotype and, 57; BSU and, 115–16; Carney and, 312; CDs and, 82, 89, 287–88; Chung, G., and, 285n3; Deem relation to, 250; deportation of, 325, *326*; at FBILA, 101–2; FISA and, 18, 37; grand jury and, 310; Greenberg and, 292, 298, 321–23, 323n11; Gu Wei and, *168*, 197n8; in Hawaii, 77; in Hong Kong, 257–58; ICE and, 320n9, 324–25; "knock and announce" and, 161; Ling Jia compared to, 338; Mrozek relation to, 137; plea bargains and, 299, 305, 308–9, 322–23; on polecam, 178; PRCIS relation to, 201n18; PRC relation to, 311–12; Pu relation to, 234; QED and, 91; racism and, 325–26; at Santa Ana City Jail, 118; surveillance of, 23, *24*, 24–26; translation relation to, 43, 44; USAO relation to, 161n2

"Choi," 86, 86n8

Chung, Greg Dongfan, 132, 163–64, 204, *351*, *381*, *382*; "Acting as an Agent of a Foreign Government" and, 337, 347, 370; aviation relation to, 163; bench trial and, 354; Bienert and, 358n2, 371, 374; Carney and, 277n55, 372–74, 380; CATIC relation to, 340n8, *362*; Chiu and, 285n3; Fung and, 340, 362–63; Gu Wei relation to, 197n8, 335, 337, 338–39; Gu Zhen relation to, 375n37; Hsien and, *343*, 348; linguists relation to, 344; Miller, K., and, 357–59; Moberly and, 295, 336, 338, 340, 349–50; Murray and, 143, 340, 350; PRC relation to, 165–66, 335n1; public domain relation to, 361; Pu relation to, 261, 347; search warrant for, 337, 338–39; sentencing hearing for, 374, 376–80; Staples and, 346, 371–72, 381; Taiwan relation to, 334; translation by, *343*; trash covers and, *338*

Chung, Jeff, 365

Chung, Shane, 349–50, 363–64, 370n27, 373n31

Chung crawlspace, *340*, 340–41, 358

Chung residence, 340–42, *348*

Chungwah Foundation, 366

CI. *See* counterintelligence agents

CIA. *See* Central Intelligence Agency

CI China squad, FBILA, 10

"Circuit Design Optimization for High Power Density Electronic Assembly," 9n3

classified documents, 54, 54n11; intercepts of, 170; for QED, 143–44; submarines and, 150. *See also* "no foreign dissemination"

classified investigations, 32, 32n4

Cleveland, Bill, 15n1

Clinton, Bill, 16

closed-circuit television (CCTV), 22, 84; covert home entries and, 61, 75–76, 77, 78–79; intercepts and, 84; microwave transmitter for, 79–80; at Power Paragon, Inc., 35; SSG and, 38

"Closing Rebuttal Points-The Sum Total Is Greater Than Its Parts," 286, 286n7

code word sheet, *128*, 161, 162, *162*, 171, 171n3

Coleman, Randy, 5–6, 64; as executive assistant director, 64n3; FBIHQ and, 20; FBILA relation to, 17; intercepts and, 84; Kable relation to, 65

"Colleen's Web," 167

Command, Control, Communications, Computers, Intelligence, Surveillance, and Reconnaissance (C4ISR), 384, 384n4

communism, 3, 244–45; American Vietnamese Patriots in the United States and, 364; Chi Mak relation to, 195n6, 257; Rosen relation to, 183, 249

compact discs (CDs), 80, 80n1, 88, 90, *105*, 109; DD(x) destroyer and, 86, 86n7, 128, 128nn7–8; "Exclusive-OR" encryption and, 126; Fuk and, 106, 106n7, 287–88;

Mak, B., and, 128, 129n12, 287–88; NOFORN and, 144–45; QED and, 122; seizures of, 125; Tai and, 82, 83, 89, 109, 287–88

Computer Analysis and Response Team (CART), 51, 177, 180–81, 222

computer forensic experts, 49–50, 180–81, 214, 215–16

"Concepts for Achieving 50% Cost/ Displacement Reductions While Retaining VA Class Capability and Providing New Capabilities," 278, 279, *279*

conferences, 9n3, 59–60, 59n1, 263n31

Congressional Notice, 315

"Conspiracy," 97, 99, 281, 294, 354, 370

"Conspiracy to Export Defense Articles," 158–59, 192

control lie question, 4, 4n3

corporate compliance, for L-3 Communications, 144n5

counterintelligence agents (CI), ix, 2; AUSA relation to, 84–85; China squad, 10; desk managers relation to, 64; "Flaps and Seals" experts and, 39–40; Lookouts and, 22; Newquist as, 211n11; non-agents and, 76n2; publicity relation to, 32; Smith, I. C., relation to, 253; SSG and, 11; translation for, 42–44

Counterintelligence and Export Control Section (CES), xii, 153; Eliot and, 98–99; USAO relation to, 178

Counterintelligence and Export Control Section, DOJ, 175

countersurveillance techniques, 25–26, 52

counterterrorism (CT): Lookouts and, 22; SARA-4 and, 3

covert home entries, 8, 37, 38; CCTV and, 61, 75–76, 77, 78–79; countersurveillance techniques for,

52; digital media and, 51; "Flaps and Seals" experts and, 39, 48–50, 53–54, 78; listening devices and, 54–55; Moberly and, 47; Newquist and, 56; Tech Agents and, 61, 77

covert technical surveys, 35

COVID-19: Chi Mak and, 331–32; Chung, G., and, 381

Cox Report, 222

criminal search, 57, 129–30

Cryptologic and Electronics Analysis Unit (CEAU), 173, 181

CSIS. *See* Canadian Security Intelligence Service

CSULB. *See* Cal State University Long Beach

CT. *See* counterterrorism

Cultural Revolution, 242, 245–46

Dahmer, Jeffery, 341n11

Danis, Michael, 360

DARPA. *See* Defense Advanced Research Projects Agency

DD(x) destroyer, 70, 73n2, 111; CDs and, 86, 86n7, 128, 128nn7–8; ICE relation to, 205n24, 295n18; Pluhar on, 222; PRC relation to, 73–74, 171, 171n7; Tai and, 263, 316

dead drops, 61

Dean, Henry, 44–45, 217, 218

Dearth, Tony, 361

Decker, Eileen, 388–89

declassification requests, 170n2

Declassified (television show), 332, 332n32

Deem, Maryanne, 140–41, 250–51

Defense Advanced Research Projects Agency (DARPA), 60; Lopez on, 235; US Department of Defense and, 235n17

Defense Intelligence Agency (DIA), 356, 360

Defense Language Institute, US Army, 3

Defense Security Service (DSS), 14

Delta IV rocket, 358, 361, 364, 370, 376

DeMille, Cecile B., 7

Dennis the Menace Park, 38, 46

Department of Facilities and Financial Support, State Science & Technology Commission, 132

Department of Justice (DOJ): CES of, xii, 98–99, 153, 178; Counterintelligence and Export Control Section, 175; executive leadership at, 136n3, 150–51; Gertz relation to, 320; Mak, B., and, 107n10; plea bargains relation to, 295, 305; "Royal Tourist" and, 16; search warrant relation to, 147–48; SRV relation to, 149–50; Tai relation to, 316

deportation: of Chiu, 325, *326*; of Fuk, 313, 315; US citizenship and, 69, 69n1

desk managers, at FBIHQ, 64

DIA. *See* Defense Intelligence Agency

digital media, 51. *See also* compact discs

Dion, John, 98, 99–100, 157; EE and, 158; Missakian relation to, 153–54; PM and, 347

Directorate of Defense Trade Controls, DOS, 209

DLL. *See* "Dynamic Link Library"

Dobbs, Lou, 297n21

DOJ. *See* Department of Justice

"Domain" program, 352–53

Dong Ngo, 364

DOS. *See* US Department of State

Dotson, Gene, 194, 243

Downey PD, 38, 38n5, 40, 46, 50–51, 51n6; Chi Mak and, 193n2; "knock and announce" arrests and, 110

Downey residence, 38, *39*, *48*, *53*; criminal search at, 129–32; "knock and announce" arrests at, 110
DSS. *See* Defense Security Service
"dual use" technologies, 201
Dublin women's prison, 323
Dumb and Dumber (movie), 323
"Dynamic Analysis with Motor with Auxiliary Windings," 232
"Dynamic Link Library" (DLL), 215

Early, John, 137; AUSA relation to, 299n2; grand jury relation to, 176; plea bargains and, 299, 306; Tai and, 173–74, 292, 316
early release, 331–32
East Asian Study Center, USC, 245
Economic Espionage (EE), 155; Bereznay and, 157–58; Chung, G., and, 346–47, 370, 380; legal precedent and, 372–73; Staples relation to, 149; USAO relation to, 354; Yang relation to, 155
ECs. *See* Electronic Communications
Edmund, Jim, 273–74
Edwards Lifesciences, 386–87
EE. *See* Economic Espionage
Electric Machine Handbook, 260
Electric Machine Technology Symposium, 9n3
Electromagnetic Aircraft Launch System (EMALS), 113, 113n6, 122; Bednarski relation to, 201; Kaye and, 194; Lipo relation to, 224; "Science and Technology community" and, 211
Electromagnetic Aircraft Launch Systems (EMALS), 60
Electronic Communications (ECs), 84
Eliot, Deirdre, 84–85, 92–93, 95–96, 98–99, 148

email: "HK" extension and, 127; Power Paragon Inc. relation to, 144
EMALS. *See* Electromagnetic Aircraft Launch System; Electromagnetic Aircraft Launch Systems
encryption decision tree, *215*
engineers, 132; at Applied Power Electronics Conference, 59–60; in China/American Friendship Association, 338; Kaye relation to, 221; Kill Chain Working Group and, 152–53; NOFORN relation to, 142; at Power Paragon Inc., 9; PRC relation to, 201; SME, 179–80
"enhancements," 318
Enough (movie), 89, 89n10
Europe, 60–61
"Exclusive-OR" encryption, 126
executive assistant director, 64n3
executive leadership, 91–92; of AUSA, 296–97; at DOJ, 136n3, 150–51; at FBIHQ, 64, 150–52; of FBILA, 63; at NCIS, 160–61; at USAO, 150–51, 152, 300n4; Valdez relation to, 352
Export Compliance Quiz, 112, *112*
export-control information, 225, 225n3
Eyer, Kevin, 181, 236–37, 281

F-1 student visa, 334
facility security officer (FSO), 360n7
"False Official Statements," 159, 159n29
Falun Gong, 27
family tree, of Chi Mak, 167, 198, 198n10
Farag, Emad, 367; on Boeing, 359–60; Staples and, 368
Fat Electronic Trading Company, Ltd., 74
FAVIAU. *See* Forensic Audio, Video, and Image Analysis Unit
FBI criminal squads, 76n2
FBI Headquarters (FBIHQ), ix, 2, 94, 385n7; blue flamers at, 63–64;

Coleman and, 20; "Domain" program relation to, 353; ECs and, 84; executive leadership at, 64, 150–52; FBILA relation to, 66, 214; FISA and, 37; Garcia relation to, 31; Honolulu Field Office, 75; Kable relation to, 65, 170; Language Unit of, 67; Missakian and, 298; SARA-4 relation to, 18–19; translation relation to, 42, 83, 83n2; Weekly Investigative Update and, 30; WFO relation to, 384

FBILA. *See* Los Angeles Field Office

FBI National Academy, 38, 38n4

FBI video cut, *83*

FCI. *See* federal correctional institution

FCI Lompoc, 329–30

FD-26 Consent to Search, 107, 107n12

FD-302, 84, 84n5, 375–76; for Chi Mak, 120, 122, 236, 330; for Gu Zhen, 378–79; for Ling Jia, 338

FD-395, 118

federal correctional institution (FCI), 319; COVID-19 and, 331–32; Lompoc, 329–30

A Few Good Men (movie), 288

Fifth Amendment, 101; Hsien and, 366; Khersonsky and, 250; Lipo and, 224

"50% Reduction in Virginia-Class Submarines," 272–73

"First Island Chain," 208

FISA. *See* Foreign Intelligence Surveillance Act

5-MegaWatt document, 227, 241; ITAR and, 281; Lee, B., on, 243

"Five Eyes" allies, 60, 60n5

"Flaps and Seals" experts, 39–40, 48–50, 53–54, 78

flight risk, 136–37, 137n4, 156

Fondren, James, 383, 384–85

Ford, Henry, 245n38

Ford Foundation, 245

Ford Weapons of Mass Destruction case, 7

Foreign Intelligence Surveillance Act (FISA), 11, 12, 174n12; Chiu and, 18, 37; Chung, G., relation to, 336, 344; conferences relation to, 59; FBIHQ and, 37; Kaye relation to, 174–76; photographic evidence relation to, 53; PRC and, 21; Tech Agents relation to, 61; Wang and, 355

Forensic Audio, Video, and Image Analysis Unit (FAVIAU), 173

forensic experts, 49–50, 95n14

Forfeiture Unit, SARA-4, 172

Fort Meade, 345

"free academic exchange of ideas," 271n44

Frye, Scott, 216, 351

FSO. *See* facility security officer

Fuk Li Mak, 169, *314*, 315; CDs and, 106, 106n7, 287–88; Chi Mak relation to, 289; at LAX, 100–101, 102; Len and, 303, 304; Ling Jia compared to, 338; Lopez and, 102, 104, 105–7, 235, 300; Luo and, 108, 216; Mak, B., relation to, 198; marriage fraud and, 26–29, 87, 90, 91, 97, 145–46; *Married with Children* relation to, 40; McDonald relation to, 172–73; plea bargains and, 299–300, 308–10; on polecam, 178; PRCIS relation to, 90, 232; Pu relation to, 261; Staples and, 269n43; Tai relation to, 85–87; "Time Served" and, 299, 303, 309, 313; translation relation to, 42n2, 44; USAO relation to, 156, 161n2

Fung, Sheldon, 7–8, 9, 96, 152n10; Carney and, 273–74; Chung, G., and, 340, 362–63; covert home entries and, 47, 49–50, 56, 77; executive leadership and, 91–92, 151–52; FBILA and, 17; intercepts and, 84; Ling-Ling relation to, 68; Luo and, 103–4; marriage fraud and, 90; Missakian and, 278–79; Murray and, 75–76; NSD-9 relation to, 67; "Pat" relation to, 33; SARA-4 and, 94; SDRs and, 24; Staples and, 288; Tai relation to, 19; technical coverage and, 14; trash covers and, 29

Future of Power Electronics Conference, 60, 263n31

Gao Zhanmin, 363
Garcia, Richard, 30–32
"Gathering, transmitting or losing defense information," 154
"Gathering Defense Information," 154n14, 155n16
"GAYLORD DIRECT," 196
Gerrity, Bob, 181; grand jury and, 208; open-source reporting and, 208n4; QED relation to, 208–9
Gertz, Bill, 176, 319–20
Get Smart (TV show), 78, 79
"Glazed Stone," 5, 18
"go bag," 130, 130, 198
Goldman, Marc L., 136–37
Gonzales, Ken, 127, 127n4, 146, 161
"Government's Exhibit List," 187
GPS: on Audi A6, 62; on Plymouth Voyager, 61
Graber, Gary Lee, 359
grand jury, 148–49, 156, 187, 190; Bednarski relation to, 199; Carney relation to, 188, 200, 232, 274n, 293–94, 310–11; Chi Mak relation to, 256–57, 267; Chiu and, 310; Gerrity and, 208; Greenberg and, 176, 311n19; ITAR relation to,

194, 277, 280, 291, 292; linguists relation to, 203; Lopez relation to, 275, 288n10; Newquist relation to, 212, 288n10; news sources relation to, 188–89; Rosen relation to, 245, 249; Schreppler relation to, 276–77; Zerden relation to, 292–93
Grandmain, Tom, 336, 353, 381
"graymail," 228, 228n4
Greenberg, Stanley, 176n15; Carney and, 320n8, 322; Chiu and, 292, 298, 321–23, 323n11; Gertz relation to, 320; grand jury and, 176, 311n19; plea bargains and, 305, 309; Staples and, 311
GS-13s, 186n1
Guerin, Rudy, 183; Bienert and, 360; Kaye and, 220–22; Moberly relation to, 356; Smith, I. C., relation to, 252–55; Staples and, 219–20
Gupta, Suresh, 251
Gu Wei Hao, 132–33, 163–66, 167, 197; Bednarski relation to, 202; Chi Mak and, 168, 219, 261–62, 285, 338–39; Chiu and, 168, 197n8; Chung, G., relation to, 197n8, 335, 337, 338–39; Staples and, 193, 290; "unfair prejudice" and, 178
Gu Zhen Luong, 375–76, 375n37, 378–79
Gwo Bao Min, 15

Hale, Wayne, 360–61, 367n23
Hampton, Valerie, 144n5, 238
handwriting samples: of Barnes, S., 141; code word sheet relation to, 171, 171n3
handwritten task list, 70, 70, 71–72, 73, 114–15
Hanssen, Robert, 220, 221
Han Xiang Song, 132

Hao, "Harriet," 45, 45n6, 341, 363
Harbin Institute, 376
hardship cases, 189, 189n6, 310
Harrington, Jack, 361n10
Harvard Law School, 355
Hawaii, 25, 75–77
Hawbecker, Ariana, 358, 365, 370
"health book," 122–23, 160, 198, 217, *217*, 264
heat shield, 361
Heller, Mike, 360n7
Hells Angels Minneapolis Motorcycle Club, 341n10
Henderson, USS, 256n11
Hilarides, William, 182, 182n5, 229–30, 229n7, 281
Hindman, Nancy, 238–41, 240n25, 241n26
"HK" extension, 127
Hong Kong: Chiu in, 257–58; USS *Henderson* and, 256n11; PRCIS relation to, 256; USN relation to, 130–31, 249, 284
Hong Kong Technical University, 130
Honolulu Field Office, FBIHQ, 75
Hsien Yeh, 341, 343, 366; Chi Mak relation to, 349; Chung, G., and, *343*, 348
Hudson Institute, 389
"Hundred Flowers" Movement, 246
Huntington Beach campus, Boeing, 335, 344

Immigration and Customs Enforcement (ICE), 13, 14, 171; Chiu and, 320n9, 324–25; DD(x) destroyer relation to, 205n24, 295n18; Mak, B., and, 313
indigency, 136
Inside (Smith, I. C.), 252n6
"insider," 33–34

Institute of Electrical and Electronics Engineers Electric Ship Technologies Seminar, 60
"instruction papers," 132
intellectual property, 148
intercepts, 83–84, 89; of classified documents, 170; translation of, 172
International Spy Museum, 4, 385n7
International Traffic in Arms Regulations (ITAR), 97, 122, 156, 158–59, 171, 171n6; appeals and, 328; Chung, G., relation to, 347; grand jury relation to, 194, 277, 280, 291, 292; Hindman relation to, 239–40; Lipo relation to, 223; SME relation to, 182; Solid-State Switch paper and, 281; USML relation to, 209–10
Irvine Law School, 204
Irvine Police Department, 7
ITAR. *See* International Traffic in Arms Regulations

Jencks violation, 361, 361n12
J. J. Smith/Katrina Leung case, 31; Len relation to, 44; translation relation to, 42
Johnson, Jeffrey, 99–101, 147
"Johnson," 130, *131*

Kable, Charles H. "Sandy," ix, 64, 96; covert home entries and, 77; executive leadership and, 91–92; FBIHQ relation to, 65, 170; FBILA relation to, 65, 172; Kuo and, 383; Mueller and, 349; Nicholas and, 92n12; Terrorist Screening Center and, 65, 65n4; Witham relation to, 36
Kaye, McLane & Bednarski LLP, 136–37, 136n2, 200, 237–38, 246. *See also* Bednarski, Marilyn; Kaye, Ron

Kaye, Ron, 184, 205, 212n18; appeals relation to, 319; Carney and, 197, 200, 233–34, 236–38, 246, 259, 263, 263n31, 266n38, 274n48; Chi Mak and, 233n15, 256–58, 262–63, 264–66, 272, 283–86; Edmund and, 274; EMALS and, 194; FISA relation to, 174–76; Guerin and, 220–22; Hilarides and, 230; Hindman and, 239; Lipo and, 226; Lopez and, 235–36; Miller, B., relation to, 207; NCIS relation to, 176–77; Newquist and, 212–14, 236; plea bargains and, 223; PRC relation to, 220n39; Reza relation to, 214n22; Rosen and, 245, 246–48; at sentencing hearing, 317–18; Smith, I. C., and, 252–53, 256, 256n13; Staples compared to, 198; "unfair prejudice" and, 178; Wian and, 297; Witham and, 195; Zerden and, 210

Khersonsky, Yuri, 250, 266

"kill chain," 138, 138n8, 152; Schreppler on, 227; submarines relation to, 192

Kill Chain Working Group, 152–53

Kim, Sean, 361

Kim, Tom, 216–17

"Kindred Spirit," 16

Kingman Ma, 162–63

Kirkland, Donald, 230n8

"knock and announce," 110, 161

Ku Chen Luong, 375n36

Kuomintang (Chinese Nationalist Party), 334

Kuo Tai Shen, 383, 384–85

L-3 Communications, 5, 14; corporate compliance for, 144n5, 195n5; Hindman relation to, 239, 241n26; QED and, 270; WashOps and, 36, 238

L-3 Ethics, 112, 112n5

Language Specialists (linguists), 31, 80, 83–84, 180, 203n20; Chung, G., relation to, 344; Dean, 44–45, 217, 218; FBILA relation to, 67–68, 83n2, 172, 327, 327n22; grand jury relation to, 203; Hao, "Harriet," 45, 45n6, 341, 363; of NSA, 345–46; proffer and, 303; of SARA-4, 12, 42–45; Yip, E., 251–52; Yoo, 45, 45n5, 172, 210. See also Language Specialists; Len Pi

Language Unit, FBIHQ, 67

Lawrence Livermore Laboratories, 15

LAX. See Los Angeles International Airport

Lee, Bob, 142, 180, 233, 244n32; Ashton and, 259; QED and, 137, 243–44; Schreppler and, 275, 278

Lee, Peter, 15–16

legal precedent, 372–73

Lemme, Clayt, 176n15

Len Pi, 44–45, 173, 205nn27–38, 206; Chung, G., and, 358; Dean relation to, 218; Fuk and, 303, 304; Ling-Ling relation to, 68; NSA relation to, 345–46; Staples relation to, 205, 206n29

Leung, Katrina, 10, 15n1, 16, 136–37, 183; Kaye on, 212, 212n18; listening devices and, 55; Rosen relation to, 245; Smith, I. C., relation to, 254n9. See also J. J. Smith/Katrina Leung case

Liaoning (aircraft carrier), 208n6

Liemeng, 142

Ling Jia Chung, 143, 163–66, 377; Carney and, 379; Chinese Nationalist Party relation to, 334; Chung, S., and, 363–64; "Conspiracy" and, 354; McKay and, 338; PRC relation to, 335n1; USAO relation to, 379n45

Ling-Ling, 67–68

linguists. *See* Language Specialists

Lin Hong, 383

Lipo, Thomas, 180; Ashton and, 259; EMALS relation to, 224; Schreppler relation to, 227; self-incrimination and, 222–23; Staples and, 224–26, 266

listening devices, 51, 54–55

Little Red Books, of Mao, 343n15

Little Rock Field Office, 253

"Little Saigon" community, 3

Liu Chang Le, 145, 241–42

Lookouts, 18, 172; covert home entries and, 48–51; in Dennis the Menace Park, 46; "Flaps and Seals" experts and, 78; GPS and, 62; for SSG, 22, 38, 39–40

Lopez, Omar, 75; Chi Mak and, 160, 211, 261, 262n30, 265, 287–88; executive leadership and, 91–92; Fuk and, 102, 104, 105–7, 235, 300; grand jury relation to, 275, 288n10; intercepts and, 84; Kaye and, 235–36; Mak, B., and, 301–2; marriage fraud and, 90; NCIS and, 172, 231n11, 351; Newquist and, 119–20, 120n12, 124, 135; Staples and, 231–32, 234–35

Los Angeles Field Office (FBILA), 3, 101–2; A/ASAC at, 4–5; ASAC at, 352; Brust and, 91, 94; CART of, 51; CI China squad of, 10; EE relation to, 354; executive leadership of, 63; FBIHQ relation to, 66, 214; Garcia relation to, 31; Kable relation to, 65, 172; linguists relation to, 67–68, 83n2, 172, 327, 327n22; SARA-4 relation to, 16–17, 32; SSG and, 22–23; Technical Agent support,

11; Technical Squad of, 21–22; translation relation to, 42; USAO relation to, 214, 300; Valdez relation to, 17, 172; Weekly Investigative Update and, 30

Los Angeles International Airport (LAX), 100–101, 102; Luo at, 266; seizures at, 125

Los Angeles Times (newspaper), 150, 214n22

Lou Dobbs Tonight (television show), 297

Luo Zhi Xiong, 101n6, 103–4, *109*; Frye and, 216; at LAX, 266; PDA of, 108, 173, 345; Staples and, 109n20

Macau, 257

machine-printed tasking list, 72, *72*, 73, 73n3, 114–15

Ma Fu Bang, 132, 167, 257, 262

"Magic Shield," AEGIS SPY-1 radar power equipment, 236n21

mailboxes, 25, 25nn4–5

mail covers, 27n7

Mak, Billy, 26, 86n7, 95n14, 99, *314*; CDs and, 128, 129n12, 287–88; Chi Mak relation to, 289; DOJ and, 107n10; encryption decision tree of, *215*; grand jury and, 148–49; "health book" of, 122–23, 160, 198, 217, *217*, 264; ICE and, 313; Kim, T., relation to, 216–17; at LAX, 100–101; at Phoenix International, 147n1; plea bargains and, 299–300, 303, 306, 308; proffer of, 301–2; Pu relation to, 125, 129, 129n10, 198; Tai and, 94–95; "Time Served" and, 299, 303, 309, 313; at UCLA, 89, 106n6, 107, 156; Wolfsen and, 310n18

Mak, Shirley, 101, 102, 102n7, 107–8, 169; on polecam, 178; Tai relation to, 327–28, 327n23

"Making a False Material Statement," 282

Mak Professional Stereo Engineering Company, Ltd., 29, 29n9, 73–74

Mandarin, 42–43, 43n3, 74n4

Mao Tse-tung, 245–46, 339, 343n15

marijuana farm case, 186–87

marriage fraud, 26–29, 87, 90, 91, 97, 145–46

"Marriage Fraud Regarding Immigration," 156n21

Married with Children (TV sitcom), 40, 40n7

Marushi, Barry, 91

MCC. *See* mobile command center

McDonald, Tom, 172–73, 303–4; NASA and, 344; plea bargains and, 309–10

McDonnell Douglas, 334–35

McKay, Colleen, 3, 102, 141, 166–67, 218n32, 338n3; Bednarski and, 219; Carney and, 218n31; "knock and announce" and, 161; Ling Jia and, 338; Staples and, 218; Vietnamese Americans relation to, 149

McVadon, Eric, 182–83, 201

microwave transmitter, 79–80

Mike (A/ASAC), 20, 30–31, 47, 133–34

Mikus, Nick, 214, 214n24, 215

Miller, Bob, 133; Chi Mak relation to, 263; Kaye relation to, 207; NOFORN and, 206; ONR and, 206n30

Miller, Ken, 370; Carney and, 365; Chung and, 357–59; Murray and, 361, 362; Wang and, 363

Miller, R. W., 140, 251

Ministry of Aviation, 132

Minneapolis, 186

Miranda rights, 110, 115–16, 119, 176

Missakian, Craig, 138, 309; Cardona and, 296–97; Carney and, 280; Chi Mak and, 281–83; "Closing Rebuttal Points-The Sum Total Is Greater Than Its Parts" and, 286, 286n7; computer forensic experts relation to, 216; Dion relation to, 153–54; Edmund and, 274; Fung and, 278–79; "Government's Exhibit List" and, 187; grand jury relation to, 188, 189; Hindman and, 238, 239–40; Kaye relation to, 178; Mak, B., and, 301–2; McVadon relation to, 183; plea bargains and, 298–99; Rosen and, 246–48; Schreppler and, 226–27, 229, 275–76; Staples and, 296, 302n6; Wang compared to, 356; Wu and, 242–43

Moberly, Kevin, 7–8, 46, 190, 380–81, 385; Bienert and, 369–70; Chung, G., and, 295, 336, 338, 340, 349–50; Chung, S., and, 349; covert home entries and, 47; Grandmain and, 353; Guerin relation to, 356; Hsien and, 366; NASA and, 336, 344; Novak and, 337; Schwartz and, 347; search warrant and, 342; Staples and, 374; as surveillance coordinator, 14; Wang and, 357

mobile command center (MCC), 46

"Mosaic" theory, 152–54, 152n11

"Motion to Vacate the Conviction and for New Trial," 319

"Motor Drive Technology," 257

Mrozek, Thom, 136n3, 137, 150, 151, 297n21

"Mr. Smug," 386

"Mr. Withers," 385–86

Mueller, Robert, 300, 349

Muntz, Sean, 368

Murray, Jessie, 41, 351; Chung, G., and, 143, 340, 350; Chung, S., relation to, 349; Fung and, 75–76; handwritten task list and, 70, 71; Luo and, 103–4;

Mak, S., and, 107–8; Miller, K., and, 361, 362; Staples and, 193n1

Nakazato, Arthur, 156, 172
NASA: Moberly relation to, 336, 344; SARA-4 and, 338; SME from, 356
NASTRAN, 165
National Day, 343, 343n14, 346–47, 366, 366n21, 372
National Foreign Intelligence Program, 11
National HUMINT Collector of the Year, CIA, 220, 220n37
National Reconnaissance Office (NRO), 381
National Security Agency (NSA), 345–46, 346n20
national security cases, 136, 136n2
National Security Division 9 (NSD-9), 16; ECs and, 84; executive leadership at, 160–61; Len relation to, 44; SARA-4 relation to, 67
National Security Letters, 12
National Surface Warfare Center, 224
National Taiwan University, 334
Naval Criminal Investigative Service (NCIS), 5; Abernathy relation to, 197; Chi Mak and, 135; executive leadership at, 160–61; FBIHQ relation to, 66; Kaye relation to, 176–77; Lopez and, 172, 231n11, 351; Newquist and, 19, 75, 172, 210–11, 329, 331, 351; "Pat" relation to, 33; SDRs and, 26; translation relation to, 83, 83n2
Naval Nuclear Propulsion Program, 138
Naval Postgraduate School, 143
Naval Propulsion Seminar, 60
Naval Reactors (NR), 10, 91, 92; Chabay and, 138; NAVSEA relation to, 180
Naval Sea Systems Command (NAVSEA), 180, 182n5

NCIS. See Naval Criminal Investigative Service
Newquist, Gunnar, 12–13; Chi Mak and, 101–2, 110–11, 113–15, 160, 211, 261, 262n30, 265, 285, 287–88; Chung, G., and, 338; as CI, 211n11; covert home entries and, 56; executive leadership and, 91–92; Fuk and, 300; grand jury relation to, 275, 288n10; ITAR relation to, 171; Kaye and, 212–14, 236; Lopez and, 119–20, 120n12, 124, 135; Mak, B., and, 301–2; marriage fraud and, 90; NCIS and, 19, 75, 172, 210–11, 329, 331, 351; NSD-9 relation to, 67; "Pat" relation to, 33–34; at Santa Ana City Jail, 118; SME relation to, 179–80, 181; Staples relation to, 211n13; trash covers and, 29; Witham relation to, 35, 274
Newsom, Gavin, 181n4
news sources, 188–89
The New Yorker (magazine), 385
New York Sun (newspaper), 255–56
New York Times (newspaper), 385
Nicholas, Chris, 65n4; "Domain" program and, 352–53; Kable and, 92n12
Nicholson, Jack, 288
Ninth Circuit Court of Appeals: Chi Mak and, 328–29; Chung, G., and, 380
Nitmitz-class aircraft carrier, 208n5
"no foreign dissemination" (NOFORN), 54, 111–12, 140–41; CDs and, 144–45; Chapman Brief, 282; engineers relation to, 142; "50% Reduction in Virginia-Class Submarines" and, 272–73; Lipo relation to, 224; Miller, B., and, 206; QED relation to, 180; seizures of, 129–30; Third Naval Symposium of Electric Machines and, 133

non-agents, CI and, 76n2
North Korea, 2, 327
Novak, Bill, 337, 358–59, 367, 369
NR. *See* Naval Reactors
NRO. *See* National Reconnaissance Office
NSA. *See* National Security Agency
NSD-9. *See* National Security Division 9

Obama, Barack, 355
O'Brien, Tom, 93, 155, 155n20
Obstruction of Justice, 370, 370n27
OCRA. *See* Orange County Resident Agency
Office for Taiwan Affairs, CCP, 348
Office of Intelligence and Policy Review, 175
Office of Naval Intelligence, Strategic Assessment and Warning Department of, 208
Office of Naval Research (ONR), 10, 60, 91, 179; Lipo relation to, 224–25; Lopez on, 235; Schreppler at, 138; "Third Naval Symposium on Electric Machines" and, 206n30
Oldsmobile Cutlass, 47n2, 52, 61
"old world" criticisms, 44, 44n4
1A envelope, 186, 186n2
O'Neil, Shelley, 360n7
ONR. *See* Office of Naval Research
open-source reporting, 208n4
Orange County Resident Agency (OCRA), 297n23, 324, 388
Orion project, 361n8
Overseas Chinese Advisory Board, PRC, 386

"Pat," 33–35, 35n2, 36
Paul, Phillip, 161
PDA. *See* personal digital assistant
Penn State, 334

People's Liberation Army (PLA), 116, 122; CAPS relation to, 201; Tai and, *123*, 124, 197
People's Liberation Army Navy (PLAN), 181, 208
People's Republic of China (PRC), xi, 2–3, 294–95, 389; Barnes, S., relation to, 197; Boeing relation to, 342; Chinese Americans relation to, 142–43; Chiu relation to, 311–12; Chung, G., relation to, 165–66, 335n1; DD(x) destroyer relation to, 73–74, 171, 171n7; engineers relation to, 201; FISA and, 21; Gu Wei relation to, 339; Kaye relation to, 220n39; Lee, P., relation to, 15–16; Overseas Chinese Advisory Board, 386; Phoenix Satellite TV USA relation to, 242; Power Paragon Inc. relation to, 5; racial profiling and, 9; "Science and Technology community," 122, 211; State Administration of Radio, Film, and TV, 245; State Science & Technology Commission of, 132; Taiwan relation to, 339n4; translation relation to, 42; Yugoslavia relation to, 310; Zhang relation to, 27
People's Republic of China intelligence services (PRCIS), 54, 222n44; Chiu relation to, 201n18; conferences and, 59n1; email and, 127; Fuk relation to, 90, 232; Guerin on, 220; Hong Kong relation to, 256; Kuo and, 383; Luo and, 108; National Day relation to, 366, 366n21; NSA relation to, 345; Pu and, 74n5; Tai relation to, 232n13
"perp walk," 350
personal digital assistant (PDA), 108, 173, 345
Phoenix International, 145, 147n1

Phoenix Satellite TV USA, 26, 107, 241, 242
photographic evidence, 53
Pitts, Earl, 220
PLAN. *See* People's Liberation Army Navy
plea bargains, 172–73, 322–23; AUSA and, 185, 299–300; Bienert relation to, 353; FBILA relation to, 214; Kaye and, 223; Tai and, 298–99, 303, 306, 308; USAO and, 295, 303–5, 308–10, 311, 354
Pluhar, Chris, 177, 180–81, 222, 361
Plymouth Voyager, 47, 49, 61
PM. *See* Prosecutive Memorandum
Point Mugu USN base, 231
polecams, 17, 21n1, 178; FBILA and, 21–22; MCC relation to, 46
polygraph tests, 4–5, 4n3, 4n4, 6
porch lights, 48, 48n4
"Possession of Property in Aid of a Foreign Government," 159
Power Paragon Inc., 5, 111, 132n14; Boeing compared to, 360; covert technical surveys at, 35; Dotson and, 194; Edmund and, 274; email relation to, 144; engineers at, 9; Forfeiture Unit relation to, 172; "Glazed Stone" and, 18; Hindman relation to, 239; "insider" at, 33–34; L-3 Communications relation to, 14; search warrant for, 118; seizures from, 132–33, 170; USN relation to, 8, 10, 238; Zahzah and, 250
PRC. *See* People's Republic of China
PRCIS. *See* People's Republic of China intelligence services
prior conviction, 186, 186n3
"Probation Office for Investigation & Report," 296

proffer, 299–300; of Fuk, 303; of Mak, B., 301–2
Prohibited Traveler Watchlist, 109
Prosecutive Memorandum (PM), 154, 155n16, 347
public domain, 278, 361, 367
publicity, CI relation to, 32
public narrative, 214, 214nn22–23
Pu Pei Liang, 73–74, 74nn4–5, 85n6, 108n18, 127n5, *199*; Cai relation to, 197; Chi Mak relation to, 123, 131, 160, 211, 257, 260–61, 261nn25–26, 282; Chiu relation to, 234; Chung, G., relation to, 261, 347; DD(x) destroyer and, 128n7; Lin and, 383; Mak, B., relation to, 125, 129, 129n10, 198; QED and, 264; Tai relation to, 74n6, 85, 122, 126, 126n3, 205

QED. *See* Quiet Electric Drive
Qing Hua University, 143
Quiet Electric Drive (QED), 10, 73, 91, 120; ASNE and, 60, 260; Calvert relation to, 231n10; CDs and, 122; classified documents for, 143–44; Edmund and, 274; Gerrity relation to, 208–9; Hilarides on, 229; Hindman relation to, 241; Kaye and, 262–63; L-3 Communications and, 270; Lee, B., and, 137, 243–44; Lipo relation to, 223, 224–26; NOFORN relation to, 180; public domain relation to, 278; Schreppler relation to, 227, 229; Tai and, 111, 114, 264

racial profiling, 9, 137, 285, 285n5
racism, 143, 295; Chinese Americans and, 203–4; Chiu and, 325–26; Hsien and, 348; Kaye and, 235–36; Staples on, 203–4, 289–90

radio communications, 40
"Red Card," 336, 336n2
"Red Flower," 291; Bednarski and,
    217, 218; Tai and, 85, 205, 251;
    translation and, 206, 210
Red Guard Movement, 245
"Red Storm Rising," 332, 332n32
Reno, Janet, 16
"reunification" speeches, 339n4
Reza, H. G., 214n22
Rickover, Hyman, 230n8
Ridley Park, 334
Rockwell International, 335, 344, 371–72,
    386
Rosen, Stanley, 183; CAPS relation to,
    245–48; Deem compared to, 250–51;
    grand jury relation to, 245, 249
"Royal Tourist," 16
Runnion, Samantha, 181, 181n3
Russia, space shuttle of, 360–61

Saba Saba, 237
SAC. See Special Agent in Charge
Saddleback Community College, 165
Saenz, Rigoberto, 244n33
"Sam," 64n2
Santa Ana City Jail, 118
Santa Ana Resident Agency squad 4
    (SARA-4), xi, xi–xii, 3, 94, 297n23;
    CCTV and, 22, 77–78; Chung,
    G., relation to, 336; in Dennis the
    Menace Park, 46; FBIHQ relation
    to, 18–19; FBILA relation to, 16–17,
    32; Forfeiture Unit of, 172; Garcia
    and, 30–31; linguists of, 12, 42–45;
    NASA and, 338; NSD-9 relation
    to, 67; SCIF for, 32; trash covers
    and, 28; Valdez and, 6; "Wrangler's
    Roundup" and, 61
SARA-4. See Santa Ana Resident Agency
    squad 4

Schiffer, Ken, 255
Schreppler, Steve, 138, 152, 179–80, 281;
    Bednarski and, 228–29, 278; grand
    jury relation to, 276–77; Missakian
    and, 226–27, 229, 275–76
Schwartz, Zachary, 347, 351–52
"Science and Technology community," of
    PRC, 122, 211
SCIF. See Sensitive Compartmented
    Information Facility
"Scott," 36, 67, 157–58
SDRs. See surveillance detection routes
SDS. See shuttle drawing system
search warrant: for Chung, G., 337,
    338–39; DOJ relation to, 147–48;
    Moberly and, 342; for "Mr. Smug,"
    386; for Power Paragon Inc., 118;
    second-look, 160–61
Sea Technology (magazine), 260
"Second Island Chain," 208
second-look search warrant, 160–61
seizures, 172; from Downey residence,
    129–32; at LAX, 125; from
    Power Paragon Inc., 132–33, 170;
    translation and, 133–34
self-incrimination, 222–23; Khersonsky
    and, 250. See also Fifth Amendment
Sensitive Compartmented Information
    Facility (SCIF), 12, 19–20; for
    SARA-4, 32
sentencing hearing: for Chi Mak, 316,
    317–19; for Chung, G., 374, 376–80
sexism, USAO and, 137n4
Shanghai Jiao Tong University, 211n15,
    362
Shanghai Mechanical and Electrical
    Industries, 132
Shanghainese, 42–43, 43n3, 45
Shapiro, Ben, 264n36
Shelly, Ken, 238, 241
shuttle drawing system (SDS), 361

Simpkins, 152–53

Simpson, O. J., 189–90

The Simpsons (TV sitcom), 40, 40n6

60 Minutes (television show), 384

SME. *See* subject matter experts

Smith, I. C., 252–56, 252n6, 254n9, 256nn12–13

Smith, J. J., 10, 16, 16n2; Guerin and, 219–20; Kaye relation to, 184. *See also* J. J. Smith/Katrina Leung case

Snowden, Edward, xii

soccer cleats, 47, 55–56

Socialist Republic of Vietnam (SRV), 2, 149–50, 364

"Soft-Switching and High-Density DC-DC Converters," 9n3

Solid-State Switch paper, 60; ASNE and, 260; Edmund and, 274; ITAR and, 281; public domain relation to, 278

South China Morning Post (newspaper), 199–200

Soviet Union, 25n5; Walker relation to, 30n1

space shuttle, 346; Chung, G., relation to, 335, 357; EE and, 370; Gu Wei relation to, 338; Hsien relation to, 348; of Russia, 360–61; submarines compared to, 229n7

Special Agent Forensic Computer expert, 50

Special Agent in Charge (SAC), 30; Newquist as, 331; Smith, I. C., 252

Special Agent vetting process, 76n2

Special Intelligence Group (SSG), 11, 14, 23; Carney relation to, 216; CCTV and, 38, 79; Chi Mak and, 103, 103n1; covert home entries and, 48; in Dennis the Menace Park, 46; FBI criminal squads and, 76n2; "Flaps and Seals" experts and, 78; Fuk and, 26; GPS and, 62; Lookouts for, 22,

38, 39–40; Murray and, 75; Newquist and, 19; Witham relation to, 35–36

SRV. *See* Socialist Republic of Vietnam

SSA. *See* Supervisory Special Agent

SSBN ballistic missile submarine, 229, 229n6

SSG. *See* Special Intelligence Group

Standard Telegraphic Code (STC), 10, 10n4, 206, 377

Stanley (Professor), 365–66, 367–68, 372

Staples, Greg, 93, 93n13, 138, 158, 249n46; Abernathy and, 197; appeals and, 328; Ashton and, 260; Bednarski relation to, 200, 202–3; Bienert and, 353, 370; Brady violations and, 378; Cardona relation to, 299n1; Carney relation to, 198, 233–34; Chi Mak and, 267–73, 274n47, 286–90; Chung, G., and, 346, 371–72, 381; Chung, S., and, 364; Deem and, 250–51; Dotson and, 194; early release and, 331–32; EE relation to, 149; Eliot and, 95–96, 98–99, 148; "False Official Statements" and, 159n29; Farag and, 368; "GAYLORD DIRECT" and, 196; Gerrity and, 208–9; "Government's Exhibit List" and, 187; grand jury relation to, 188, 189–90, 288n10; Greenberg and, 311; Guerin and, 219–20; Gu Wei and, 193, 290; Hsien and, 366; Kaye relation to, 178; Lee, B., and, 244; Len relation to, 205, 206n29; Lipo and, 224–26, 266; Lopez and, 231–32, 234–35; Luo and, 109n20; Mak, B., and, 301–3; McKay and, 218; Miller, B., relation to, 207; Miller, K., and, 359; Missakian and, 296, 302n6; Moberly and, 374; Murray and, 193n1; Newquist relation to,

211n13; plea bargains and, 172–73, 298–300, 303–4; PM of, 155n16; on racism, 203–4, 289–90; Rosen and, 246–48; search warrant and, 338; at sentencing hearing, 317; Smith, I. C., and, 253–56, 256n12; Stanley and, 367–68; Tai and, 269n43, 270, 309, 316; Tattooed Love Dog relation to, 190, 192, 198, 293; Valdez and, 307–8; Wang relation to, 356; Wenfeng and, 387; Wian and, 297; Witham and, 195; Wu and, 242; Yip, E., and, 251–52; Yoo and, 210

State Administration of Radio, Film, and TV, PRC, 245

State Science & Technology Commission, PRC, Department of Facilities and Financial Support, 132

STC. *See* Standard Telegraphic Code

Strategic Assessment and Warning Department, China Naval Forces Division, 208

Struyk, Jim, 92n12

Strzok, Peter, 384n3

subject matter experts (SME), 69, 177, 179; CIA relation to, 182, 324; Danis as, 360; Lee, B., as, 142; McVadon as, 183; from NASA, 356; Pluhar as, 180–81

submarines, 272–73, 281; Bednarski and, 228, 228n5; canceling harmonics for, 276; Chabay relation to, 230–31; classified documents and, 150; Hilarides relation to, 182, 229–30; "kill chain" relation to, 192; Schreppler and, 275; space shuttle compared to, 229n7; Virginia-class, 10, 120, 138, 180, 180n1

Suet Li Mak, 26

suicide watch, 118–19, 118n9

Supervisory Special Agent (SSA), 16, 84n3

surveillance, 76; of Chiu, 23, *24*, 24–26; of Chung, G., 336; covert home entries and, 49–50; polecams for, 17, 21–22, 21n1, 46, 178

surveillance coordinator, 14

surveillance detection routes (SDRs): of Chiu, 23, 24–26; of Fuk, 26–27

symposium articles, *121*

Syria, 41n10

Szady, Dave, 30, 30n1

Taiwan, 208, 311; CCP relation to, 348; Chung, G., relation to, 334; PRC relation to, 339n4

Tai Wang Mak, 11, *12*, *315*; appeals of, 326; Audi A6 of, 62; Bolick and, 104, 105; CDs and, 82, 83, 89, 109, 287–88; Chi Mak relation to, 87–88, 122, 127n6, 128–29, 289, 328; DD(x) destroyer and, 263, 316; Early and, 173–74, 292, 316; FISA and, 18; Fuk relation to, 85–87; Fung relation to, 19; Goldman and, 137; at LAX, 100–101; Luo and, 108, 216; Mak, B., and, 94–95; Mak, S., relation to, 327–28, 327n23; Mak Professional Stereo Engineering Company, Ltd. and, 29, 29n9, 73–74; marriage fraud and, 90, 91; *Married with Children* relation to, 40, 40n7; at Phoenix International, 147n1; PLA and, *123*, 124, 197; plea bargains and, 298–99, 303, 306, 308; PRCIS relation to, 232n13; Pu relation to, 74n6, 85, 122, 126, 126n3, 205; QED and, 111, 114, 264; "Red Flower" and, 85, 205, 251; SDRs of, 26; Staples and, 269n43, 270, 309, 316; translation relation to, 42–44; trash covers and, 29, 69; Wu relation to, 145

Takla, Mark, 388

Tattooed Love Dog, 190, 192, 198, 293, 293n15

Tech Agents, 49, 61, 173; CCTV and, 79; covert home entries and, 61, 77; GPS and, 62

"tech cuts," 43–44

Technical Agent support, FBILA, 11

technical coverage, 14

technical papers, 59–60, 59n2

Technical Squad, FBILA, 21–22

TECS. See Treasury Enforcement Communication System

Teledyne, 251, 258

teletype, 10, 10n5

Terrorist Screening Center, 65, 65n4

"Theft of Government Property," 99, 150

Third Naval Symposium of Electric Machines, 133; "Algorithms for Reduced Scale Permanent Magnet Synchronous Machine Propulsion Drive" at, 259n21

"Third Naval Symposium on Electric Machines," 206n30

Thompson Twins, 259, 267, 287n9

thriftiness, 24–26

Tian Lai Hu, 365

Tidwell, Stephen, 155, 156–57, 156n24

"Tiger Trap," 15

"Time Served," 299, 303, 309, 313

Toyota Celica, 62

translation, 42n2, 45, 356; by Chung, G., 343; of handwritten task list, 70, 71–72; of intercepts, 172; of machine-printed tasking list, 72; "Red Flower" and, 206, 210; seizures and, 133–34; SME and, 180; Tai relation to, 42–44; USN relation to, 83, 83n2

trash covers, 27–28; Chung, G., and, 338; handwritten task list and, 70, 114–15; Moberly and, 336–37; Murray and, 41; Tai and, 29, 69

treasonous activity, xii–xiii

Treasury Enforcement Communication System (TECS), 13

Trevett, Karen, 360n7, 364–65

trial transcripts, 203–4, 203n22

Twelve Angry Men (movie), 189

UCLA. See University of California at Los Angeles

"under duress" challenges, 114

"unfair prejudice," 178

United Front Work Department, CCP, 372

United States Attorney's Office (USAO), 63, 84; AUSA and, 355n27; Cardona and, 148, 148n3, 347; CES relation to, 178; DD(x) destroyer relation to, 295n18; Dion relation to, 98; Early relation to, 299; EE relation to, 354; executive leadership at, 150–51, 152, 300n4; FBILA relation to, 214, 300; Fuk relation to, 156, 161n2; Goldman relation to, 136; ITAR relation to, 171; Ling Jia relation to, 379n45; Missakian and, 298; plea bargains and, 295, 303–5, 308–10, 311, 354; sexism and, 137n4; SRV relation to, 149–50; Staples relation to, 95–96; Tai relation to, 316; Wenfeng and, 387–89

University of California at Los Angeles (UCLA), 89, 106n6, 107, 156

University of Minnesota, 334

University of Southern California (USC), 245

US 7th Fleet, 281

US Air Force, 7; Moberly and, 336

USAO. *See* United States Attorney's Office

US Army, Defense Language Institute of, 3

USC. *See* University of Southern California

US-China Institute, 245

US citizenship: of Chiu, 324–25; deportation and, 69, 69n1

US Defense Security Cooperation Agency, 384

US Department of Defense, 235n17

US Department of Energy, 16

US Department of State (DOS), 156; Directorate of Defense Trade Controls, 209

"Use of Property to Aid a Foreign Power," 97

US Marshals, 315, 326

US Munitions List (USML), 144; Hindman relation to, 238, 240; ITAR relation to, 209–10

US Navy (USN), xi, 111; Chi Mak relation to, 193; EMALS and, 113n6; FBIHQ relation to, 66; Hong Kong relation to, 130–31, 249, 284; L-3 Communications and, 5, 238; Lopez and, 231; ONR of, 60; Power Paragon relation to, 8, 10, 238; SME in, 69; translation relation to, 83, 83n2; Walker relation to, 30n1

US Navy Purchasing, 130

US Probation Office, 379n47

US Probation Presentence Investigation Report and Sentence Recommendation, 316

US Space Shuttle program, 165

US State Department, 361

US Supreme Court, 329

US war games, 201

Valdez, Sal, 2–3, 63, 84n3, 303; Bereznay relation to, 157–58; Chung, G., relation to, 340, 349; Chung, S., and, 350, 370n27, 373n31; executive leadership relation to, 352; FBIHQ relation to, 66, 214; FBILA relation to, 17, 172; Fuk and, 300; Garcia relation to, 31; Kable relation to, 65n4; NSA relation to, 345–46; NSD-9 relation to, 67; polygraph tests and, 4–5, 4n4; SARA-4 and, 6; Staples and, 307–8

Varyag (aircraft carrier), 208

VCF. *See* Virtual Case File

Vietnamese Americans, 149–50, 364

Virginia-class submarines, 10, 120, 138, 180, 180n1

Virtual Case File (VCF), 18

Walker, John, 30n1

Wang, Ivy, 355–56; Miller, K., and, 363; Moberly and, 357

Washington Field Office (WFO), 4–5; Bereznay and, 93; FBIHQ relation to, 384; Gertz relation to, 320; WIU and, 383

Washington Operations (WashOps), 36, 238

Washington Times (newspaper), 176, 319

Weekly Investigative Update (WIU), 30, 156n22, 383

Wenfeng Lu, 387–89

Wen Ho Lee, 16, 94, 95n15, 136–37, 142, 244n32

WFO. *See* Washington Field Office

White, John, 256

Wian, Casey, 297, 297n21

Witham, Fred, 36, 118, 132n14, 138; Hindman relation to, 238, 241n26;

Kaye and, 195; Newquist and, 35, 274
WIU. *See* Weekly Investigative Update
Wolfsen, Thomas, 301–2, 310n18
"Wrangler's Roundup," 60–61
Wray, Christopher, 308n12, 389
Wu-Tai Chin, "Larry," 15, 219–20, 219nn35–36, 252–53
Wu Xiaoyong, 145, 241–43

X-33, 361
X-37 Space Plane, 361
Xian Aircraft, 340n8, 363

Yan Feng, 145, 197, 271
Yang, Debra, 148n3, 154–55, 157, 158n28; Bereznay relation to, 158; Cardona relation to, 158n27

Yeager, Chuck, 163n4
Yip, Eddie, 251–52
Yip, Stephen, 180
Yoo, "Rick" Zachary, 45, 45n5, 172, 210
Yugoslavia, 310

Z., Vince, 64n2
Zahzah, Mohammad, 250
Zerden, Mal, 182, 209–10, 292–93
Zhang, 26–27
Zhao An Tai, 132
Zhongshan University, 108, 108n18